1991

The Planetary Man

Other Books by Wilfrid Desan

THE MARXISM OF JEAN-PAUL SARTRE

TRAGIC FINALE: AN ESSAY ON THE PHILOSOPHY
OF JEAN-PAUL SARTRE

THE PLANETARY MAN

Volume 1
A NOETIC PRELUDE TO A UNITED WORLD

Volume 2
AN ETHICAL PRELUDE TO A UNITED WORLD

Wilfrid Desan

GEORGETOWN UNIVERSITY PRESS
Washington, D.C.

Cover photo: This view of the earth was taken by the Apollo 17 crew in 1972 during their journey toward the moon, approximately 100,000 miles away from the earth. Courtesy National Aeronautics and Space Administration, Washington, D.C.

Georgetown University Press
Intercultural Center, Room 111
Georgetown University
Washington, D.C. 20057

Library of Congress Cataloging-in-Publication Data

Desan, Wilfrid.
    The planetary man.

    Originally published: New York: Macmillan, 1972.
    Includes bibliographies.
    Contents: v. 1. A noetic prelude to a united world —
v.2 An ethical prelude to a united world.
    1. Philosophical anthropology.   2. Ethics.
I. Title
BD450. D44   1987   128   87-10
ISBN 0-87840-437-6 (pbk.)

to Betty
and
to those who were
both my students and my teachers

Contents

[9]

Foreword

THIS book contains the first two volumes of *The Planetary Man.* A third is due at a later date. Volume 1, published in 1961, has been revised and appears together with Volume 2, which is published here for the first time. The topics of the two books are clearly distinct. But this intended diversity does not cancel their unity, for the same principles run throughout, with the ultimate purpose of positing, on different levels, a new definition of man, man as planetary. What this planetary dimension implies, and what it gradually reveals, is the focus of this study.

If certain themes are recurrent in the two parts, this is intentional, and it will be noticed that they gain in amplitude as the reader moves into Volume 2.

To the question of whether or not the author himself has evolved in the writing of a book which has been spread over so many years, I can only answer by saying that the power of the collective has become more and more cogent. As a result the "planetary man" denotes more than ever the end of the Cartesian era and the death of the "modern man." In writing this, I should add that I write not what I wish were true but what I believe to be true.

Modern man was born in the Renaissance. Having fulfilled the dream of Prometheus and robbed the fire of the gods, he finds in the end that individual man must not play with godly tools unless he is himself divine. Perhaps it will be seen that men are gods only when working together, that the divine when well understood results from an addition of the diverse, while Spirit is actually not so much a nature as an operation, an operation, that is, which results from cooperation. In all this the planetary man is both Actor and Observer. To some it may appear that the ultimate fulfillment is a dream and that the hopes which run through these pages, especially through the ones which discuss the ethical, are part of the myth and of the absurd. My only answer is that what appears absurd today may no longer appear so tomorrow. For as Heidegger has said, "philosophy is untimely . . . [but] what is untimely has its own future."

WILFRID DESAN

VOLUME 1

∴

A Noetic Prelude
to a
United World

*I walk among men as among
fragments of the future.*
NIETZSCHE

Introduction

THIS book is an attempt of integration in the order of knowledge. Although having no ethical purpose, it confesses to some ethical implications. It does not reject the need for analysis, but its foremost aim is to bring together the things of the mind to satisfy a desire for unity. Perhaps it requires an immigrant to write about these matters because although he does not want to give up being here, he can never forget that he was there. If writing is not about what one is but about what one wishes to be, I can say that this writer writes about unity because he looks for it.

The center around which our integration is built is not a supernatural one. This is a philosophical work, and although the possibility of revelation is not excluded, it is viewed as not relevant here. Man may indeed belong to the sphere of the sacred, as some claim, but this consideration has no place in our philosophical research. This is an attempt of man on his own, and the dialectic unrolls without the help of revelation, as far as it can go. Some may think that it does not go far enough. This is not the philosopher's fault. His world is autonomous but not complete.

In developing the view here defended, I have based myself not so much upon deduction as upon observation and description. A fundamental topic of observation is that of the survival of the species itself. The thesis propounded considers survival to be its very cornerstone, survival viewed not in its scientific aspect but as mere empirical fact. Since the method employed attempts to describe the implications of this fact, I call it a phenomenological essay. However, I should be reserved in making this claim. When a term is very much in fashion, it can no longer be used without some specification, for its meaning and applications have become multiple.

First of all, no book is merely such or so in its method, for even the most extreme phenomenologists "reason" a lot and there is more than one syllogism hidden in their descriptive approach. Nor is reasoning absent, ironically enough, among those who want to prove that reason is of no value. In looking back now upon the growth of this book, I believe that its method can be called phenomenological in the sense that it analyzes an observable phenomenon.

The phenomenon which my description gradually brings to light is the fragmentary structure of man, the limits of his noesis and the power of total noesis. The point of view which is taken during this inquiry is not, as might be expected, the viewpoint of the individual man but that of the collectivity. It is the totality as such which attempts a phenomenologization. Just what this implies I shall initially attempt to explain, although the main body of the book will show it more abundantly.

At the beginning of the modern era we meet Descartes, who in the philosophical disorder of his times was looking for an unshakable starting point which he "could safely accept as the first principle of the philosophy (he) was seeking."[1] This unshakable point of departure he discovered in the existence of his own self. This in the eyes of Descartes was an absolute foundation, and as a new Archimedes, he lifted the world of thought, having found its fulcrum. Taking himself as starting point, he strove to construct a philosophy in the way a science is built, eliminating both the probable and the occult and accepting only what evidence could allow. "The explicit awareness of the self is the greatest discovery since Plato and Aristotle," wrote Whitehead, and although the multiple deductions drawn by Descartes have not survived in their integrity, the importance of taking the subject as starting point has proved to be tenacious. After Descartes, several great philosophers—to name only Berkeley, Locke and Hume—have chosen this same path, each following it in his own way.

---

[1] *Discourse on Method*, 2d ed. rev., trans. Laurence J. Lafleur   (New York: Liberal Arts Press, 1956), p. 21.

Among recent philosophers this trend has not declined. Edmund Husserl, the founder of modern phenomenology, has given to the book containing the last and perhaps the best synthesis of his thought the title *Cartesian Meditations*, for in Descartes' *Meditations* Husserl saw the prototype of all philosophical investigation. He, no less than his predecessor, insisted upon the *ego cogito*—"I think"—as the starting point of all careful philosophical inquiry. This went not without problems, for his descriptive method differed notably from that of Descartes, who in his own deductive way went looking for the atoms of evidence (Hamelin). What counts for Husserl is the description of that which appears in so far as it appears, with the hope of gathering in this way a collection of essences. I should add, of course—and this has sometimes been forgotten—that my description of phenomena will always be the way they appear to me. Great efforts have been made by Husserl himself to shake off the suspicion of subjectivism, unavoidably connected with such a method. It is doubtful whether his efforts were ever rewarded, for it is practically certain that he ended up in an idealistic position. So strong was the impact of the ego upon the essences moving in its orbit of description that for all practical purposes their existential dimension was completely overlooked.

Husserl's disciples, enchanted though they were by his method, nevertheless made more determined efforts to keep their philosophical doctrine free from all imputations of idealism. The phenomenology of Heidegger, Sartre and Merleau-Ponty has its variations, but all three in one way or another make use of intentionality as a definite means to hang onto an objective world. Only in the grasp of an object can the subject be born. This is a very interesting point, indeed, and to an extent it does protect the objectivity of the data. The viewer has his world and is born into it. Actually the world becomes world by his being born into it, and he himself becomes subject in this very birth. Unfortunately, as everyone can see, by being born into his world, the viewer sees no other world. His "objectivism" is real but narrow. He emerges into a universe which he makes not in its brute reality but in its "humanization." What human reality does to the brute existent is amazing, as the most skilled advocates of phenomenology have shown with great effect. But one thing strikes me, namely, that each of them is constantly moving within some sort of spatial "angularity," out of which he cannot lift himself. He is unable to break the limits of a world which is himself. Even when at the very start he accepts the other and the world of the other, it is as part and part only of his individual constellation. The individual subject, standing at the center, gives vision and meaning to a world of his choice. His freedom lies in his creation of a world.

In order to protect the movement against the accusation of essentialism, existentialists claim that they are actually the philosophers of existence. I confess that, after years of study of this particular philosophical trend, this formulation still puzzles me. If by this it is meant that existentialism aims at a more complete approach than that afforded by Aristotle, Aquinas and others, one which attempts to discover in man certain emotions such as hope, despair, anguish, etc., or to reveal the mode of his becoming, the word "existential" is rich in meaning. If, on the contrary, it is implied that from now on the individual man will be studied as he is in his concrete existence—as it is often asserted—then the notion becomes unclear. For it overlooks the fact that of the notion of existence or of the individual as existent nothing can be said. Existence is not an object of knowledge unless it is somehow essentially incarnated. I am incapable of knowing existence unless it is the existence of something. The revolt against essentialism, when pushed too far, can be suicidal, for it remains necessary to ascribe existence to something in order to make it understandable. When existentialists, therefore, in order to escape the accusation of idealism insist that their aim is existence, they must of necessity endow this existence with some feature, whether it be anguish or hope, boredom or nausea, something around which existence can be wrapped. But once they have discovered and described these or other "essences," they find themselves surrounded once more, like Husserl, "with a region of essences." Whether the center be called *Dasein* or *Pour-soi*, it will always be a subject looking around itself for a conceptualizable order, and although they insist and claim that their revelation is the discovery of an existing world, it will nonetheless always be their world. This author holds no grudges against Heidegger, Sartre and others. His regret is that they are Heideggerian only or Sartrian only. Being the skillful describers of what appears to them, they have seen a lot, but I cannot say that they have overcome the subjective. As Professor Lauer aptly puts it: "[The followers of the phenomenological method] agree in their contention that philosophy can only consist in an analysis of what is present to consciousness prior to the philosophical inquiry . . . Each then, limits himself to a description of what he finds revealed in consciousness—each is at the same time aware that the description itself is somehow an instrument of revelation . . . [However], if the thinker undertakes to describe experiences, it is inevitable that many of them will either be his own personal ones, or at least those which belong to this intellectual, political, social, religious, or historical milieu—or a combination of all."[2]

At this point, the reader will agree that in the writing of this study, which is actually an attempt of philosophical integration, the phenomenological outlook as preached by Husserl and practiced by his continental followers was of no avail, as far as the "subjective" point of departure is concerned. Only the totality can integrate itself without taking one side or another. The only way to integrate a philosophical diversity, therefore, was to take the viewpoint of the *totum*.[3]

This identification with the *totum* requires in my opinion a double stand: first of all, what I call an acceptance of the limitation of the one, i.e. of any singular position; and secondly, as an unavoidable consequence, an acceptance of the plurality. To accept the finitude of man and of all that he is and does is the first requisite. Our study hopes to show that no pronouncement on behalf of the totality of truth has been made and that every representation is caught within a circle. But this very attitude of accepting limitation is a first step towards overcoming it. To overcome means to introduce the other. Only when we are disposed to multiply the circles shall we cover the surface of our human territory.

To confess to one's finitude and to accept the plural is tantamount to accepting the *totum*, for the *totum* is not a collective consciousness or some form of world mind—I observe nothing of the sort—the *totum* is nothing but the plural. For man, identification with the *totum* means nothing more than the acceptance of

---

[2] Quentin Lauer, S.J., *The Triumph of Subjectivity* (New York: Fordham University Press, 1958), p. 185.
[3] *Totum* can be understood as "totality." This term, of course, does not explain all the nuances of the concept. This is what the book gradually attempts to do.

this plurality. When human "absolutes" have been multiplied, the only answer is their juxtaposition. And perhaps the view from the summit down, which in this study will be attempted, will show that the totality implies parts or fragments and that these parts and fragments not only are juxtaposed but complete one another as well.

The breakaway from the subjective in this study, or what might be called a reaching for the objective, must be understood as a total human grasp, resulting from an addition of the plural and of their mutual correction. The objective is the subjective multiplied. Truth then, it will appear, can only in one way or other be synthetic. A world of all, by which I mean numerically all, must give us a complete human world. It is this world which our study wants to explore, a world which actually is nothing but the *totum* looking at itself, for if phenomenology as understood by Husserl's disciples carries the subject by means of intentionality outside himself towards the exteriority of a world and in this very act makes the subject get hold of himself and of what is not himself, the phenomenology as practiced here—if this term is still permissible—presents the *totum* as subject, but in so doing, the *totum* reaches the total human world, for when the *totum* as Subject gets hold of itself, it reaches the human universe, which actually is the sum total of the many individual awarenesses considered *in toto et in uno*. Outside the human world there is nothing, for to claim that something *is* implies that it falls in one way or another within the noetic reach of the human *totum*.

I would now like to add a few remarks for further clarification.

First of all, the acceptance of the possibility of the multiple approach within the totality does not at all mean that one should feel obliged to embrace each and all. What counts here is the observation of these plural views and their eventual contribution when juxtaposed. No value judgment is herewith expressed. Nor do I claim that each and every approach contains an equal share of truth. This ambitious evaluation I am not at all able to make. But there can be a priori no reason to refuse the contribution of the "one and the many," when on the human level, a noetic integration is at stake.

A second remark is that from the viewpoint of the *totum*, the "problem" of Descartes has no meaning. He who accepts the *totum humanum* does not start from the subject (I mean the individual subject), since in starting from itself or more exactly in looking at itself, the *totum* reaches what is object for the individual. As has been said above, the *totum*, looking at itself, in this very deed reaches a whole human existing world with its many (individual) subjects constituting together the totality. The efforts of Descartes to emerge out of the cell of his own thinking are well known; it was not easy to reconquer that world which was so joyfully abandoned at the start of the Cogito. To avoid the problems of Descartes one must avoid his point of departure. The acceptance of the *totum*, however, implies the acceptance of the individuals existing and moving within that *totum*. Just as Descartes discovered a world existing within himself which in the eyes of some was surprisingly and exaggeratedly rich, so also the *totum humanum* finds existing within itself a multiplicity, spread over a spatio-temporal measurable quantum, reaching out in a variety of directions, yet caught, notwithstanding its motion and commotion, within the limits of a human dimension. Its one and great aim seems to be to survive as totality. But that, of course, our study must try to clarify.

We may here add—and this is our third remark—that the parallel with the Cartesian position can be drawn further, for just as Descartes, once he was certain of the world within himself, began an inquiry concerning the possibility of a world outside himself, so also the human totality, certain of its "content," yet not entirely satisfied with its own dimensions (the existing human universe) not seldom is interested in finding out whether or not some "other-worldly" entity exists. Our chapter 8 of this volume will attempt to show how a phenomenology, when undertaken by the collective over and against a similar approach when performed by the individual subject, does reach a metaphysical object. It will appear not only that the "collective" approach gives more satisfactory results, as a whole, but also that a phenomenology when performed by the *totum* does indeed reach the Transcendent, called God. This discovery will not be called a demonstration, but it will be more convincing, I believe, for it will result from an interrogation perpetrated upon the deeper meaning of the *totum* as *totum*. The *totum humanum*, turning its vision inward, discovers a multitude of existing individuals and their utterances, but, turning its gaze outward, discovers another dimension, and in this dimension it may very well find God.

The reader may well wonder at this stage whether the individual has been completely overlooked in this study and has been once and forever locked up in some biological matrix.

To this my answer will be threefold. I confess that this book is an attempt to defend the collective, but the collective as understood here is not a menace for the individual; actually, in the world of tomorrow it will be his only defense. For in fact, the only way for the individual to survive is to be recognized as an individual, that is, as unique. The integration here presented, as it will appear later in the study, is one where diversity is not only accepted but even required. It is indeed a unification of the multiple unique. It will be clear from the start that unification is built upon complementarity and as such requires the different. Only that which is different can complete and achieve. This book, then, in protecting the uniqueness of the individual constituent, is ultimately a defense of the latter, although it is simultaneously an attempt to integrate the multiple noesis. Although the point of observation taken here is precisely the immobile position of mankind as *totum,* it will appear that looked at from this chosen place, what counts is the individual, the individual not wishfully idealized but as he really appears to be.

Moreover, as we will see at the end of chapter 4 of this volume, the individual man and not only the *totum* is the seat of integration. Actually a double current runs all through the book: integration carried out by the totality, which could be called objective, and integration accomplished by the individual, which would be called subjective. As long as the individual is not the *totum* of mankind, the unity of knowledge will have to ride that double span. Since the fragment will never be the *totum*, any overlapping of the subjective and the objective is out of the question.

And finally it should be added, in defense of the individual, that an entire chapter under the title "The Planetary Man" is devoted to him. The planetary man is that ambiguous entity which wants to be both the *totum humanum* and himself as well. This may appear to be presumptuous, and so may indeed be the title of this essay. We will see by the end of this book that this double presumption is actually one and the same and that neither, alas, can have all of its wishes fulfilled. Yet if it does not reflect an accomplished ideology—this is no longer what we are looking for —I believe that it reflects an attitude, the attitude of the man of the future. "We are no longer 'all of a piece man.' "[4] This, then, is the planetary man: he asserts himself in order to contribute, for he is unique, yet he destroys himself in order to understand, for he is not alone. No one can speak for all and speak the whole truth.

It cannot be emphasized enough that this is not an historical study. No excursions have been made in a variety of directions, but the unity of purpose has been constantly kept in mind, and I have followed as well as I could the golden rule of the old Sertillanges: to push everything towards the end. Consequently, if other writers on the same topic are not mentioned, it is not because of lack of due respect, but simply because this is not an historical work and I have seen no reason to summarize their views. They can be read on their own. Obviously some of the things under discussion are not new; so, e.g., the principle of complementarity, which I consider fundamental, has been used by several in the past, to mention only Bergson, Oppenheimer and Bohr. I have made great efforts not to fall under the Hegelian seduction, however. The reader will discover whether or not I have done so successfully.

Let me make it clear from the start that in this effort of mine I want to remain faithful to the theory developed in these pages, hence confess to its own fragmentary character. Although the result of many years of thought, it is no doubt itself liable to completion. Criticism from any quarter will be welcome, for it is clear by now that philosophy is a dialogue. Philosophy once more is the agora, where opinions meet. The agora stands eternally, but its visitors come and go.

---

[4] F. Dostoevsky, *The Idiot,* trans. Eva M. Martin (New York: Everyman's Library, 1957), p. 498.

I

A Phenomenology
of Survival

The Totality as Surviving

"THE human species will disappear, little by little the small star which is our sun will lose its lightening and warming force. Of all these human and superhuman civilizations, discoveries, philosophies, ideals, religions, nothing will subsist. In this minuscule corner of the universe, the pale adventure of the protoplasm will be eliminated forever . . ." Jean Rostand's text is famous and has seduced many, perhaps because deep in his heart man actually enjoys the tragic, with death at its very core. However romantic it may seem, however, despair is not an inevitable response. For although extinction on this planet is still a possibility, up to now life has proved itself the victor. In fact, the "pale adventure" of the protoplasm has grown more robust since its birth, and if life has consistently buried its dead, it has taken care of the future with equal fervor. Survival is a fact.

If then it is a fact—and the statement is its own proof, for the dead are silent—it deserves close study, particularly in the anguish of our times, when the continuance of life seems to be threatened once more.

We might begin by examining the etymology of the word *survival*. The Latin origin is obvious: *supervivere*, to live beyond . . . To live beyond what? The first answer seems to be that *supervivere* implies the meaning of living beyond the present state. Yet this is merely a play on words, since everything lives beyond its present state, otherwise it would not live. To live beyond one's present state is merely to live, *vivere*, not *supervivere*. The implication of the prefix *super* is stronger and points towards a living beyond something. It is in the definition of this something that ambiguity has to be avoided. This something may be another existent which one merely *outlives*. This meaning of *outlive*, although acceptable, has lost the connotation of the original sense of *supervivere*. For *supervivere* actually means to remain alive beyond a problematic situation, whatever that situation of crisis may be. One survives an accident or an illness. One does not survive one's death. This would be a contradiction, since no one would claim to be at the same time mortal and immortal.

Some, it is true, claim that there is an immortal element in the person who dies and that this element survives the destruction of the organic totality. In this case the term *super* keeps its natural meaning, but the term *vivere* comes in for a difficult if not impossible interpretation. The immortal element cannot be said to live since such a characteristic is proper, by accepted definition, to an organic material totality. For that state in which some part of the individual endures after his disappearance from life as we know it, the term *immortal* is more suitable than *survival*. This is merely a matter of semantical clarification, for it is not the purpose of this study to investigate whether such an immortality exists.

Returning then to the meaning of survival defended here, we may say equally well that an individual survives (an accident) or that the human species as a whole survives. . . . We discover a common meaning, the meaning namely of *to persist notwithstanding*, . . . *to outlast regardless*. . . . There is, therefore, an obvious implication that in the case of survival, in its authentic and original meaning, some opposition is overcome or some menace is offset. It is not our concern to examine what made the victim of an accident survive—causes may be diverse—one thing is certain, a threat was present, but the individual came through notwithstanding. . . . He *survived*.[1] A similar meaning can be discovered in the case of the survival of the human species as a whole. It will be our task in the following pages to do so.

---

[1] In the Latin authors we find both meanings of *supervivere* in use, e.g., in Justinus (28,3): *Olympias non diu filiis supervixit*, the meaning of *supervivere* as to *out-* *live* is used, while in "*expeditioni superfuit et supervixit*," it is the second sense of living beyond which is predominant.

Let me make it clear from the start that I do not have in mind concrete examples, such as the invention of a remedy when some fatal disease grips the human species, or the discovery of a defensive weapon when a nation is under the menace of destruction. These random cases of survival result from a deeper structure of the totality as such, and it is this deeper structure which I wish to pursue.

When I talk about the whole of mankind or *totum*, I do not refer to the *totum logicum* or logical class, where a universal concept because of its content is applicable to its inferiors, in this case to human beings themselves; without denying the existence of the class as logical entity, I consider here the *totum* as *totum physicum*, i.e., a whole made up through the addition of fragments.

Of course, the possibility of the class as a logical whole always remains, for once in the presence of a plurality, I can discover common characteristics and essential similarities. The rejection of the class as a logical entity would result in a blurring of classes, a confusion which I want to avoid. Aware of the fact, therefore, that by abstraction the logical whole takes care of those elements which human beings have in common, I shall not explicitly handle mankind as *totum logicum* (although accepting it implicitly) but instead devote my attention to the *totum genus humanum* as physical *totum* and to its constituents or fragments. For the sake of accuracy, I shall add that in my understanding the fragment was never identical with the *totum*. This is, of course, a postulatory statement and implies that there was always more than one fragment in the *totum humanum*.

The fragment into which the *totum physicum* breaks down is obviously the individual. This has to be understood literally. The human individual is, indeed, individual or *undivided*. Such is also the meaning the Greek word ἄτομος or undivided fragment, that fragment, namely, which so far as structure and inner life are concerned, appears to be indivisible at the peril of destruction. This supposes, as everyone can observe, a living content where a center is present, where all feelings, thoughts and actions are consolidated and viewed as belonging to one. Such an entity is rightly called an individual. The *totum genus humanum* is made up out of individuals or undivided fragments.

Surviving Through Time

To be undivided, however, does not imply to be indivisible. In fact, the human fragment is divisible, and upon its destruction needs replacement. The replacement of man is man. This consideration brings us to our first form of survival, which I shall call survival of the *totum* through replacement. The totality as a whole survives because of a continual loss and a no less continual repair. Without this inner danger and the remedy deriving from the complement, we could not talk of survival. The multiplicity of men, therefore, however strange this may seem, is a lapse into imperfection, but it is a protracted salvation of the totality as well. It is the very imperfection of the continually replacing fragments of the species which has driven them towards multiplication. A mutual correction is continually exacted upon our planet, for our species is a kingdom of fragments, and its will for survival is a will towards multiplication.

As such, survival is a play of life and death. From the individual viewpoint, life is only life, death is only death, but from the viewpoint of the surviving *totum*, life is made up out of both. There is no place for an immortal man, for his destruction is as important as his birth. Survival implies both the menace and the remedy, but the remedy lies not in the menace. If we speak of a fragmented *totum*, we signify that if the disappearance of *A* constitutes the threat, the protection of the *totum* lies in the other *(B)*, not in himself *(A)*.

Although replacement might have taken place in a variety of ways, the human totality, like any other known organic *totum*, takes care of its replacement through procreation. This affects the whole structure of the *totum*. Calling the appearance of a new fragment its "birth" and the disappearance its "death," we find strikingly present between the two extremes a persistent care of the future of the totality, through growth, marriage, birth and education of children, etc. Since replacement is through procreation, the *totum humanum* is made up out of fragments which are in turn child and parent. As child they are from, as parent they are toward. The fragment is crossed through and through with relational dimensions, dimensions which express themselves both through completing and through being completed. The child "completes" a declining parenthood in most cases; at the very least he, through his presence alone, completes the *totum humanum*, since through his birth the extinction of the *totum* is once more delayed. The parents on their side "complete" what-is-not-yet, for without them no child would ever have been born, nor would it, once born, without their help have survived. In conclusion, the individual man is the one-who-is-from-the-other and also the one-from-whom-the-other-is, or in terse Latin *qui-ab-altero* and *a-quo-alter*. Relation is built-in.

Surviving Through Space

In addition to this survival through replacement, we can also discover what may be called a survival through juxtaposition. Here the same principles apply. We notice once more how it is the individual fragment which pays, and by this I signify that while in our previous analysis, survival dictated the complete death of the fragment, here survival requires the limitation of the self, or what may be called "partial death." Looking at vertical succession (or survival through replacement), we observed how the individual was caught in "time" and was unable to break that external limit. Man, however, is as much here as he is now, he is as much a prisoner of space as he is of time. Caught within a spatial ambiance, man is obliged to remain within this circle; yet notwithstanding this limitation, or rather because of it, the *totum* survives. In the very act of limitation of the one lies the possibility for the other to fulfill his function. This limitation or finitude of the fragment is double: it is constitutional and built-in—one is born neither omniscient nor omnipotent—and, as a consequence of the first, it is also confirmed by choice in those restrictions by which man limits himself to be this and only this. The individual can only be himself, as in the choice of a particular career, leaving through this restriction upon a horizontal plane of simultaneity room for the other, who is only himself and in being what he is, in turn allows a third man to be his own self, etc.[2]

This "mortification" is similar to the actual death of the indi-

---

[2] This calls to mind the process of specialization, with which we are so familiar in our day.

vidual which was imperiously asked for in our previous considerations, since here again, the survival of the *totum* depends upon this very act of self-restriction or partial death. An omnipotent being within the framework of the human *totum* would through its presence upset the structure of the latter. Only the "partial" selves build up a physical *totum*. To conclude, if the individual were unlimited, i.e., replacement (in time) or juxtaposition (in space) were superfluous, the fragment would be the *totum*. This is obviously not the case and was excluded as a postulate from the start.

Yet it would be wrong to consider these "partial" or limited selves as merely juxtaposed. In fact, they are dependent both upon one another and upon the space-continuum in which they move. The death of Albert Camus is an example of this latter dependence. Camus was a defender of existential freedom, yet he was himself caught in the unavoidable when his car headed towards destruction. His death was "unavoidable" and we call him a "victim." Obviously unavoidability implies essential dependency, and to be a victim means to be conditional upon what-one-is-not.[3] What we have observed might be formulated into a rule: a dependence in origin transforms itself into a dependence in subsistence, i.e., the individual man is made out of what-he-is-not; subsequently he can only live from what-he-is-not. That which went into the structure and development of an individual is a congeries of elements, all of which were not-what-he-is. The reconstruction results in what-he-is and makes that result unique. But to remain such, he is, without intermittence, caught in an exchange with what-he-is-not, whether in a physical, biological, intellectual or moral form. In fact, he *is* this perpetual dependency upon what-he-is-not. Here again, as in the chronological succession, the relational element is pervasive. In this lies his perpetual contamination and ever-present menace. Aristotle's insight into making the Prime Mover independent from the world of man and from the world in general was very clever indeed, but this could only happen to a god.

Within the space-continuum moves our *totum genus humanum* or human totality, and just as the individual man is dependent

---

[3] Freedom, of course, should not be ignored and will be more fully discussed later. We should point out here, however, that freedom must not be confused with independence.

upon what-he-is-not, so also, and for the same reason, is he dependent upon who-he-is-not. Once more dependence of origin has transformed itself into a dependence of subsistence: man is born from man, and once there, leans upon man. Breughel's tragic painting of the blind guiding the blind comes to mind except for the fact that there is no pit, for our pit would be only for the isolated man. One cannot survive where the other is absent, nor can one remain sane of mind among the insane. We observed above how the self is "mortified" or in one way or other "self-restricted"; we can now add that, while the inner structure of the *totum physicum humanum* requires this multiplicity of "partial" selves, it appears equally that the "partial" selves require the *totum*. The individual must be a fragment in the present structure of the broken *totum humanum*, yet in order to survive as fragment, he needs the *totum*. He appears, on the horizontal no less than on the vertical level, *qui-ab-altero* and *a-quo-alter*. Limitations in time and space go together, for the only way to be part of an organic *totum* is to be born from that *totum* in time, but once one is born from a *totum*, one is part of it in space.

From our previous considerations, it appears that no greater mistake can be made than that of ascribing to the individual human "fragment" some form of metaphysical independence without sufficient consideration for its collateral connections. All terminology which isolates the "fragment" can no longer be used in fairness and precision to describe the individual existent. The latter can only be completely understood when "comprehended," i.e., placed upon a line of past and future and within a supporting frame of left and right. To "comprehend" implies to posit within its chronological and spatial dimensions. Man is *from* and *toward*, and he is this by way of completion. Through his very being, the individual man either achieves, replaces, corrects or supports.

One cannot prevent the intellectual, of course, from playing the game of solitude—it gives him a sort of Cartesian self-sufficiency and the joy of holding in the inner self a fulcrum of certainty—but he must remember that any assertion of the *I* which excludes the *we* commits a sin of omission, since it forgets that it is only through the *we* that the *I* is there. At some point or other in any dialectic the wisdom of the *totum* catches up with the subtleties of the fragment. And on the basis of our point of departure—the collectivity of mankind as physical *totum*—Cartesian subjectivism, or for that matter any solipsistic trend, needs correction. A look into the remote history of the *totum genus humanum* will confirm our position.

Totality and Reflection

WHETHER or not the species as a whole may reach farther than the individual in the ultimate conquest of knowledge is a question which will be examined later, but in the act of reflection the individual undoubtedly leads the species. For the human fragment —unlike the *totum genus*—has a capacity for self-introspection, or the return of thought upon itself. The human individual passes away, and his lifespan is shorter than that of the species; but for a brief moment he is a center of solitude, where, utterly alone, he must face himself. This, his greatest asset, is also his gravest pain, for in the power of reflective consciousness, which the individual possesses over and against the species, lies the realization of his finitude as well. Self-awareness awakens the implicit awareness that one is made for juxtaposition and that one's finitude "invites" the other.

The development of *reflection* in man had a striking impact upon his evolution and history. Paleontologists have advanced the theory that the early evolution of primates took place in the form of dispersive movement; branches of life at certain more active moments separated themselves from the main stem. After a certain time these branches were in turn ready for a new scission. This was the pattern before the advent of reflection.[4]

Upon the gradual emergence of a more explicit self-awareness, the "hominized" animals came together. As soon as man knew what he was, fragment of a *totum*, and realized what he could do with others of his sort, the dispersive movement towards further branching out was dramatically reversed, and replaced by a *rapprochement* and a dwelling together. The sadness of self-awareness

---

[4] See on this point Pierre Teilhard de Chardin, *The Phenomenon of Man*, trans. Bernard Wall (New York: Harper & Row, 1959), p. 301.

was made more endurable by this mutual attraction. A variety of new approaches to life resulted from man's cooperative efforts, such as the ability to plan for the future, the invention of tools, and the introduction of community life, with its division of labor. Plato's primitive state was enabled to come to light. "Reflection" inside man gave birth to the man outside *as* other.[5] And if reason revealed to man the loneliness of his solitude, it gave him at the same time a knowledge of the power of collectivity.

Although it cannot be asserted with absolute certainty, it appears as if all through history participation has grown. In the increasingly complex way of life of our modern day, the human fragment is more than ever part. As soon as the child is born, he becomes entangled in a web of traditions, languages, customs, a body of laws and rules, sciences and religion, constituting a tightly closed environment which takes over as soon as he leaves the womb. The species offers him the inheritance of millions. He is part and fragment, and if he is wise, he *plays his part*. At times he may want to escape his boundaries and be, all by himself, the whole of man. Actually he does not break his own contours. In that wisdom which is born from self-awareness, he does not exclude anything *next* to him, since nature excludes so much *in* him. The assembly line, which has been so severely decried, incarnates a philosophy of the future, whether we want it to or not, for it shows what men can do to a product when they approach it simultaneously and when they complete one another.

Totality as Chain of the Unequal

THIS insight into the structure of dependency should not make us lose sight of that which is subsistent in man. For although man is thoroughly relational on both a vertical line of descent and a horizontal plane of simultaneity, he is nevertheless distinct from—and opposed to—that upon which he is dependent. He is, although a relation (completing and completed), a subsistent relation. He is towards-the-other but he is not-the-other.

Whether or not this subsistent character has metaphysical im-

---

[5] And we shall add later that the *other* is *my* reflection or the way through which I reflect. (ch. 6.)

plications lies outside the scope of my method, but within the observable dimensions of our descriptive analysis, it appears that this character is his from his very birth. At the moment of his entrance into the *totum—totum universum* and *totum humanum—* he is marked forever. His birth is his destiny. This is not to advocate some dire fatalism but only to point out that which can easily be observed; from that moment on he travels a certain world route that is his and his alone. He is he, and not you or I. The amount of freedom which this implies we shall discuss later, but we can observe already both a uniqueness in origin and a distinct *curriculum vitae*—a wholly individual life course. He is definitely not the other; his relational structure is both exclusive and unique.

This exclusive character will be his until his death. Even in the act of procreation, he will pass on only what we have in common, not what he himself is and has become. He is fragment, no doubt, but he is irreplaceable fragment. He is complement, but he is so in a unique way. The existential impact of the act by which he completes the *totum* and in this very completion is what he is, must be a never-again. Thus the individual existent completes the *totum genus,* he does so uniquely and he is the necessary condition of the world being as it is. At the same time, he is only provisional, and unable alone and in himself to finish the *totum*. He is both transitory and irreplaceable. In his uniqueness lie both the dignity and the dependency of man; he is such, but he is only such.

The unique multiplied in the texture of the *totum genus* results, of course, in inequality. Inequality is fundamental. We touch here upon the core of our study: each man cooperates in the structure and the survival of the human ensemble as a fragment only, but he cooperates as no one else can. Plato's Phoenician tale seems to corroborate this opinion. The citizens of the ideal republic are to be told that their youth and education are but a dream and that they really are autochthonous, i.e., sent up from the earth, which being their mother they are bound to love and defend. This is a fiction, of course, which Plato admits is an audacious one, but he seems even more hesitant to introduce the second half of his fable. "Citizens, we shall say to them in our tale, you are brothers, yet God framed you differently."[6] Whatever may be the

---

[6] *Rep.* 415 a.

value of the other applications he wishes to make, two things strike us: first, the fact that "in the earth" we are molded differently, and second, that outside ourselves a fate exists, governing our life and being and molding us by a force beyond our power to conceive and certainly beyond our ability to alter. This is evident from such phrases of the tale as: ". . . God has framed," "God proclaims, . . ." "For an oracle says. . . ." In making this second point Plato seems to imply not only that inequality is a fact, but also that it is as inevitable as destiny and as impossible to eliminate.

On both themes Plato is right, however unpopular the idea of inequality was in his day and is now. In this world, with its spatio-temporal architecture, salvation of the *totum* is possible only through a variegated contribution coming from a multiplicity of unequal fragments. Survival, de facto, is concatenation of the unequal. Upon the ontological basis of the unique and the unequal rests mutual completion, whether in succession or in horizontal simultaneity. Man lives in a world of exchange. Life is possible only under the form of a trade of the unequal, each one being and contributing what the other lacks. The *totum genus humanum* must be made up out of the heterogeneous.[7]

Totality as Eternal, or Sex as a Sign of Mortality

IN conclusion, the concrete individual is the atom of the species, fragment of the *totum*, referential in his temporal and spatial dimensions, unique in his relational structure, and made for completion. Ultimately he does not survive; the totality does. It does

---

[7] Nietzsche has dramatically emphasized this in calling for what he terms "Love of the remotest," which is a way of insisting that our tendencies must go towards that which is beyond and far, i.e., the best, omitting the nearest and the mediocre. Inequality, then, becomes the basis not only for mere survival but also for survival with progress, for only upon inequality is evolution upwards possible.

"Where there exists a love which fosters what is best in the few who are best, progress is the result." (N. Hartmann, *Ethics*, vol. II, trans. Stanton Coit [New York: Macmillan Co.; London, G. Allen & Unwin, 1932], p. 321.) We need not add that Nietzsche's *Fernsten-liebe* in its denial of *Nächstenliebe* overshot the mark. One value should not make us forget another.

so, however, as fragmented *totum*, the elements of which, being fundamentally imperfect, replace one another in a linear succession and uphold one another on a horizontal span of simultaneous existence. Both dimensions taken together (existence in depth and existence in width) result in the *totum genus* or species taken as a whole. This *totum* obviously does not exist all at once (the dead are innumerable, as are the unborn), and concerning its eternality we should be reserved. Nothing proves, indeed, that it possesses what I call an eternity by right, since we have no sign that the human species is eternal by sheer necessity of its essence, but it has an eternity by fact, since it is technically structured in such a way that the individual functions as a link and procreates, before dying, a being similar to himself, fulfilling in this way an essential function of relation as defined that-which-is-from-the-other and that-from-which-the-other-is. Sex, therefore, is ultimately a recognition of mortality and an attempt to survive through the other.

2

History as Completion

Human Acts as Fragmentary

THE fragmentary structure of man unavoidably implies the fragmentary structure of his works; these activities are deserving of an equally close examination.

Whether we have in mind the elementary inventiveness of food and shelter, or a more complex performance, such as automation or some artistic achievement which answers man's need to live in beauty, we are struck by the fact that human activity appears above all to be anti-suicidal. It aims towards protecting men, whether individual or in groups, against a menace or discomfort in one form or another. This protection, therefore, ultimately points to survival.

This survival can be a survival in the strict sense of the word, which is a mere survival without progress, or it can be a survival in progress. The former is a protracted existence of the group, characterized by procreation only, with little or no attempt of creation. The quality and tempo of creativity over and above mere procreation expresses the level of one's survival. Creativity occurs when wishes for higher values become needs, and these needs provoke attempts towards fulfillment. This survival in progress—and here again I observe the factual—is the present phase of survival in a major part of our planet.

Yet, even when performed in a rhythm of progress, human actions carry the stigma of imperfection and need a complement under the form of replacement and additional support. In the unfulfilled character of each undertaking, considered in itself, lies the urge for its completing continuation, and in this limitation, moral and physical, the need for its multiplication. It appears, once more, that life works through the many and not through the one. The juxtaposition of human undertakings makes for eventual correction just as succession makes possible a certain success. It is not without reason that success originally had the meaning of succession, for the favorable outcome is due to a completing succession or co-related sequence of fragments.

These observations, which actually are merely factual, posit the relational character of the events. The mere juxtaposition of historical events in time and space is insufficient to explain the rhythm of survival. Event B not only comes after event A but also has a complementary dimension, i.e., it makes up for and corrects the unavoidable deficiency of the preceding and neighboring event. Each historical event, therefore, constitutes through its position in time and in space a complement or element of completion. The factual basis of this assertion is obvious: if we accept the finitude of the human "fragment" and of his works on the one hand and the fact of survival of the *totum* on the other hand, this correcting and replacing activity through history cannot be denied. History is completion. By "completed" we do not mean, however, "brought to its entirety or perfection." Such a meaning would transpose us into an artificial semantic created mainly for utilitarian purposes. In fact, nothing is ever brought to an end. What is meant, then, is that by the act of completion, a "deficiency is somehow remedied." This definition now needs further analysis.

In order to grasp the conception of history as unfolding through completion, one must visualize: (1) the *totum genus humanum* (or any *totum* for that matter) as fragmented, and (2) the fragments themselves, whether persons, groups or events, as not self-sufficient. Since these fragments have only a limited impact in space and time, they must complete and be completed (by replacement or correction), with the result that the *totum* itself survives, although in an altered state.

It is important to insist that the *totum* can be any *totum*. Although we are usually concerned in this study with the whole of mankind, our analysis can be applied to any other whole, e.g., a political, racial, or national group. Such a minor whole, however, obviously stands in a double relation—the relation from *totum* to fragment (its own internal members or elements), and the relation from fragment to *totum* (the *totum* of which it is itself part and fragment). No *totum* which is fragment also (as in the case of the minor wholes, e.g., nation) can have any claim of eternal or absolute standing, much as its members might like to think so. It is permissible to hope for a long-lasting subsistence of a nation —such is indeed the power of all myth—but it is presumptuous to claim for it an unconditional and perennial survival. For such is the nature of the fragment—whether it be nation or any other group—that sooner or later it will be in one way or another completed; it must be replaced or altered, and in this very act, serve the survival of some higher *totum*. The planetary man—who will be introduced in the last chapter of this volume—has an insight into the possibility of surrendering all of the *totum* which is at the same time fragment. From the viewpoint of the *totum*, its own inner fragmentation and equilibrium provide security and can be considered an absolute. However, from the viewpoint of the larger *totum* of which it is a part, the smaller does not survive. All minor groups—and this includes nations—do not survive intact, or without alteration; only the human species or *totum genus humanum* can be said ultimately to survive. No doubt, the objection can be made that the *totum genus humanum*, which we have considered to be fragmented but not fragmentary, is itself part of a world-structure, hence is destined for replacement. Without denying this possibility, I do not at present study it as an eventuality.

Human Acts and Their Mutual Completion

A distinction should now be made between immediate and remote completion.

Completion is immediate when it seems to function within our individual orbit, i.e., within such a spatial and chronological propinquity that it can be checked through empirical observation. We might consider, as a concrete example, the history of France and of Europe during the Napoleonic period. When Napoleon, as first consul, took in hand the reins of the French government after the coup d'état of 1799, he faced a country which, still shattered by the terrible crisis of 1789, stood on the verge of disaster. The treasury contained a mere 137,000 francs; neither taxes nor pensions were being paid. Industry and business had virtually come to a halt, and the jobless were ten times more numerous than they had been in 1789. Bridges and public buildings were in a state of neglect, arable land laid fallow, the harbors of Marseilles and Le Havre were empty of all traffic. Soldiers, neglected and unpaid, were deserting in droves, in many cases to menace the countryside as brigands. Vendée and Brittany had still not submitted to the central government. The need for authority and organization to rescue France from this extraordinary chaos called for some unusual intervention. And Napoleon appeared on the scene.

Seven years later France had drastically changed. A revolution had taken place politically and morally, for during the consulship of Napoleon, France gained most of her famous institutions and the essentials of her machinery of government. Under his leadership order and discipline were reestablished, education reorganized, religion permitted, through the Concordat, to become influential once more. The *code civil* was introduced to protect France against the excesses of the Directoire. There was even time for superfluity; during this period builders gave Paris her most beautiful boulevards, such as the Champs Elysées, terminating in the magnificent Arc de Triomphe. The emperor's army, the best in Europe, was able to step from victory to victory—Marengo, Rivoli, Austerlitz.

France had survived, and when we look closely, we discover in the very fact of its internal *dismemberment* the reason for its salvation. What was corrupt and a menace for the whole could not be salvaged by itself, but only by what was not so. This rescue implies that the one was not the other. There is an inevitable loss incurred by internal multiplicity, for as we have mentioned before, there is a loss for *A* in not being *B*, but in this very handicap lies also the root of redemption, for it allows *B* to complete *A*. We need the multiple and the diverse. But the same structure also explains why any intervention is, in fact, limited and provisional, for what is fragment itself can never have the durability and wide range of the *totum*.

However—and here is another application of our principles—

France through her recovery became so strong a country that it asserted itself as a menace to the continent of which it formed a part. That which was the completion of France as a totality became a threat, or an assumed threat, for Europe. In order to meet that threat, the successive coalitions of Austria, Prussia, Russia and England were formed. Now the roles were reversed, and that nation which had asserted itself as powerful and independent was defeated by the many, and in this act of defeat admitted its dependency upon an unremitting European totality. Its ontological status of *totum*, however cogent, took on the status of member and fragment, with the survival of the European totality resulting. Waterloo symbolized the rescue of the larger *totum* that was Europe because of the fragmentation and internal repairability of that *totum*.

The application of our theory is double. On the one hand, Napoleon constitutes a complement for a debilitated France; and on the other hand, the Holy Alliance, springing up from a troubled Europe, disciplines a nation considered to be a threat to its continental equilibrium. The continent will retain its present kind of organization until some day, in a more world-wide conflagration, the *totum genus humanum* may eliminate or alter Europe to save itself. A totality survives as long as its "membership" is diversified enough so that health and disease are distributed among the many and the different. To grasp the referential attitude between sickness and remedy means to have an insight into complementarity at work.

The sense of the historical, therefore, implies a double awareness. First, one must have a sense of *time*. Without time there can be no succession and without succession there can be no history. The historian, therefore, in manipulating events, cannot overlook their time-consuming character, nor the fact that they come in a sequence of before-and-after. When precision and care for factual reporting is fashionable, as it is at present, the historian prides himself upon carefully describing this temporal sequence, and we do not have to worry overly about this first requisite.

However, in addition to this awareness of succession in time, the historian must also have an insight into the referential structure of human act. Human activities appear to be dispersed chronologically and spatially. In order to understand them, one needs that reassembling act of the mind whereby one sees the fragmentarity of the elements and their mutual completion. He must understand that a *totum* survives as long as within itself it can step from one "imperfection" to another, the latter being less imperfect, to be sure, but provisional nonetheless. Napoleon affords us a magnificent example of a fragmentary strength which has saved a nation and has no less spectacularly surrendered it when reaching inevitable limits. The deepest grasp of history implies a sense of its contingency and of its indestructible potency of transmission.

The second part of our double form of historical completion has been called *remote* completion. This takes place when the completing activity arches over space and time in such a way that an individual cannot discover and categorize it with certainty. Through this completion persons and events, though they be continents or centuries apart, nevertheless outbalance and correct one another. This implies an impact of the distant and the future upon the here and the now: "What will be and must be is the ground of that which is," Nietzsche says pointedly.

A global view of history which would present the birth of cultures, their growth and decline, their death and replacement and the ultimate survival of a *totum*, whether national or planetary, would ideally be able to show this remote completion in action, but it might also fail to do so through presumption or through submersion in detail, as is the case with the Spenglerian vision. Let us avoid this danger and merely state the general principle: observing immediate completion—by replacement or addition—to be an integral part of survival, we may assume, on the basis of that survival as fact that a similar process is at work beyond our observable limits. The *totum* will survive, since what is in need of completion will be completed, though we dare not at present attempt to predict in what way—as did Spengler. A remote future shapes the present, as on the tennis court, where the future accomplishment of the tennis player dictates his present gesture. Prophecy lies in the act itself, however, not in the awareness of the act, which is quite often performed in ignorance of its real motivation. The given reason for an act or the attempted "explanation" for an event is often merely self-deception. For the real reason lies far away in time and space, out of reach of the individual awareness. In chapter 6 of this volume, a further corroboration of this position will be attempted.

Pawns on a Chessboard Complete One Another: They Do Not Cause One Another

IT may be well at this point to caution against any confusion of complement and cause. A complement is not an efficient cause. Within a mosaic representation the individual segment does not causally produce the *totum*, but by way of complementarity each segment corrects and extends the limitation of its neighbor, which in turn "achieves" what the next has to offer. Each is complement of the other. Nor can the individual segments be said to cause the painting when taken collectively, for in their totality they are the painting. Just so, when we look at pawns on a chessboard, we notice how they complete one another, yet there is no causal interaction between the pawns of one camp. One cannot speak of a direct causal dimension of any one pawn with regard to the ensemble, for the pawn does not cause the totality, whether the latter be considered in its immobility or in its movement. It merely is part of a *totum*, and within that *totum*—whether the immobile alignment on the chessboard or the game in action—it supports and extends the limitation of the rest of the group. None of these pawns has absolute value by itself; each carries an impact only in cohesion with its neighbor. The fragments reinforce one another and in doing so constitute a texture; this texture is the *totum*. There is no *totum* over and above this interweaving of fragments which mutually reinforce one another.

It may be stated, therefore, that the phenomenon of completion takes place only when a totality is implicitly or explicitly accepted. Only against a background of a *totum* can one speak of completion. The *totum* can of course be present, but it can also be absent or, to be more precise, only partially present, as is the case with the *totum genus humanum*, which all through history comes into being in succession. But even this absence has a way of being present on the horizon as potential achievement or as a finality, which although never attained is always in the process of achieving itself. There is, therefore, in the phenomenon of completion a reference of the part to the *totum*.

To call this reference a form of finality or activity of the final cause is, in my opinion at least, presumptuous. It may indeed happen that the fragment has the avowed intention of devoting it-

self to the "salvation" of the totality, a possibility when that fragment is a living and conscious entity. However, we, as outsiders
who claim an identification with the *totum*, can merely say that
with the data at our disposal, things are what they are in their
ineffable variety and relational structure and that although we
have no conclusive argument for or against finality, we can in
many cases observe completion at work, even when finality is not
there. It is not a diminishment of man's value and intrinsic dignity
to underline his indigence, for it will appear from further reading
that modern man is indeed led to forfeit his isolation in return
for his own survival, whether he wishes it or not.

One can approach finality from still another angle and inquire
whether the acceptance of completion, especially when it results
ultimately in survival, does not presume the existence of some
Planner as well. It may be tempting to place above and beyond
the activity of the *totum* (the totality of mankind surviving) a
Mastermind or Supervisor, just as above and beyond the mosaic
representation stands the artist and behind the chess game is the
player. This conclusion cannot be drawn here, for one cannot
know with certainty whether that "arrangement" which one can
observe to result in the survival of the *totum* requires a Planner
distinct from the world or whether the planning is actually identical with things and can be called Nature.

This much on complement vs. cause. Although in the preceding
discussion, efficient cause was understood in a more traditional
way as that which through its influence actually produces the
effect, and not merely as a constant antecedent (in a Humian and
more modern way), this distinction does not affect our argument.
Cause whether as producing or merely as anteceding is not in the
strict sense a complement. The latter has certain nuances which are
not brought out by the concept of cause. It is this difference which
our analysis wants to bring out and which the rest of our study
will attempt to underline even more. As far as the metaphysical
dimension of the notion of complement is concerned, this is not
our concern here, since such an exploration lies outside the scope
of our method.

If Human Acts Are Human Only (and Not Divine), Do We Need a Manifold?

THE question may arise whether sometime in the future, completion will work only collaterally and not in succession. Or stated differently, if the "imperfection" of the fragment—whether it be man or his work—diminishes and gives way to a growing perfection, is the staggering multiplicity of fragments in succession still imperative? Once men are gods, do we need a multitude? If their works are divine, could they last forever?

Where the question touches man himself, it becomes so theoretical as to be almost meaningless. As long as man is man—we cannot of course guarantee indefinitely the fulfillment of that definition—the survival of the human species must be insured through the multiplication of its constitutive elements. However, as far as human achievements themselves are concerned, man has a right to dream of a perfect world in which all the values and accomplishments which a slow and struggling past gave us in succession are realized simultaneously, a world in which he sees classicism and romanticism, the mechanical and the humanistic, on a single stage in the same continuous act. A qualification must be made. Material accomplishments, which in their very essence participate in the finitude of the maker, are particularly doomed to disappear and be replaced. This is true as well for scientific work, which, because of its incessant growth and close dependency upon observation of the matter, must drop the imperfect theories that newer insights have replaced. It is in the realm of philosophical and artistic achievements that a greater claim to eternity can be made. For the higher human labor climbs towards the domain of the spirit, the more it partakes of its perennial value.

Philosophical and artistic works suffer less from chronological contingency, and the greatest of them may even be considered to be omnitemporal. Their success is not a mere result of succession. Although their individual approach is fragmentary, this omnitemporality allows them to fulfill a supplementary and outbalancing function all at once. One is tempted once more to wonder whether man cannot actualize one vast image, the fragmented components of which can be apprehended as a unity, structured out of a simultaneous addition of values which the past has lived in succession. It is still a question of fragments completing fragments, of course, but the completion is purely collateral and no longer successive.

For man may attribute his suffering, his errors, his lack of understanding, in large part to the excesses and the deficiencies of life as it must be lived, each act or idea being forced to wait for its counterpart or being supplemented by a counterpart which, in spite of its qualities, carries with it some defect. A mechanical age should not eliminate humanistic values, nor should speculative thought exclude scientific investigation. Succession can be an instrument to success, but it can never through its very ontological structure be other than an obstacle to perfection. In making survival possible, it is of course better than nothing at all, but in doing so through the means of replacement or addition of fragments, it rules out the perfect world. For the replacing fragment as fragment can never contain all the qualities of its predecessors. The "perfect world" does not at present interest us—actually the very fact of succession makes it nonexistent—but the attainment of a more perfect knowledge, or of an improved version of our fragmentary knowledge, does seem more closely within our reach. One would see it brought about if man could control temporal succession and keep in a tense juxtaposition what in the past "has lived the time that live the roses, the time of one morning" (Malherbe). This is precisely what I have in mind when I will call for a juxtaposition of different philosophical views or artistic achievements; how this can be done will be the topic of further analysis. For this would, if successful, be one way of counteracting the inevitable flaw of survival in succession. The history of philosophy, then, like history in general, would still involve completion, but unlike ordinary history would not depend upon succession.

3

Truth as Angular

Truth as Possible

THE understanding of complementarity at work in the realm of ideas cannot be grasped without a prior examination of the notion of truth. Since this is a difficult and broad topic, we must first restrict our inquiry.

For the past two thousand years philosophers have come back repeatedly to the general statement that truth is conformity—the Latin word for it is *adequatio*—of the mind with the real. However, they have endlessly debated the manner in which this conformity is fulfilled. For the deeper meaning of conformity as well as of the terms *mind* and *real* has ever eluded them. The purpose of this chapter is not to reexamine these perennial problems, but rather to strike out in a new direction and to suggest in what way a knowledge of the concrete existent individual may fulfill the definition of truth.

Let us make clear from the start that the defense of an "individual" truth, the character of which will be explained later, should not be understood as a rejection of all "objective" or "absolute" truth. For in asserting that "there is no objective truth," one implies the contradictory statement "there is truth." This initial attitude, as a protection against intellectual despair, is fundamental. Man must be able to assert that there is a Truth as ideal, or what one can call the "truth of God." This is a prerogative of his type of knowing, the prerogative of going speculatively beyond his limitations to accept the possibility of an ideal Truth without meeting it positively. And although in its integrity it eludes his grasp, that Truth should not be distorted to meet man's limited power. Judgments made in its light are inescapable, not by virtue of its being God's Truth, but because, whether there is a God or not, it is also man's absolute ideal.[1]

However—and our second preliminary remark brings us immediately to the human level—truth is unmistakingly fulfilled in proportion to the amount of knowledge. "To have a true idea signifies nothing more than to know something perfectly and very well," writes Spinoza. All our knowledge, however, is human, and as human, it is limited. Man is not divine: he did not make the world, and he neither lived "before" time nor will he live when time is "gone." In order to know a beginning and an end, one needs a presence to the hereafter. This limitation is common to all men, and we must accept the fact that without revelation of God, man's truth will never go beyond man's humanly acquired knowledge.

We may not conclude from this that human truth, however limited, is a divine lie. Human knowledge has, to an extent, a universal content that is common to all; for example, certain basic principles such as that of noncontradiction, and the assertions of mathematics. To these assent cannot be denied, for it is given not in virtue of the individual insight as such, but on the basis of a belonging to—and sharing of—the common rational nature. On this Aquinas asserts, it seems rightly so, that there exists a command of nature by which the assenting to or the dissenting from certain principles is not within our power but takes place necessarily.[2] This command of nature is that to which the species as *a whole* submits. It would be wrong, therefore, to call the science of mathematics inhuman because of its unemotional clarity; it is not inhuman, it is merely impersonal. For the second adjective points more accurately to the nonindividual structure of mathematics and the unquestioned acceptability of its principles to every human being capable of grasping their content and verification.

In addition to this universally accepted conformity to the real, there is also the unique vision of the concrete individual. Meta-

---

[1] The problem of "absolute truth" and its existence will be elaborated upon in chapter 8 of

Volume I.
[2] See *S.Th.* I.II. 17, 6.

physicians of the past have concentrated upon the *ought* to the extent that they have frequently overlooked the *is*. Within our approach, with its claims of being descriptive of the existential and its attempts to analyze things as they are, not merely as they ought to be, the individual phase of truth must be more fully explored.

Truth as Angular

MAN has appeared to us in our previous pages as the undivided fragment of the human species. In the realm of empirical knowledge, the vision of one man because it is here-and-now-and-such-only contains in its act of perception certain elements which he sees and others do not see. And the other man, similarly, perceives certain elements from his vantage point which he sees and others do not. That part of the real which is opaque to one is so owing to his "absence," just as that which reveals itself to another does so owing to his "presence." The individual, ever trapped in a determined location, must of necessity miss the panorama of omnipresence. We might add that the gradual and partial human discovery of empirical data betrays a certain ignorance, since the Omniscient, if He exists, does not discover; He already knows. Whether considered in space or in time, the individual vision is limited to what I call an *angular vision*. This term *angular* will be of continual use from now on in this study. There is implied no moral meaning, but only the meaning of restriction which it originally possessed, i.e., vision in the form of an angle, hence limited because of the limitation of the viewer.

As soon as the individual man proceeds deductively beyond the merely empirical into the more elaborate interpretation of the empirical, he is seen even more clearly to stand behind his conclusions as a man and a fragment, not as a *totum genus*. In an argumentation, he sets out literally on his own. He can of course attempt to convince others of the plausibility of his reasoning and may very well succeed, but he will never convince the *totum,* which never takes that which did not originate within itself as an expression of the whole. The history of philosophy, with its undeniable variety, is the conclusive proof of our statement. Whether it be in his everyday knowledge or in a philosophical interpretation, the vision of any one individual bears the stigma of his fragmentarity.

However—and this is an important corrective—to be partial (understood here etymologically, i.e., as opposed to complete) does not mean to be false. My knowledge may very well involve an insight which other individuals do not have, it may or it may not be available to others, but whatever its exclusiveness and its incommunicability may be, it cannot for these reasons be considered to be inconsistent, or not in conformity with the real. Subjectivity does not necessarily imply falsity, for in the sense here presented, it merely emphasizes the individual insight of the individual existent and is, for that reason, not necessarily in conflict with reality. Subjectivity points, in our case, to the unique objectivity, or a conformity with the real, which possibly can be comprehended only by the one "visionary." The conformity with the real to the extent of its presence in an angular vision, I call an *angular truth*.

In order to clarify this unique and segmental adequation to reality which is the result of man's inalienable limitation of vision, I would like to borrow Heidegger's term "discovery." I do not herewith want to follow the German philosopher all the way in his description of truth. Yet it seems that the term "discovery" indicates better than any other the very limited, and at the same time the very specific, approach of the individual man. The individual existent *reveals*: from a phenomenological viewpoint, he is continual revelation and opens the world to himself, and thereby himself to the world. Unlike Heidegger, however, I do not yet call this truth, but merely a prelude to it.[3] Truth itself is conformity resulting from discovery or revelation. No conformity can extend beyond the scope of revelation or discovery. Hence no

---

[3] Heidegger rejects the idea of conformity altogether as being obscure and meaningless and limits himself to the notion of truth as being discovery based upon freedom. Yet this is not satisfactory. The very defense of the notion as he understands it implies some form of conformity for the militant attitude by which the mind asserts that something is such and not so, implies that "discovery" progresses into some form of conformity. To assert a position concerning truth really denotes that in one way or other one's own position "conforms" to the real and is the right one.

truth or conformity with the real can go beyond the angle, whether obtuse or acute, of man's noetic vision. It naturally follows that if there is a certain amount of discovery, there is concomitantly a huge amount of concealment, which carries with it the unavoidable consequence of nonconformity. In this case, since it is not positively asserted, it could best be called "privative nonconformity." Man, the concrete existent, is necessarily condemned to wander within an angular visual limit, beyond which this privative nonconformity is prodigious; his brief day lights but a portion of a vast night. Since the grasp of the object upon the individual mind is no less powerful than the hold of the subject upon the object, noetic limitation is rarely recognized. The term *fascination* is not too strong to describe the state of those who are caught within their own knowledge. The individual man, spellbound by his own light, wanders for the most part in a crepuscular world.

Angular Visions as Unequal

IN this state of affairs, it is important to recall that the inequality of different views is grounded upon the finitude of man's vision. To be *such* excludes to be *so*, and although my truth has a face, it never wears the face of another. If it has the stigma of being mine, it has also the honor of being different. Hence, if the total *genus* of men is to have any knowledge of the total reality, this datum has to be and is, in fact, divided. The world is a common ground from which a multitude of thinking centers appropriate their share of knowledge, each mind facing its particular portion. This portion may of course be expanded through learning, but eventually as one's vision becomes less extensive and more and more intensive, the moment comes when the boundaries are clearly marked, and the circle enclosing the knower with his "object" is complete. Man is caught within the limits, however extensive, of his own noesis. That which the *totum humanum*, as a timeless and aspatial entity, receives all at once, it renders slowly and interminably through the diversity of its individual fragments, which divide unequally among themselves the global datum, quite often ignoring what the other knows and above all unaware that the totality alone, not the individual, constitutes the fecundity of the globe.

This in no way diminishes the contribution of the individual mind, which always remains unique in its complementary support. In fact, its complementary contribution is built upon its ontological inequality and noetic uniqueness. If all and each of us knew all the knowable, communication would be rendered superfluous and convergent contribution made impossible. Silent contemplation would be the only issue, as it is for the mystic who faces the Absolute. A fragmented species implies a fragmented vision and only in the glow of unequal vision shall we play the game of conversation, for only the different can shake off our indifference. We need the dissimilar or angular truth.

Yet this singular vision of each one of us is communicable only when conveyed by that vehicle which alone can make it understandable, namely the similar. Communication is made possible through the use of conventional semantics: agreement upon the similar and its use conveys the dissimilar or angular vision from individual to individual.

When this function is betrayed, i.e., when the similar is no longer merely the means of communication but becomes the end itself, we obtain a form of extreme unification at the price of individuality. This is essentialism, with its cult for essences and possibles and its implicit contempt for the ontologically and noetically diverse. There is, undoubtedly, a strange urge to discover the "similar" in men by means of the "similar." Historical observation, however, reveals that this endeavor is outbalanced by another; man feels the need, either through emphasis upon the "reasons of the heart" of Pascal or upon the existential unique, to break up a homogeneous noetic bloc into a variety of perceptions and a multiplicity of awarenesses. Mankind is subject to this double law, with its contrary drives. Since the *totum genus* calls for survival in fragmented variety, it must explode into inequality, hence respect the angular view of the individual and the unique. However, since communicability and unification are no less important, it must protect the semantic commodities of the similar as well.

That which constitutes the inner tension of the species reflects the microcosmic tragedy of the individual, who is a unique fragment, possessing a personal outlook and an angular truth, yet who craves to be all. However, in desiring to be all, he must choose, and being himself, he forever chooses himself. Tension there is and always will be, for both the similar and the dissimilar are present in the ontological makeup of the individual man and result from his belonging to the physical *totum genus humanum* without in himself being that *totum*.

Both dimensions have to be respected, if survival can be guaranteed. In the domain of the angular truth and its expression, it is through the vehicle of common understanding that the "dissimilar" or existentially unique is enabled to come to the surface and that some attempt towards universalization and unification can be made. I say "attempt," for more cannot be expected; nature has skillfully taken care of that. Contemporaneous agreement in a universal way would result in a homogeneous intellectual bloc and kill that noetic inequality which is the charm of a fragmented species. Universal respect—if not agreement—rewards only those who are gone, and one better tolerates a dead Plato than a living Platonist.

Art as Creation of the Angular

THE problem of angular truth is no less acute in art. Malraux, for example, believes truth to be the expression of one man. "The great painter is a prophet as regards his art, but he fulfills his prophecy himself, by painting," he writes. "The truth that was van Gogh was for him a plastic absolute towards which he constantly aspired; for us his truth is what his pictures signify as an ensemble. The truth of the classical painter is a concept of perfection and is not the truth of the world of visual experience nor that of the artist's vision but the truth of painting *qua* painting. Little did Gauguin care if the Tahiti beach was pink or not, or Rembrandt whether the sky above Golgotha was really that of *The Three Crosses*; or the Master of Chartres whether the Kings of Judah were really like his statues; or the Sumerian sculptor whether Sumerian women were like their effigies of Fertility." . . . "All his life Frans Hals had painted with a stubborn independence that heeded nothing but the truth that was in him; he was impervious alike to poverty and wealth, anguish and peace of mind. A truth that was inexpressible in any language but its own language of forms; that truth which is no less self-assured and successful than in 'pariah' art, for we find it in Poussin as in van Gogh, in Racine the courtier as in Rimbaud the vagabond or in Villon the footpad. It engenders in the case of Goya, monsters; in that of Rubens, the portraits of his children."[4] "Truth for the artist," continues Malraux, "is painting which frees him from his disharmony with the outside world and his masters."[5] One can discuss whether the Hegelian allusion which Malraux includes at the end of this quotation is a useful addition—it might be. The important part, however, is that Frans Hals, according to Malraux, incorporated his private universe in *The Governors of the Almshouse,* while Goya incarnated his in the evil spirits haunting him, and Fra Angelico sought to create a world that was hardly of this world. No one artist has set out to create a total truth or an exhaustive conformity to the real. Once more, truth was fragment.

When the work of art is a cooperative effort, it expresses an epochal view of the world of its own period. The Parthenon both reveals a world and *is* through this world; it is indeed the monument of a civilization (I dare to hope that the trite epithet has fresh meaning), the witness of a faith, the synthesis of a whole period of history and of the way the Greeks of that time viewed certain values. It is a discovery of a world, and as such results in a truth. As an absolute, art is a failure; its disclosures must be segmental, not only since no victory over the matter is complete, but also since the insight into an epoch is tied to that epoch. Ironically, in the very reason for its failure, lies also the reason for its success. For if the failure of all art is due to its finitude, so also is its beauty; the work of art caught in the matter, prisoner of time and space, can be this, and only this. The poem or the painting or the statue is individual, unique, unduplicable—if it is not these things, it is not art.[6]

---

[4] *The Voices of Silence*, trans. Stuart Gilbert (Garden City, N. Y., Doubleday & Co., 1953), pp. 356, 358.

[5] *Ibid.*, footnote, p. 359.

[6] We face here once more the problem of communicability, of course, and since artistic truth has to be perceptible, we need the medium or vehicle of the "similar." The *similar* and *communicability* have to be there, for we belong to the one species, and without it, the artist is buried alive, a lonely emperor under an empire of colors.

Angular Vision as the Ground of Freedom

WITH these considerations concerning angular truth in mind, we are prepared to discuss a topic which we have hitherto skirted, that of man's freedom.

Although life as a whole has appeared to us as an ascending adventure, consistently more optimistic than the living, we know that this ascent is a devious one, with all the detours and circumventions, the retreats and advances of a multitude of self-conscious centers. The individual existent, notwithstanding his relational structure, is the mobile segment of the *totum*. His mobility is not merely physical but also psychic; against and notwithstanding a background of belonging to the *totum genus*, he is able to assert himself, i.e., to choose within certain limits the form and the mode of his uniqueness. His ability to choose is a manifestation of freedom, though freedom in itself eludes definition and is by essence unjustifiable.

Choice or the possibility of choice is a distinctive quality, perhaps even the quality of human freedom. And it exists because of the existence of angular truth; choice and angular truth are correlative. As the individual man goes beyond that insight which he, as a human being, sharing the common rational nature, must accept, he lands upon the terrain of angular vision, where compulsion of adherence no longer exists and where man is, what we call in human terms, "free." When the cognitive power confronts what-is-not-absolute-but-merely-relative, one can freely prefer one thing to another. This does not imply that within angular truth no absolute truth-value can be contained, but only that *this* absolute caught by the angular vision does not have the impact of the absolute; it is obscured by the shadows in which moves that human achievement which is outside the compellent clarity of numbers and first principles. The object of the angular vision becomes the contingent, and our reaction upon the awareness of this contingent character we call freedom.

With possibility of choice, however, I do not claim to have defined freedom, nor am I certain that I have reached its most essential manifestation. One can easily imagine the existence of a being which, being everything, is pushed around by nothing; and although that infinite being would not be confronted by the necessity of choice, it would nonetheless be free. One can also think of a being—let us call it an angel, without asserting its actual existence—which, because of its total grasp (by hypothesis a non-angular vision), has understood in an instant what could be chosen and has done so, once and forever. For that being, existing outside of succession, there is no more alternative left, no more choice to make, there is no longer any awareness of indetermination; nevertheless, its inner structure is one admitting freedom. For that fragmentary entity called man, however, freedom of choice is and remains a necessity.

The necessary exercising of his freedom by the human fragment becomes a favor when executed. So, for example, every great philosopher's achievement synchronizes with the fulfillment of his freedom, of which his theory or angular vision is the proud attestation. But to allow the angular expressed in freedom implies an acceptance of the diverse, just as to face the diverse in a fragmented world means a tolerance for the angular.

That which is true for the philosopher is true for the artist as well, for the unusual is part of the beautiful. When the philosopher or artist breaks away from a tradition, more is involved than a dissatisfaction with a past; there is also, consciously or unconsciously, a manifestation of freedom at work, or a vision of the unique and personal.

The philosopher or the artist in choosing to be himself through his forceful assertion of inequality serves at the same time a completing function. On the basis of the survival of the *totum*, which is the empirical ground of our study, this function should not be considered to be a merely sportive one. The discovery of a new outlook upon the world corresponds in fact to a certain need. One does not choose the need, but the most able choose the answer. Hence, although the philosopher is fundamentally free in the choice and the creation of his theory, the latter will, nevertheless, be directed precisely towards that which, for this place and at this moment of history, needs to be expressed. Survival requires this variegated succession of fragmentary discoveries. The most subtle paradox of survival is that the individual, in protecting his own security, fighting for his own survival, loving and generating for his own ends, simultaneously causes, whether he wants it or not, a rhythm of survival in progress. Life is tolerant for individual whims, but not forgetful of its ultimate purpose. The irony of the *totum* consists precisely in the fact that it exploits the pride and the lust of the fragment, and upon occasion makes it noble against his will.

The following chapter will contain a first attempt to resolve the apparent contradictions of the multiplicity of angular truths and thereby bring a return to unity. Our age is one of analysis. We do not admire, we analyze. "The modern world has mutilated art, compelling it to examine details, small cubes, small ironical poems, small lyrical candy. . . . Our poetry lacks the incarnation, it should belong to heaven and earth, and to hell where it has to descend,"[7] writes Bernanos. The philosopher of our days has forgotten that if philosophy is analytic, it is also synthetic; and that if truth is angular and fragmentary, it is ipso facto additive. "We are only wrecks," exclaimed Rodin, admiring Chartres. This was his avowal that beauty is above all architectural. And so is philosophy.

The problem, therefore, consists in finding a point of view which will not sin through fixism, but will offer the human mind a possibility of unification and synthesis, while still respecting the continual need for analysis and fragmentation. The man of faith accomplishes the miracle by which he can overlook the "one" from all angles in realizing a unification through acceptance of revealed Truth, herewith introducing into his soul what John of the Cross has called "the experience of center." Faith brings him to his central point, which is God. To the philosopher, this attitude is ruled out at the start and he must try to achieve in another way this "experience of center."

---

[7] In a letter of January, 1942, | to the Brazilian poet di Lima.

4

Paradox and Unity

Paradox as a Tool of Unity

IN literary circles a paradox has often been defined as a statement which shocks through its audacity of expression yet is correct in its fundamental meaning. The etymology of the word favors this signification. Παράδοξος means "contrary to common expectation," hence, unusual. Plato himself used the term in the sense of *extraordinary*.[1] The paradox will often point to an apparent falsity, which can be restored to a meaningful sense upon a closer investigation. Improbable at first, the statement becomes plausible upon second examination. When Christ tells us "Blessed are the meek, for they shall inherit the earth," He formulates a paradox, for it seems extremely unlikely that he who makes constant concessions will become the conqueror of the world, yet in giving it a second thought, one discovers that the opposition between meekness and conquest of the earth can be overcome. Many a skillful orator has taken it upon himself to prove just that. The content of the paradox can even be unlikely to the extent of being absurd or completely incongruous, yet later appear to be true. The fact that I say *later* implies that I caught up with the paradox with some delay, that is to say, in succession. Its psychological impact results both from my mental limitation and from the complexity of the real. The multivalent can only be absorbed in time. The paradox exploits this slow procedure and combines, in speed, elements which I perceive only one by one. From this springs its ability to shock.

---

[1] *Rep.* V, 472 a.

As we have said, the elements of the paradox are at times strikingly diverse, and result in a flagrant opposition. For example, in the person of Jesus Christ we are confronted by the double aspect of kindness and power, expressed by the author of the Apocalypse in the metaphor "the wrath of the Lamb." The mind must not only balance the terms in succession to grasp their implication but also sustain a certain tension in the operation itself. Renan considered it necessary to break up this semantic complexity, and separating the gentleness of Jesus from his combativity, called the latter a nervous crisis occurring after the idyllic hope of the Galilean phase— as if it were a contradiction to love humanity and at the same time to grow impatient with its sluggishness. Skepticism is only for those who are unable or unwilling to reconstruct the segments of the knowable and to bear up under the tension. One who wishes to grasp the heart of reality must rise above noetic fragmentation and come closer, in continual purification, to the unknown qualities of the real. Whether this recuperating effort of the mind can be accomplished tirelessly is unlikely. Yet the very stress involved constitutes our joy in the paradox.[2]

We must now examine whether this encompassing function of the individual mind, facing the paradox and constituting it by its very vision, might extend itself beyond the synchronization of concepts and attempt the synthesis of two or more philosophical views.

It must be asserted from the start that eclecticism is not what we have in mind. We are not brewing some concoction made up of hybrid elements in order to reconstruct a unifying view. Only doctrines taken as a whole, however angular or narrow their respective insights may be, can be used as constituents of our unifying approach. In any case, eclecticism is too often imputed to those who use certain concepts of others in order to build a new whole of their own. Every theory has a past. Even the greatest thinkers have taken over from their predecessors a method or a principle, but they have transposed these elements into the framework of their own vision, regrouped them under the obsession of a personal intuition into a unity, which although not a systematization, con-

---

[2] In a similar sense Augustine: "*Cum discerno, purgatum, cum connecto, integrum volo.*" "When I divide (and analyze), it is out of purity, when I bring together (and synthesize), it is out of integrity."

stitutes nonetheless a real defense against the accusation of eclecticism. The philosopher sculptures his doctrine like a statue. Once the work is finished we can walk around it and discover its qualities and weaknesses, but we cannot take it to pieces without destroying it. Analysis is the test of a doctrine's resistance. Synthesis is the way to its understanding.

If eclecticism is rejected as a method, so also will be a mere additive approach such as that proposed by Lactantius in his *Institutiones*. Under the title *De Philosophorum Varietate eorumque Veritate*, the Christian apologist gives an interesting view on philosophical diversity, the main idea of which can best be summarized in his own words: *Particulatim veritas ab iis (philosophis) tota comprehensa est.*[3] Truth as a whole is possessed by the diversity of philosophers, each of whom owns a particle of it. There is no sect so divorced from it, nor any philosophical doctrine so vain (*inanis*), that it does not share some truth. If there were someone clever enough to gather these fragments into one body of knowledge, the result would not be different from what Christianity teaches.[4] But no one could do so unless he knew the truth in advance, and no one knows the truth in advance unless he is taught by God himself. *Solus potest scire qui facit*, said Lactantius. And this is of course true. The only debatable point is whether Christian revelation corresponds to divine truth—a philosopher is not necessarily an apologist—and if so, i.e., if revelation is divine truth, whether the philosopher should be permitted to use its data, since he need not be a theologian. Lactantius' additive approach is both intelligent and inspiring. However, it will not be followed here, since we wish to reach our conclusions solely through philosophical means.

Descartes vs. Pascal

OUR attempt of unification starts with the implication that all integration presupposes some form of opposition. Two suppositions may be envisioned. In the first hypothesis a *minus*-stand is

---

[3] Migne, *Patr. Tome IV, Lact. Div. Instit.* VII, c. 7.

[4] *Ibid.*

taken where one says less than he should have said, leaving room for a complement; no real opposition between the two doctrines is at stake. A second hypothesis is constituted by a *plus*-stand; in this case more is asserted than can be defended, inviting criticism and rejection as a complement. The critic repudiates, but in repudiating fulfills.[5]

As we have said, the first hypothesis does not constitute an opposition in the full sense of the word and implies only what might be called a "surface-contradiction." Although the philosopher asserts his view with conviction and claims to be complete and exclusive in his approach, he actually leaves room for others, for he is exhaustive neither in method nor in content. Such oppositions as those of Descartes vs. Pascal and Voltaire vs. Rousseau typify such a complementarity.

It is almost a commonplace to say that Descartes is the rationalist par excellence, and his opposite quite naturally the author of *Les Pensées* and "The heart has reasons which reason cannot know." When we define Descartes by saying that as a rationalist, he attempts to explain the world and ourselves by means of reason, we imply three things: (1) rationalistic philosophy tends to be objective, i.e., independent from emotional subjectivism; (2) it strives to be universal, that is, presented in such a way that everyone can accept and eventually verify it; and finally, (3) it has to be clear, in such a way that it imposes itself upon the mind by its inner intelligibility.

In claiming that Descartes was a rationalist, however, we do not mean to say that Descartes was only a rationalist, or even that he was a successful rationalist. The extent of his rationalism is a problem of historical interpretation, and as such, subject to debate. Some historians would claim that for Descartes the whole universe is "thinkable and hides no mysterious bottom."[6] Others,

---

[5] There is, I confess, a certain arbitrariness in the choice both of these categories and of the philosophers concerned. Others could have served equally well as our examples. Furthermore, when we oppose Aquinas to Hume, we have attributed a *plus*-stand to Aquinas.

Yet his position could be said to be a *minus*-stand when it is opposed to that of the existentialists. The two "stands" must be viewed in relation to one another.

[6] Hamelin, *Le Système de Descartes* (Paris: Alcan, 1921), p. 281.

like Laporte in his very thorough *Le Rationalisme de Descartes,* in an attempt to mitigate that statement, claim that for Descartes—although it is indeed true that all things which can be solved must be solved in a fashion which is similar to that followed in mathematics—there is a limit to what *can* be solved. We should tackle only those things which we can handle (Reg. II), and although God's veracity is a guarantee of the existence of terrestrial things, it is not a guarantee of their complete cognoscibility.[7] Descartes furthermore seems to accept an element of infrarationality in the thorny topic of the union of body and soul.[8]

This debate does not affect our main statement concerning Descartes' fundamental rationalism. The fact remains that qualities like objectivity, universality and clarity are being fulfilled more completely in mathematics than in any other field and that it was Descartes' main ambition to introduce a mathematical method into problems of philosophy. This attempt, especially in its application to "simple natures" such as thought, extension and God, appeared to be overambitious. Especially concerning thought and God, human knowledge is far from clear, and to apply to nonquantitative objects a mathematical method was to hurl an audacious challenge, one which could not escape the attention of one of the most brilliant minds of this period.

It has been observed that there have been two types of philosophy in history, those which try to eliminate mystery and those which establish themselves in mystery and are neither able nor willing to rid themselves of it.[9] Pascal obviously belonged to the latter. He was not natively inclined towards the irrational, for he was in his earlier period the mathematician, the inventor of many geometrical discoveries, the physicist of genius who in his treatise *On the Geometrical Spirit* undertook to defend Descartes against all accusations of plagiarism in connection with the famous *cogito, ergo sum,* for he admired and loved Descartes. Yet an older Pascal, having explored things outside the realm of quantity and

---

[7] J. M. F. Laporte, *Le Rationalisme de Descartes* (Paris: Presses Universitaires de France, 1954), p. 218.

[8] *Ibid.,* p. 220 ff.

[9] Nédoncelle in the introduction to *Oeuvres Philosophiques de Newman* (Paris: Aubier, Editions Montaigne, 1946), p. 19.

scientific measurement, would write this fatal sentence: "Descartes useless and uncertain."[10]

Through this sentence Pascal and others who will develop this radical condemnation have a place in history and are at the same time independent of history. They express the need to build up a paradox and to outweigh the Cartesian extreme stand, which they confront. Pascal's intuition emerges as a reaction against an exaggeration, and in turn constitutes through its own exaggeration the necessary counterpart. His struggle against all-dominating mathematical evidence was, at the same time, a concession to Jansenius and to Luther's distrust of reason: "Man is a subject full of error"[11]; "If man will look at himself, . . . the sight will terrify him, and, seeing himself suspended, in the material form given him by nature, between two abysses of infinity and nothingness, he will tremble."[12] Pascal was at times frightened by the visible world: "For, I ask, what is man in nature? A cypher compared with the infinite and all compared with nothing, a mean between zero and all. Infinitely unable to grasp the extremes, the end of things and their principle are for him hopelessly hidden in an impenetrable secret, for he is equally unable to see the nothing whence he springs and the infinite in which he is swallowed up."[13] Pascal incarnates a growing opposition to Descartes' enthusiasm for reason and mathematical clarification. We are all familiar with the story of Descartes' Pentecost, when he had the "vision" of his almost supernatural mission: he had the key to universal knowledge. There was no conscious presumption in Descartes' attitude, just as there was no lie in the Pascalian reaction. It belongs to a later generation, however—ours, for example—to visualize this conflicting attitude of two geniuses, each of them walking at the opposite ends of a scale and keeping it through their own spiritual weight balanced upon the pinpoint of human history. They conflicted, and their conflict was a mutual completion.

---

[10] *Les Pensées*, ed. Léon Brunschvicg and Pierre Boutroux (Paris: Hachette, 1904), no. 663.

[11] *Ibid.*, no. 601.
[12] *Ibid.*, no. 600.
[13] *Ibid.*, *l.c.*

Voltaire vs. Rousseau

WHAT appears to be true in the purely theoretical domain is no less applicable to the theories that become the ideology of an event. Voltaire and Rousseau did not alone carry the Western world towards its greatest revolution, but each had his appointed place in the shaping of it. They thus form an interesting example of what we intend to show: in the creating of any great occurrence, there are no solitary forces. Voltaire and Rousseau were not friends; indeed they were rivals, but as unwitting bedfellows they are irrevocably linked. For a great writer is not original because he is autonomous—his solitude is only apparent; a great writer is original because he is opportune and brings at the right moment and in the right place that portion of truth which history needs.

Voltaire's rationalism was not on the technical level of Descartes' exactitude, but he had other talents—he could see the defects of his society, his nation and his generation and write about them in a prose which has never been surpassed and rarely equalled. The Voltairian mockery tore down everything—regime, royalty, church. Voltaire's insight was fiery, witty, light-footed; as Nietzsche put it, "the dance of the stars." Others brought it to earth and called it the firework which culminated in the lighting of the French Revolution. Never had the world been so amused at such a formidable expense.

Voltaire lacked a capacity for the emotional, however, while Rousseau possessed it abundantly. If Voltaire was a lesser Descartes, Rousseau might be compared with Pascal, less deep and less precise, possessing more sentiment and a more optimistic drive. For Rousseau feeling was a source of knowledge. He had a naive trust in the goodness of man, and as a consequence preached a return to nature as the condition of happiness. The beginning of the degeneration of man, according to Rousseau, was caused by the institution of property, which resulted in the division of labor, the separation of classes and the birth of evil passions. Reason, continually in the service of our self-seeking instinct, was not to be trusted. It was not true, as Voltaire ironically remarked, that Rousseau wanted us to run on four feet again. He hoped, rather, for the perfection of man, but the right way to that perfection lay not in the unnatural condition of intellectual understanding but in the simple and natural state of feeling. In opposition (and in completion) of Voltaire's enlightenment of the intellect, the lines of which all converge towards the revolution, there appeared in Rousseau a philosophy of feeling, of such elemental power that it consciously pushed towards a violent revolution, confident that man's innermost nature would assuage the clash and reunite the social elements which would be scattered by turmoil. If laws were taken away, man, naturally good, would step into a reign of justice and equality. If Voltaire was severely critical, he was not naive. He could only smile at Rousseau's candor. "Men are rarely worthy to govern themselves," he wrote (in *Dictionary*, article Fatherland), and, "when people undertake to reason, all is lost."[14] In fact, he was against revolution, but others, less timid than he, drew the necessary conclusions. An individual inference, however powerful, is only one voice in the tumult which prepares a great event. We have chosen Voltaire and Rousseau as examples of our theory of "mutual completion" because although each was firmly convinced that the other was wrong, they mutually achieve one another. There are others, of course, in number who, unaware of their fragmentary contribution, fulfill a function which they believe to be exclusive, yet which is only a portion in the eyes of the one who is able to judge—the onlooker, particularly that onlooker par excellence—posterity. "The young are fortunate," wrote Voltaire, "they will see fine things."[15] The "young," however, did not see the stirring events; they lived them. It was posterity which saw them. Under the eyes of those who follow, the individual of the past has sunk to the bottom and is frozen in a rigor mortis, perpetuating the angular truth which he was. It is the task of the historian to discover, no less than the partial contribution of each, the global donation of all. There is a touch of irony in the fact that, in the view defended here, to be incomplete is not a sin, but to be incomplete in one's incompleteness constitutes the real failure, for it is one's duty to live up to the very limits of one's finitude.

---

[14] *Correspondance*, April 1, 1776.

[15] *Correspondance*, April 2, 1764.

Auguste Comte, or the Paradox Within the One

AUGUSTE Comte is another who, like Pascal, has lived in succession.what others divide among themselves and carry forever separately. Between 1830 and 1842 he published his six volumes of *Cours de Philosophie Positive*. The point of departure in these works is scientific, for he begins by an observation of the most simple phenomena. However, he states that one must go beyond the mere phenomena and attempt the formulation of laws which in turn need coordination. The knowledge of these laws allows us to foresee, and foresight enables us to act—*"Voir pour prévoir, et prévoir pour agir."*[16] Although laws make things more intelligible and more consistent, they are not the deeper nature of things. This deeper nature escapes us.

This positive approach inaugurates a new phase, the last of three phases contained in Comte's so-called sociological law. There was at first, according to Comte, the theological stage, where man explained everything by the will of deities, as when the stars were the chariots of the gods or the gods themselves.[17] A progressive rationalization of theological beliefs led man from fetishism to polytheism, from polytheism to monotheism, and gradually to the second phase, the metaphysical stage, in which abstract causes took the place of the gods or of one god as an interpretation and answer to the problems of the world.[18] For Comte, metaphysics is a corrupted form of theology and has only a provisional and transitory value. The third phase, mentioned above, comes when metaphysical explanations, such as Plato's ideas or Hegel's absolute, yield to the laws of science, when interest in the why is replaced by curiosity concerning the how. Laws, not causes, are the only explanation for society and for the world. What Aquinas had done for the theological stage and Descartes for the metaphysical stage, Auguste Comte was convinced he would do for the last stage, and in so doing help the world into that final age in which humanity was to live forever. Although this view was often arbitrary and prejudiced in its application, and obviously

---

[16] *Cours de Philosophie Positive,* VI (Paris: Bachelier, 1830), p. 618.

[17] *Ibid.,* I, p. 4 ff.
[18] *Ibid.*

undertaken for Comte's reformatory purposes—the victory of positivism—it nevertheless drew quite a few disciples.

Surprisingly enough, as if the circuit of the three phases were to be verified first of all in the author himself, Comte, in the last period of his thinking, fell back into the theological stage. The explanation of this volte-face has been a topic of debate. At times a romantic explanation has been suggested. For when Comte wrote, "We tire of thinking and even of acting, we never tire of loving,"[19] it did seem as if some sentimental encounter were behind the wavering of the positivist, and the discovery of Clothilde de Vaux, with whom he fell in love in 1845, confirms the supposition. At any rate, the old positivist started to place feeling above intelligence as a reforming power, and subsequently spent years devising a new form of religion, the function of which would be to strengthen love and altruism among men and elevate Humanity to the position of a divine object worshipped in a ceremonial cult. He contrived an intricate system of priesthood, sacraments, prayer and discipline and set himself amidst all this as the capital high-priest of his religion-devoted-to-humanity.

All this would have appeared harmless to a neutral observer, but it was for his followers and admirers, such as Mill and Littré, a frightening prospect.[20] Having overthrown metaphysics and religion once and forever, they refused to be dragged by Comte from positivism into a substitute form of theology and religion. The result of the ensuing debate among the masters of positivism is accidental to our purpose. What is crucial, however, is Comte's motivation. And on that point, it seems to us impossible to explain his conversion solely by the presence of a woman in his life. She was at most an occasion, not a cause. The ultimate cause was the manifest insufficiency and one-sidedness of a mere scientific approach. "If we look at the world from the point of view of science alone, it appears that the world has no unity of its own," writes Gilson.[21] Some may feel that this unity is superfluous. Yet unfailingly the human mind is tempted to find some unifying dogma

---

[19] *A General View of Positivism*, trans. Bridges, reprints Stanford, p. 1.

[20] J. S. Mill, *The Positive Philosophy of Auguste Comte* (Boston: William V. Spencer, 1866), p. 127 ff.

[21] E. Gilson, *The Unity of Philosophical Experience* (New York: Charles Scribner's Sons, 1950), p. 257.

behind the variety of scientific laws. If not a fetish, then a god; if not a god, then some metaphysical principle; if not a metaphysical principle, then . . . what? Comte's intent research to go beyond phenomena and to formulate laws (the function of science), and furthermore, to find the law of laws (the function of positive philosophy) betrays his real anxiety to introduce an ultimate principle.[22] The need for unity, Comte concluded, could be fulfilled only by considering all sciences as preliminary, sociology as foremost, but above all, mankind as the *Grand Etre*, to which all things have to be subordinated. Above the mind, therefore, is the heart; love for Humanity directs everything. Mankind is divine.[23]

The success of Comte's second career, as it is often called, may be considered to be debatable. Our thesis is served neither by Comte's success nor by his failure, but by his attempt in itself. An ideal is served by its parody as well, for underneath lies the silent consciousness of what is absent and lacking. In Comte's doctrine the ultimate insufficiency was obvious: one may consider philosophy to be a description of what is, but can justification of what is not also be asked for? Comte's turnabout has been ridiculed beyond necessity, for at bottom it was only a concession to the urge for completion. A man may finish his career quite differently from the way he started it, not because he wanted to be better or worse, but because he wanted to be different and, in being different, consciously or unconsciously to be more complete. If Clothilde de Vaux provoked the second part of Comte's career, she accomplished more than could reasonably be expected, for it was not Clothilde de Vaux who pushed for an achievement of her lover's doctrine, but the doctrine itself which, in being inadequate and insufficient, by sheer organic necessity called for completion.

Hume vs. Aquinas, or a Completion from Afar

IN previous oppositions, whether contained within a single individual (Comte) or existing between two or more individuals, we

---

[22] Lucien Lévy-Bruhl, *La Philosophie d' Auguste Comte* (Paris: Alcan, 1900), p. 116.
[23] *Ibid.*, p. 133. See also Comte,

Cours, VI, p. 610, and *Politique Positive*, I (Paris: Larousse, 1890), p. 266.

noticed that the opposition resulted from the fact that there was room for complementary addition in one form or other. Descartes and Voltaire were considered to have taken *minus*-stands, where underassertion left room for addition, whether they wanted it or not; Pascal's intuition of the heart completed Descartes' rationalism, Rousseau's emotionalism outbalanced Voltaire's irony. Aquinas, on the other hand, represented what has been called a *plus*-attitude, the assertions of which invite criticism; it was David Hume who responded by contradicting.

Hume, in attacking traditional metaphysics, represents that part of the human species which undertakes a precise and critical examination of what others have seen or believe that they have seen. The appearance of this negative attitude at a particular place or a particular time can answer an immediate need. A certain age may struggle to work out its own perfection, and in so doing, counterpoise—all the more effectively for its unawareness of it—the metaphysical acceptances of a previous generation. Or space may play a part; it seems to be a predominant attribute of Anglo-Saxon thought to display an instinctive distrust for all uncontrollable speculations and an exceptional care for experience. Notwithstanding the fact that individuals are caught in a space-and-time fabric, the complementary function of their angular views can be above both. Hume, a Scot, was "born" during the Middle Ages when Occam, rejecting the reality of the universal, pushed Western philosophy into nominalism, did away with any distinction between conception and perception, and reduced all abstract and universal ideas to terms of sensory experience. The distance between Occam and Hume, however, was crossed all at once by one of those *enfants terribles*, to be found in all ages, who say with great candor what others prefer to leave unsaid. Nicholas d'Autrecourt propounded a double thesis: immediate understanding of the concrete and, as a mode of reasoning, analysis and nothing else. Causality was dropped and accident and substance were "phenomenized."[24] Hume's fundamental positions were already present in the work of d'Autrecourt, who, I hasten to add, had no desire to found a school. His was merely the joy of

---

[24] Joseph Lappe, "Nicolaus von Autrecourt: Sein Leben, Seine Philosophie, Seine Schriften," *Beiträge Zur Geschichte der Philosophie des Mittelalters*, Band VI, Heft 2 (1908), pp. 1–31.

a dialectician. Hume's philosophy will have a deeper and more elaborate content and a farther-reaching influence. Occam was condemned, d'Autrecourt was condemned, Hume has been "refuted" many times; but notwithstanding, the nominalistic thesis installed itself in the philosophical stronghold, and neither condemnation nor rational demonstration has succeeded in dislodging it.

Many have reproached analysis, whether ancient or modern, for being less "productive" and creative than the work it attacks. However, it should be remembered that this is not its duty. A masterpiece is often the result of both positive contribution and negative control. In the domain of sculpture, the medieval craftsman did not himself handle the chisel. "As far as I can make out," said Renoir, "there was one fellow with a hammer and a chisel, hammering away at a statue for all he was worth, and another fellow in a corner just looking and doing nothing. And the one who looked on, so they tell me, was the sculptor."[25] The comparison has its value. It is not suggested, of course, that the speculative philosopher is the laborer who constructs the theory, while the empirical analyst merely looks on, points at the mistakes and, ipso facto, becomes the craftsman; nevertheless, it is true that a speculative theory has the obligation to destroy itself as *separate* doctrine. It must bury itself in its triumph. Standing alone and pushed to its extreme consequence, it proves fragmentary in its solitude, for its function lies in achieving and outbalancing its opposite. Empiricism cannot be checked without the brakes of some speculative principle, nor does pure speculation make sense without empirical control.[26] It may be well to add that the use of the terms *positive* and *negative* is often relative; so, for example, when in our presentation Hume's attitude is considered to be negative and a speculative theory positive, the reverse can be asserted on equal grounds. In the shadow of Hume's doubting—which is as positive

---

[25] As narrated by André Malraux in *The Voices of Silence*, p. 308.

[26] A typical case is Bacon's assertion in *Opus Majus* (P. VI, c. 1) where his empiricism and his insistence upon the necessity of experience is outbalanced by the acceptance of a spiritualistic doctrine or a metaphysical background. This is especially striking since Bacon includes in what he calls "experience" rational evidence as well as the grace of faith and even mystical illumination.

an attitude as any—continental thought builds its speculations, for where one philosopher asserts his doubt, the other finds room, surprisingly enough, for an absolute assertion, like a bird building its nest in a crack of the other man's house. Whatever the name, the fact remains that all position implies an opposition, that every philosophical achievement stands under the menace of its negation and has to be viewed together with this negation, and that, as a consequence of all this, St. Thomas cannot be truthfully evaluated without mentioning Hume.

Paradox and Sin

WE discover a similar structure in the ethical domain. No act of virtue would be meritorious without the seductiveness of the opposite. What would be the patience of the martyr without the cruelty of his torturer or the value of humility without the pleasure of vanity? "What is frightening in life," writes Péguy, "is not only the juxtaposition of sin and sanctity, but their interpenetration, their mutual nourishment." Augustine, who more than anyone else has attempted to penetrate the motives of evil, insisted that both opposites constitute a parasitic relationship: "For as the beauty of a picture is not dimmed by the dark colors, in their proper place, so the beauty of the universe of creatures, if one has insight to discern it, is not marred by sins, even though sin itself is an ugly blotch."[27] Shades serve the light and dissonances play their part in the harmony of the score. Only a global view is authentic—only a global view kept Augustine an unrepentant admirer of this creation. Conversion, furthermore, does not introduce the converted to a totally different world, for a paradox of opposites seems to constitute the core of the supernatural dimension as well as the natural. The dogma of the Redemption, essential in Christian doctrine, implies a similar cadence, and the Liturgy speaks of a "happy fault, that was worthy to have such and so great a redeemer."[28] The paradox of the "happy fault" reflects the ethico-ontological structure of man's universe, although it does not, of course, reflect God's intimate nature. The fall of man and

---

[27] *De Civ. Dei*, XI, 23.   [28] Preface of Holy Saturday.

the Redemption belong to the order of men, and they are accomplished by men—even Christ took on the nature of man—in time, with its inevitable succession and division.

This dichotomy of opposites which permeates human ethics is not a major concern in this study. If it is mentioned here, it is because I want to point out its similarity with the infrastructure of the human noesis, which, as it was explained in this chapter, is merely an application of our theory on angular truth. However interesting a philosophical discovery may appear in the realm of truth, it leaves an immensity unexplored and concealed. The philosopher himself ignores his ignorance, however, and judges that his theory is all-inclusive and absolute. All creation takes place under the spell of the absolute. This myth does not necessarily affect the outsider. If *A* is an angular truth, I can say that *B* is born in its concealment. *B* is a daughter of the night which *A* could not see, or stated differently, the finitude of *A* results in the complementary correction of *B*. Thus the problem of opposites is metaphysically connected with the finite and the multiple. Only for man does opposition make sense, only for him is its grasp *paradoxical*. Since God has a total grasp, the paradox, with its unavoidable implication of segmentary and successive vision, is meaningless.

Paradox and Its Noetic Locus

THE ontological locus where the meeting of opposing theories takes place is the human species itself, which under the urge of survival, manipulates the multiplicity of individual fragments and their views as so many correctives. Although the finitude of the individual is the ultimate metaphysical explanation for the dualism of position and opposition, it is the *totum supervivens* which exploits the fragmentarity and, in a slow but continual attempt to protect itself, builds up this interaction.

The function of unification itself is accomplished by the individual observer, or "third man." He is the noetic locus, since only in an individual consciousness can the meeting of opposing theories knowingly take place. Whether we consider a philosophical "opposition" like that of Descartes vs. Pascal, the complementarity of which is, at bottom, one of additive enrichment, or whether we have in mind doctrines like Thomism vs. Hume's empiricism, where the opposition is more strained, it is the task of the outsider or third man to compose the opposing positions. Facing the multiplicity, he attempts a synthesis.

This synthesis is not, it must be emphasized, a Hegelian one. In the view defended here, the organic unity and structure of each theory requires neither disintegration nor reconstruction in order to become the constituent of a new composition. On the other hand, the composition is not a mere numerical addition either, with theories juxtaposed like bricks. It is actually a synthetic view where two or more positions are seen to illuminate and to transfigure one another through their mutual presence. Once B, the counterpart of A, has been stated, it may at first sight appear that merely one more idea has been brought into circulation. Actually B has modified A, which derives its true meaning only when considered in relation to B. "Truth has its beginning only at the moment when the writer takes two different objects and notes their relation to each other," wrote Proust. The relation of two or more theories is discovered in a similar way; one takes two objects . . . (in our interpretation two philosophies), attempts to discover the individuality peculiar to each angular vision, then searches for possible roots where the two are united and possess something in common. Finally, one must study where they differ and achieve their counterpart. If the angular vision contains some angular truth, it is in completing its opponent or in being completed by the latter that this truth value will appear. Truth emerges in and through the relational operation. For the way of paradox is the way of truth.

The grasp of the paradox, which involves both extreme positions, requires a special movement of the mind, which might best be described as a kind of pendulum movement by which one, in attempting to attain a maximum of discovery, swings from one angular vision to another. Without this oscillation there is no balanced knowledge. To see reality, we must see it as on a tightrope, claims Oscar Wilde. He is right. When verities become acrobats, we can judge them, he adds. Here he is wrong, I believe. For it is not the verities which are the acrobats, but we swinging endlessly back and forth, from one extreme to another.

Although the *locus* of this operation is in the human consciousness, the paradoxical extremes which one wants to embrace can only be reached in their plenitude when all the faculties of man are put into action. Since philosophical methods, particularly in modern-day philosophy, are variegated—i.e., either descriptive or deductive or even emotional—it follows that for the third man some verities can only be understood by an emotional awareness, others by the reason alone, still others by a sense of accurate observation and an affinity for the experimental. One has to go through the whole of oneself to understand the world. Only the paradoxical structure of the self can hold the multivalent paradox of philosophical (and other) discoveries. And, although Aristotle is right when he writes, "What says that two things are different must be one, . . . what asserts the difference [between sweet and white] must be self-identical,"[29] I believe that this undivided self-identity belongs to the self, even though the tools (mind, senses, heart, etc.) may be diverse. The unifying vision itself, as explained above, is not a simple synthesis which can be grasped in one noetic expression. The synthesis is necessarily complex because of its content, for although the whole operation belongs to complete knowledge, the knowledge itself concerns contraries, which can only be attained in succession.[30]

---

[29] *De Anima*, 426 b 20; see also *S.Th.* I, 75 a 6.

[30] Pascal typifies this attitude. He not only promoted mathematical clarity, but also defended mystery —"Man is an incomprehensible monster"—and, in so doing, fulfilled his role as an anti-rationalist. Yet, in strange perplexity, his mind runs back and forth between the splendor and the wretchedness of man (*Les Pensées*, ed. Brunschvicg, no. 416); between dogmatism (acceptance of natural principles) and pyrrhonism (*Ibid.*, no. 385), (distrust of reason and nature); and, between the being of an angel and the being of a beast (*Ibid.*, no. 140), bearing inside itself this perpetual soaring from pole to pole, forever engaged in an internal conflict which was itself only part of a more global conflict. The paradox he contained within himself alone was a form of intellectual maturity and an intitial attempt to grow beyond himself and all human fragmentation.

Angular Truth as the Call for Its Opposite

THREE remarks result from the preceding analyses. First, angular truth cannot be understood to have an isolated and self-sufficient content. It is impossible for man to posit in the realm of speculation an absolute theory, i.e., one which needs no outbalancing or further correcting. Angular truth always has an equilibrating function against an opposite extreme, absent or present, and must, for the sake of completion, be understood together with its opposite. The *mean* in its existential and speculative fulfillment (I do not allude here to its ethical meaning) is the privilege of the Omniscient. Man himself walks back and forth, sees aspects only and sees them in succession. Sometimes he sees not even that much, for certain philosophical adventures may be complete failures. However, they have to be attempted as so many dead-end streets which must be explored. They help the paradox by their utter nought. A philosophical theory, therefore, although erroneous, constitutes a detour towards the absolute; it has penetrated into a new cycle, of which it was not itself aware, but which the outsider will detect.[31] Every exploration is not a discovery, but it may very well prepare the way for one. It is for this reason that error should be appreciated, for in most cases intellectual stagnation is due to the refusal to admit trial and error and to the illusion that absolute truth has already been acquired. Failure, therefore, is not an obstacle but an essay which must be absorbed in the paradox, as an unavoidable result of the inadequacy of all knowledge.

A second remark follows with no less insistency. The composition or holding-together-in-the-mind-of-two-or-more-theories does not resolve into a stable and mathematical equation. The relation between both components remains open and tense; the situation is enriching, yet not productive of what is generally called tranquillity. Man remains the "restless head." His is a continual attempt

---

[31] On a similar topic, J. S. Mill writes: "If there are any persons who contest a received opinion, . . . let us thank them for it, open our mind to listen to them, and rejoice that there is *some one to do* *what we otherwise ought* . . . to do with much greater labour for ourselves." *On Liberty* (New York: Liberal Arts Press, 1956), ch. II (italics mine).

to correct his incompleteness, even though to look at the world with the eyes of others, or as Nietzsche puts it, with a hundred eyes, must result in pain. In viewing the opposing theories, the third man feels the contrary effort of the elements at his disposal, which, in a perpetual tug-of-war, are reluctant to join the forces of either side. But this unrest *is* the mind of man, reaching its center; it is what I would like to call, in imitation of John of the Cross, the "experience of center." From this center the splendor of the multiplicity is visible. It is not, at least not at this stage, the experience of God, as the mystic might suggest, but it is human consciousness itself grasping the relative value of a manifold expression and measuring this plethora in its mutual outbalancing power.

Finally, it may appear by the end of this chapter that the classical objection, according to which both opposing philosophical doctrines cannot be true—hence, that one must be right and the other must be wrong—has no meaning in view of what has been said. Each theory is formulated by a certain individual who, being such and such only, in his very uniqueness incarnates the different. A theory is the abstract moment of the incarnated uniqueness and difference. The different, however, implies the negation. In the global process of survival, each position is an accusation; it cannot be an absolute and exhaustive truth, since its very structure implies limitation and concealment, or what might in a traditional way be called error. This error will be denounced by another intimation which in turn will need some corrective. It is imperative to remember that the angular truth contained in angular vision *A* is not exhaustive and that the organic structure of the latter cannot be dissected with the vain hope of extracting the particular truth in its purity from the false elements it contains. For its guarantee is ultimately angular vision *B*, the contribution of which will be positive, no doubt, but presented as different, hence inclusive of negation.

Since the third man has a right to visualize the synchronization of the apparently conflicting theories, our chapter at this moment closes upon itself. Unity can be accomplished in the mind, the mobility of which is such that it can include the paradox. That this operation affords us more truth and more extensive discovery is evident. That as acquisition it is still angular—hence, from an existential viewpoint, still individual rather than "specific" (or belonging to the species)—is no less certain. It will appear from further research that this is a provisional stage in our dialectic.

5

The Problem of
Generic Truth

Truth of the Totum

ALTHOUGH in the preceding pages a form of unity was reached, it was, notwithstanding its value, still subjective in character. This subjectivity, although not implying distortion as a necessary consequence, does point at the limited portion of truth that can be seen by an individual. The understanding of the most extensive world-views, a fortiori the combination of these views, results ultimately in a personal insight, and an addition of angular truths neither frees the individual man from his angular vision nor lifts him for that very reason to the level of the species. The apprehension by way of paradox, although more inclusive, remains an angular vision. Pursuing our descriptive dialectic, we shall in the present chapter observe what the collective powers of men can achieve, and examine whether an all-encompassing truth can be found—a truth that is possessed by the *totum genus humanum*. In order to distinguish it from angular truth, we shall call it *generic* truth.

To our question concerning how a global human knowledge can be obtained and what sort of generic truth can be expected, the answer may appear to be obvious: discover the common denominator between individual X and individual Z and their respective insights and present your result in the form of a universal statement. This solution cannot be altogether rejected, for some common parcel of truth is always found. There are, as we have already agreed, a certain number of principles to which assent cannot be denied, not because of an individual insight, but on the basis of a common nature.

However, a deductive method, with its universalization, tends to ignore the original contribution of the individual participant. The achievement of the concrete individual remains partial, yet it is revealing by virtue of its uniqueness, not of its similarity to the thought of others. Individuals constitute a variety facing variety, like portions of the ocean reflecting a different world of stars, each wave unaware of what other waves mirror. Since each participant posits himself as subject and center, absolutely original and inimitable, reflecting the universe in a unique way, it is through the complementary addition of these percepts that a global and generic dimension will be reached. Generic truth, therefore, can only be exhaustive and authentic when obtained not only by a blunt summary of that which concrete individuals have in common, or a consideration of the similar, but also by a description of the results of an additive complementarity. It is in a closeness to the existent that our research must be pursued.

Truth as Additive Completion Both on the Level of Time and on the Level of Space

The global knowledge of the *totum genus humanum* can be seen to contain a double dimension: it is a result of a horizontal addition, i.e., one in space, and of a vertical addition, i.e., one in time. This brings us back, of course, to a similar division used in chapter I of this volume. Actually the same principle applies: whether in succession or in juxtaposition, a diversity is present, each segment continuing where the other leaves off, eventually repairing where the other was deficient and the whole movement itself resulting in what may be called survival in progress. There is, however, a nuance which at present requires our attention. While in chapter I the result of completion was the survival of the *totum*, we notice in exploring the realm of the human noesis that the additive complementarity of *angular* truths results in generic truth. Actually, survival and generic truth can be said to be related, for generic truth provides the technique of survival. We do not mean to signify by this that generic truth has survival as its conscious and immediate purpose, but we can say that a pragmatical purpose, whether conscious or unconscious, whether immediate or mediate, is always there. He who survives knows how to do so.

It is furthermore clear that generic truth is the fitting ornament of a *totum genus humanum,* which through its power of thought transcends mere animal life and will only continue to do so, i.e., survive as *humanum,* if and when individual minds are bent upon intellectual research and through their mutual contribution build up this generic truth.

Whether we look at this global human knowledge in its horizontal or in its vertical fulfillment, we observe that it is broken within itself and made up out of a multiplicity of angular truths. Your specialization covers my ignorance and my knowledge covers your limitations. Division of labor within a fragmented *totum* is ontologically justified, just as a universal do-it-yourself could only end in disaster. This is observable from an emotive point of view as well. The metaphor which considers our world to be a valley of tears is a questionable one, for within our "valley" there is no less sunshine than there is shade. The two are strangely connected, for your joy is my sadness, your gain is my loss and your victory is my defeat. Only through this mutual correction of angular "moods" can the species as a whole keep up its tempo. Even competition shares in this strange rhythm, for to compete is actually to complete. We live upon a surface where many fight one another, unaware that in their opposition lies a source of growth, which is ultimately a guarantee of survival.

This cadence strikes us on the vertical line as well. While John is a specialist in electronics, his grandfather, ignorant of all mechanics, read Virgil in the Latin, and his ancestor, in the glorious days of Pico della Mirandola, found his delight in Greek versification. John and his grandfather and his ancestor are supplementing one another. "We are not better than our fathers," complained Jeremiah—only different, we might add, and in being different, able to complete them.

This succession of father-son, father-son, etc., implies a completion by way of repair for the ignorance of some predecessor (or in atonement for his follies); at the same time, a new void is being hollowed, for our children will have to compensate for the deficiencies of the present generation. "In your children you will make up for the fact that you are the children of your fathers." In this paradox Nietzsche confirms our thesis: it is my duty to protect my children against the errors of my father. Survival of the race is explained by this successive completion in depth, though within a single generation the form of survival is not always highly successful. For when the heir fails to fulfill the definition of heir and becomes merely descendant, the family (or group) sinks into decadence. To be heir implies more than to succeed to the estate or property of the deceased; it points also to the incumbent responsibility of repair, whether or not this duty is consciously perceived. This factor of repair is important in the dynastic succession of generations, for it illustrates the shrewdness of life, which distributes its assets as if aware of their fragmentary value. It has a profound significance in the domain of the spiritual, as when Aeschylus saw human suffering as something that descends upon the whole family of the wrongdoer, not merely upon the wrongdoer himself, or when Dostoevsky made his world one in a common sense of guilt, hence of reparation. "Believe me, everyone is really responsible to all men and for everything."[1] In the notion of atonement, the very core of Christian theology, we discover an idea closely related to our study, for in its deeper metaphysical meaning, atonement implies the *inflicting of a contrary* with the hope *to remedy*, as when someone mortifies his own flesh for the sins of others, believing that only pain can equilibrate illicit joy and that if sin is man's greatest evil, expiation is the remedy and complement.

The Mona Lisa *as a Work of the Many*

WE have previously observed how survival in progress signifies a slow but continual transformation of new wants (grandfather wants it . . .) into new needs (the father needs it . . .) and of new needs into new ways of fulfilling them (the son makes it . . .). We are now in a position to see the noetic implications. The word *need* implies an awareness of the problem, but an ignorance of the solution as well. However—and this is an essential observation concerning our division of labor in the order of knowledge—the Species buries its dead today and takes care of their problems to-

---

[1] *The Brothers Karamazov* (New York: Modern Library, 1950), p. 344.

morrow. If my children and grandchildren are able to answer some of my questions, they do so while posing new problems themselves. Only the future realizes the dreams of a dying past. Question and answer do not belong to the same man, nor does the execution of the masterpiece and its inscrutable prelude. "Since the power [of being intellectual] cannot be completely actualized in a single man or in any of the particular communities of men above mentioned [family or city or state], there must be a multitude in mankind through whom this whole power can be actualized, . . ."[2] writes Dante, and a little further on continues, ". . . the proper work of mankind *as a whole* is to exercise continually its entire capacity for intellectual growth . . ."[3] Dante's insistence upon the *totum genus* as being alone capable of exhausting *all* the potentialities of humanity can, it seems, be applied on a smaller scale. We may assert—and observation confirms our assertion—that only a plurality (group or epoch) is capable of any sizeable achievement, whether speculative or artistic. Although creative ideas spring immediately from individuals and not from the group, although "Hamlet was written by Shakespeare and not by a committee,"[4] in most cases nevertheless (if not in all), it appears that the genius lies on the summit of an epoch and is a child of that epoch. If he is not the product of a primitive nation, it is not because the unusual is lacking in that milieu, but because the milieu itself is lacking in its ability to stimulate the unusual. I cannot, therefore, agree with those who ascribe all progress in civilization to the superior man and attribute to the "common" man mere docility and submissiveness, as if the genius himself were not part and product of the plurality of "common" men, who not only bring him into existence but offer him an ambiance and an audience and surround him with that wisdom and common sense which he may very well lack.[5] There is a nuance between the meaning of wisdom and intelligence. If our classics are works of

---

[2] Dante, *On World-Government or De Monarchia*, trans. H. W. Schneider (New York: Liberal Arts Press, 1950), I, 3.

[3] *Ibid.*, I, 4. For Dante, actualization of the intellect has not only speculative purposes but active ones as well.

[4] Alfred W. Griswold, *In the University Tradition* (New Haven, Conn.: Yale University Press, 1957), p. 156.

[5] See on that topic Henri Bergson, *Les Deux Sources* (Geneva: Skira), p. 164.

geniuses, the creators are nonetheless indebted for their balanced perspective to the slow-moving environment which neutralizes some of their speed in exchange for its delay. Here, once more, we discover that X has what Z does not have and that the *totum* is a result of variegated fragments. Actually there is no "common" man. The term is at odds with the fundamental principles defended in this study, for its deeper significance points to a definition of man where uniqueness is overlooked and a standardized view of the many is accepted for purposes of easy manipulation. It is not the type, the "common" man which contributes to the achievement of a work, whether intellectual or artistic, but the multiple unique through its convergent complementarity. This contribution operates in mysterious, usually incalculable, ways. For those who from a distance evaluate what is considered to be the achievement of one man, there is no succession but result only. For the many who, in fact, constitute that power, there is succession. In the *Mona Lisa* lie consummated as in their ultimate end the efforts of the many who preceded and the many who surrounded da Vinci. The groundwork, buried in the silent depths, escapes our vision. Only when all is ready does the immortal work rise above the earth.[6]

Vertical completion, whether in the form of mere continuation or of repair or of progress, is an intricate complex no less than its correlate, horizontal completion. Both together result in the global knowledge of the *totum genus*. It is impossible to discover a collective consciousness distinct from the individual consciousness that carries this knowledge. But there is obviously a consciousness which, although not existing in a state of separation, is multiplied and individualized in the body. This multiple consciousness carries the total knowledge or technique of survival.

Generic Truth and Collective Judgments

THERE is a definite analogy between, on the one hand, the *totum genus humanum* facing its constituents or human individuals and,

---

[6] Sartre is right, I believe, when he says: "The question is to know whether or not there exists in this falsified world one deed of which we can say: I did it," in the Preface to André Gorz, *Le Traître* (Paris: Editions du Seuil, 1958), p. 19.

on the other hand, the human individual facing the plurality of ideas within himself. Both the *totum genus* and the human individual contain the multiple under a variegated form. Since we are attempting an integration in the realm of noesis, the multiple under discussion is, of course, multiple knowledge. Within the *totum genus* the distribution takes place among diverse human beings, while within the one individual it occurs among a plurality of ideas. There is a plurality in me just as there is a plurality in the *totum genus*. The multiple noesis in myself slowly molds me, just as the multiplicity within the *totum* gradually gives it its cultural shape. In the very act of reflection (or mental return upon myself), the duality between me reflecting and me reflected upon presents a strange similarity to the mutual otherness between two persons.

The differences between the *totum genus* and the *totum individuum* are obvious. A human being, although a fragment of the *totum*, appears to be a much more independent entity than the ideological bits within himself. I control the multiple in myself, it seems, more efficiently than the *totum genus* controls the multiple fragmentation within itself. My control lies in the possibility of choice or the exercise of freedom as we know it.

It is now our task to explore whether or not the knowledge of the Species, not unlike its fragment, the individual, at times formulates what we call a judgment. The individual has ideas concerning which he makes a pronouncement. Is it possible that the Species or *totum*, carrying in a silent way its immense knowledge, from time to time expresses a truth-formulation by way of a collective judgment which may be said to emanate from the Species (or *totum*) as a whole?

The term *judgment* will first need clarification. At present, it belongs to the semantics of the individual and is defined as that act of the individual mind by which the predicate of a subject is denied or asserted. It contains a truth-formulation, that is, it presents *for* the consciousness the conformity with the real which by hypothesis was already present *in* the consciousness. It makes the individual aware of his conformity. We ought to remember that, however important this operation of the mind is, a judgment has no more value than the vision which made it possible and that this vision can only be an angular one. No individual pronouncement, whether speculative or ethical, can extend beyond the angular vision of this particular individual. This does not impair the judgment of an individual, which actually has an immense area in which to work; however, the individual judgment is less convincing where immediate evidence is lacking or where some complex human behavior requires an ethical evaluation. In such cases the *totum genus* takes over and judges, not only because it knows better (this point will be developed later), but also because the individual act belongs to it. The latter is true since the individual act has a relational impact; in a world where the multiple is present in succession and in juxtaposition, it goes beyond the agent and reaches others. Once perpetrated, the act belongs to the many and its agent is committed. This is the real reason for all judiciary intervention. The etymology *"jus-dicere"* points to an authoritative arbitration which decides something in dispute. This supposes a legal tribunal, based upon collective choice. It is precisely to escape the insoluble reversibility of the individual man punishing the individual man that in the *Oresteia* a judgment is asked not of a few judges, but of a whole people in session around Orestes. An appeal is made to the City. And when sentence is given, it is the word of Wisdom, the word of God and Father, to whom alone revenge can belong. It is to Him that Apollo and Athena mysteriously allude. We have, on the one hand, the supreme will of God tacitly affirmed and recognized, and on the other hand, the multitude placed above—and around—the particular drama or individual act upon which judgment or collective arbitration will fall, as if only the many could authoritatively interpret the Divine will. One can also recognize here the deeper meaning of ecumenical power, where the authority of the multitude is asserted and individual belief made dependent upon its decision. In this sense also must be understood the unusual depth of St. Paul's words "we are made a spectacle to angels and men," for to be looked at by many is to be judged by many. This was not invalidated by the admonition "Thou shall not judge" (Matt. 7:1), for Jesus' words were addressed to the human individual. He saw deep into the heart of man, where he is alone with himself, poor and naked: He understood (metaphysically) the imperfect man, the individual fragment, immature and limited. A fragment should never judge a fragment. Only the Unfragmented, only the One who made us, can judge us; and in His absence, the totality in His name. The *totum genus* judges the individual, categorizes him and his work, or in sheer indifference drops him into oblivion. Even the most fanatical individualist is in the hands of the Species: he belongs to the other man, however much he may have hated him during his lifetime. Whatever may be the problem of individual immortality, a problem which we do not have to discuss here, one thing is certain: the individual upon his death falls into complete dependency.

Having stated this judgment of the Species *de jure*, we shall next attempt an analysis of its *de facto* procedure. A general remark should be made at the start. Although the knowledge of the Species is a global affair, its (explicit) formulation requires the individual existent. He is the "spokesman" for a silent Species; mankind as physical *totum* must find its linguistic expression in and through the individual. The term *person* can be understood in its literal sense as well, as the "mask" through which the dialogue of the silent *totum* is carried on. The voice of the people, forever mute, can only be metaphorical. Whatever I inherit, I have inherited from a tacit Species; whatever I say (or write) as personal and original will, in the purification of time, be added to the unspoken treasure of the knowledge of the Species. The effability (by the individual existent) of a specific judgment—and by specific I mean "pertaining to the Species"—constitutes an important criterion, for our observation will show that the judgment of the Species takes a double form: (1) there are human events and human debates concerning which a specific judgment is reached in an articulate way, and (2) there are others where a definite pronouncement appears to be ineffable. Both deserve our full attention, for it is one of the aims of this study to examine whether a specific acquisition can become an individual enrichment.

Generic Truth and Its Modes of Expression

WE do not have to look far to find examples of where the Species has been able to articulate a judgment, for they abound in the field of art appreciation and in estimates on various historical events.

A definitive judgment of Michelangelo's Sistine Chapel was not made by Raphael, who, in his jealousy, saw mostly defects in the work of his rival, nor was it made by the partisan appreciation of

Julius II, but it has grown out of the opposing judgments of many partial approaches. For many years there were hints towards a rightful appreciation, but hints only. However, one fragmentary allusion after another, conflicting yet constructive, independent yet correcting one another, constituted a succession of levels, by which the work of art and the artist himself made their ascent in the esteem of men. In some cases the pristine view is the right one and the "judgment of history" only a confirmation. In others, the global final judgment is a far cry from the first individual evaluation. How many of the beheaded and burned would come back to life if an uncommitted posterity could have its wishes fulfilled? The trial and death of Jesus Christ is an instance of very great significance. Jesus was, at the moment of his passion, a lonely man. It is not our task to decide whether his trial was a fair one and whether all means which could have been placed at his disposal by the minutious Roman law were indeed offered. We have not to worry about that point at present. What strikes us, however, in regard to our thesis, is the undisputed overthrow of Pilate's judgment by posterity. While Jesus at the moment of the sentence was alone, some five hundred million people now claim to be his followers and his admirers. Humanity has reversed an individual judgment, even in the quarters where it was least expected. An act of the past is irrevocable, but the judgment of that act belongs to the future.

It is in the light of similar principles that a notion like tradition should be considered. Tradition is usually defined as "a set of ideas and habits handed down from the past." As such, it is not always considered to be reliable, and we are inclined to oppose it to the experiments of modern-day science; or, to put it bluntly, we oppose traditional to empirical, forgetting that tradition in many cases is as empirical as any present-day experiment. The term *traditio* points explicitly to that which was passed on—*quod est traditum*—but implies also that many experiences were not transmitted, having been dropped because they were ineffectual. Tradition, therefore, is the empiricism of the species.

In its experimental aspect, tradition constitutes an enormous asset, for it has been submitted to the test of the multitude, and although susceptible to an incessant correction, posits nevertheless the result of an age-old experiment which is as empirical as any, though the modern experiment is often a faster and far less expensive operation than this undertaking that is spread over centuries. "Modern" experimentation is likewise building up a tradition, since its multiple coadunate works actually result in that which in the days to come will be "what is passed on."

The newborn never starts from zero, culturally speaking, for tradition, the result to date of vertical and horizontal completion, is gradually communicated to his awakening consciousness. It goes without saying that it is more advantageous for him to stand upon the accumulation of millennia than upon his own two feet, for whatever may be his dignity and talent as an individual, there is much more in what he is not than in what he is. Yet—and this is no less important—he too is a complement and a unique vision, and since the discovery and presentation of global knowledge implies a succession of angular truths, it follows that tradition is a continual conquest no less than a preservation. The concrete individual fulfills his function of transmitter, yet no two transmitters are alike. The succession of the multiple unique results in a slow but continual change: each new fragment introduces a new aspect. Tradition implies growth.

In our discussion of the different dictates of a judging Species in the domain of art and history, and in the development of a tradition, we discover a certain number of similarities.

Tentatively, the law can be formulated that the activity of a certain being is in inverse proportion to its duration. The shorter the lifespan, the more feverish is the activity; or, stated differently, the sooner replacement is needed, the faster is growth and evolution. This may not always be valid for individuals within the same species, but it appears to be common on a more general level. Insects are more active than mammals, and a species as a whole is infinitely slower than the individuals which compose it. The human Species, turbulent in its members, operates slowly as *totum*, requiring centuries to bring the eternal and the valuable to the surface and to let the second-rate sink to the bottom forever. Within the medium of time, the narrow (and at times the partial and prejudiced) insights of the individual become impartial through amendment. In other words, an element of correction is at work: each angular vision becomes the object of some reevaluation and is given its antidote through horizontal and vertical completion.

It now appears more clearly how the angular truth discussed in chapter 3 had relational value only and is actually a function which needs completion. Angular truths outweigh and correct one another. The resulting equilibrium is what we call generic truth. It comes not from a mere addition, but is born out of the convergence of the multiple unique. If a plurality of individuals agrees on the artistic standing of Michelangelo, it is not because of the similar in the plurality, but because of the convergence of the multiple dissimilar on that topic.

The generic truth, the genesis of which has been through incessant improvement and completion, contains a conformity to the real far beyond that of any individual conquest. For if its knowledge is thorough, so consequently is its *adequatio*.

All this often results in a shifting of emphasis. That which appears important for the individual is no longer so for the *totum*. The individual estimate may be obliterated, to be replaced by the judgment of the total human approach, which is more objective. Yet we should remember that this objectivity belongs still to a human approach, and that generic truth, however enriching, can by no means claim to be exhaustive. It sets the *totum genus humanum* apart just as individual discovery sets me apart; or, if speculation is permissible, just as a collection of some supra-human sort of beings—for example, angels—would be cognizant of a world proportionate to their nature and cognitive power, but still not exhaustive or absolute, since no finite approach can contain everything.

Generic truth, with its conformity with the real, is formulated, as we have said, in the judgment of the Species. Just as individual sensation and idea establish an implicit conformity, which, through reflection or through the more complex operation of the judgment, presents us with a full awareness of truth (the conformity was there *in* the consciousness, but not for the consciousness), so also generic truth receives its explicit formulation through a judgment of the Species; that judgment, however, although there, becomes effable only when taken over by the individual.

The individual can formulate certain judgments of the group (or of the *totum*) on historical events or particular dictates of a tradition, even though he is not in a position personally to check their growth through the ages. We notice here a return to the concrete existent, who was also the remote origin of a "specific" judgment. The generic truth is in the *totum*, but the explicit aware-ness of it exists only where its formulation resides, i.e., in the human fragment. The latter is the "spokesman," and often he is so without discovering the unusual power of the mandate which he utters, for the latter is invisible in its becoming. A scientific method may not be able to measure the genesis of such a judgment; hence, it is inclined to neglect the argumentative power which it, de facto, possesses. Yet it is not always advisable to reject a state-ment of tradition, of which the historical origin and subsequent growth cannot be checked by the individual, caught as he is within the limits of the here and the now. Only the *totum* can cover such a span and guarantee its authenticity. The concrete individ-ual must build up his own synthesis and constitute himself as a center, but he must also be aware that ontologically and noetically he is but part and fragment, hence, that decisions coming from the *totum* should be seriously considered for possible conversion into his own life, since they offer it thereby a vaster and more "objective" truth.

Generic Truth as Ineffable

AT times the "specific" judgment, although present, concerns historical events which are still surrounded by mystery or by de-bates that appear to be insoluble. There is no "universal" agree-ment. A judgment is said to be ineffable when no one individual can understand the answer all by himself.

The Battle of Verdun provides a case in point. The true Verdun is not that of Jules Romain, nor of Marshal Pétain, nor of the German historian, but each of these approaches has seized upon a totality, only the fringes of which were given to one person. The whole was reserved for the group. In a similar way the philosoph-ical conflict between Aquinas and Hume may appear to be insolu-ble, except by the method suggested in the preceding chapter, that of a paradoxical apprehension kept together in the mind of a third man. This, however, is not a stand *in terra firma*. Beyond a certain limit this psychological attempt for unity dissolves. The compo-nents become strictly opponents and the third man chooses a part.

At that moment another form of unity must be found and there is only one possibility—the *totum genus* itself.

For the *totum* as *totum*, however, no paradox is problematic. Either the paradox is an apparent contradiction or a real one. In the first hypothesis, the effect of shock it produces results from the fragmentary vision of the individual, who assimilates his notions in succession and is struck by their unexpected juxtaposition. The species as a whole is never taken by surprise, since the very knowledge of its members prevents the wonder of the *totum*. There is, therefore, no paradox that is an apparent contradiction for the *totum*. When the contradiction is real, the *totum genus* takes over, with the ontological replacing the psychological. What *is* replaces what *appears* (to me as individual). And what *is* contains no contradiction. This needs further elaboration.

Since traditional philosophy has not presented man as fragment, nor mankind as *unum* and *totum*, the difficulty here is mainly imaginative and pedagogical. Only the correct perspective, which we attempt to re-establish, can afford an answer.

To help us to gain this perspective, we must imagine the existence of an entity—we may call it God—who, as one and absolute, faces the manifold. For such a perfect being, the totality of the real would not need a cumbersome multiplicity of expression, but would be reflected in one single idea. Such knowledge would not come from the real itself, but would be somehow pre-existent to it. It would also, I imagine (I insist that all this is merely hypothetical), be detached from time and space and have none of the fragilities which mark an angular vision. Hence, it would include the manifold of the concrete, not in its spatio-temporal unfolding, but merely in fulfillment of the principle *qui potest plus, potest et minus*.

When we turn to the unity of the *totum humanum* and its global knowledge, we discover that its content is not pre-existent to the real, but, as has been sufficiently shown, originates through the multiple segments or angular truths present in concrete individuals. Confronted with a contradictory explanation of one and the same event (e.g., Verdun), the "specific" knowledge is the sum of the individual pronouncements, each individual pronouncement coming from the unique (individual) facing the unique (datum). Individual X asserts what he sees, but since his angular vision

limits the datum, he denies or rejects the aspects which he cannot
see; those are taken up by individual Z, who in turn repudiates
what individual Y has discovered, etc. The concatenation continues in a horizontal and vertical way, each view correcting the
other through assertion and denial. Negation is, indeed, essential
in the corrective function of the complement. If there are opponents
within the *totum genus humanum*, it is because the single reality
itself can only be represented by many (angular) visions, each
one *in*cluding and *ex*cluding. All this denotes the complexity of
our multiple approach, though not the complexity of the real. For
the contradiction is built by the multiple viewers not by the
ontological oneness. The *totum* (like God, although in a lesser
degree) faces this oneness.

From all this it appears that the knowledge concerning an event
like Verdun is ours but not mine. A plurality is required not only
to write about Verdun, but also to grasp it. Only the species, therefore (or eventually part of it) can grasp a number of ambiguities
which one enlightened individual cannot combine with his own
insight, however keen his eye and broad-minded his disposition.
Several individuals juggling with the cumbrous complexity of the
world divide among themselves an understanding which does not
so much exceed them quantitatively as it crushes them contradic-
torily. Hence, although we still defend the thesis of the previous
chapter with its "subjective" solution of antinomies, whether applied to the field of historical interpretation (Verdun) or to the
domain of philosophical explanation (e.g., Aquinas vs. Hume),
we must agree that at a certain level the antinomies need a multitude for their complete understanding and approval. This does
not imply that for the *totum* the principle of contradiction does
not exist, nor that for the *totum* something can be and at the same
time not be, but it implies that the *totum genus* has to allow, within
itself, the true to be expressed in a fragmentary and impure form,
i.e., such that it needs completion and correction. This is, unlike
the simple glance of God, the internal fragmented dialectic of the
totum. In certain cases the true drifts to the surface, i.e., the contradiction resolves into an effable (by the individual) pronouncement. In other cases, it does not, and it remains a plus-and-minus
assertion in the life of the single individual. Yet what is mystery
for one man is not so for the *totum*, and what is mystery for the

totum is not so for God. In the case under discussion, the solution
is there but is not effable. The world of the future is obviously a
world where a solution in many cases does not belong to one person, yet it is there—it belongs to the many within the moving
sphere of the *totum genus.*

In conclusion, we should add that if it is the pride of the individual to be himself, it is his sadness to be only himself. Incapable
of overcoming dual trends or of expressing generic truth in every
case, he should take comfort from the fact that, whether generic
truth be effable or not, it constitutes an equilibrium and self-
protection, since it is made from the correction of the many. All
through the misfortunes and errors of history runs the silent and
continual urge of mankind to protect itself. At times it is but an
undercurrent, a very sensitive presence in that vast sea of human
consciousness which spans the centuries. Mistakes are committed,
but where they occur, a correction is forthcoming, even if it takes
centuries. For the fragmentary unit which we call man, one mistake can be fatal. For the *totum* which we call the human species,
mistakes are repairable, since the *totum* itself is fragmented and
the fragments replaceable. Catastrophes exist, but they are local,
not planetary.

6

Semantics and the Species

WE are now sufficiently equipped to attempt the formulation of a certain number of semantic rules, which are based upon the views presented above. The aim is to make explicit the individual stand as opposed to the generic or specific, with the hope also of offering a lead towards further correction of the merely angular approach of present and past philosophical and cultural apprehension. This is not intended to be an extensive analysis of semantics. Semantics will be considered only insofar as it fits into the limited topic of our study.

Rule I: The fragmentary units of the *totum genus* are connected through meaningful sound. Semantics is the study of these sounds with their meanings.

In language we discover the physical element, or sound, and its psychic connotation, or meaning. The first is unavoidably connected with the material infrastructure of man: the involvement of man in space-and-time dimensions results in the use of the (sensible) sign. To imagine beings outside a space-and-time dimension is to make the sign superfluous. For the human world, sound is one sign, and although other signs are a priori not excluded, it is the prevalent one. To use a sound as the carrier of a meaning supposes: (1) a being which is intelligent, i.e., detached enough from material involvement so that for practical purposes at least, it manipulates successfully the one and the many or (in this case) the sound as understandable or meaningful; (2) another

[98]

being which is capable of understanding, i.e., capable of perceiving sound and grasping its meaning; (3) the necessity for both of these beings to attach the same meaning or signification-value to the same sound; (4) the necessity for both dialoguers to be fragmentary and relational. (Dialogue is in itself an acknowledgment of insufficiency and mutual need. As such, it is the expression of ontological poverty; one *is* not alone, one is as fragment of a *totum*. Language expresses this structure.) Finally (5) it supposes the underlying unity of the dialoguers. Semantics is a result of the multiplicity of fragmentary percepts within the one group. There is no conversation between men and trees, nor is there between God and men. "God spoke to men" is a biblical assertion, one which cannot be taken literally. Only in a god-made-man can contact be established, and it can be seen that the incarnation was a philosophical necessity to bring God down to the level of man, with the hope of bringing men up to the level of God. God-made-man is a semantic necessity, whatever its other benefits may be for a struggling mankind. Conversation is an exchange in understanding and understanding is possible only where there is a deeper underlying unity.

Yet although it is an instrument of men, language is a deceptive tool. And it is so for two reasons: (1) It is necessarily the same for all, hence, gives the illusion that the minds are not more different than their linguistic tool. The danger lies in the limitation of all abstraction: the one-and-the-many becomes the one-being-the-same-as-the-many; and, (2) Language often gives the erroneous impression that the use of a word is a guarantee of its understanding. Actually the individual man grasps only a part of the full meaning, and even then he does so in his own way. What he obtains is not what the other man sees. However, everyday life runs smoothly notwithstanding the superficial grasp of the meaning of a term. We all know what *nation* is, what *justice* is, etc., even though very few of us are able to define those terms with precision.

Rule II: Semantics is either an individual semantics or a group (or generic) semantics.

It is of course evident that semantics always implies a plurality of men. Language is a tool used only within the framework of a social structure and is therefore meaningless without a plurality of men. The question, however, now arises whether, with this basic qualification, terms used by the individual do always receive their full meaning when used by an individual. The answer here is negative, and a distinction must be made.

A term belongs to the individual semantics when it is used by the individual and obtains in this use its full meaning. A term belongs to the group-semantics (or generic-semantics) when it requires the global and complementary expression of the multitude to have its full meaning. It is obvious that a term which essentially belongs to the group-semantics is often used by the individual. In such cases the meaning of the term is either partly or totally lost.

The term *atheist*, for example, is an individual epithet, since the negation of God is an individual attitude, which rightly or wrongly can be taken by the individual man. So also are terms like *blind, sick* and others which affect the individual in his singularity. This does not imply that those terms exclude the other man. In fact, they connote indirectly the existence of others, for to be sick implies not to be like the rest of the species. On the contrary, the term *theist* and others which we shall discuss later belong to the group- or generic-semantics, for a full grasp of such concepts transcends the individual understanding.

Rule III: The group- or generic-semantics is either: (a) the *we-language* which is *parallel-additive*, when the term merely expresses the simultaneity and additive plurality of a certain act, e.g., we are walking; or, (b) the *we-language* which is *complementary-additive*, when the addition, coming from a multiplicity of fragmentary sources, is also complementary, e.g., we-manufacture-a-car. The *car* is the result of the convergent complementarity of many unique interventions, a uniqueness which, in the case of the assembly line, becomes repetitious, but which in its achievement of the one car is and remains unique. In this sense our present-day trends of unification and collectivism are very significant. The political and social growth of the masses, the increase of financial and intellectual trusts, the melting together of political unities, the increase of the number of conventions, conferences and other forms of "solidary" thinking, the growth of laboratories or centers of collective research, all point towards a growing compenetration and towards man's growing insight into being-part-of. The surface of the sphere makes this even more urgent. A Ptolemaic surface, indefinitely extending, might have made this coming together and the resulting awareness of ontological fragmentarity less pressing, but upon a spherical planet unification corroborates oneness more than ever. This oneness, at present, is semantically redundant. By this I mean that according to the present rule, the meaning of certain terms rests in its full bearing upon the many. The speculative understanding of a concept therefore becomes a group affair, as is its practical understanding or execution, which can only be fulfilled through the individual-and-unique contribution of the many. At this moment a distinction must be made.

(1) As far as science is concerned, the *complementary-additive we-language* is already at work in terms of speculative understanding and will be immensely more so in the future. We-conceive-and-we-make-the-spaceship is a division of language (and of labor) where specialization, hence individuality, is recognized and integrated into a whole because of the encyclopedic amount of knowledge and labor involved. The multiplicity of insights at work in a scientific achievement is a fact, and although here as elsewhere, the genius produces the new, his creation, once it has seen the light, belongs through its mathematical expression to the many. This implies not only that it will be integrated into the work as complement, but also that the many will recover what fundamentally, because of its human character, i.e., its mathematical expression, belongs to the *totum genus* and originates from the depths of the *totum*. The mathematical genius, although contributing the new and the unique, is less detached from ordinary human society than the artist, since his equation, however complex, is quantifiable and thus ultimately reducible to a vision of the human species. In conclusion, we must say that although the individual subject is at work here and although the multiple variety of the subjects produces the highest in its field, we have not yet reached that which the complementary-additive we-language can produce when the dialoguer produces within the *opus* that unique which remains unique and mathematically untranslatable, and yet in its unequalled way contributes to the ensemble.

(2) In the domain of art, where the subject and his unique

vision intervenes in a more pronounced way, the application of our rule concerning the complementary-additive we-language becomes more complex. Actually this application depends upon the genre of interference of the subject in the achievement of the *opus*. From this point of view, a distinction between architecture and other modes of artistic expression is important.

As far as the latter are concerned, we observe, without denying the part of the unique, that they all contain the presence of the communal in their depth, in a way of vertical completion. Only thus are they understandable. A poem, for example, contains in its unknown origin the poems of Homer, Shakespeare and others;[1] the communal lies buried within it. A whole unseen creation precedes that which is seen. The communal, furthermore, supports it contemporaneously by horizontal completion. We may say that Hamlet is carried on the summit of the Elizabethan Age. Only in a particular epoch, or restricted world, where many poets labor, does Hamlet appear and do they, through their combined effort, produce in us a response to the *opus majus*. This participation of the secondary and the remote has often been forgotten because of the fact that the reality of a world-of-beauty as organic *totum* has been overlooked. A world-of-beauty is, indeed, the great achievement and the ultimate limit of the complementary-additive we-language in the world of art in general. We-create-a-beautiful-world is as far as the coadunate effort can go. Each work of art is an absolute by itself in the sense that, unlike the quantifiable object of science, it cannot be translated into numbers and remains essentially a mystery in its birth and in its esthetic impact. It transcends the scientific impact through the power of the unique, which will forever be unique; yet—and this is a point which should be underlined—it fulfills its referential function in helping to make an epoch. Even though the components of a world-of-beauty lack that easily discernible and clear-cut relational dimension which we discover in the diverse elements which constitute a scientific achievement, they constitute, nonetheless, a totality and will be so identified later in such designations as the Golden Age

---

[1] On a similar topic, see T. S. Eliot's essay, "Tradition and the Individual Talent," in *The Sacred Wood* (London: Metheun & Co., Ltd., 1920; New York: Barnes & Noble, 1964).

of Pericles or the Quattrocento or *le Siècle de Louis XIV* or the Elizabethan Age. We discover in them the unity which they ignore but amidst which they lived and produced, through collateral support, their greatest works, whether the Parthenon, the Sistine Chapel, Phèdre, or Hamlet.

There is one creation, however, where the complementary-additive we-language results in a closely unified work, and although the term *language* cannot be understood here in a strict sense, it can be said that architecture may very well fulfill the dream of artistic production carried out by a team. Architecture occupies this honor for two reasons. The first reason is that the participation of mathematics in its planning and execution is greater than in any other art. This quantifiable aspect of architecture makes it ultimately a common possession, for, as we have said above, mathematics is human yet impersonal.

The second reason needs to be sought in the very essence of architecture itself. That which is multiple but merely juxtaposed can never impress us as does the multiple which converges and results in one. A symphony is more beautiful than a melody; an oil painting has a greater impact than a mere sketch; an unfolding of stone and pillars which results in a division of space called the Parthenon has, all other things being equal, a more imposing beauty than an obelisk. The more audacious the multiple and the more powerful its synthesis, the higher the beauty which is achieved. The multiple components of the work, however, each with its *"particulata pulchritudo, sicut et particulata natura"* ["Fragmentary beauty and its fragmentary nature"] (Dionysius Areopagita), requires the intervention of the many. Even the initial vision and planning is not the work of one man but in most cases is the result of a continual correction and completion where several masters interfered. This is the way, I believe, it was understood by Rodin, when standing in front of the Cathedral of Chartres, he made the remark which we have already quoted: "We are only wrecks." He was admitting that his work is mere fragment compared to the artistic achievement of a team.

In a world gradually closing upon itself, the complementary-additive collaboration will produce the highest and most complex forms. When the polycephalic and multi-voiced artist will produce them in beauty, dams and bridges, turnpikes and skyscrapers will compete with cathedrals. Yet these accomplishments will achieve their esthetic purpose only if the contributing agent is welcome as *individual*, just as the contribution of the latter will reach its highest result when integrated into the ensemble. This is where museums, in pilfering monuments of the past, have in many cases been destructive to the ensemble. When the Parthenon was vandalized, museums were enriched with broken relics, and by broken I mean not only mutilated through age, but also through removal from the main work, where they truly belong. The admiration which we feel for a relic like the statue of Victory is esthetic, no doubt, but it contains also an element of pity because of what is lacking, and of nostalgia for the world-of-beauty from where it originates. In the modern trend towards the collective and towards a greater reliance upon science, architecture, gratifying both these tendencies, will reach its highest fulfillment in the days to come, on the condition that the many who contribute will complement one another in an arrangement where each will have his own place, fulfilling thereby a fruitful inequality. It will be an addition of the unequal resulting in the unequalled or the beautiful. Without this contribution of the multiple unique, the future will degenerate into an age of mere machines.

(3) In the world of philosophy variety does not serve the same purpose as in the world of art. For, if variety or multiple angular truth is present in the multiplicity of philosophical achievements, it is ultimately aimed at the conquest of an absolute truth, even though each achievement is only angular. For this reason, as was shown in our preceding chapter, integration is imperative and the complementary-additive language fulfills its role. The individual of the future, facing the achievement of the past, will gradually give up the claim of absolute interpretation and visualize his accomplishment for what it is worth. Partial insight will be seen as a segment of global completion and generic addition.

The following rules, starting from an acceptance of generic knowledge of reality, will attempt an inquiry into the generic meaning of a word. This will constitute the complementary-additive we-language in the strict sense.

Rule IV: Certain terms can be evaluated both on an individual scale and on a "specific" scale. Their meanings, therefore, will be dependent upon the user: terms which express the individual striving and his fundamental limitation will have a different meaning when expressing the potentiality of the species. Examples are the terms *difficult, immense, impossible, humble* and all others expressing power and weakness. What is immense (or *im-mensuratus*) for the individual may very well be *mensurabilis* for the species—well within its sphere.

Rule V: Words which imply a chronological or spatial quantity must also for future usage be confided to the *totum genus* for better evaluation, e.g., time and space. More concrete applications such as hour, day, month, year, foot, yard, mile, etc., were made for a world where the individual existent was an exclusive dimension. The past was a one-man world, while the future will be a group-world, wherein the individual will find his fullest actualization.

The understanding of this assertion requires a closer look at the phenomenon of the *totum genus* (or species) as we have used it in this study. The term covers the physical additive totality of all human beings, and as such it covers past, present, and future. It is identical with the sum of all human beings from all time and all places, identified with none, but built up out of all individual "fragments" which had, have, and will have historical existence. As *totum* therefore, its connections with time and space are nonexistent, yet as far as inner growth and decline are concerned, the *totum* is *in* time. This distinction is important. The *totum genus* as such does not succeed to itself, is not renewable, hence measurable, but its internal fragments are subject to alteration; that is, they appear, grow within the *totum*, and disappear. Once the *totum* has started, however, it can be said to make its way through time; that is, an internal unfolding of the *totum* takes place through a multiplication of individuals. Although this is accomplished in time and space, we must repeat that as *totum* it is not, in its total dimension, time-involved, since the conception implies all three: past, present, and future. The difficulty is merely one of imagination and results from our "individualistic" pedagogy. I shall, therefore, introduce two examples to attempt a clarification of my own thought.

When I talk of the past, present, and future, I express a view which has meaning for me as an individual fragment and for my

mind, which considers the *totum* through time and divides the latter into past, present, and future. My position, however, is not
unlike that of a prisoner. The prison is not a prison for itself, but
only for the prisoner. Just so, time and space are not a limitation
for the *totum* but only for its fragment. I can assign to the prison
no time-limit, for transposed in our problem, it has a form of
timelessness. And although the prison in its entirety can be destroyed, so long as it exists, its inhabitants will be prisoners,
hence time-and-space bound.

To escape from the prison, I do not use the Platonic exit from
the cave, but another metaphor which, although fictitious and un-
realizable, may help me to understand in a tentative way how it
feels to be *totum*, i.e., everywhere at once. For the one who is
everywhere at once, there is no change. His perceptive power might
be compared to that of a battery of movie cameras spaced closely
next to one another around the perimeter of a bullfight ring. If, by
impossible hypothesis, a human eye could see simultaneously that
which is portrayed by these manifold visions, it would discover no
change. The example extended and multiplied would find an immobile world. This world is discovered only by the one who is
everywhere at once, i.e., by the one who does not change himself.
But the use of a terminology like that used in our present analysis,
as, e.g., *everywhere-at-once*, keeps us in a world of individual
semantics. Everywhere-at-once could be expressed more truthfully
in generic semantics by saying *nowhere* and *never*. The one who is
everywhere at once, furthermore, would accomplish everything at
one glance. Time as the medium for accomplishment would be
nonexistent for him. The individual fragment, left to his own
capacities, is time-bound, and for any action is imprisoned in the
rhythm of succession.

At present we have caught up with the application of our *Rule
V*. Time is the thing absent in the *totum genus* as *totum*. Time is
the internal successive growth of the *totum genus* (growth being, I
insist, already an anthropomorphic term). And finally, time is the
presence *sine qua non* of the concrete individual. To return to the
complementary convergence for the accomplishment of a work,
therefore, implies to put forth the first step towards time for the
generic *totum*, i.e., towards a dimension where there is no time. It
is a return to the non-dimensional or to an infinite-dimensional
which from our point of view is the same. Aristotle's notion of

time, "number of motion in respect of 'before' and 'after'"
(*Physics*, 219 b 1–0), is applicable only to the individual
"counting." As soon as *we* enter into the game, our overlapping
of "before" and "after" cuts down on time in proportion to our
omnipresence. *We* eliminate part of the contradiction which *I* face,
just as the complementarity of angular judgments reaches a
generic truth which no less than any other feature of the *totum*
has a timeless character. The we-language is a revenge upon the
fragmentary capacities of the concrete existent and implies a division of labor, whether simultaneous or in succession, with a shrinking of individual time as a result. The task is performed on a
different scale, since for *us* time is different from what it was for
me. The philosopher of the future will have to take into account
the performance of mankind acting as a growing *totum* or as a
group "assembly line" and accomplishing thereby the unseen, i.e.,
the heretofore-never-accomplished-in-such-a-short-time (individual
time, I mean).

This process of acceleration expresses itself in diverse domains
which will not be discussed here, since we wish only to present, in
a systematic way, a certain number of principles, not their applications. It suffices to mention the difference between the reporting
of an event made by hundreds and that made by one. If by many—
and that seems to be the trend of modern news agencies—the
manifold (and simultaneous) approach of a great number of
thinking units results, literally, in an amazing conquest of time
and space. Our very amazement, however, shows how we live on
this side of our accomplishments and are judging by individual
semantics a work which, because of the complementary contribution of the many, should be judged in a generic way. The machine
affords another example of the powerful shrinking of space-and-
time, again due to the convergent cooperation of the many. Indeed,
it consolidates within its metal structure innumerable thoughts and
attempts and failures, and in so doing, saves and alters the very
nature of time. This alteration—it should be emphasized—im-

$$\text{plies, first of all, a quantitative diminution.} \frac{\text{We}}{\text{Time}} \text{ unlike } \frac{\text{I}}{\text{time}}$$

and the coadunate *we* present within the performance of the machine transform time through abating or even eliminating that
which is considered to be its main feature, its element of succes-

sion. We do not know, at present, where this process of elimination will end, but we can observe, nevertheless, that with the maximum intervention of the complementary-additive we-language, the amount of succession is drastically diminished. Secondly, the alteration introduced by the machine confirms in its way the metaphysical structure and the psyche of man, as envisaged in our study. The planetary world of tomorrow will insist that the individual, although unique, is fragment and that if his potentialities are immense, they are so only through the conception and application of the we-language. Surprisingly, the small child will often live this conception more authentically than the adult. For when he shows no nervousness for an ulterior occupation beyond that which he is doing at the time, we adults call him slow. This is the wrong epithet. For his absence of any time awareness implies not only that the notion of time is one of time-for and that he has no other motives beyond those which keep him interested at that very moment, but also that, by instinct, he has an insight into living in a world where division of labor and inequality of talents is honored. Actually both factors go together; one is "slow" because he knows that he is only responsible for his own task and that others will take care of the rest. This conception will be growing in the days to come. In a world of an all-out performance of the *we*, the *I* is unique but unique only. The complementary-additive we-language is an assertion of the inequality of man and of the intrinsic dignity of the individual existent (his uniqueness) as well. It is difficult to predict how the gradual conquest of generic time will affect individual time, but even so, it can be said, without the rejection of individual semantics, that in a world of survival in progress, generic time will be predominant and pervade the individual accounting of time. That this constitutes a total inversion of world political and economic thought is obvious, but that problem and its psychological implications do not constitute the topic of this study.

To conclude, we observe a reduction to unity in spatial and temporal dimensions in proportion to the convergent intervention of the group or of the *totum*. This reduction to unity has a double sense: (1) it implies a return to the primeval unity of the *totum genus*, not an undifferentiated unity, but a unity that is internally differentiated because of the multiple unique. The generic, therefore, not in its pre-ontological homogeneity, but in its internally diversified variety and mutually completing diversity is the attraction par excellence of the future; and, (2) it implies, furthermore, that at this stage, space and time have a tendency to disappear as separate dimensions. The ontological effect of acceleration, or time understood in a complementary-additive we-language, implies that a task is accomplished by more people but within less time. Space itself is a shrinking dimension and is brought from an individual level to a group level (or generic level). What was *there* is now *here* and it is *here* because *we* are *here* instead of *I*. This means that *here* and *there* because of the complementary-additive approach stand for *now* and *later*. Both these terms belong by nature to an individual semantics—*you* were *before me*—but have a tendency to disappear once the *we* over-bridging *now* and *later*, *here* and *there* takes over. Time and space are media of accomplishment for the individual existent, and their primordial meaning no less than their measurement was originally made strictly upon a basis of individual operations. Where the latter are giving way, we observe not only that time-and-space dimensions condense, but also that they make less sense as separate and distinct; for the complementarity, conception and planning of the we-language erase the *here* and the *there* no less than the *past* and the *future*. To move away from the *I* means to drop chronological and spatial restraints. It is obvious, however, that any conquest of the coadunate *we* affects me: *I* move less when *we* work. *Our* labor is to *my* advantage. My wonder in contemplating modern accomplishments results from the fact that I tend to translate into individual semantics that which was conceived, planned and executed by the group- or generic-semantics.

It cannot be denied that in the preceding analysis *time* has been understood pragmatically, i.e., as time-for. This does not preclude the acceptance of a more affective meaning such as that defended by present-day existentialism, where dimensions of past, present and future are sometimes viewed as resulting from feelings like remorse (past), attention (present), and hope and desire (future). This explanation is simply ignored in the present study because its specific power and additive complementarity are less pronounced than in the case of a pragmatic understanding of time. It is precisely this second understanding of *time-for* which gets its full meaning in the semantics of a complementary-additive we-language.

Rule VI: Terms which imply a complexity far above individual insight have always belonged to the species, although they have often been drawn within the individual orbit, e.g., God, Truth (in its generic or its absolute sense). This rule needs no special comment at present, since a special chapter will be devoted to the notion of God, and Truth, already examined, will be further investigated later.

Rule VII: Most abstract words have their full meaning in specific bearing only.

By *abstract* I understand here the notion as apprehended by the mind and resulting from an operation of the mind in which it is detached from the real. In that sense, every idea is abstract. It is not our purpose at present to examine the psychological structure of this abstractive operation or in what precisely the abstract notion or idea (or universal) consists. This much can be said, however. An idea is an individual attempt of universalization, but this endeavor, guided by the angular vision of the concrete existent, can be only partially successful. Some universals are elementary and through their daily usage can easily be grasped with a superficial understanding, but others are much more complex. Even the idea of a tree, superficially simple, needs the help of several for a more precise understanding. The notion of tree formed by the biologist and botanist is quite different from that of the gardener; the philosopher has his own view, as does the poet, both of whom mean something entirely different from that which the physicist has in mind when inquiring into the ultimate structure of matter. The conviction that each of these approaches is fragmentary has permeated the common-sense understanding of what an idea is to such an extent that even when the average man claims that he has an idea of X, he does so in the realization that his knowledge of X is only limited and shallow.

Other ideas which are abstract in the full sense of the word and express a "form" without "subject," like Beauty, Justice, etc., are in strict terms undefinable by the concrete individual. They are so complex and contain so many facets that when an individual claims to know what they are, his apprehension must be considered as an individual appropriation of what originally belonged to the *totum genus*. Such terms are in their full and unfragmented meaning a possession of the Species. In actuality, however, they are the object of the individual's desire and are unconsciously transposed into his own personal understanding. The specific realization becomes the individual's dream, and as such, is a stimulus for his activity and for his collateral competition, hence, for his complementarity. In its specific realization (always on a human scale, of course) and specific propriety, the abstract term is, in a way, not unlike Platonic participation, fragmented among the different individuals. This Platonic absolutization, however, does not dwell in the realm of essences, but is in our case merely the result of an additive-complementary convergence fulfilled in the totality of the human genus.

It becomes apparent now that the failure to understand the universal lies in the failure to consider its real origin. The universal is not individually but specifically possessed. The individual thinks universally through the others. He borrows a universal notion which he himself cannot exhaust because of his finitude, and the *we* becomes not only an epistemological protection, but also a psychological fulfillment. A complete definition is only made up by the many, and since the universal, in the strict sense of the word, is that which corresponds to a perfect definition, it can only be carried by the many, even then being still susceptible to inner growth. A universal, therefore, is a group possession, and is as a cupola arching over time and space, enclosing the *here* and *there*, the *now* and *later*.

It follows that a restatement of the concept of the universal is necessary. In the past the universal was considered to be a concept applicable to many, implying a oneness, yet a communicability. This oneness may be understood as a distinct entity existing outside the mind and outside the thing (Plato), or as having a certain existence in the mind although drawn from reality (Aristotle), or as a term or word which, although particular itself, has, because of its similarity or evocative power, a relation to many other particulars (the nominalistic school). Without discussing the variety of opinions, we may say that although a oneness and a communicability are always required, this view can no longer be defended as adequate. We do not deny the possibility of a universal concept which can be multiplied among the many, so long as that concept expresses the rudimentary knowledge of the idea, since there is indeed a oneness which is multiplied or multipliable among the many. There is, however, a oneness which is common to many in the way a room is common to several occupants. In this prospect, it follows that that which is common to many is not necessarily the same in an exact mathematical amount. Any individual in a group possession owns a part of the total (universal) concept. This part, however, cannot be demonstrated to be identical with that which his neighbor possesses. It is, in most cases, complementary to what the other lacks, and by the same token, respects the uniqueness of an approach which in traditional assertions, although not denied, was certainly overlooked. In a similar way, the theologian would never claim that the divine nature behaves as a universal towards the three Persons: it is common to the three Persons, but does not as a universal descend to its inferiors. The traditional universal has its value in an individual semantics (see *Rule II* above), but is no longer applicable where an intellectual team achieves global understanding. At present, the group-language, an expression of the complementary-additive semantics, comes into its rightful place and can be understood as the total expression of a fragmented universal, resulting in a universal the oneness of which is, at bottom, a common possession and not a multiplication. From this it follows that the predicability or immediate result of universality in the traditional sense of the word must be redefined. This problem will be examined in the following chapter.

Rule VIII: Survival constitutes a fundamental universal, expressed through the complementary-additive we-language. History is the actualization of survival in time.

If we try to examine in detail the content of the complementary-additive universal, the notion of survival presents itself as typical. As previously explained, *to be* means to endure and to endure implies that a remedy was provided for a provisional situation.[2] To provide the necessary complementum requires knowledge.

---

[2] See chapter I of this volume.

Whether this knowledge of "how to survive" is distinct from the effort of survival itself is not clear, but I am inclined to believe that the application of the traditional distinction between to know and to will is artificial here and that survival as an elemental instinct includes both knowledge and drive. It is not essential whether knowledge itself is conscious and rational; what does matter is the insight that specific survival is made up from the addition of millions of centers of knowledge and constitutes as such, de facto, a universal—even the first universal. The realization, in most cases, is oblique, i.e., through an inversion of the individual purposes and a reversal of the end to the level of means (what I consider end can become means for the *totum*), and vice versa. As part of the intricate machinery of the species, the individual may often lack the precise awareness of how his knowledge or instinct for survival will ultimately serve the *totum genus*. This is, in most cases, a mystery for him, although at times, he becomes explicitly aware that his life fulfills a functional and referential purpose, whether by protecting itself and surviving, or by losing itself for the other and, in this very act, fulfilling its highest referential function. A deeper comprehension of the complex activity of the *totum genus* in its immense effort towards self-preservation would reveal a mysterious cooperation of the living in the most remote and unexpected way. This approach, admittedly, alludes to an absorption of the universal in the individual existent. This important aspect of our notion will be discussed in the following chapter. All that needs to be underlined at present is the importance of the complementary-additive knowledge as the fundamental and first universal, which constitutes, in fact, man's survival.

It appears now that our notion of history can be defined in the light of the terminology used in the present chapter. In particular, the distinction between *res gestae* and *narratio rerum gestarum* needs to be examined. The very existence of *res gestae*, or the ontological succession of human events, rests upon the broken and heterogeneous structure of the total line of mankind. For it is the transitory individual who is the ultimate explanation of history. He does not, of course, constitute it in his loneliness; only the many in succession with their individual differences, their eventual conflict and mutual correction, can constitute history. In calling this ensemble the *res gestae*, we should give some attention to the deeper meaning of *gestae*. The usage of the past participle implies the perspective that what is bygone is "there." Such a prospect is possible only because of the *we*; i.e., the very use of the past *gestae* implies that there is plurality and that within this plurality one can discover those who are gone and those who are still in existence; or in a more restricted way, when I say *gestae*, I consider those who live before me *and* myself turned towards them. There is no past without present. But since what is gone is gone for me (unavoidably so), the noetic is obviously involved in the ontological. My consideration of the *res gestae* is actually a backward look and signifies a viewing of that which is gone by that which still is.

It would be illusory to consider the *narratio* (*rerum gestarum*) as totally distinct from the *res gestae*. In fact, both overlap, the *narratio* simply being more elaborate and scientific. In performing this return upon the past, the historian, no less than the layman, is not and cannot be identified with that past; he makes a personal inquiry into that which is absent. Nothing more. To recognize this is to accept the need for a noetic plurality to conquer that which is absent. History, no less than survival, belongs in its full meaning to the semantics of a complementary-additive language. As *res gestae* (if I consider myself as detached from the *res gestae*), history results in survival as an accomplished feat; as *narratio rerum gestarum* (we of the present knowing a past better and more scientifically), history is a result of survival, for only bygone things are objects of my *narratio*. Survival, therefore, occupies that unparalleled and unique position of an entity which contains its own effect, yet results from that effect. Such is the unusual position of a *totum* which is *totum* but exists in succession only. It survives, hence has a history as soon as a past emerges; but it can only survive as a result of a disappearing succession of temporary fragments and their accomplishments. Notwithstanding their close relation, however, survival of the *totum* and the history of man are not identical. For survival is above all a quality of the *totum* as *totum*. History, on the contrary, is the protracted existence in time of the *we* with their multiple adventures. The multiple individuals do not survive, but they have a history and know a history; paradoxically, the history they have they do not know, and the one they know, they do not have; for their own history will be achieved only when they themselves are no longer, and their historical knowledge, as a complementary part of the global and complementary-additive ensemble, concerns those who are no longer and already belong to history.

Rule IX: (a) When the complementary-additive we-language applies to words and not to theories (as in the preceding chapter), the individual apprehension of the meaning of these words can only be fragmentary.

(b) The complete grasp by the individual of a term belonging to the group-semantics is not one of direct intuition, therefore, but ultimately one of faith.

Part (a) of this rule is based upon our assumption that the individual fragment cannot replace the *totum genus*. This does not deny that the common possession which results from the very belonging to the one *genus* does not belong equally to all and every one. Nor does it deny that the single existent cannot and should not attempt to grow beyond himself. This reaches, indeed, the very core of our study, and part (b) attempts one step more towards its elucidation.

We are now suddenly taking the viewpoint of the *totum* which, as *totum*, faces the meaning of certain terms, with the result that the meaning of these terms appears ambivalent, i.e., we discover in those terms a meaning which is individual (belonging to an individual semantics) and one which is generic. The nine rules of this chapter elaborate upon the latter. *Rule IX* is nothing but a more explicit transfer from the semantics to the individual, for that which has been conquered by the insight of the *totum genus* is now tentatively brought back to its undivided fragment, or man, who ought to see things in a generic way. This first conclusion implies a psychological orientation, in which one man's achievement can no longer be taken as the central criterion. In exhausting his limitation through self-awareness, man passes beyond that limitation. For the acceptance of the fact that individual insight is partial insight is part of overcoming it, and where man reaches his limit consciously, he steps onto a higher level. Whoever reaches the top level of the lower part by the same token reaches the lower part of the top level.

As the concrete individual faces the activity and expression of the complementary-additive we-language, we notice that although the very complex structure which results from the multiple unique and its skillful specialization escapes him in its *why* and *how*, nevertheless he enjoys the result. *I* am unable to grasp what the combined *we* has conceived and expressed, but I accept its incarnation. Cathedral, spaceship, and any end-product of the complementary-additive we-language, although a mystery for the individual in its becoming, is a common possession in its achievement. Like the judgment of the Species hidden in its birth and growth, but becoming at a certain moment an individual's effable possession, so the artistic or technical achievement grown to completion through the completion of the many will be recognized and enjoyed by the single man. What lies buried in its phase of genesis is the secret of the *we* or *totum genus*, a secret which is open to collective knowledge but hidden to individual ignorance. This ignorance is actually never completely lifted, for even where the end-product which is conceived and achieved by the we-language is enjoyed, it is never thoroughly understood by the individual. He enjoys and accepts it in faith.

To our previous implication that the *totum genus* as *totum* is everywhere at once, we can now add that this human omnipresence is a human omniscience as well. That which, by hypothesis, is extended through all time and all space can perceive all that there is to perceive. The individual fragment, however, is not where the *totum* is. His faith in others is a makeshift to fill the immense gaps of his perception. In short, life requires the witness whom we trust. If there were only one man upon this planet, he would be an unbeliever, of course, but he would be ignorant as well. The thinking units of the *totum genus humanum* are interwoven by trust and faith. One could even say that the act of faith in the other is the epistemological argument par excellence. The forceful impact of the *we* upon the *me* in the realm of the noetic has too often been forgotten. No mathematical argument has ever been offered to convince me of the presence of the real, but if I constantly go beyond the impression and accept the multidimensional object, it is perhaps due to the fact that, although I view one aspect only, I unconsciously take views from several angles, thus assuming the fictive presence of the many. It may be this which conveys to me a realistic insight into the external world. If this is true, I could assert that faith in the many lies at the very start of any epistemological guarantee. *We* (you and I and he) give density, or depth and volume, to a world far more strikingly than does any ordinary epistemological security based upon the "I" alone. Without the multiplicity of a fragmented *totum*, the world would lack the dimension of depth. Only a globe inhabited by the *we* lies bare for a multivalent approach and acquires the bulk or foundation for quantifiable space. The multiplicity of individual fragments, therefore, whether real or fictitious, outlines the density, or depth and volume, in the universe, at the same time shrinking its distances when working in a complementary-additive we-language. This density of volume and its geographical delineation is accepted "in faith."

The witness is not always fictitious, nor is his testimony merely to depth. I also accept events and things, whether distant or bygone, through a concatenation of witnesses, the first being the one who observed them, the others being a series of witnesses in a descending line reaching to me; I can believe in the event only because I believe them all. If I believe in the "absent," under whatever form, because of a chain of witnesses, I believe also in man's creations—whether they be a machine, a work of art, an architectural performance—even when they are a mystery to me. Their highly complex structure, resulting from the combined skill of many, escapes the "angular" me, but my faith continues and covers my ignorance. This attitude of trust is ultimately a transfer from the generic semantics to the individual semantics. That which the we-language asserts may be partially seen and even partially understood, but only in faith is it completely accepted. It is my right, of course, to check the chain of witnesses which introduces the event to me, or to investigate the intricate arrangement of a machine, but the results of my investigation will never surpass the method, which in its essence is fragmentary.

In conclusion, the philosopher who accepts this claim of faith makes an act of submission to the group (or to the *totum*), for if he were to trust only what he himself sees, he would no longer trust, but merely see. This dependence does not destroy the unicity of the individual man's vision, so often defended in this essay. On the contrary, the uniqueness of his vision is accepted upon a basis of trust in his own organs of vision, whether sensory or mental.

Similarity of tools has, however, never meant identity. However dependent it may be upon the semantics of a we-language for individual enrichment, man's vision is his and his alone. If he accepts a conception and product of the we-semantics, it is only because individual semantics are inconclusive and need completion.

7

Logical Applications

A Logic of the Team

SINCE ideas are, in many cases, a common possession and result from the contribution of the diverse, it is no longer possible to consider these concepts to be an individual monopoly in the exclusive sense used by Aristotelian Logic. Where a team achieves understanding or the execution of a work, the result, condensed into a "universal," can be said of the team only and not in its entirety of each of the separate members. When I assert that the roses are red, a sufficient apprehension is obtained by the one who makes that judgment, so that with good reason the term *red* can be predicated of the subject roses, or of each rose separately. With no less authority the individual can state that *the missile is ninety feet long,* for although the missile itself in its noetic conception and in its practical achievement is an example of the complementary-additive we-language, the statement *the missile is ninety feet long* is not exhaustive, but a fragmentary description only, which can be made by an individual. When the predication, however, presupposes a thorough knowledge of a complex universal, as is the case, e.g., in the statement *this is a missile,* it appears that such a statement needs the many to possess a guaranteed and authoritative value. Our claim gains strength when instead of using the indirect formulation *this is a missile,* we present our judgment in a direct way: *we conceive-and-make the missile.* In the example *we are walking,* which in the previous chapter illustrated the parallel-additive we-language, the predication is in the usual way, since *walking* can be asserted of each of us. In such examples, however, *as we won the game, we conceive-and-make the missile, we won the battle of Verdun,* a collective approach is presumed, and obviously the predication can only be done when and if the *we* is taken collectively. The use of the first person plays no decisive role, for the substitution of the second or third would not weaken our thesis. It is the plurality which matters, for in any of these performances the communal is at work and within the community each contribution is unique. The predication must, therefore, be done collectively and, within the collective predication, in a differentiated way for each participant. Both conditions are equally important: the predicate is not applicable in its totality to each one of the constitutive elements of the subject, but only collectively; yet within the team or crew (or *totum genus* eventually), the individual contribution is varied and must be recognized as such.

At this moment it appears that an Aristotelian Logic is deficient for the manipulation of a concept which is the result of coadunate planning and execution by a team, crew, group, or *totum genus.* Traditional logic handles concepts in such a way that they can stand a clear-cut manipulation with the notions of comprehension and extension each in its traditional position. The comprehension of the complex universal, however, cannot be known by one man but is possible only through the additive noesis of the team or *totum genus.* Nor can the traditional meaning and use of extension be of any use, since the singulars are not inferiors of a uniform predicate, but rather are fragmentary carriers of partial concepts and of their partial execution. In the strict sense, no technique is available for showing the birth of the partial concept in each of the contributing fragments and its complementary convergence in a unique way towards the resulting complex and communal universal. If it were, the unique and the ineffable would then be categorizable. Yet a real Logic is here at work. The striving of a team towards a global achievement, whether it be a cathedral or a scientific product, is not unlike the manipulation of an idea in the mind of an individual, who elaborates his premises and deduces his conclusions. The premises here, however, are living men and the partial insights of those living men. The syllogism is polycephalic, and the conclusion can be either concrete (the work of art or the scientific achievement) or abstract (as the judicative evaluation of the group or of the *totum*). The end-result or "universal," which the individual was unable to construe alone, contains his unique complementary contribution. This latter aspect—a very important one—traditional logic does not recognize, nor is it capable of dealing with that total result which comes from the addition of a distinctive variety of cooperating men.

The reason for this is that an individual has hitherto only been understood by the logician insofar as he resembled the other.[1] The concept belonging to a class in Logic is such that it is repeated in a way homogeneous to itself; any qualitative difference between these inferiors of a particular concept are not taken into consideration. Whatever may be the status of the traditional universal, real or nominalistic, its very foundation consists in its aptitude of being in many, a condition which can only be achieved through separation, hence through destruction of the unique. The technique of complementarity, on the contrary, prevents this, since it absorbs the unique into the convergent addition of the many. The content of the universal is no longer homogeneous but heterogeneous. The technique of complementarity, unlike the traditional technique of theoretical reason, *includes* the *exclusive*. In fact, it applies the principle of the assembly line, resulting not in a deplorable standardization, but rather in a higher form of productivity, made possible only through the collaboration of the many. The timing, of course, lags behind that of the individual reaching his conclusions through syllogistic deduction, but the time lost while group or team (or *totum genus*) slowly comes together and adjusts its many-angled thought is amply compensated for in the result, which is, indeed, a victory over time. It seems, thus, that in the future, complementary "logic" will overtake its predecessor, and without excluding the abstraction and deduction of the solitary thinker, will absorb him and his activities into accomplishments of unimaginable magnitude.

A further analysis of this convergent procedure must once more make a distinction between the different "universals" of a generic semantics. That which is predominantly scientific is, to the extent of its measurable element, also subject to a closer calculation of the individual participation within it. That which is less so cannot be

---

[1] See Henri Bergson, *Time and Free Will*, trans. R. L. Pogson (London: G. Allen & Co., 1950), pp. 129, 136.

measured and divided with the same precision. For its technique is mysterious, as is always the case where the unique interferes. The work of art lies at the end of an unseen process, as does the judgment of the *totum*.

This judgment which we have called "specific" is fundamentally an evaluation. Without aiming at that which is immediately pragmatic, it is nonetheless connected with the basic notion of survival, since even the most detached speculation is transformed into an additive growth upon the evolving species and ultimately contains some element through which life corrects and protects itself. Life understood as more than bare survival is considered here to be survival in progress as well, i.e., survival where a want can become a need, and where subjective need (my need) can become objective need, i.e., a right. Not every individual want can make that claim, but some, through the combined efforts of the specific judgment, reach that level. It is also in this direction, I believe, that the notion of natural law, as the global expression of the will of survival of the species, has to be looked for. Since this is not the topic of the present study, it suffices to say that this notion, no less than any other collective concept that is carried by the multitude, might be a growing entity and in its very depth an evolving succession of rights and duties. The judicative power of the species is immense, to the point where it might be called the criterion and molder of civilization itself. This being so, it can never be entirely divorced from practical concerns.

Political Applications

THE question now arises whether complementary "logic," especially in its judicative function, can be artificially provoked or at least accelerated. In seeking an answer, we might turn to an ethical problem.

Traditional abstraction and the easy manipulation of its components have found an echo in the political elections of modern democracies, which are, as everyone admits, not based upon your or my personal advice, knowledge, or opinion, but merely upon you or me being one of the many constituting a number. In the future, our elections will be considered to have been the most crude and elementary approach to free thinking and free individual expression. In truth, "we are still not better than our fathers," in whose days not the voter's opinion but, as Socrates put it ironically, his "bean" was asked. The future will want the opinion or viewpoint of the voter, and this unique viewpoint will in a complementary way be added to the opinion of the other. A law will not be promulgated through an elected candidate but will result directly from the sum of the very individual expression of a multiplicity of individualuals, each expressing his preference in a personal way, the way, namely, of individual knowledge and opinion. The law, or *vox populi*, will express the nuanced additive thought of human beings who are free, yet not entirely equal. Egalitarianism, as the undemonstrated postulate of our primitive elective methods, is also the metaphysical assumption of two thousand years of logic, and salvation can come only through an approach which allows the unique to become relevant. The unique and the individual will become relevant only when a universal is formed, not through the addition of the mere numerical presence of the individuals, but through a synthesis of their singularity.

How can this dream be fulfilled? Existentialist philosophy has emphasized, more than any other brand of philosophy, the value of the existential unique and the failure of deductive abstraction to capture the existing free individual. Although, with that purpose in mind, it has made large use of Husserl's descriptive method, it still has not been able to render that which is most individual. Its attempt to solve the problem by means of plays and novels has suffered from the same limitation, an imperfect and defective rendering of the concrete datum. Description will always have its limitations, for no one individual can express with utmost precision what he is or what he knows. In the supposition that he is capable of doing so, the outsider approaches this objective report in a subjective way. He is, and he incarnates, an angular truth.

It is an intricate problem, therefore, to construct a universal which gathers within itself the opinion of the many, yet respects all, and to make this universal communicable in one way or another. The solution which follows is at best speculative.

In a most interesting but too rarely read passage in *de Angelis* (in the *Summa*), Aquinas speculates that communication among the angels results merely from a motion of the will, with no material impediment ever distorting or limiting the purity and integrity of their dialogue. Since angels are not individualized in matter, each is a species unto himself. Man, however, being imbedded in matter, must depend upon some material means to be the conveyer of his most personal thought. Furthermore, it must be remembered that the Self is a mystery to itself and can only be known through its relational character. It is precisely through what is not the Self that the Self can be known, or in other words, it is by means of what might be called a negative replica of itself that the Self can be reached. It is not impossible to envision a complex machine used as a tool to collect man's inner thought, to add up these thoughts with a due regard for their individual nuances, and to reveal its sum when desirable as the collective concept containing the unique expression (and wish) of the many. The future should explore the means of manufacturing some form of electronic computer with the hope not only of a simplified calculation and statistical investigation, but also of revealing, insofar as possible, those personal nuances which have always been neglected in any condensation of the general will of the many. General will would then become what it ought to be, noetically (in the order of knowledge) and appetitively (in the order of wishes and desire): the unique expression of the many, each one within the many being not merely a numerical unit but, above all, a relevant individual.

If the term *general will* emphasizes the political applicability of the theory set forth, it is only because this example comes immediately to mind. It does not exclude other applications, for general will has to be understood as any judgment (appreciative judgment) reflecting the many minds which in their originality have helped to compose it. It is a form of the complementary-additive we-language. Yet, the applicability of our theory to politics is interesting, I believe. It is obvious that the usual collecting of votes is an infringement of the rights of the individual as such, since it accepts him only as a numerical unit. A law will express and successfully condense the nuanced opinion of the original promoters only when, in its moulding, direct expression and personal participation are made possible. The result will also contain those tensions which, in outbalancing one another, create the most perfect achievement. The judgment of the *totum* (or of the group) will be obtained in an accelerated way, its result will be communicable; but most important of all, for the first time, the individual as individual will be recognized. The individual of the future will be relevant rather than equal, for equality was at bottom a negation of singularity. Only unequal dimensions within the general will can reflect the presence of the unique.

We are coming close here to what we may call an encounter of the existential unique and the machine. This is a very complex problem, which cannot be discussed now. Let us notice, however, that any "communicable" knowledge of the self requires the self to be broken down into parts. But if the *I* is thus broken down into universal parts and is what we may call universalized, this *I* becomes entirely "predicable" and is then also entirely "predictable." But where, then, are the uniqueness and the freedom of the individual? If those characteristics which we have called the unique and the ineffable in man are to be protected, the role of the electrocephalic machine cannot be accepted as exhaustive. For if the time should come when angular and generic truth overlapped at every point—that is, if the fragment and the *totum* had exactly the same vision and were identical in the realm of knowledge—this would mean the end of the individual as individual knower, and hence also the end of the individual as irreplaceable fragment. If knowledge could be totally reduced to mathematics, the angular would be generic; but, by the same token, it would no longer be individual. Therefore no machine should ever be able to compel us to accept that tragic conclusion.

8

God and the
Human Totality

Is Human *Truth the Limit?*

IT has been said earlier that "terms implying a complexity far above individual insight have always belonged to the Species, although often drawn within the individual orbit, e.g., Absolute Truth or God."[1] We have now reached a point where it is possible to comment more fully upon that statement.

It would be well, first, to restate our position. Angular truth, or truth of the individual as individual, is a conformity of the unique and "subjective" with the real. Individual insight, however, recognizes the limitations of all incarnation. Since it cannot with certainty judge about itself, it is dependent upon the unfolding of the *totum genus*, with its global truth-assertion. This leads us into a new dimension, which has been called generic truth. The latter, however extensive, cannot claim to be exhaustive; and in not being exhaustive, it cannot, however immense, be placed on the level of the absolute. Actually generic truth can only be: (1) that truth belonging wholly to the *genus humanum*, as the assertion that $2+2=4$ or the first principles (e.g., the principle of contradiction),[2] and (2) that truth resulting from the complementary addition of individual or angular views. In the second case, the global addition of the multiple "unique," in making room for ideological variety, eliminates the need to combat it.

We must now either admit that we are brought to a standstill and

---

[1] See chapter 6, *Rule VI*, p. 110.
[2] We do not say to the *genus* humanum only.

[126]

that *generic* truth is the limit and ceiling of our exploration, or using our method of descriptive analysis, attempt to arrive at the existence of an Absolute Truth. By the latter we do not merely mean that some assertions are absolutely true (without this presumption this essay could not even start), but we signify that some Being exists which embodies Omniscience and Absolute Truth in its total fulfillment. This Being would be God or Truth itself. Once we have reached this uncreated light, the natural implication will be that the amount of Truth contained in the angular and the generic visions will be dependent upon their participation in its Absolute fulfillment, without claiming for that reason that a definite criterion is available to discern within the angular and the generic visions what is absolutely true and what is not. It is useless to state that if God existed, He would not have to make use of the paradox, which is merely a concession to the frailty of man. On the other hand, it would be comforting to know that just as the Species takes over where the Individual breaks down, so also God continues where the Species fails.

Diverse Modes of the Deity

OUR approach will continue to be, above all, phenomenological and descriptive. The point of view will be both angular and generic: angular in the first part of our study, when the datum is available to the individual, and generic in the second part, when the *totum* itself constitutes the viewpoint.

Our first observation notes that the immense majority of mankind accepts a god but that this admits of exceptions. The existence of atheism is a fact, and constitutes, admittedly, a weakening of the universal consensus. We shall take up the phenomenon of atheism at the end of our inquiry, but we can mention in passing that in most cases the atheist falls into either of two categories: that including those who are indifferent, or that of those who, by no means indifferent, are nevertheless unable to admit a Supreme Being. As for the first category, a certain number of men simply do not feel the need for any inquiry at all. They put religion altogether out of their minds, and it does not even occur to them to inquire why or in what they believe. Newman would say they have a "dormant intellect" in that field. Others have a tendency to deify some other elements, such as money, Reason, Science, etc. Out of these elements some form of Absolute is constructed, not bearing the name of God, yet fulfilling His function. The second category, embracing those who are unable to accept God's existence, includes the atheist who rejects God absolutely and loses all concern for further inquiry. We shall attempt to show that the main reason for this lies in the atheist's insistence upon getting that which no one can give him—generic vision—instead of resting content with the angular, and in the realm of generic truth, upon his seeking a clarity similar to that obtained in a mathematical assertion instead of accepting truth which is built up through complementary addition.

We notice, furthermore, that the religious expressions of men have much in common. Living on the same planet, under the same sky, witnessing the splendor of dawn and the mystery of sunset, the light of day and the poetry of night, noting the growth and death of vegetation and of other living things, men have come to a certain resemblance in formulating their religious feelings. Certain elements recur, such as an idea of the beyond, of god or gods, of redemption and salvation, of communion, similarities which do not necessarily imply an interdependency. Since the mimicry of men, furthermore, is limited, they cannot indefinitely vary their liturgical rites. Yet, here already the diversity is as impressive as the similarity. There is no form of worship which man has not cultivated. Everything at some time or other has been divinized or declared sacred, from the growth of a tree to the thunder of a storm, from sexual intercourse to cannibalism, from the most naive myth to the most abstruse speculation. Diversity is no less apparent in the motivation or intention of religious rites: worshipping or atonement, thanksgiving or penance, pure love or selfish calculation. Side by side are the vagueness of religious dreaming, the immanent infinite of a Spinozistic pantheism, the transcendent God of Christian theism—three worlds quite different and yet all implying a religious position.

When there is variety, there is fragmentation as well. "Perfection is unique," writes Lactantius with great wisdom. Those who worshipped the sun or declared a tree to be taboo had no grasp for the abstruse speculation of an Aristotle or the Pure Act of an Aquinas. On the other hand, those who explored the realm of the invisible to "locate" their concept of the deity found matter unworthy, thus introducing the term *immaterial*. This implied that if the god were not what we are, he could only be different, that is, completely detached from the vicissitudes of matter. God thus became "immaterial" and out of reach. When this distant god filled the hearts of men with fear, however, a reaction came and brought the gods back among us. Incarnations multiplied and introduced the familiarity of god with men. And so each religion, at first powerful and impressive, by the very law of its fragmentariness soon appeared to be unconvincing and elusive.

Nor does it appear certain that the conceptualization of God is an exclusive possession of the civilized mind. A monotheist may easily be led to believe that a primitive is a polytheist or a believer in a plurality of gods. Yet, closer scrutiny often shows that the so-called polytheist merely favors a belief in a higher power that is spread out over a diversified matter, as if the divine attributes needed incarnation in a multitude of personages for the sake of easier comprehension. This corresponds to a deeper need of human nature, which rebels against the understanding of the many in the one, but, living in a world of matter and material diversification, visualizes the many in the many. The philosopher himself, who attempts the demonstration of God's existence, does not fundamentally alter the divine concept. He is merely an individual man who corroborates a stand taken long ago, which his approach now aims to give a legitimate status. Demonstration is a conscious motivation, not a creation: it does not create an acceptance but merely confirms a choice.

Total Concept of God as Composite and the Example of a Film in Reverse

ONE thing appears certain: outside revelation, the notion of God, whether conceived by the primitive or by the civilized man, remains contaminated by the tragic impotence of all human achievement. For this, the believer should not be made responsible. Notwithstanding his fragmentary grasp of the deity, he asserts his belief as an absolute. Not only is this a psychological necessity—without absolutization no worshipping would take place—but ul-

timately, this attitude can be legitimate, for in his subjective vision
some truth is contained. "Subjective" and "personal" do not mean
distortion or error; both point merely to fragmentary discovery and
angular truth. In this sense, true religion is as old as the world and
has pre-existed any revelation. "The reality which one today calls
the Christian religion was present among the ancients; it has never
ceased to exist since the origin of mankind, until Christ came in the
flesh, the period when the true religion already existing began to
call itself Christian." Augustine found this expression to be ambiguous and judged it necessary to correct his statement by asserting
that he did not want to imply that there was any way of salvation
except through Christ. This correction was superfluous, however,
since well understood, the one statement did not exclude the other.[3]

The variety of human conceptualizations of the divine object and
the subsequent fragmentary character of any one conceptualization
are due to the limitations of the human recipient and the absolute
perfection of the deity itself. The fragmentary character of the
human recipient and his angular vision have already been sufficiently described. The absolute perfection of the object is postulated
here as a definition of the deity, necessarily transcending all angular
conceptualization. Only through an inner cumulative addition of the
many angular visions can this concept of God approximately reflect
his immense Simplicity. This collective concept, which at this stage
of our analysis is only a phenomenological entity without a firm
ontological counterpart, is an open concept, since the concrete elements which comprise it are continually being added. This is not a
mere addition, with the emphasis upon quantity, although the fact
that millions have worshipped is indeed an impressive argument
confronting the sceptic. We look qualitatively at a collective concept of God, however, one made up out of elements which are
unequal and semantically heterogeneous, yet which mutually complete and correct one another. In this sense, the religion of the
totum genus might be called an exemplarism in reverse, by which
the multitude of mortals, whether aware of it or not, attempt a return to the Power that brought them into existence, as if an explo-
sion were filmed in reverse and the different fragments, scattered in

---

[3] The reason for Augustine's
hesitation: "It was of great importance not to shock the ears of the
religious." (*Retract.* I. IV, N 3.)

every direction, were drawn back to that unseen middle point from which they originally started. In their collective conception, indeed, the mortal fragments attempt to fit the broken pieces together into an Image of the Absolute.

It may be well to insist that our collective concept does not preclude any individual approach to the divine. If it is the individual's concern to speak for himself and to worship the way he wants, it is no denial of his individual rights to remind him that in the very act of worship, he is *part of*. . . . Whether kneeling in front of the altar or alone in the Sahara desert paying his respects to Allah, he is part of a form of universal liturgy, the orthodoxy of which it is not our function to defend. The liturgical act in a stricter sense, however, can more easily be understood in the light of these remarks: man has always felt that adoration was a communal undertaking. "Where there are two or three gathered together in my name, there am I in the midst of them" (Matt. 18: 20) has profound philosophical implications, for it betrays the fact that man is fragment, that his vision of the divine is angular and that only with others is he able to overcome the limitations of his singular vision.

We have made no effort to clarify the inner content of the collective concept of God. For beyond a vague notion of God, of a noumenal entity that is perennial and powerful, his essence remains ineffable for the philosopher, though it is not necessarily so for the theologian. The internal mobility of this concept, which we have just observed, goes together with its pervasive obscurity. It is precisely this elusive character which provokes the human fragment to his angular attempts to comprehend it. We may add that, even if the internal clarification of our concept were possible, it would not further our present purpose, since what matters here is merely the fact that mortal segments do construe such a collective concept. It may be well to point out also that this concept should not be confused with common belief. Common belief is based upon empirical insight, which in some cases may later appear to be erroneous. If and when the mistake appears, no attempt is made to return to the previous false representation. An example is the pre-Copernican notion of our planetary system, which, no longer credited, will never regain its common acceptance. On the other hand, no argument has ever convinced man that the inquiry into God is vain, or that, since no solution has ever been entirely satisfactory, one should give up the quest once and forever. The explanation for this is that the collective concept of God, although at times material in its representation, is in its object trans-empirical. Progress in the realm of the empirical does not *per se* illuminate the mystery of the trans-empirical.

God as Eternal Presence to the Totum

WE have now to ask whether the collective concept containing the multiple unequal, the fragmentary, the unachieved but growing reaches an existing God or whether it merely attempts to express his ideal essence. In other words, is this God of the many—the result of our horizontal and vertical completion—ultimately the God of none? Does phenomenology reach an ontological counterpart or is it merely empirical, and metaphysically impotent?

The answer lies in a re-examination of generic truth. To give that answer, we must first tighten certain definitions used previously and then carefully examine whether their deeper meaning does actually lead us to the assertion that an Absolute Truth *exists*.

Generic truth has been considered in this study to be that knowledge which is gathered by the *totum genus* and the conformity of that knowledge to the real. Of its double approach—that based upon mathematical evidence and that resulting from the condensation of the multiple subjective—it is above all the second that we have been examining. This approach is more extensive than that of any abstract knowledge, which claims to discover by separation that upon which all of us agree or imagine ourselves to agree. Since abstractive activity in itself implicitly denies that which it implicitly asserts—namely, the existence of angular truth—the result is, as experience shows, that we rarely agree upon its abstract result. Angular truth, which results from the viewing of the unique by the unique, differs from person to person and pervades all abstractive knowledge and all deductive performances. Contaminating any noetic achievement, it stops only for those first principles which the *totum* as *totum genus* in its very foundation has in common because they *are* in common. Beyond and above that communal and fundamental perspective, the *totum genus* reaches a new dimension only through the addition of the unique and angular.

To grasp this process to its full extent, we must take into consideration the carrier, which is the *totum genus*. This notion has been presented as the sum of individuals, whether dead or living, resulting in a physical *totum* or heap-universal. In the evaluation of the relation between *we* and *time* made earlier, the notion of *totum genus* was extended and, by implication, future individuals, those who are not yet, were considered to be part of a complete definition. *Totum genus* then became a conception where part had already been fulfilled and part was merely potential. In short, the *totum genus* partly exists, partly does not exist as yet. We have also presented earlier the supposition of a *totum* which does not grow, for the *totum genus* can, strictly speaking, be considered as *totum* if and only if the notion of this internal duration in time and space is overlooked. That this omission of both space and time is non-sensical in a universe where duration and quantity are essential, no one would deny. But it is no less important to point out that if duration is an internal dimension of the *totum*, an external consideration for mere speculative reasons is not necessarily meaningless. It cannot be demonstrated that although the *totum* evolves in time by way of successive internal fragmentation and spreads open in space by way of gradual implementation and occupation of an extended universe, the consideration of the *totum* as *totum*, free from the dimensions of time and space, is contradictory.[4]

Who is able to grasp the *totum* in such a non-progressing dimension? The outsider, and the outsider only? Does a week progress? Does a month progress? Does the history of mankind progress? It seems that an affirmative answer is imperative. Yet upon closer scrutiny, it appears that they only progress when considered as incomplete and growing towards what they are supposed to be. No attempt is made to deny change, yet a week is only a

---

[4] It may not be useless to remind the reader, who is surprised by our stand, of Kant's position in the *Dissertation* (1770), where space is declared to be subjective and ideal, nothing but a coordinating scheme of external sensations and derived from the structure of our mind (*Dis.* sect. 15). Similarly in the *Critique of Pure Reason*, trans. N. K. Smith (London: Macmillan & Co., 1958) p. 86, Kant considers it indubitably certain that space and time are subjective conditions of all our intuitions. I should add, though, that Kant's approach is different from that which I attempt to develop in these and the following pages.

week when the seven days are "there." A week is not constituted by three or four days nor by its growth, but by the achieved totality of seven days. Nor does a month as month progress, but it simply is or is not. Similarly, mankind as *totum* (physicum) does not progress, although it does so in its internal fragmentation and successive actualization. Terms like "progress" and "duration" fall into the category of individual semantics. They are "overcome," however, through the synthetic grasp of the outsider. In the case of week and month, the outsider is the individual man who, in looking back upon the time elapsed, has no problem in viewing a week as week and a month as month in their respective totalities.

The *totum genus* is a similar totality, although a more complex one, since both space and time are present. Yet, as preceding chapters have shown, both those elements have something in common. The insufficiency of the particular is the raison d'être of complementarity, for it is upon the individual insufficient character, in whatever way present, that the "complement" or remedy is added. In its *present* aspect—and by this I mean present to us, its witnesses[5]—that *totum* is succession and juxtaposition. As such it is subject to duration and is carried over from fragment to fragment in an incessant vertical continuum. It is also spread open over a surface which it incessantly conquers. But is it not obvious that such statements are made only by witnesses who themselves are part of this continual succession and conquest, and who contain in their very being this flux of temporality? Is the meaning of witness not one of presence, hence of involvement in a structure made up of past and future as well? If—and this is for the moment sheer hypothesis—a Being exists outside time and space, it can *not* be called "witness," for it is actually present to nothing—no present exists for that being—nor does it witness any succession, since it is not involved in duration. If that Being exists, it does not wait until the sugar melts, to use Bergson's example, since this very waiting is a witnessing in succession, and to the one who is *before*, *during* and *after*, the sugar does not melt in succession. He is simultaneous to all these stages. Since the being in question exists outside

---

[5] To be in the present (opposed to past and future), means to witness. See on that topic Sartre,   *L'Etre et le Néant* (Paris, 1943) p. 164.

space and time, he does not face succession, but exists all at once, hence contradiction is only apparent. God, if I may use this name, although his existence is still hypothetical, faces the *totum genus humanum* as *totum* without viewing internal fragmentation in succession. The possibility of such an Outsider—whoever he may be— is here postulated, since the a priori denial of his existence or of the existence of any suprahuman entity beyond and above material involvement, is not more justifiable than the assertion. If such an Outsider exists, he obviously views the *genus humanum in toto*. For him the history of man *is*, and so *is* mankind in its physically accomplished *totum*.[6]

The Totum *as Viewer of the Deity*

PURSUING our dialectic, we may say that the divine viewing of the *totum* corresponds to the consideration of the *totum genus humanum* which we have described above, that is, as an entity which although unfolding internally in time and space, yet is susceptible of being considered as a *totum* outside this involvement. The possiblity of a god viewing his creation compels us to consider this creation in its totality. Although this way of existing is not within our individual noetic reach, since we are caught within its internal unfolding, it nonetheless belongs to that same *totum* which exists in time.

---

[6] Of course, Sartre would not agree with the argument as I have developed it. There is, however, one term used in his book *Critique de la Raison Dialectique* (Paris, 1960) that is interesting in our case. It is the term *totalization*. By this term Sartre means *to comprehend, to take as a whole*. On pp. 668 and 702, Sartre denies the possibility of a *totalization* of the human genus on the basis of his atheistic postulatory position: there is no external entity which can from the outside comprehend the whole of mankind. With this attitude, I can, of course, not agree, as the whole of my argument clearly shows. I have discussed Sartre's book in my book *The Marxism of Jean-Paul Sartre* (Garden City, N.Y.: Doubleday, 1965).

Let me also remind the reader that the "totalization" here presented is not to be confused with the one discussed by Kant in the first Antinomy, for there the problem under discussion is concerned with the magnitude of the world, not with the totality of mankind as such. (See *Critique of Pure Reason*, p. 396.)

This very same entity, outside all space and time impedimenta, not only is known by its creator, but knows him as well. If there is a God, any being outside time and space cannot possibly fail to recognize His existence, for it cannot possibly remain ignorant once it is outside the dimensions of matter, where knowledge, no longer being distributed among a multitude of corporeal things, is no longer bound to be fragmentary, angular and non-compulsory. Yet the very awareness of the deity by a *totum genus humanum* outside time and space corresponds to the accumulated knowledge concerning God by those who are, were and will be. If God is a vision of the *totum*, only a concept of the *totum*, or what we have called a collective concept, can express this vision. This one collective concept, expressing vision and knowledge of the deity by a *totum* aware of God, *is* the multiplicity of fragmentary concepts concerning God, multiplicity this time visualized outside time and space, hence by this very fact as *totum* and as one.

The collective concept is not to be interpreted as a Platonic form, however, but as the knowledge of the multiple condensed from an unequal and variegated knowledge. The present, past, and future knowledge of the many reverberate this collective concept concerning God in fragment and "in faith." The one and same concept ignores succession and fragmentation, when viewed in its external shell by the Deity; but once engulfed in time and space, it shares a variegated and individualized actualization, and in this very act of multiplication echoes the other aspect of its existence, namely, that of the atemporal viewing the eternal.

Its internal unfolding, however, in time and space, or what might be called its de facto existence, is the proof that it exists as "otherworldly," and our hypothesis of a collective concept on the confines of the nontemporal is the only plausible explanation for an event which in the history of mankind has been as stubborn and recurrent, fragmentary, yet continually self-correcting, as the phenomenon of religion in its diverse manifestations indeed is. From its external extratemporal and total intuition results an internal, successive fragmentation among the multiplicity of existent individuals. Their understanding of the divine is individual, non-intuitive, quasi-fideistic and quasi-compulsory. However much the believer attempts to rationalize his faith, he never succeeds completely. Beyond and above all rationalization, he bears deep within himself the awareness that his acceptance of God is part of a communal movement, out of which he cannot pull himself. If he succeeds in doing so, it is only at the cost of great pain. He is caught in the web of a theistic belief and is strangely unable and even unwilling to break the web. It is this strange phenomenon which is the best proof and confirmation of our hypothesis. For it is precisely because an awareness of an existing God takes place upon some unknown level that we can feel here upon earth the magnetic pull of belief, worship and cult.

God as Eternal Absence to the Individual, or Faith as Free Choice

IT now also appears why the collective concept concerning God can and must be accepted "in faith" when unfolding in time. Only as *totum* can mankind under its present status intuit the deity. Since its communication (outside revelation) is distributed in time and space, it is necessarily fragmentary. In this fragmentary distribution no conclusive evidence is provided, but acceptance reaches beyond intuition. It is an act of faith of the individual existent, who by his very nature is made for angular truth only, but who in accepting God's existence asserts that which only generic vision and generic truth can acquire on their own terms. All individual attempts reflect a partial truth-dimension but are ultimately unaware of their final conformity. Involvement in matter constitutes an impenetrable wall for the average individual, and never can internal unfolding and segmentation reach on its own power those insights which in a different dimension are available to the human ensemble. Time is an organ of vision, indeed, and *I* cannot do without it. Only *we* in a different dimension face the Eternal. The *we-Thou*, therefore, expresses a more authentic attitude of a mankind attempting to formulate its God than the *I-Thou* proposed by certain modern-day thinkers. It is the *clamor* of voices as a whole which is impressive, in the complete meaning of the word. This clamor can only be considered to be "impartial" because of its continual self-correction, and perennial because of its never-ending unfolding in time and global vision outside time.

While an angular approach is "partial" and fragmentary, the qualification attached to the collective concept is that of generic truth—truth resulting from the additive complementarity of the *totum genus* but limited to that genus. A different genus (non-human I mean) could conceivably have a different conformity to the real, resulting from a different discovery of the real. A classic formula states that no matter what is received, is received in the shape of the receiver, and although the interpretations have been various through centuries of philosophical speculation, we can agree upon its general tenor and accept the possibility of a different species of beings which would differently formulate a concept of the universe and of its Maker. This does not suggest that *generic* truth is false, but only that it is incomplete, and a different vision, entirely unknown to the human totality, remains possible.

At present we are better equipped to understand the fundamental technique of survival, a topic which has been recurrently approached in these pages. Viewing the global knowledge of mankind in its totality as extratemporal and extraspatial, we perceive that the *totum humanum*, although behaving in time, ignores time, but it orders the multiple fragments and their accomplishments in such a way that the *totum* survives. Survival, thus, may appear to be a form of finality, and it indeed is. Yet, finality is an expression proper to the individual, who, in using an individual semantics, imposes the label upon that which serves his individual grasp. In fact things are merely what they are, but in being what they are, they constitute a surviving *totum*. Of this immense game, we, individual fragments, can discover neither the beginning nor the end, although within the act of duration and becoming, we can discover what we call finality, which is, at bottom, nothing but survival in a space and time continuum, executed by the human noesis performing in time what it knows in the supratemporal. Survival, history (as *res gestae*), and finality, as space-and-time achievements of the *genus humanum*, make sense for individuals speaking the language of individual semantics. For the outsider, who has the grasp of the *totum*, the earthly adventure is nothing but a complex event which, although existing in time and space, is known by him outside these impediments.

God's Absence as Necessity

FROM the foregoing argument some conclusions may be drawn. It appears, first of all, that if phenomenology has offered us an ontological object instead of a mere description of the apparent, it is due to the fact that we did not lean upon individual perception, but entrusted the vision of the *totum* as *totum* and were able, through an analysis of the latter, to envision a phenomenon which is beyond space and time. The revenge of the collective upon the individual is that it could reach the ontological, where heretofore "individual" phenomenology has ever failed. Our study claims to have reached an intuition from the "we," not from the "I." It cannot be denied, however, that at this point we face an insoluable paradox: the Species, lacking the power of reflection, is unaware of its divine possession, while the individual, although capable of reflection, cannot completely embrace a conclusion drawn by the *totum*. That which is unconsciously owned by the "we" cannot exhaustively be owned by the "I." God remains, therefore, tragically ineffable for the angular approach. He does not walk with us one by one, but remains the *deus absconditus*—the hidden god. For the individual is left the empirical observation of the phenomenon of worship. It is his privilege to observe the gigantic effort of the *totum genus* to conceptualize God and to become part of that to which he is witness. Although the individual man can measure neither the beginning nor the end, he can observe the continuous interrogation of mankind all through the ages and the myriad proposed answers, the strange mystery of conflicting ideals, the long effort continually improved and desperately amended. Faith in God is above all a result of faith in man. The individual is not the *totum*, hence he should be satisfied and consider himself fortunate if in his very trust in mankind, he has tapped the wall behind which the Absolute has chosen to hide itself.

In our second conclusion lies an attempt to clarity the notion of atheism. Atheism is, I believe, not so much a denial of God as a negation of the species. As Jaspers puts it, "Nietzsche has not loved anyone in an unconditional way, which is why for him God is dead. . . ."[7] A form of individualism in the extreme, atheism may in some cases be a resentment against men. From a rational viewpoint, the atheist requires an insight into the metempirical which equals that of the *totum*, i.e., he wants an intuition of the generic within the limits of the angular, forgetting that the *totum genus*, if it finds

---

[7] Karl Jaspers, *Nietzsche* (Berlin: W. de Gruyter, 1950), p. 388; (Tuscon: University of Arizona Press, 1965).

its balance as *totum genus* in God, *leaves its unrest and suspense to the individual fragment.* The salvation of the latter, therefore, lies in an acceptance of belonging. Since there can be no revolt against God by the *totum*, such terms as "the rebellious man" must be classified under individual semantics. Only where vision is angular and the wrath thereof grows, does protest arise against the *totum* and its "vision" of the Absolute. Yet whatever may be said in favor of a theistic attitude, atheism remains an individual's free choice, and no compulsion whatsoever can make an intellect reach a conclusion which by essence is specific.[8] The possibility of the rejection of God is tied up with the notion of angular truth, which is built-in in the dimension of the individual man. For these angular visions, God is *absent.* (Our expression is, of course, a concession to individual semantics, since one is absent only for the individual who is *here* and *there.*) It is this absence which prompts atheism.

What the atheist seems to forget is that God's absence is an absolute necessity, for if He were *there*, He would no longer be God. In the actual shape of man, God can only constitute in the flesh an impoverished image of His infinite splendor, and in a world of matter, where things are juxtaposed and come in a slow succession of unequal values, He can offer only the image of a "fragment," in which the divine presence could be guessed, but never witnessed in its entirety or with certainty. *Present* and *absent* are derogatory terms. God is not present as God, though he may be as man. But once he is as man, he is no longer compelling as a god. Thus Jesus with his perfection, and in the words of Catherine of Siena his *netteza* ("lucidity"), has his doubters. As long as a theophany presents itself in material form, the "god" thus appearing must share in the frailties of matter. Even though he may transcend it at times, he cannot do so perpetually, for in that supposition, he would no longer "belong" to our kind. It is no exaggerated claim to assert that God has no means to make Himself heard the way mathematics can make itself heard.

God's absence, furthermore, is not only a necessity, but reveals

---

[8] Owing to a greater sense of belonging, there are fewer atheists among women than there are among men. *She* belongs more than *he* does, has a more profound attachment to the soil, symbol of the race, and is, through motherhood, committed more than the male to the species.

wisdom as well, for only on the condition that the divine satura-
tion not be *there*, does the human genus within its internal fragmentation keep up its "struggle for survival." The co-presence of
God and man would mean the end of the latter as generative
power, since the ultimate urge of completion through successive
generation would be lacking. Procreation is bound up with imperfection, or as Aristotle aptly puts it: "Since no living being is
able to partake in what is eternal and divine by uninterrupted continuance, it tries to achieve that end in the only way possible to
it, . . . so it remains not indeed as the selfsame individual but
continues its existence in something like itself—not numerically
but specifically one."[9] The survival of the human *totum*, therefore, requires the God who is absent. In this God, mankind places
the realization of its noblest dreams; the form, however, in which
it posits Him is bound up with historicity. Here, as elsewhere,
men disagree in the angular and agree in the generic, but as usual
we ignore our agreement and are even incapable of formulating
it, for this would be the complete grasp of the generic.

In our third conclusion, we are able to bring to a final meeting
point, through the notion of Absolute Truth, two lines of thought
which run all through our study: the idea of paradox and the
notion of truth. The use of the paradox as a mode of knowing
implies the existence of angular truth and makes sense only for
human beings, i.e., for those whose vista is limited by the space-
and-time continuum. Where tension overflows the individual grasp,
still kept however within the boundaries of the *totum genus*, we
reach what we have called generic truth. The *totum genus* because
of its fragmented diversity becomes "the sculptor who sees the in
and the through, the four sides" (Ezra Pound), not the painter
(the individual) who sees one face of things only. The present
chapter has led us a step further and introduced "us" to the
Absolute Truth. The eventual existence of a suprahuman paradox
—a contrast of ideas such that even the *totum* is unable to resolve
the noetic conflict (theologians would call it a mystery)—would
find its solution in the Omniscience or Absolute Truth of God,
for whom, of course, any paradox is meaningless.

If both paradox and truth are intertwined in the way described,

---

[9] Aristotle, *On the Soul*, 415 | b 5.

the relation between the hierarchical structure of the triple form of truth is no less evident. When truth is angular and individual discovery is alone at work, truth cannot judge about itself, but must wait for the collective concept to build the best of the angular into lasting value. This is tantamount to saying that time is the medium of noetic survival or that generic truth is the criterion of the angular. At this time, we may further add that God *is* what human thought approaches fragmentarily, consequently becomes the criterion of generic truth. Absolute Truth is the standard of all human noesis, and if there is another universe, a nonhuman world with a nonhuman truth (which is still truth in its own way), the latter can also only be tested in the last instance by the Supreme Truth. The existence of this Absolute Truth, however, cancels neither the generic nor the individual approach (of whatever universe), for a deity who creates can do so only through the multiple diversified, never through a duplication of his own Simplicity. If God makes a recipient of knowledge which is not Himself, fragmentary truth must arise under one form or another. Just where fragmentary vision coincides with Absolute Truth, however, often remains elusive for man.

9

The Planetary Man

IT may seem to some that with our speculation on the generic and on the divine we have forsaken the individual. This is actually not the case. If the purpose of this study has been to show where man belongs, it has also by the same token shown the transcendent towards which he should tend. This transcendent implies both the generic and the divine. The individual man is not the *totum genus,* nor is he God, yet he is to an extent capable of emulating both. We have shown that along the way. It remains for us to bring together the main threads of this noetic redemption and to show to what extent it is possible for man to escape his boundaries and to imitate the *totum genus* and God. This imitation of course should not be understood as one of practical behavior—we are here in the realm of speculative knowledge—but rather as a psychological attitude. This attitude is precisely the concern of the planetary man and admits of three phases: one of detachment, one of coordination and one of preference. All three together constitute the itinerary of the individual mind in its attempt to overcome and correct its original "angularity." The planetary man, then, is the embodiment of the conclusion of this volume.

The Stage of Detachment, or the Planetary Man as Homeless

THE first phase begins with a recognition of the fragmentary and the angular as simply that and no more. In confronting the internal diversity of a *totum* (any *totum* for that reason), man should never attribute the value of the Absolute to that which he knows to be merely fragmentary and angular.[1] The naiveté of the angular is to consider itself generic. It belongs to the myth to absolutize that which is only a segment and to consider as eternal and unlimited that which is merely angular and of short duration. Yet a human accomplishment, finite and limited, does not merit the unquestioning devotion of the fanatic. Nations and racial groups, although in themselves constituting totalities—made up of fragments—are in the global structure of the *totum genus* only segmental and must be treated as such, once in the tumult of nations and groups the survival of the *totum genus* is at stake.

If a mortal creature were a god, he would—and this is the second implication of our phase of detachment—divorce himself from partial subjugations; facing the cultural variety of this world, he would not choose to be on one side or another. To choose is not necessarily a sin, but to choose exclusively is a confession of man's fragility and implies absolute adherence to a position of angular discovery. For the gods, there is no angular discovery to the exclusion of any other. If we attempt to express the divine noesis in human terms, we should emphasize its multidimensionality where, at the start at least, no preference is asserted nor any theory a priori doomed. The planetary man, in his growth towards the stage of unification, has first to bring himself upon that level of impartiality. It is a detachment not unknown to the mystic: "In order to arrive where you are not, you must pass through what you are" (John of the Cross). Oedipus, too, had to undergo a painful experience of self-knowledge, through which, his pride and ἀρετη shattered, he was prepared for the divine epiphany.

For at this stage suffering is needed, that suffering of the mind

---

[1] The term *fragmentary* generally has an ontological connotation in our study, and the term *angular* a noetic.

which is provoked by a contact with opposites and by a growing insight into our own fragmentary structure. He who stands on the threshold of planetary understanding might be compared to the convert just before his conversion, or to the immigrant immediately after his arrival in the new land. His mind is empty, he has broken the last link with the past, and yet he has forged no new ties. Having known different, even opposite views, he questions much of what men think. His mind, although in pain, is in a healthy state, and its capacity for divorcing itself from previous convictions and intellectual particularism is a mark of strength rather than of weakness. This suffering is a necessary prelude to a wider outlook, that outlook which embraces the atemporal and the aspatial. For such is, indeed, the presumptuous claim of the planetary man. He *is* nowhere and never. And although he may never reach these ideal dimensions, he nevertheless submits himself to this purgatory of opposite experiments with an intention of achieving detachment and freedom. He is "non-engaged."

The Stage of Coordination, or the Planetary Man as Builder of the Synthesis

THE planetary man is now prepared for the second stage—the stage of coordination. As Plato's demiurge ordinates the chaos, so too does our observer, for he ordinates philosophical views and cultural expressions as so many elements of a scale which outbalance one another. Appearing as extremes of our thought, they compose that thought.

However, before weighing these views together, one has first to study what they are alone. An understanding of the elements is as important as a view of the synthesis. We have already noticed how angular truth belongs to the angular vision, whether philosophical or otherwise: every individual has his view of reality, which becomes philosophical when it tends towards an elemental interpretation of the datum. To understand the philosopher, therefore, we must place ourselves at the angle from which he peered and was able to gain *his* peculiar vision. No detail can be overlooked, "for the insignificant must be narrated in order to bring out the significant" (Augustine). An effort of the mind is required to install oneself inside the organic unity of a theory (or a culture) and from this center to follow and to understand its growth and movement, its internal details and its results. To find out what the philosopher wants to do, what his method is, and his milieu, is no less essential than to study what he has achieved. In fact, the achievement will often be understood only through its setting. For behind every system stands a man.

Yet the study of a system has also shown what it lacks. In many cases, it is not what is said that counts but what is omitted. The planetary man must look beyond that which is commonly accepted by a certain epoch or a certain school or a certain group in order to discover that which is not "said." When the atheist claims that there is no god because only the factual has meaning, one may wonder why only the factual has meaning. When the Thomist claims that the contingent implies the necessary, one may ask whether this statement does not hide the postulate that the contingent is distinct from the necessary. Each theory has unveiled one aspect but covered up another that is no less important. The planetary man must be a relentless hunter of that which is concealed and—this is a typical point of his approach—he will find this hidden fragment in another philosophy or group developed, explored, brought into the open, though at the inevitable expense of a new omission.

It is this insight of the lack which makes one realize that any single philosophy can offer only false security. Yet it is no less correct to say that the mere knowledge of many is a source of despair and scepticism. Only an insight into the many angular visions as components of a wider integrated vision can constitute an approximative approach to the Truth. The planetary man has that insight, for he has a grasp of the diverse, perceives the integrating value of all fragments, and even discovers a place for the absurd and the contradictory. But his insight results from an observation—namely, an observation that the *totum genus humanum* has survived. This is indeed one of the main themes of this book. We know that survival means self-correction through complementarity and that this outbalancing process pervades all domains, the intellectual no less than the more material. To survive as an animal requires merely food. To survive as a human being requires truth. *Hence, in the domain of knowledge we observe a similar process of self-protection through incessant repair.* This process has been sufficiently analyzed in our preceding chapters. The planetary man sets out in search of that noetic equilibrium. His phase of coordination is above all a discovery: he discovers the corrective function of two or more theories, and surveying the activity of the *totum* in that domain, he himself survives in truth. Once more the individual *is* plurality. Carrying within his mind the multiple noesis, he reflects the structure of the *totum* and like the *totum* survives because of the plurality in him.

The result bears some resemblance to Husserl's description of the Transcendental Ego, but with notable differences. Husserl's Transcendental Ego stands at the center, or rather at the summit, of a philosophy; the planetary man, on the contrary, aims at occupying a central point from which different philosophies (or rather fragmentary entities) are seen as complementary. Husserlian Ego is purified and freed from all personal "interiority," resulting in a *Bewusstsein Überhaupt*, or form of general consciousness facing its thoughts, the planetary man has also been freed from himself; not through any philosophical reduction, however, but through a phase of detachment. Placing himself outside and above the multiple and the diverse, he confronts not a world of essences, but a world of angular discoveries and theories (eventually of groups and epochs). He indeed believes that an event or a theory in its organic unity requires the acceptance and the study of its historical setting, but he is no less convinced that in order to co-relate events or theories an abandonment of the historical framework is in many cases required. History is completion indeed, as we have shown in chapter 2, but completion does not always occur in immediate succession.

The phase of coordination is a psychological attitude, let us repeat, but in our case psychology is a means to attain the ontological, for in the very act by which I approach reality through a plurality of (angular) visions, an ontology or philosophy of being is constituted. It is an ontology which is mediated through the visions of others but which reveals nonetheless a new and wider world. The study of being is thus largely a result of my choice. I can limit it and narrow it down, giving to the angular truth the status of generic or even of divine truth; or more realistically, in the conviction that the angular is not the generic, I can multiply my visions with the hope of approximating the generic truth concerning the real. An ontology built upon the choice of the multiple coadunate transcends any one ontology caught up in the angular. Yet it does not sin through relativism. Our insistence that (1) angular vision is the seat of angular truth, (2) that angular truth, although unique, is absolute, and (3) that an Absolute truth exists gives adequate protection against relativism. Neither do I think that our psychological attitude leads to psychologism, for nowhere has it been asserted that truth is the result of brain-structure, or that the principle of contradiction has a biological function.

Yet for all its qualities, it would be erroneous to state that this psychological coordination is a disposition without inner conflict. The residual ground of two or more angular visions contains a more extensive truth than any isolated insight, no doubt, but it remains in the individual thinker an effort of reconciliation and is not productive of peace. Peace is not an earthly term. With great wisdom the liturgy of the Church has brought together "peace" with "eternality" under the beautiful epithet "eternal rest." There can be no peace within the temporal so long as the human fragment faces a variegated noesis, which itself is an unavoidable consequence of a fragmented *totum*. In lifting itself up above the angular to approach the generic through a multivalent vision of the real, the individual mind reflects the quiet state of conflict of the *totum genus*, and survives in truth if not in peace.[2]

There are of course situations where, over the ages, certain conflicts have reached a form of unity. These are acquisitions of the *totum* and represent a deposit of conflicting statements which have become indistinguishable to the individual observer. Hence the point of rest from which the human fragment can dominate the transitory and the diverse is often the *totum genus* itself. Tradition, theological belief, ethical mandates, esthetic appreciations

---

[2] Augustine's famous definition of peace, "peace is the tranquillity of order," is above all applicable to the city of God (see *De Civ. Dei*, XIX, 17) while peace in Dante (*De Monarchia*) is an ideal, not a fulfillment. Similarly in Kant it is an end (not a state of nature), in order that man may be secure from man. (*Zum Ewigen Frieden, Kleinere Schriften zur Geschichtsphilosophie, Ethik und Politik*, p. 125.)

and estimates concerning historical events are in the power of the *totum*, and it is from that extratemporal and aspatial position that the individual can gather at once what it took mankind centuries to acquire. This universal owned by the *totum* is not a Platonic entity, nor is it the result of an Aristotelian abstraction, but—it may be well to remember—it is a deposit of the complementary-additive we-language.

The Stage of Preference, or the Planetary Man as Creator of the Angular

THE man of our times, because of his higher sensibility and because of his awareness of a world where space is quickly shrinking, might approach the ideal of the planetary man more closely than the man of ancient times, although the Roman knew a lot more about political and cultural universality than most of us. (As Paul Valéry put it, in order to extend and to preserve that cosmopolitan approach, he checked the intestines of his chickens and found there more ingenious ideas than we in all our political books put together.) However, Roman or not, the planetary man did not and does not become a god. Emulate a god though he may (and must), there are moments when the distribution of all points escapes him and he finds himself crushed by a collision of worlds. Through sheer force of construction he has constructed himself—his planetary vision was a tutelage of the highest quality —yet he is and remains a "fragment." However sincere his desire to coadunate the paradoxes and to protract within his mind the dialogue between thinkers, there comes a moment when the dialogue stops and the attempted coordination gives way.

This is the third phase, the phase of preference. There and then, the planetary man is a fragment, unique and free but a fragment, nonetheless, which chooses its own view, struggles for its defense in a world of competition and as a *competing* instrument, mysteriously completes the others. Notwithstanding his detachment, he is enveloped in duration, and struggle as he may, cannot turn into an unhistorical man. To meet this challenge, the planetary man will choose; and if he is creative enough, he will prefer himself.

The act of creation, however, results from the desperate synthesis which the phase of coordination has propounded. Copulation of contraries being the law of life, the presence of conflict inside the mind can only favor reflection and perhaps the growth of a new insight: "One still must have chaos in oneself to give birth to a dancing star."[3] One should never consider it urgent, therefore, to bring conflict and contrariety to repose and final unity, for the natural sequel to the phase of coordination is indeed the phase of preference and of creation. Once the personal insight emerges, however, it is not, I insist, a Hegelian synthesis or "reconciliation": not the digested content of opposing theories, but their tension giving birth to an entirely new vision. This vision, then, will derive its originality not from those elements of previous theories which are still present, but from the uniqueness of the individual visionary who gives them a new meaning. And although no man is uncontaminated in his attempt to explain the structure of this world, it is not the influence of the past which matters but the psyche of the prophet himself. Only he who is different from the present "world" will undertake the building of another.

Here, then, we have the planetary man finding his joy in the divine occupation of creation. Consciously or unconsciously, he is seeking to gain vengeance upon the congenital angularity within himself. For once, so he believes, the fragment is beyond itself. He is unique and his creation is the powerful expression of this uniqueness. Yet at this moment, he is caught in a paradox. As a candidate of the first phase, having abandoned the angular, he is homeless; later on, in the second phase, he looks for coordination and for the "additive universal" of the *totum*; at present in the third phase, he chooses and clutches his portion of a disruptable universe and of its noesis, falling back into his original mold of angularity. Even individual creation, stripped from its metaphors, is a positing of the angular vision and cannot, when uncorrected, claim the value of the all-encompassing absolute. It seems then that the individual man turns in a circle from angular back to angular and that his finitude is, philosophically speaking, incurable!

Actually his journey through the three phases is cumulative

---

[3] Friedrich Nietzsche, in Prologue of *Thus Spoke Zarathustra*, trans. R. J. Hollingdale (Baltimore, Md.: Penguin Books, 1961).

no less than successive. He is, simultaneously, inquirer into the generic and, through his necessary choice, prisoner of the angular; he is detached from any particular solution, yet striving towards it; he is dedicated to the planetary and the universal, yet engaged in his own choice and creation. It is not necessary that this paradox be solved, for it contains a definition—the definition of the *planetary man*, who is both a flexible understanding of the many and a selfish drive against the many. In this antithetical attitude lies his grasp of the *totum* and of its value in the realm of knowledge, for to be both egotistical and altruistic in the noetic sense implies in the individual man the insight that any approximation of truth requires himself *plus* the other, and men are fragments and complements, and that only from the multiplicity of the angular can generic truth issue.

Beyond this, nothing more can be said. Subjectively in the very act of his creative obsession a god, objectively he remains a man. So, at any rate, is he doomed to be classified by mankind at large, for at the end of all human achievements patiently waits the impartial judge, the onlooker, who is our *totum genus humanum*. Within his limits the planetary man is an able instrument of global survival. Upon his completive contribution he will be judged. The *totum humanum* survives as long as it contains fragments *and* the fragments correct one another. Beyond that there is nothing, and by this I mean there is death and the end of survival.

VOLUME 2

∵

An Ethical Prelude
to a
United World

Wir Heimatlosen. . . .

We, homeless from the outset,—have absolutely no choice, we must be conquerors and explorers: with the hope that what we are missing, our descendants will perhaps inherit,—that we may leave them a home.

NIETZSCHE

Introduction

IT is becoming increasingly clear, in this second half of the twentieth century, that moral sentiments are radically changing, the sphere of consciousness is enlarging, boundaries are dissolving, and our earlier certainties—even the certainty that certainties are possible—have been swept away. To find some sort of foothold on the shifting terrain and in face of the changing landscape, we need a new definition of man. Probings in that direction were made in an earlier study in which the planetary man was described as the one who, through nonengagement, attempts to be *nowhere* and *never*. In some mode he escapes his own limits, and although he is neither God nor the human totality, he strives to emulate both. This emulation was described in Volume I insofar as it pertained to the realm of human knowledge, or noesis. Whether or not it would be possible for the planetary man ever to succeed in his endeavor we did not say. It may appear to some that such a man does not exist. To others it may seem that he is no less than the collective, To still others it will appear inevitable that, however divine the aspirations of the planetary man may be, he must remain a man so far as fulfillment is concerned. His very aspirations to disengagement and Faustian omniscience place him among those who—far removed from disengagement—choose and prefer, those especially who are *here* and *now, then* and *there*. In other words, to desire of oneself to constitute the human totality is wishful thinking; to desire to transcend it, godlike, is utopian.

Yet the idea of being a planetary man is not devoid of meaning.

Even if it falls short of total fulfillment, it is capable of attainment as an attitude, an orientation. The planetary man has a grasp of the human *totum* and of the diversification of its texture. He will no longer attribute the value of the absolute to that which he knows to be merely fragmentary. He knows that it is the character of myth to absolutize what is only a segment and to consider as eternal and unlimited what is merely angular and of short duration. And in that sense, he is more than a dream: he is a "transcript of reality," of reality to come.

The new man is discovered to be planetary in another sense as well. He is the Wanderer. Such is the meaning of the Greek word: πλανητης. The one who is nowhere and never is a wanderer, *planetes*. But he is a wanderer with a purpose, so we can truly call him a pilgrim. Aiming at becoming the *totum*, yet failing in its achievement, he is and remains the pilgrim enroute towards the ideal fulfillment.

In this volume, I attempt to portray the same man, this time in the realm of human behavior. We explore his ethics, which is, of course, man's actions insofar as they affect another man. The planetary man will become not only Observer but Actor. We asked in our earlier study: What will he *see* as an Observer? In this study, we add another question: What will he *do* as an Actor?

In developing the views here presented, I have attempted to write not what I wanted to be true nor what I was taught as true, but what the present and future tell us is true. In choosing facts over wishes, I may appear to be less subjective in my approach and more authentic as well. Nevertheless, the individual subject, carefully avoided in order to give clearance to things which are, in the way they are, is perforce brought into sight again. This occurs not only because in his attempt at objectivity he betrays then and there his deepest concern but also because in the process of objective reporting, those whom he discovers as objects of his vision nonetheless behave very much as subjects. Writing objectively does not imply forgetting the individual subject. A book on ethics is written by a human person about human persons; we must keep this in mind.

Yet it will appear that this term *human person* needs reexamination. Consequently this study may to some extent break away from a view of the past in which the individual subject was conceived as a center on which everything in the universe turned. During the last three hundred years, ever since the famous night on which René Descartes discovered that individual man, in his very act of thinking, was an indestructible fulcrum, man has increasingly been becoming a center. People and things, and even the supernatural itself, have increasingly been converted into means for him: God Himself has assumed the form of an instrument for man's eternal beatitude.

Such is the structure of Western civilization as a whole. It is a comfortable world. It cannot be shown that capitalism is inherently vicious—such radical claims are hard to prove—but it can be seen that it reflects a similar trait. Its power is self-interest: individual man works for himself relentlessly, and successfully if he is strong enough. Yet, if the morals of men mean what they say, that is, if they truly seek a way of living which allows all men and not just the better-endowed to live, one may wonder at times whether the West, which as a whole has taken care of itself with economic splendor, has done so with moral rectitude. A philosophy of the future must not ignore the unfathomable depth of the individual subject, his power and his relentless initiative, but an ethics aware of the past, yet not ignorant of the present and future, cannot help observing that a world where individual man was shown to be the center is also a world where man appears to be most selfish. For one epoch, this attitude may have seemed to be the answer; whether it is the solution of the future is not certain. This study will not give a direct answer, but it may attempt to formulate the principles whence an answer can be deduced.

Just as we will abstain from political dictates, we shall be reserved concerning the religious and the sacred. But in attempting to observe the behavior of men, what they do and what they ought to do, it will appear more and more (1) that the supernatural has been unduly stressed as a means for personal and eternal happiness, and (2) that as a result it has mistakenly been conceived as belonging only to remote and invisible spheres.

Man constructs his own alienation; that much can be said with certainty. He does it in both the social and the theological orders, for he fails to see that the redemption of man comes from man himself and that the supernatural is not something divorced from the natural and opposed to it but is part of the reality of the here-

and-now. We shall refuse to see an opposition where there is none, and if nevertheless a certain real opposition and separation remain—and obviously they cannot wholly be denied—we shall accept them as the "given" for the human totality, or *totum*, as part of the reality to be taken into account, enabling the *totum* to find itself, and having found itself to exist and to survive. For in the final analysis, ethics is nothing other than the attempt to understand what is, and in so doing to dictate the rules for survival.

This may appear to be simple. It is not. It is not because of a world which is incessantly changing. The claim that ethical content is eternal and that only its semantics are changing is a gross oversimplification. The fact is that semantics is the vehicle of the eternal, and the eternal has a way of being present in provisional semantics which makes it impossible for the philosopher to separate semantics from its content. The eternal is now; it has a way-of-being-now, and try as we may, we cannot be certain of its way-of-being-later. From this, it appears that although we accept a different semantical formulation from one epoch to another, we shall speak of a philosophy of ethics only when, paying due respect to the temporal and the provisional, it reveals the eternal in the temporal; for only in revealing the eternal will the philosopher explain his own epoch.

Hence there is presumption in the role of the philosopher. His undertaking involves nothing less than an inquiry of the *I* into the *we*. However sincere he may be in this endeavor, he knows that he is exceeding his sphere of competence, for he is aware, in the ultimate depths of his being, that he is incomplete, and from these ultimate depths the knowledge of his incompleteness will come to him daily. Nevertheless he must take a stand in the face of this incompleteness, for only when he has taken a stand is he open to the correction which comes from the *totum*. If this statement sounds diffident, it is not because its author is too modest but simply because he is aware of not being alone. The viewpoint of an individual is never born in solitude, nor is it ever self-sufficient, whatever one may believe. Were an intellectual position to be self-enclosed, it would suffer from a mortal impotence; for it can exercise its function only in relation to the views of others, its force depends upon its being heard.

This is, of course, a way of confessing that the planetary man has a philosophy but that this philosophy holds him as much as he holds it. Individual man is not a monad but a mere fragment in his structure and his vision. Such a claim is not a harmless statement, for it turns around, lays hands upon its maker, and makes him prisoner of a metaphilosophy out of which there is no release. What he says about others is true of himself.

I shall add that as we move with the present study into the ethical sphere, the impact of the collective has increased. Thinking may be the privilege of the individual. Acting is not. Action includes mobility, it touches the other and in this very contact is either beneficial or harmful. Action is, more than thinking, a collective affair. We have stated in the preceding volume that the individual has an "experience of being a center" by which, confronting two opposing theories, such as those of Hume and Aquinas, or Pascal and Descartes, he sees their mutually completing function at work. This vision places his individual self at the center of a paradox.[1] *But to be at the center of two conflicting theories does not mean to be at the center of the world.*

The greater stress upon the collective does not per se point to the existence of God, nor does it per se exclude His existence. The notion of God, although often mentioned in this study, is not a requisite for the acceptance of the principles it sets forth. Although an attempt was made in the earlier volume to present God as a discovery of the *totum*—or better still, as that which only a collective intuition could reveal—that conclusion has not been used as a basis for an ethical discourse. Whether God made man or man made God, whether He is present as the underlying yet invisible force or whether He simply is not at all, will have no direct effect upon the ethical vision of the following pages.

Yet for all this show of independence, it will appear that the wealth of the past has not been left untapped. If Judeo-Christianity *was* a development or still in the mind of many *is* a major development within this world, if that form of religion has gone through hard times in current days, its spirit has not died. This spirit, or what is deemed valuable in it, this book must attempt to use; but it will only do so when it shamelessly takes over a terminology that

---

[1] *The Planetary Man*, Volume I, *A Noetic Prelude to a United World*, chapter 4.

includes such concepts as *sin* or *responsibility* or *sanctity*, which up to now have been carefully avoided among most philosophers as being merely devotional, or, worse still, as part of the clerical preserve. Unbeliever so far as the nature of his profession is concerned, the philosopher may be more than a philosopher and say his prayer as a human being, but even that does not prevent him from philosophizing upon what some consider to be the data of revelation. It will appear in most cases that revelation was merely a bringing to the surface of what the human *totum* carried within its depths as untested potential for redemption. To the philosopher, it appears that what Jesus of Nazareth said was truly revolutionary, and that if it has gone unheeded for so long, perhaps this is partly due to the fact that the mundane world (which is, after all, the true world) had not become aware of what he meant to say. His "revelation" went unnoticed because it was appropriated by a few and reserved as the privilege of a celestial city. In fact it was meant to be valid for all, sinners no less than saints, the secular no less than the sacerdotal, the terrestrial no less than the angelic. Now that the structures of the religious hierarchy are in crisis, we the philosophers shall divide the spoils among us, and duty-bound, bring into the profane and the secular what certain groups of the religious had considered to be otherworldly and supernatural. Religious semantics has a natural use. We do not claim that it has no other use. The sacred is visible. We do not claim that only the visible aspect exists. But this is not our present concern.

This book makes no sociological or anthropological claim, yet some of the points proposed may very well corroborate the conclusions of both these fields. Philosophy by its very nature constitutes the underpinning of the more empirical sciences, and if in the past philosophical speculation sometimes conflicted with empirical data, more careful observations will be able to correct this. The philosopher still speculates. He still attempts to construct that by which the data of experience become intelligible. But he does not so much invent the invisible to explain the visible as place the visible datum within a co-related ensemble. The philosopher *sees* the coherent. Metaphysics, if metaphysics there is, must be seen as that which explains X by Y and Y by X, for this is what we call a grasp of the coherent, or the explanation of the part by the whole and the whole by the part. What this implies further study will attempt to clarify. But one thing we already know. We can no longer be impeded by the concept of the absurd, for the absurd is the ghost which plagues the one who is unable to reconcile his desire for omnipotence with the finite being he is. There is no reduction to absurdity for anyone who sees the *totum*, and himself as part of the *totum*. This position has moved away from the existential. What Existentialism has done for many, and for this writer in particular, will not be forgotten. Its impact is invaluable. Yet what the future has in store is something more collective, and as a result, more objective as well. "Je sais ce qui nous sépare," Sartre told me at Eastertime 1969. But what separates Sartre and his former commentator is also what unites both: the eternal coming and going of human thought, which fully belongs to none because it belongs to all.

I

A Phenomenology
of Descent, or the Observer
from Afar

WHILE the individual man, as we observed in the first volume, is part and fragment of the human totality, he was also shown to be a center. He is *part* of an ontological dimension, since he is fragment of the *totum genus humanum*; yet he is also a center, because he and he alone is able *noetically* to visualize and to totalize the multiplicity of this world. This power of totalization has a qualification, however; it is caught within the optic of an angular vision, and a vision that is in the form of an angle necessarily limits the horizon of the viewer. The planetary man was seen to be the ideal achievement of the angular and to come onto the stage wherever and whenever the angular happens to coincide with the generic, i.e., where the truth of the one is the truth of the totality. We call him ideal because his complete actualization, that is, the identification of the reach of the individual with the noesis of the totality, is not and cannot easily be presumed. The attainment of the dimension of planetary man, although it is not achieved, nevertheless remains the *paideia* (I use the word in the Greek sense of the instruction of the young) of modern man. It is the fundamental discipline from which he must receive his intellectual orientation.

On the threshold of an ethical study, we must concern ourselves with the orientation of present-day—and future—man towards the dimension of the planetary, for only when individual man has reached this summit will he be able to see the fragmentation and the diversity within the immense *totum* and the survival of that *totum* by virtue of this internal fragmentation. We shall call individual man in that position the *Observer from afar*. Here again, no claim is made that this dimension is ever entirely attained. Yet, whether totally achieved or not, the Observer remains an ideal towards which we must forever tend. This entire first chapter will be devoted to his pursuit. We begin by attempting to seize him in a definition: the Observer from afar is the one who, as uninvolved entity, sees the fractured *totum genus humanum* from the periphery of that same *totum*.

The Totum *Under Observation*

THERE is a famous folk tale of a dialogue that once took place between the Jungfrau and the Matterhorn that may start us on our way to an understanding of the term *totum genus humanum*. According to the legend, for millions of years the two Swiss mountaintops stood immobile in their icy solitude. Conversation between them was infrequent, and reduced to very few words. Once in a while, the Matterhorn looked down into the valley, as did also the Jungfrau, but their reaction for years was the same: nothing new down below. This went on until one day, man was born. The Jungfrau noted, "There they are." The Matterhorn, looking down, merely nodded in reply. The traffic down below went on for a number of years, centuries even, and then all was still again. The Jungfrau, always the more curious, noticed it first. "They are gone," she said. The Matterhorn smiled. Silence came down once more over the mountain range, and in the valley below.

In reflecting upon this fiction, we shall obtain a definition of *totum humanum*. That which had appeared in the valley constituted a *totum*. A *totum* is that which is made up of connected parts and which, considered in its entirety, is contained between a beginning and an end, in time and in space. Whether it is more than an addition of parts, we shall at present choose not to answer.

From a philosophical point of view, it is not important to know where these limits are. We confess that the beginning of the *totum* is inevitably obscure, but this does not cancel the fact that there was a beginning nor, most probably, does it eliminate the end. What happens between beginning and end we shall call *history*.

The *totum* unfolds in space as well as in time. Here again, we shall not attempt to define its limits. One thing appears to be certain. Man is no longer frightened by the silence of "infinite spaces," like Pascal in his day. Since then, the scientists and explorers have conquered this planet and set out beyond its borders. Whatever may ultimately be the frontiers of the conquerable, we shall call *geography* the science of that area of which conquest has been made.

Individual man is not definable in and by himself. He can only be defined within the *totum*, as part of the *totum*. He is a fragment of the *totum*, incomplete yet unique. This definition of man does not claim to be a total and exhaustive one, but it suffices for our approach if at this point we define him through the *totum* to which he belongs, a *totum* which, after observation, we shall be able to qualify as *humanum*—human.

In attempting to discover what makes a *totum* or totality a human totality, we immediately observe features which are in strong contrast with those of animal behavior, activities which attempt to change, control, or interpret the environment. Once a collective is religious, for example, one may presume that whatever form this religion takes, the constituents of that collective have asked a fundamental question concerning the remote origin of life and its ultimate destination. Art appears to be another specifically human achievement, for however elemental, it transcends the given in its creation of beauty. It improves upon what is, and is thus a conquest of the environment. Similarly, science attempts to discover and exploit the laws of "matter" for its own purposes, while political organization attempts to build stable structures for the defense and protection of those within a particular group. Whatever the nature of the undertaking—political or religious, scientific or artistic—as symptomatic of the human element, it must be viewed as a collective one. Insights in any of these fields are never the achievement of one man, however much they may appear to be. Quite often, the great achievement of one man or of a few seems to be detached from the past and from a milieu. This is deceptive. Those few are nevertheless spokesmen speaking out of and for the *totum*, never detached from it. Even their own awareness of solitude, however deep and sincere it may be or may have been, still does not disrupt the ontological tie with the *totum*.

In conclusion, a *totum* which engages in religious acts or creates art, or in one way or another builds up political or social structures, and does this collectively, we shall call a *totum humanum*, a human totality. It is a continuum, made up of parts called fragments, each fragment unique and incomplete, yet capable, when working with other fragments, of achieving certain kinds of acts which transcend the act of any other collective of our experience. The claim is not that it *exists*, all at once. It *is*. What *is*, however, explains that which *exists*.

The stress upon the function of the collective does not mean that individual human behavior is unselfish. On the contrary, one can even go so far as to say that the cooperation of men is calculated on an individual basis, and that unlike animal cooperation within the same *totum*, it is to an extent even selfish. Whether it has to be that is a question we shall examine later. It may appear that if the *totum humanum* wants to survive as human, it will have to alter its form of cooperation from one which, at present, can be said to be egocentric to one that is *totum*-oriented. But we are not that far as yet.

The individual fragment has been described as incomplete and as a part, yet as a unique part. It may be necessary here to clarify our insistence upon this quality of uniqueness, for in the history of philosophy there have always been those who have stressed the opposite—what human beings have in common. Aristotle, in constructing his categories, asserted clearly and forcefully that only in discovering the common element could the universal be detected, and that only in the gradual elimination of the diverse and in the incessant uncovering of what we have in common could the human mind reach towards the one and universal. The result is indeed the universal. But it is now clear to us that in discovering this universal, or in uncovering what we have in common, however satisfying this was to the Greek mind, we have lost track of the diverse. Greek philosophers are like Greek sculptors, who were forever looking for a few specimens of perfect bodies. They examined the multiplicity around them, and wherever possible reduced the many aspects to the one idea, or at least to the very few. It was in the contemplation of the few that the Greeks found the divine, for the philosophers no less than for the artists.

But obviously—and here we want to come back to the philosopher's problem—the reduction of the many to the one and the attempt to discover what they have in common took place at the expense of the unveiling of that which makes them unique. To say of men that they were rational was and still is an acceptable statement, yet in this very proposition, the peculiarity which makes each of them that particular unique individual is lacking. It is precisely in order *to include* the incommunicable and undefinable qualification of the individual subject that the construct of the totality is introduced and the individual is seen as unique fragment of the totality. Through this totality and through the achievements of this totality he will be *comprehended*; that is, the *totum* will reveal what he can do. Within the structure of the *totum*, moreover, it will become evident, on the basis of comparison with others in the same *totum*, what he is in his singularity and what his peculiar way is of doing what others are doing. To comprehend, as we understand it here, does not signify to understand through abstraction only, or— what is the same thing—to take apart the individual and categorize the composite elements under universal classes. This can be done, but it does not reveal the singular and the incommunicable. To comprehend signifies to see the different within the common and to see it in its uniqueness. An act of vision is here involved which reaches and knows the concrete on a basis of comparison. This implies that the singular is *part of.* . . .

So far, one thing is certain: the *totum humanum* is observed here in its physical sum total and not as a logical class. Certain airlines, when they calculate and compare the proportion of weight and of passengers which their plane will take for a long flight, call the addition of the latter "humanity," and hence speak of "9000 pounds of humanity." The comparison may appear disrespectful. In fact, it is more respectful when well understood, since it implies that adding the individuals together as the *totum physicum* instead of the *totum logicum*, or class, one does indeed presume that the individual himself is considered as a whole—that is, as a living reality with *everything which is peculiar* to him and makes him in depth the *individual* which he is. The method of approach here defended considers men as fragments indeed, but as unique fragments of a physical *totum*, wherein they are enclosed not only with certain traits which can be considered common but also with that which is supremely unique to each of them. There is no other dignity for individual man than his uniqueness within the *totum humanum* and, consequently, his unique contribution to that humanity which survives as *totum* because of the unequal and diversified contribution within its own structure.

If the individual man is unique, he is in one sense irreplaceable; for if, after a certain length of time, he is taken away and replaced, it will be by another *like* himself. "Like" does not imply total identity. The replacement of the irreplaceable—which is indeed the basic technique of the human *totum*—results in what is commonly called change. Whether this change should be called progress or regression is not for us to discuss. The change of the fragments, which is triggered by the uniqueness coming in succession, does not disrupt the ultimate cohesion of the one *totum humanum*. It is this *totum humanum* as a physical, global entity with all its qualifications, its fragmentation and its diversity, its endurance and its survival, which will constitute the object of our "vision," that vision of the Observer in which will be revealed the means of survival of that *totum*.

The Observer from Afar

IN attempting to define that particular function, we shall from the start eliminate introspection, or observation of the individual self by the individual self. Introspection is not unlike an individual face looking into a mirror. What sort of mirror? The mirror of one's past as remembered, one's present as now felt, and one's future as obscurely feared or hoped for. Yet, there is more. The look within is not merely a look at oneself in past, present, and future; it is also in many cases a look which removes the world without and replaces it with the world from within, that is, with a world as seen by me, through my love or hatred of it. Introspection as a source of cognition paves the way for a world as imagined, not necessarily the real world. This form of introspection will not be used in this study, but rather, introspection will be viewed as the return of the *totum* upon itself.

When we make the statement that the *totum* observes itself and practices what may be called a sort of self-reflection on a large scale, we should be circumspect, for the simple reason that the individual man himself has no clear awareness of such a thing. This is, of course, not a sufficient reason to reject it altogether. After all, the brain cell itself is totally unaware that it is part of a complex operation which is called the reflection of individual man. Yet, if there is no reason for accepting such a phenomenon on the immense scale of the *totum*, there is no cogent argument at this point of our study to reject it either. There are indications that the *totum genus humanum* as a whole behaves with a certain self-awareness. It is striking indeed that it has the know-how of survival amidst the hard struggle on this earth—in our first volume we have called this the first universal[1]—but the question remains whether or not this self-knowledge of the *totum* as such, however skillful and efficient, ever reaches the level of clear awareness somewhere in a mind, or a collective consciousness, which may be termed a generic mind. On this no definite answer is as yet available, although we have made it clear that in the philosophy of the planetary man, the existence of a generic truth is taken for granted. On this, there can be no doubt. The question whether this generic truth has any habitat other than within the intellects of many individual men remains open. Similarly unanswered is the problem of whether the Observer is one man or many men, whether he is one individual who by some peculiar disposition has reached this pinnacle or a coadunation of several individuals who, although each having limitations, through their multiplicity correct one another and thereby reach what might be called the promontory of the objective. Earlier,[2] we asserted that any movement of the individual fragment towards fulfilling the aspiring dreams of the planetary man was doomed to failure, since the individual self in reaching for the stars could not and would not be able to transcend the limitations of his own angular vision. It will always be from the *here* and the *now* that he will observe. On this, we agree. Yet, his attempt to reach the nowhere and the never must be perpetually reiterated in order to reach that promontory of the uncommitted, be it alone or with others. In our attempt to examine the concept of the Uncommitted and the place from where he explores his object and the nature of this object itself, it would perhaps be more fruitful first to explore just what the task implies and only then to inquire whether one or perhaps many individuals are required to fulfill it.

---

[1] See Volume I, p. 112.   [2] *Ibid.*, chapter 9.

The Promontory of the Uncommitted

In order for the Observer to find the place from which the *totum* as *totum* is laid bare to his eyes, he must first outdistance himself and occupy that point in space from which he can embrace the totality and that instant in time whence he can be said to be present to all moments of time. Is this within the limits of man's ability?

It must first of all be remembered that man is in the particular position of being both cause and effect of the *totum*; that is, he causes the totality to be—there is no doubt about the fact that the *totum* implies the parts—and at the same time, he is also the product of that totality. We shall call this a structural, or better still, an ontological fact. That is the way things are. When we say that the individual is both producing and produced, we mean that he is prisoner of the prison he helps to make. Yet, although chained within, he is also able to climb outside. The individual noesis transcends its ontological imprisonment, for individual man is a perceptive unit which is able to take a position outside itself, stretch itself to the utmost and observe the *totum humanum* as *totum*. The perceptive powers of the human individual are extravagant indeed, in the etymological sense of the word *extra-vagans*—to wander away from—for they enable a man to reach outwards and forget himself.

This self-oblivion deserves our attention, for it will in the long run constitute the core element of what we call the phenomenology of descent. Self-oblivion, it must be stressed, is more than the noetic sequel to the ontological structure: the noesis centers without because the ontological structure is one of within. The segmentation of the *totum* in itself makes it clear that the individual man, in his function of ontological fragment, cannot be an absolute center of noesis.[3] This self-oblivion, as the necessary condition of the position of Observer, can in no way be equated with the Cartesian or even the Husserlian point of departure, where the individual is con-

---

[3] If he does fulfill a central function, it always is and always will be of relative value, and although in Volume I we attempted to constitute the *paradox* as a solution to overcome the angular, it was obviously not an undertaking aimed at replacing the generic truth. See Volume I, chapter 4.

sidered to be central and as a consequence is regarded as absolute. On the contrary, as we view the ontological structure, individual man is ex-centric, and it is the *totum* that is absolute. The whole effort of self-oblivion is to transfer the weight of the observation from the part to the *totum*, so that it is not merely in the realm of the ontological but also in the domain of the noetic, or of the *totum* observing itself, that we are able to construct the image of the Observer. The Observer, then, abandons the centrifugal position of the individual as the image of somebody and becomes nobody, and through this very act of forgetting the self and the angular, reaches the position of the *totum*.

Self-oblivion is a first requisite, then, in our attempt to build up a phenomenology of descent, but its full meaning can only be understood when it is made clear that the abandonment of the self presumes that the Observer will proceed to take a position at several points in space and time. In order to know things as they are, the Observer is obliged to take his position at points indefinite in space and time, for observation will be objective only when it occupies different points in space and observes an event not merely from the optic *here* but also from the point of view *there*. Obviously, the *totum* is here *and* there, not in the sense of being a spirit, as one tradition would have it understood, but merely in the sense that the expanse of the *totum* as *totum* covers different points in space which can only be occupied by the individual fragment one at a time.

Self-oblivion therefore requires self-multiplication. Self-multiplication in space on the part of the Observer presumes an attitude of mobility and of outdistancing on the part of the self, in order to be present to the habitat of the *totum* as *totum*. This performance calls for a lack of engagement to any one location. The Observer, in training himself for judging objectively on the ethical value of the *totum* or parts thereof, must judge from here and from there, or what may be called from afar. Only when we judge from points indefinite in space shall we judge as not belonging, which is what it means to judge from afar. As an inevitable result, of course, we shall be able to attach only relative value to certain pronouncements which were once considered to be eternal and absolute.

Descent has to be practiced not only from points indefinite in space but also from more than one moment in time. An event must be judged not merely as it is seen now but also as it will be seen in the future. How does the *later* look at the *now*? By this we do not imply that the act of the present must be of any particular kind in order to avoid the condemnation or gain the praise of those still to come, but merely that no act stands alone. An act of the present can and will be successful only when it is viewed as unfolding in succession, that is, as part of a time sequel where things come one after another. The act will not be a success because the future praises it; rather, those of the future will praise it because it is a success. The Observer must view the event from beyond the present moment and take a position from afar in time while looking at its present accomplishment.

The Observer, then, occupies points indefinite in space and in time, and from these points descends upon the *totum* or parts thereof. These instants of past and future or points of here and there are by no means points of repose for the Observer. They are merely points of relay or provisional immobility, from which he pursues the movement which I have called "descent" in order to know and to judge a particular event in toto, or in *total* knowledge, the way the *totum* knows. This is the exact opposite of the Socratic dictum to "know yourself," for only in the identification with what is not-me can I, *from there*, judge myself.[4] The object of our inquiry, of course, need not be *oneself*, it can be any event or person which is judged in objectivity from a point distant in time and space. So, e.g., how would Socrates have judged Jesus Christ? How does one living in the present, yet not a follower of Christ, judge him? How does a Buddhist judge Jesus Christ? How will an inhabitant from another planet judge him a hundred years from now?

In the answer to these and similar questions (concerned not necessarily with a person, but it may be equally with an event, or a way of living, a conventional code or "morality"), a phenomenology of descent constitutes a medium by which generic truth is discovered. Generic truth is the knowledge of the *totum* concerning event Z (by hypothesis, the object of our inquiry).[5] It may at first appear as if the noesis merely followed the ontological becoming,

---

[4] And I should add that only through the *absence* of his past does the immigrant *know* his past.

[5] See Volume I, chapter 5.

the ontological becoming being, of course, nothing but the genesis of Z through the sequel of cause-and-effect until the very moment of its coming into existence. The observation of this chain of antecedent and consequent seems natural and would lead the Observer from the past to the present actualization of Z. Yet, it should be kept in mind that this ontological becoming of Z is itself subjacent to a manipulation of a higher order, which is dictated by the *totum* as such. This study considers the *totum* as enclosed. Within this container, time and space are dimensions of an essential order, since they provide for the diversification of the parts or fragments that constitute the *totum*. From the point of view of the fragments themselves, there is no doubt about their time-awareness—I mean of their awareness of past, present and future—but from the point of view of the *totum*, there is merely at work a manipulation of the parts such that it results in the survival of the *totum*. The *totum* merely *is*. Consequently, when in connection with Z something is said to be future, it merely implies that from the point of view of the atemporal *totum*, Z has a relational connection with that future something, just as it has a built-in relation with all points (in space and time), and the reverse is equally true: points future and past have a relation with Z which in one way or another corrects or completes Z. The fact that time and space play a role in the actualization of that scheme and that things come in succession does not really affect the structure and the survival of the *totum* in depth, for that is the way the *totum* is. The *totum* as *totum* is like a chess game; although the pawns move and eventually disappear, in their very being they support the total game and play their role. Since the future no less than the past is present in event Z, *descent* upon it, to be complete, must take into account the judgment of *a totality which is not yet but some day will be*.

Let us not forget that the Observer replaces the *totum* and that what is in question is the *totum* looking at the *totum*. From the point of view of the *totum*, the fragments, whether they come sooner or later, remain nevertheless fragments and as such play their part, a part which we have described as one of the mutual correction leading to the being of the *totum*. It can therefore be said without exaggeration that from the point of view of the *totum*, time is no longer succession but simultaneity, and history appears as panorama.

Epistemology as a "False Problem"

UNLIKE the Cartesian and the Husserlian points of departure, the phenomenology of descent as proposed here does not encounter the epistemological question, with which any philosophy that begins with the Subject or individual Self is unavoidably confronted. Since the *totum* reflecting does not question the *Totum* within (neither did Descartes' *Cogito* doubt the existence of the Self and its content), the only question that might arise would concern the eventual existence of that which lies beyond the orbit of the living and existing *totum genus humanum*. What this means we shall attempt to clarify later. As for the *totum* itself, it is enough to state that the *totum humanum* "turning its gaze inward discovers a multitude of existing individuals and their utterances."[6] To turn its gaze inwards means to look within and to observe the observable, whether it was, or is (now) or will be. From the point of view of the individual fragments, the triple time-dimension is starkly real, and the term "exist" is reserved only for those who are now. From the point of view of the *totum* reflecting, however, past and present and future constitute one expanse. The *totum* observes itself as *totum* in its atemporal dimensions and discovers within it no epistemological questioning, for the simple reason that the *totum* has never questioned its own being. As the *totum* reflects, it discovers its inner constituents and the density of the inorganic between the organic as the unavoidable extension of that which was alive and of that which will be alive. The *totum humanum* as *totum* contains within itself the living as its constitutive parts—this has been sufficiently stressed—but it also carries the density of the inorganic between individuals as the necessary "whole cloth" out of which life grows and towards which the life of existing individuals returns. Death is the whole weight of the inorganic which is suspended between the living, and as such is part of life. There is no authentic questioning of the cosmos for anyone who has not torn himself away from the whole cloth called humanity and constituted himself a monadic Self confronting, by this very fact, the rest of humanity as alien matter, the "existence" of which has to be dem-

---

[6] *Ibid.*, pp. 24–25.

onstrated. The phenomenology of descent therefore discovers naturally within the walls of the *totum* that which is, whether it was, or is (in the present) or will be.

We do not have the same confidence once the *totum* "turning its gaze outward, discovers another dimension."[7] Although it is not the purpose of our study to discuss the nature of this "world beyond," several observations made possible by our method of inquiry should be put forth. (1) By "world beyond" we shall understand any entity which explains this world or makes it in one way or another intelligible. In that sense, God would belong to the "world beyond." (2) It does not follow from the preceding statement that this "world beyond" is totally distinct and totally different from the world that we see. Whether it is a world tied to ours or totally distinct is a question worth asking. (3) In the opinion of this writer, only the collective can eventually bring an answer to that question, for only collective praxis, or practice, brings into being collective noesis. It is very well possible that our past failure in metaphysical explorations results from the fact that we have taken the concepts of an individual semantics for granted.[8] The metaphysical entities, whatever they are in themselves, are beyond the reach of the individual man, because he is himself caught within the quantifiable and measurable. As an isolated individual, he cannot transcend his prison. Only when a group praxis comes into being do we have a multiplicity of fragments which covers a multiplicity of *heres* and *nows*. The individual is always time- and space-bound, but the *totum* is not, since it is made up of parts which are at different moments and in different places. *We* are not time-bound because I *am* now, you *will be* and he *was*. *We* are not space-bound, because I am *here*, you are *there*, and he is *elsewhere*. The time barrier can only be broken when the multiplicity covers every instant, for then there are no longer instants, since there is no longer succession. The same can be said about space. Space becomes infinity when the *totum* is everywhere, and it is everywhere when its constitutive parts or fragments occupy all points.

A group praxis, when evolved far enough, will some day accomplish this feat. But its noetic result, we should hasten to add, will be a group noesis. Only the group will know what the group does,

---

[7] *Ibid.*, p. 25.   [8] *Ibid.*, pp. 132–135.

and in this sense, collective praxis will beget collective noesis. Some day it may become evident that such invisible entities as the soul are nothing but extensions of the visible. And they will manifest themselves as such because their fabric, still a mystery for our times, will reveal itself to the collective noesis, that is, to an instrumentation which is both "*tota et simul*," an instrumentation which in transcending time and space discovers that which is spaceless and timeless. We shall, of course, reserve the terms *spaceless* and *timeless* not for what in the past was called "spirit," but for that which transcends the *measurable* of individual semantics. Only that which in its approach reaches the "absence" of space and time will reach that which is nowhere and never, yet which nevertheless *is*. It is immaterial whether we shall call this discovery physics or metaphysics. Physics may very well be the suitable term, but a physics which is no longer tied down to a quantifiable calculus.

Obviously, this too falls within the domain of a phenomenology of descent because it is a vision from afar, or from the periphery of the *totum*, which considers the *totum* as *totum*; and it is at this level, and at this level only, that the dimensions become atemporal and aspatial and prepare "us" for the grasp of that which is beyond a quantifiable physics. Although such metaphysical preoccupations could very well constitute an object for a phenomenology of descent, they will not be pursued in the present study. If this topic is touched on, it will only be to the extent that it affects our ethical stand. Our approach aims, rather, at the observation and description, by way of descent, of the *totum humanum*—its fundamental structure, its diversity and mobility within, its tools for survival.

The Mode of Descent, or Vision from Afar

SINCE we have no epistemological problem and since we have decided to set aside metaphysical preoccupations, it appears, then, that all that remains for the Observer to do is to look at things as they are. It is here that the term "vision" seems to be appropriate.

In his acts of knowledge, individual man remains caught in time and space. Knowledge reaches out from the individual knower as from an optical lens and covers only a certain amount of time and space. The expanse may be large, it may be small. The world of a child is small: it stretches between his home and his school and into a past that is very short. Even within that past, he does not reach far. An invisible lasso encircles his vision. He feels happy within it. Even when he travels, he does not readily break out of that circle. Indeed, if he travels continuously, neurosis may set in because in that incessant moving around, he cannot for any length of time cast anchor and settle his noesis upon an immobile space. The knowable expanse of the adult vision covers immensely more territory, but whatever the breadth and the depth of the human act of knowledge, it reaches from the individual knower and descends unto a maximum which is translatable into a space-and-time quadrant; in very old people we sometimes observe that the circle of vision narrows down until the periphery coincides with the point. This is the moment of death.

All knowledge is caught in the concrete and is never totally divorced from it. The mistake of the philosophizing of the past was that the abstract idea was removed from the concrete and the multiple to reside in the mind or in some remote heaven. There was an inversion of values when the Platonic method, with contempt for the percept, attempted to reach beyond it to the One which is the independent form or Universal. What mattered for Plato and his followers was the discovery of what beings have in common, together with the annihilation of that which makes them distinct and unique. We have already noted a similar trend in the Aristotelian categorical structure. Plato was the destroyer of the visible.

Our study, on the contrary, will keep as its object the earthly city, using the term not in the Augustinian sense of an evil city but as that which is there, and in being there, is in its manifold variety the object of our vision. It is upon the earthly city that the act of knowing ultimately lands. The *cognoscendum*, or object-to-be-known, belongs there and then both as unique and as fixed in the *totum*. Although abstraction continues to have a function, that of discovering what the diverse ave in common, angular vision will include a grasp of the concrete as well.

The literal meaning of the word *vision* is, of course, simply the physical sense-activity by which color and light are apprehended. The human eye is constructed in such a way that light is projected upon the retina, as in a camera. Yet, the vision of man is more than mere photography. The meaning of the word stretches beyond that immediate way of knowing, beyond the sensual grasp, to include the act of comprehending the external world. In the exercise of any of the external senses—whether seeing, hearing, feeling, smelling, or tasting—there is at work, when the individual is awake, an activity which transcends the mere grasp of the datum. What this activity is we shall not attempt to delimit for the time being, but it can be said to be either an initial form of inquiry, if the object appears for the first time, or a movement of comparing and weighing its "connection" with the surrounding world. One does more than merely see, hear, feel, smell, or taste: one knows. If this is true of all sense perception, it is even more striking in vision. The etymology of the word attests to this. "Vision" comes from the Latin *videre*, to see, and through the Latin, is connected with the Greek stem *yiy*, which lies at the origin of the family of words implying knowledge. To see is to know. But the act of knowing includes both a movement of abstraction—that is, a movement of the mind towards revealing what X has in common with Z—and also a movement of the sense towards its proper object. The act of vision includes both the percept and the understanding. It is a form of intuition or grasp of the concrete with a simultaneous sense of its universalizable content— the term intuition is innocuous enough, but it should not be reduced to the Bergsonian intuition which seizes reality in flux. It is, rather, an intuition which in the grasp of the concrete X discovers its uniqueness and its difference from Z. It is imperative for the philosopher to explore this method of approach in a world where the impact of the visual is overwhelming. Television, photography and the cinema are the media of our times, and contemporary man is more and more trained to acquire knowledge through the visual and the perceptive. This implies that he constantly transcends the vision of the concrete image that he sees. To transcend is to go beyond the given and to compare it with what has been seen before or elsewhere. The individual man has his own way of knowing: he incessantly universalizes the given, and his universalization is one of comparing the concrete with the concrete. His education no longer emphasizes naked syllogistic reasoning but attempts to discover the different in the concrete visual. It is the merit of McLuhan to have drawn attention to the impact of modern media. Our position would not claim, however, that the medium is the message, but rather that the message transcends the medium and reveals the content of the percept and much more.

Not only is there a gradual shift in man's approach to absorbing the outside world, but the amount of knowledge which the communications media offer him is massive: what is going on in all parts of the world is a matter of everday knowledge to him. All events can be seen immediately and on a grand scale. His knowledge of the earth and its cultural and geographical divisions is more thorough. Even history is made present. In some ways, he knows more than his ancestors did. One should not conclude that by virtue of this, he is necessarily a better-educated man, or that his approach to the outside world is more penetrating. We merely claim that it is more visual and on a more immense scale.

The position of the Observer from afar is not placed on the same footing as that of the Observer of a television screen or a documentary movie. Yet, there is some similarity, in that for both, the concrete empirical data in their unique character play a considerable role. What matters for us on the threshold of the ethical is a certain preparedness to visualize from afar things as they are, and in this observation to discover the unique and the place of the unique within the *totum*. The recognition of the unique and of the plural has major consequences for an ethics that is truly of our times, as will appear in later chapters.

The Man of San Pancrazio and the Chief of the Balubas

THE man of San Pancrazio is individual, *X*. He is unknown. In order to discover him, we shall come down to him from time present and also from time past. We shall approach him from the left and from the right, for only when he is framed within a certain epoch and within a certain place can he be known. From indefinite points in space and time, the Observer will uncover the individual tomb or the hidden *X* as that unique point where in an irreplaceable way geography and history intersect. One could with good reason call him the individual tomb, for he is hidden within several layers of the collective, or groups, each one englobing a portion of time-space quadrants. The Observer burrows several centuries down and comes up from several centuries in the past to the time when *X* was alive. One moves likewise from the North to "him" and from the South, from the East and from the West. An unremitting, painstaking excavation uncovers the tomb and releases the living *X*.

He lives in Rome on the via San Pancrazio, in the year 1508. In reaching the man of San Pancrazio there and then, the Observer concludes that there is no absurdity involved; for the closer one looks, the more one becomes aware that he could live only there and then. He is a painter of great talent. He works for popes Julius II and Leo X. He wears the dress of his time and a black cap over his long hair. He paints in the style of his time: he has moved beyond the simplicity of Perugino but not yet into the genre of Guido Reni. He is an Italian and he is a Catholic. He is a believer, but he is not averse to the life of luxury of a man who has great wealth. For the Observer, X or the man of San Pancrazio is "intelligible." There is nothing "absurd" about him. The *totum* has placed him at that time and on that spot, and through this very act, it has placed the ground for what is not X. The *totum* presses him to be *such* so that something else might be *so*. The presence of the unique is the negation of the absurd when it has been understood that at that time and at that moment there could only be X. There is no absurdity for the Observer, however absurd life may have appeared in the eyes of X himself. The awareness of the absurd is the confession of ignorance. No one lifts up the lid of his own tomb, for tombs are approached from the outside only.

To become intelligible in the sequence of history does not mean to be universalizable. Uniqueness precludes distribution among others. The man of San Pancrazio is not Z, chief of the Balubas tribe living on the edge of Tanganyika around 1875, two years after the death of Livingstone. Z is tall, erect, the bearer of a spear, polygamous. He lives in the center of the village, in the tallest hut. He commands the tribe, smokes a pipe and sits in the sun, worships the spirits of his ancestors, believes in the gods of his tribe and observes the rituals. Z, too, is unique.

To be unique does not imply to be independent. It is permissible for the man from the via San Pancrazio to sign his painting X, since a name is the conventional mark of the unique. A signature is an act of independence, yet X cannot sign his work of art X without tacitly referring to all those before and after who brought him into being and gave him his prominence. This, of course, only the Observer notices, for X is not clearly aware of the *totum* in which he is suspended. A very few people see themselves as a point in the current of time or upon the expanse of space. Very few run ahead of their time and come back to themselves by way of descent.

In most cases, the individual fragment constitutes the screen hiding the *totum* from himself. In his very incarnation, the man of San Pancrazio constitutes a wall sealing off the dimensions of past and future. To the extent that X reveals and exemplifies the *totum* he is ignorant of the *totum*. His uniqueness creates the penumbra of what is not himself.

At this point, one may ask whether it would help to become less oneself in order to become more the *totum*. Such is, ideally, the attitude of the Observer. He sees the unique and the dependent: he sees X as a knowing and living point hanging at an intersection of space and time, caught in ever-narrowing circles: his continent, his nation, his city, and his street. He sees that individual above all in his century, his epoch and his time. In reaching the man of San Pancrazio *in* the Rome of the Renaissance or the chief of the Balubas *on* the coast of Tanganyika, the Observer as explorer has reached what is concrete, hence, different from any other concrete. This descent is not condescending in the moral sense of the word—no humiliation is intended—it merely follows the immense movement of all incarnation and its course downward from the non-existent or the suprahuman to the singular. To discover the incarnation has never meant to mortify the incarnated. The Observer can merely discover what is. *What is* is not the idea, as Plato or Aristotle would have it. The philosopher of the future will not set himself to discover the similar. On the contrary, in opposition to the Greek contemplation of imperishable forms or of the universal, he will find his joy in the acceptance of the diverse and in the contemplation of the unique as fulfilled in the existent.

At this point, the Observer reaches a conclusion which is salient in this study: what is observed as unique must be judged as different. The stress lies upon the words "judged" and "different," for clearly the Observer will be the judge of the different.

Observer and Judge

WHETHER or not the Observer is more than just an Observer and becomes judge as well will depend upon the task which is expected from him as judge. The function of judge under consideration here is not the one usually identified with the man who presides over a trial and, after the decision of the jury, pronounces the innocence or guilt of the defendant. Much less is he the coercer.

The Observer is the judge to the extent that, being the onlooker from afar, uninvolved and nonengaged, he acquiesces in the different within the *totum*, yet at the same time protects the *totum*. It is his duty, therefore, to observe the different and to respect the different in the conviction that only on the basis of the diverse will the *totum* survive; but it is no less his function to forbid the different when it becomes incongruent or incompatible to the point of constituting a danger to the *totum* itself. The Observer is the Guardian, and the conclusions of his insights are a protection for the *totum*. Morality is protection.

Morality can only be effective when it reaches to the sources of destruction. A moral treatise, therefore, will be a guiding light when it is an illumination from afar. And it will be such when under its searching eye, the structure of the *totum* appears visible in its entirety "in descent." Only to the one who occupies the position of the atemporal and of the aspatial will it appear whether or not the one is one and whether or not, within the one, the man of the via San Pancrazio emerges as "justified," as does with equal equity the totally different chief of an African tribe in the days of Livingstone. Justification of the unique will be judged in the light of the total composite.

Knowing in greater detail the task required, we can now be more specific in answering the question which came up in earlier pages: Is the Observer one or many?

The complexity of the act of judging and evaluating results from the unresolvable paradox that the individual fragment conveys the utterance of the *totum* and yet is not, of himself alone, the *totum*. He speaks for it, yet he is not (totally) what he represents. The result is that this partial judgment must and should be put in brackets until it is completed by the judgment of the "other" individual self. The mark of infallibility does not belong to *one* man. His voice can never be a definitive judgment; it is only an informed opinion. "Opinion" contributes to the building up of what we have called the complementary-additive we-language. An opinion does not by itself reflect the *totum*, nor does it by itself impose itself upon the *totum*, but, along with other "opinions," it forges a position which reflects the judgment, or else the opinions diverge from one another. This mobility betrays the internal structure of the *totum* itself, whose fragments adopt attitudes which are pro or con. This point will be developed later, but it is sufficient now to note that every idea or opinion is in fact incarnated in an individual fragment. Earlier, we made it clear that to the (ontological) fragment fits the (noetic) angular view. What we would at present like to add is that the individual fragment supports his "opinion" by reasons. As we say, "he has his reasons." The fact that an opinion is skillfully presented and reasoned out by way of argument demonstrates the skill of the individual dialectician, but it does not per se subjugate the minds of other people. One can admire the "reasons" without admitting defeat. The "reason," and reason itself in depth, is the self-defense of such or such an individual uniqueness. The *totum* itself, without necessarily being anti-reason, transcends the "reasons" of individuals, corrects the narrowness of their angular vision, and constructs the view which one commonly calls "objective." In most cases, therefore, the individual self formulates his "opinion," but in doing so, he merely submits material for the formation of a collective thought. In the meantime, he waits, as does his opinion. It is this *waiting* of the ideas for their corrective which must be stressed, for such is indeed the fate of the Observer as well, when the function is occupied by *one* man.

From the outset, the position of the Observer and of the planetary man in his function of Observer, especially when it is a position occupied by one man, must be considered as the object of an intense *paideia*, a paideia which by hypothesis is never totally finished but is incessantly worked upon. As we have already noted, we understand the word *paideia* in the Greek sense of the word as "education of the young." In the grasping of the world as one and as diversified, our world is still in its infancy. Paideia implies the capability of assuming the different faces of the human *totum* of whatever time and space. These faces are the many shapes and forms of the *totum* with which the would-be planetary man attempts to identify. Perhaps we might compare this endeavor to the efforts of Paul of Tarsus, who claimed to be Jew with the Jews, Greek with the Greeks and Gentile with the Gentiles—all things to all men. The magnificent *cor Pauli, cor mundi*—the heart of Paul, the heart of the world—was not undeserved. The paideia of the Observer aims at similar results without as yet striving for the universal charity of Paul. So far, the Observer is Observer only. His goal is knowledge. And, if he attempts to elevate himself beyond the parochial and the national in order to touch on the planetary, it is as yet merely for the sake of objective evaluation. Whether or not this curiosity and form of detached altruism will prove to be fatal to him, we do not yet know. Further study will enlighten us on that point. One thing appears certain at this stage. Whatever the efforts of individual man to reach the promontory of the Uncommitted, he is condemned to a fate of waiting, for however detached, he cannot ever totally overcome his own unicity. This "waiting" is a submission of his own vision and the acceptance of the other as the ultimate complement. The ideal fulfillment of the Observer and Judge presumes the moving of opinions towards one another, with the result that the Observer of the *totum* becomes ultimately what the *totum* itself is, namely, pluridimensional.

2

The *Totum* as One

"THE fragment does not survive: the totality does. It does so, however, as fragmented *totum*, the elements of which, being fundamentally *imperfect*, replace one another in a linear succession and uphold one another on a horizontal span of simultaneous existence. Both dimensions taken together (existence in depth and existence in width) result in the *totum genus* or species taken as a whole."[1] Our examination in Volume I, both of the oneness of the *totum* and of its fragmentarity, was merely speculative. Now, we will consider the *totum* and its internal structure with an eye upon the behavior of the constituents. Oneness will be found to have moral implications, and the interdependence of the parts will be an important factor when the moment of final judgment has come. This "last judgment," or judgment of the *totum* concerning the behavior of its constitutive parts, forms the core of our moral system.

Our present concern is the *totum humanum* and its oneness. We have no intention of denying the obvious fact that the *totum humanum* itself is part of the *totum universum*. Men, immersed in the inorganic, live from and communicate through the inorganic. Only within the inorganic can the organic subsist. Yet, we only acknowledge in passing this endless and incessant exchange of the organic and the inorganic, since our primary concern is with the living.

---

[1] *The Planetary Man* Volume I, pp. 39–40.

It is natural to start with the question: What is oneness? Traditional approaches would bring us to such answers as that oneness is the quality of being one, the one is that which is undivided, and since there are many ways of being undivided, there are many ways of being one. There are, for example, entities which are undivided in a logical sense, such as the oneness of the class or category. The concept or idea of table has such a oneness: we obtain it through an abstraction from many tables, and what we obtain is applicable to all tables. This universal is a form of oneness or "undividedness" that is homogeneous, indicating what tables have in common.

But suppose now that instead of following the path of abstraction that enables me to discover the one and the similar in the many and to end up with a logical oneness (*unum logicum*), I become the Observer from afar, and from this vantage point observe the human totality additively. I discover not merely what a human being has in common with another human being, but a new form of oneness, an *unum physicum* that is made up of the diverse, not of the similar, as was the *unum logicum*.

If the homogeneous entities become one through the levelling of logic, how can the diverse become and remain one? There is only one answer: through communication. The rejection of the Aristotelian category and its replacement by the *totum physicum* will in turn reveal a new mode of oneness. Oneness will be no longer the oneness of the logical class, but a oneness through communication. Finite fragments within the *totum* communicate. Communication makes the oneness of the *totum*; the closer the forms of communication, the more intimate the ensuing oneness.

This communication of parts is extremely diversified, and we shall use the term "interlocking" as the one most apt to describe the interrelating of fragments. From this, it will appear that having given up the *totum logicum* as the ultimate achievement of our mental activity—reducing everything to one law and rejoicing in the contemplation of that law, as did the Greeks—we shall not now look for what the parts have in common, but rather for the multiple ways in which and through which the parts communicate and are unified in the one *totum*.

(1) This basic interlocking, which of course constitutes the

most essential communication as well, is the interlocking of parts through origin: the many are born within the one. As such, the *totum* has the elemental unity of the tree. The tree in the forest stands one and compact, its fruit held closely on the stem and the branches. Only when the fruit is ripe for independent reproduction does it leave the tree. When we compare this to the structure and operation of the *totum humanum*, we perceive a manifest difference. The human being has intelligence and a far greater mobility; he is able to walk away from the genealogical tree. This mobility does not, however, mean independence. The genes of a man walking are still genes, and wherever the individual moves, he carries within himself the attachment to the tree. The genealogical tree is a rich metaphor, for descendants of the same couple, although diverse, are the bearers of an undeniable continuity, and to be human means to retain permanent and indestructible ties with the tree.[2]

(2) "A dependence in origin transforms itself into a dependence in subsistence, i.e., the individual man is made out of what-he-is-not; subsequently he can only live from what-he-is-not."[3] This presents us with a second form of interlocking or fundamental communication. Dependence in origin makes man an invalid for life, not in the pathological sense of the word, but merely in that which affects him normally. Individual man in order to be, and to be beyond the present moment, must hold onto the hands of others around him. We have all observed how the very sick like to hold

---

[2] This is in no way a scientific treatise, but it is worth observing that certain findings in biology confirm our philosophical remarks. A culture of bacteria made overnight results in approximately the same number of generations as is required for human beings to fill a span of a thousand years. A generation of bacteria takes twenty minutes, more or less, while a human generation fills thirty years. What is noteworthy, though, is the fact that in the culture, certain characteristics of the night before are still present the following morning. This seems to imply that as far as human beings are concerned, the present generation still carries the mark of an ancestor who has lived a thousand years ago. Naturally, that particular trait is no longer there in a pure state, since many collateral influences have affected it. Yet it seems safe to say that the human individual keeps this connection with a past which goes back a thousand years and longer.

[3] *The Planetary Man*, Volume I, p. 34.

someone's hand. The gesture in these moments may be one of despair, yet it is significant of what our whole lives are, even those of us still in good health. Men have always held onto each other's hands, although in the full vigor of life, this interdependency of the diverse is less dramatically symbolized and there may be less clear awareness of it.

Among the various forms of interlocking, one of the most important is that of language communication through sound. The *totum*, silent as a whole, carries within itself an incessant colloquy of fragments. The term *person*, or *persona* ("mask") to denote the individual self is well chosen, for the person is indeed "that through which the sound comes." The person can also be said to be the mask of the *totum*, for he is in fact that through which the *totum* asserts itself, not fully or unconditionally but in a contributing way. The *totum* is not a homogeneous block moving slowly and steadily through the ages; it is, on the contrary, an entity internally fractured and at times torn apart by strife and hatred. One person is one expression: he is an utterance of the *totum*, and he is so in a unique way. "Expression" here has its full meaning: the individual person is, *and* unwittingly discloses, or reveals in some way, the inner depths of the *totum*. Words are instrumental to this revelation, since they are sound with a meaning that points to something. Their advantage is that they contain the possibility of "promise" and "contract," and in being such, prepare for an action which transcends the act of that which is fragment only. This "interlocking" through sound enables men to work at a level which is much more complex than that of the animal. On the other hand, anything threatening the oneness constitutes a menace to the totum as well. *It is not diversity as such which threatens unity*—the one, as this study has repeatedly stressed, is made up of the diverse—only the diversity which is unable to communicate becomes the fatal danger. Diversity can never become so polarized as to destroy the possibility of communication. Take, for example, the case of massive immigration with a nation. Massive immigration threatens unity because it interrupts, in the philosophical sense of the word, full communication or interlocking in depth. Assimilation is hampered because communication is at a standstill. In order to reestablish—or establish—the ideal "one," cultural,

economic, perhaps even biological exchange is a prerequisite.[4]
The one is continuum, not commonality, at least not essentially.
Communication as the tool of continuity is there even when not
consciously perceived.

The Unconscious, or the Ground of the One

THE multiple subjects of the *totum* confronting one another in an
incessant encounter, of which they are clearly aware, are doing
this precisely because they are caught pre-ontologically in a deeper
oneness which escapes them, yet which to a great extent guides
their lives. This is the oneness of the subconscious. We have previously defined the person as the unique mask of the *totum humanum.* As such, he is endowed with consciousness, hence aware
of his surroundings and above all of the fact that he is distinct

---

[4] The Negro problem in the United States is a peculiar problem. Although the blacks have been in America for over two hundred years, communication between black and white is poor. Both communities are merely juxtaposed. At present, in an effort of assimilation—an effort which is essential if the nation wants to survive as one—the problem is seen in all its acuteness and can only be solved through communication on all levels. What has made this case much more complex is the fact that the Negro, even in official documents, was not considered to be human the way the white man considered himself to be. The presumption was that the difference was too great to make assimilation possible, for it was strongly, however erroneously, believed that the Negro was not part of the underlying One which constitutes the *totum humanum* itself, as we have described it.

The principles presented here find their application not only in the making of the collective, but also with regard to the oneness of the individual man. The transplant, at present a topic of medical research, may or may not threaten the existence of an individual organism. It does not per se threaten his existence. But it may prove to be fatal; and it will be fatal when the oneness of this small *totum* called individual man is at stake. When communication with the alien part cannot be re-established, the individual in an attempt to reject the foreign body is in great danger. Or—and this is another hypothesis—in attempting to assimilate the new organ, the candidate does not so much lose life as he loses himself. In case of replacement of the brain—which is not a totally utopian concept—this individual in his uniqueness would no longer be what he was, and communication with the outside world—let us say, with the members of his own family—would be excluded.

from these surroundings. In his mind terminate the lines of a certain vision which we have called angular. This vision is unique and is rooted in a unique self. To the Observer from afar, he appears as that entity which uses the semantics of the "I" and the "mine," and only to a lesser extent the "we" and the "ours." When he constructs a grammatical conjugation, he starts with the "I" and only later comes to the "we." Grammatically, he places himself first. And he does so economically, politically, and in every other possible way as well. The individual man, although clearly aware of the presence of the other, remains *unconscious* of the subterranean oneness which ties him to the other. But this reality, which is made up of the multiple ties linking the fragments together in depth, exists as the subconscious, the obscure place where the fragments meet, unaware of their encounter. This encounter must not be understood in any spiritualistic sense, nor in the Freudian form, nor as the Jungian concept of the collective unconscious of mankind. Our claim is merely that oneness is built up through communication, that in some unconscious way some form of communication takes place. This becomes clear when we consider the dimensions of time.

Although the *totum* is considered immobile and atemporal, this cannot be said of the internal fragmentation out of which it is made. The *totum* considered from within moves in time. In this viewing of the *totum humanum* from within, one can distinguish between those who were, those who will be and those who are. We shall reserve the term "to exist" for those who belong to the last category: the *totum* exists in the living. Furthermore, we should add that it exists in succession and is not at all hampered by time. Actually, as far as its unfolding is concerned, time is of its making—or, better still, is of its essence. Time must be defined as that which allows the *totum*, although atemporal as a construct, to move from nonexistence into existence and from existence back into nonexistence. Hence time must be considered as nothing more than a function of distribution. Observation shows how the dimensions of time are closely related, and how through and in them fragments reach "subconsciously" at each other.

1. For one thing, there is no doubt about the impact of the past upon the living. Western man carries within his body and soul the influences of Greek and Roman civilization and of the Judeo-

Christian world vision. But two remarks must clarify the under-standing of this impact. (1) When we say the man of the West is a sum-total of that past, we do not imply that he merely totalizes that past in the sense that his conscious presence constitutes the past as a whole—a meaning which in present-day thought has often been given to the term "to totalize." We claim that although the contribution of the individual is undeniable in keeping that past alive, it can not be forgotten that if he makes the *totum*, the *totum* makes him as well, and that within the *totum* the past is an important dimension. (2) Moreover, in granting the presence of the past within the modern scene, we must stress that the living can be of the past only through being different from that past. The past puts at a distance not merely its own sequel but above all its own corrective or *complement*. The present was already "chosen" not merely as that which is potential within the fabric of bygone times but also as that which, in being what it is, is different from that which was in order that the *totum* as a whole may survive. *Melius is sic esse quam non-esse*, wrote the medieval philosopher; it is better to be such (meaning "only such") than not to be at all. But we shall add that, although one has to be *such* in order to be, in order to be over any length of time, the *totum* itself will replace the *such* by the *so*. Otherwise, in perpetuating a fragmentary and imperfect state, the *totum* would in the long run disappear. An empire subsists by replacing its emperors, but emperors, being what they are, will only uphold the empire by being different.

2. When we say "the future is now," the meaning is even more complex. This proposition does not mean the elimination of the future, which, as such, will always be "elsewhere." Having ex-cluded this rather obvious interpretation, it seems that we can still point to two things. First of all, we must underline the fact that when we state that something is not yet, we clearly imply its ab-sence as visible reality; nevertheless the same words point to the event as coming. We shall call this way of being a potential one, or better still, shall say that the present is merely a repository of the future. The latter statement is broad and general, and for that reason innocuous enough; we shall keep it so until the study of individual freedom allows us to make it more specific. The gen-eration of the living *is* the capsule of what will be, and the future pilot carries within him, at his birth, that which forty years later

will lead to his death and that of the passengers on his plane. Examiners will call this flaw a case of human error, but they should know better, for the flaw was in the captain all the way. It merely went unnoticed.

There is a more incisive way, however, in which the future is now. In Volume I, we discussed the concept of completion "beyond time," calling it immediate and remote completion.[5] This peculiar propensity of the future to reach into the present by way of completive force will appear more clearly as we get a firmer hold on our view of the oneness of the *totum*. The term completion was introduced earlier as that particular quality by which finite X is liable to correct finite Z regardless of time-and-space considerations. Obviously, the very act of correction which "we" discover in the succession of fragments is a complex one. It is fair to say, first of all, that the act of replacing the individual who dies is already one form of correcting a situation, hence of protracting the existence of the *totum*, but this is manifestly insufficient, for it is not enough to replace X: one must also provide for that which, in replacing X, corrects what by hypothesis was missing in X. At this moment, the diversity of the fragments, or what we have called their inequality and uniqueness, provides the solution, for only what is different is liable to correct. Z, therefore, in being different within the limits of the one, is the corrective of X.

Only if we transcend time and view this completion in action will it appear that complementarity is not one of space only, as if the diverse on the horizontal surface of the earth were the only element which results in keeping the *totum* on the move. Actually, the same is true when considered in the succession of time, or what is commonly called history. The diverse in history responds to a need for incessant repair, resulting in an equilibrium called survival. The *totum* survives as a fractured One because the fragments dispersed in time correct one another, and in this incessant correction postpone the entropy of death. Not only does the present at times correct the past, but we can say—what amounts to the same thing—that the future commands a present situation. Let us take the example of Caesar crossing the Rubicon. This action may

---

[5] *The Planetary Man*, Volume I, | pp. 45–46.

appear to be merely the result of the general's own decision, stemming from the victories of his past life and triggered by his ambition to run the nation singlehandedly. This we have no intention to deny. Yet above and beyond all this, there appears the immensity and the power of the Roman Empire, which dictates its beginnings from afar, or better still "calls for" those very beginnings.

We deliberately choose the verb "call for" because it brings to mind a pictorial representation in which one color calls for another, as in a painting of Rembrandt. From the pivotal spot which the Observer occupies, the history of the *totum genus* appears as completed. From there, the *totum genus* appears as a tableau where the diverse is requisite. Yet there the comparison stops, for while in Rembrandt the voluptuous red calls for the pale yellow to bring forth the unparalleled beauty of the canvas, in the mural of world history which "we" at present confront, it is survival not beauty that counts. But survival no less than beauty requires the diverse.

The deeper meaning of the verb which we have used—*to call for*—needs further clarification. It will *not* do to consider this as a mere application of cosmic finality, as if it were predestined from all eternity that a certain act, such as the crossing of the Rubicon by Caesar and his armies, should be only one more step towards the fulfillment of a masterplan devised by a Mastermind and executed over the centuries. The completive action as here described runs in a multilinear direction, since it can be said that a human event posited in the present is indeed exigent of a praxis which will be performed five hundred years from now, but it must be added with equal accuracy that the future and unique event X calls for a present and unique event Y. The complementary moves in different directions, and just as a smaller *totum* (let us call it a *subtotum*) survives through the diversity of its accomplishments, so also the *totum genus* on a much larger scale equilibrates its performance through a variety of human actions resulting in its survival. Obviously, the end does not mean the end of time, as a linear concept of history would lead us to believe. Eschatology, whether Christian or Marxist, sees a falling into place of persons and events towards the progressive achievement of an ultimate End, be that end natural or supernatural. These views make every-

thing instrumental towards that ultimate End, but do not direct
the End itself towards that which has preceded it in time. And
this is where their mistake lies. It is not per se erroneous to construe a vision where an End is reached and to consider the gradual
implementation of human events towards that End, but it is onesided to stress a future as ultimate and the intermediate steps as
only instrumental. The fact is—and this will be stressed in a
forthcoming chapter—that *instrumentality is reversible.* Just as
the crossing of the Rubicon calls for the building of the Roman
Empire, so also the Roman Empire postulates the crossing of the
Rubicon and from afar even commands this action. Looking at it
carefully, we observe that the end is here no less than it will be
later. Once more the vision from the atemporal nowhere shows
this with clarity. Rembrandt makes a masterpiece and through a
harmony of colors keeps the spectator spellbound. It cannot be
said that one shade is more important than another. Likewise, it
appears to the Observer that in the global survival of the *totum
genus humanum* no one individual fragment is superfluous, nor
can any human act be said to be without repercussions. From
afar, considering the *totum* as surviving, we see that what will be
later is instrumental to what is now, no less than what is now is
instrumental to what will be. The suchness X of what-will-be
dictates the suchness Z of what-is. This command from the future
to the present to be such or so is not merely a phenomenological
meaning-giving function, as if in the light of things to come, things
present get their full meaning. In that sense, one could say that
only the reign of Marcus Aurelius, for example, could give the
full meaning to the crossing of the Rubicon several hundred
years before. If Caesar must be viewed together with Marcus
Aurelius to be understood, he must also be so viewed *to be*, for in
the light of the *totum humanum* manipulating the diverse to
achieve its own survival, it can be said that the future ontologically commands the becoming and the being of such or such as past,
just as, in the realm of space, this shade of red requires a coloring
of black velvet to create a harmonious ensemble, and in the
realm of sound, the second movement of Beethoven's *Fifth Symphony* demands and obtains the astonishing overture.

Behind the canvas of the *Night Watch* stands the artist master-
fully distributing shades and colors. Behind the *Fifth Symphony*

stands the composer building up notes in succession and achieving "the sound that shouts for mastery." Who is the Rembrandt or the Beethoven when the masterpiece is the *totum humanum* and its expansion through time and space? There is only one answer: the *totum* as one yet subconscious.

Before commenting upon our answer, let me make clear that *subconscious* is a term which by its very nature presumes the conscious individual. The subconscious is the reality which affects the human individual but of which he is not himself conscious. The *totum* itself is not unconscious: the *totum* knows, but its members taken individually are unaware of that which moves them. One is unaware *qua* fragment, yet one acts in line with the forces within the *totum* without knowing them. Hence the ambiguity of our statement used above: the *totum humanum* is one yet subconscious. In fact, the *totum* can only be considered subconscious when considered as that which underlies individual consciousness; yet the same *totum* considered as the sum-total of the many individuals is far from ignorant. It knows.

We should add that the *totum* as subconscious reality is not passive but, on the contrary, is very active, since it is through the creation of the diverse and the fragmentary in succession that it achieves an incessant repair and offsets the menace of death and extinction. Individual consciousness is the subconscious emerging from the darkness into the light. This event, which takes place incessantly, with the appearance of every new man, does not cancel the subconscious, which in its oneness underlies the dimensions of past, present and future. The subconscious does not belong to one dimension only. It reaches from the past into the present, carrying with it the influence of times past. It is the *totum* and has the omniscience of the *totum*, since with and in the *totum* it shares its omnitemporality: it reaches into the future no less than into the past and from afar shapes the present as that which someday will be the complement of things to be. It accepts the deficiency of the present, knowing that some future event will correct it. Although its sagacity by far transcends all individual calculation, we see in the individual man signs of its presence. A great amount of planning takes place in each of us unconsciously: this planning is directed towards a future which we ignore in our conscious life. More than anything else, the wise man is the one

who knows what will be, although he does not know it consciously
and cannot rationally motivate his attitude. Wisdom is not always
articulated: it lacks a rational defense in the present instant, but it
has a knowledge and an experience hidden in the depth of the subconscious. Yet whatever may be its privileges at times, the in
dividual consciousness, to the extent that it brings the subconscious
to the surface, remains itself caught in the instant.

It can now be seen how individuals are opposed to each other on
the surface only, for in fact they are rooted in the oneness of the
subconscious. We shall no longer say *ego cogito*—I think—as
if this were a totally solitary performance, but *totum cogitat per
me*—the *totum* thinks through me. Through individuals the *totum*
absorbs knowledge of this cosmos (the inorganic) and of its
content (the organic). This knowledge contains a form of truth
which we have previously called generic truth, the truth of the
totum genus humanum as such. The Cartesian discovery of the self
as an unshakable rock was no doubt an important one. Now, how
ever, from the point of view of the Observer, it appears that the
rock is part of the mountain and that the individual self is engulfed in the *totum humanum*. Individual man is no longer absolute center. He is ex-centric. In abandoning Descartes, we have
said farewell to the obsession of the central. Our observation turns
instead to the theme of Pascal and sees the individual man as
existing from *then* to *then* "the short duration of my life absorbed
in an eternity which precedes it and follows it. . . ." and from *here*
to *here* ". . . the small space which I fill . . . lost in the infinite
immensity of spaces which I ignore and which ignore me. . . ."[6]
Fragments are finite and caught in the One. In this one and underlying reality minds meet beyond time and space, unaware of their
encounter. Someday, perhaps, science will illuminate this obscure
abyss and show how individual X living in the present must be
seen as the sequel and corrective of individual Z who is no longer,
and how individual X is himself instrumental towards a future
as yet unfulfilled. It is in the oneness of the subconscious that one
must look for an explanation of the strange affinity between people who have met only once and may never meet again. There remains between them a silent form of communication. The reason

---

[6] Pascal, *Pensées*, ed. Brun-   schvicg, no. 205.

for this strange and at times romantic intertwining may be found in a past which has affected both or in a present of mutual completion (which never was) or in a future where their descendants will meet. We do not know this with certainty, but there is no reason to believe that one will never know.

From an atemporal and aspatial point of view, if we accept the *totum*, the subconscious is always conscious somewhere, or better still, what is subconscious for one has sometime and somewhere emerged unto consciousness. It is only fair to conclude that my ignorance is another man's knowledge, and in reverse, that my vision, clear as the day for me, may be totally ignored by my fellow man. All this was already implied in our examination of the concept of angular vision discussed in Volume I.[7] Our present speculations upon the hidden or subconscious merely confirm the conclusions reached before.

Dialectic and the One

How can dialectic—a term at present very much in vogue among existential phenomenologists as well as among Marxists—be compared to the interlocking of parts within the One? Is there any connection between dialectic and the conclusions reached so far in this chapter? Does the concept of dialectic present us with the basic structure of growth and change?

Dialectic in its elemental fulfillment presumes a relation, be it a

---

[7] Chapter 3. The problem of whether or not the human *totum* as a sum-total is in fact "more" than the addition of its parts must, in the opinion of this writer, be answered as follows. The *totum* is a sum-total of the diverse, indeed, but the working together of the individuals must be viewed as that which transcends the dimensions of time and space. It is to the extent that the parts operate collectively, and in this cooperation break spatial and temporal barriers, that we can speak of the beginning of the "spirit." Spirit must not be considered as a dimension which is totally alien from matter, but merely as that which although organic, hence engulfed in the matter, is obtained through the collaboration of minds. To the extent that the individual cooperates, he achieves the spiritual. The self-forgetting member of the *totum* spiritualizes. This "spiritual" achievement is that by which and through which the *totum* is "more" than the addition of its parts.

relation from man to matter, or from man to man, or from man to group. The way in which this relation works is a matter of debate and does not at present concern us. What clearly appears, though, is that a relation between different entities implies communicability of the entities which are related. The nature of this communication may be extremely diverse, but it must be there if one can speak of dialectic at all. It is precisely at this point that the concept of the One presents itself as the infrastructure of dialectic. Before all dialectic, there is the One. Since we are concerned here with the living, we can make the further qualification that before any dialectic there is the one *totum humanum*, the parts of which are pre-ontologically structured for communication. It is only because there is by way of ontological priority a *totum*, the parts of which are able to communicate and thus constitute its oneness, that we can speak of dialectic.

We can add that in line with what we have observed so far, wherever a form of "dialectic" takes place among the constitutive parts of the One, the communication which takes place is one of completion. "Dialectic" must be seen as a corrective force which by nature is atemporal and which through the manipulation of the diverse keeps the whole alive. It cannot be demonstrated that this tension among two parts results *necessarily* in the formation of a third element which has commonly been called a synthesis, since survival or the mere fact of being does not per se call for a merging of *A* and *B*. It calls for an equilibrium, which results from the corrective impact of different parts. It neither includes nor excludes dialectic as the movement which unavoidably ends up in a synthesis.

By this no claim is made that nothing new is ever born. But the claim is made that the new coming into existence must not necessarily nor exclusively be brought into relation with its antecedent. It may very well be considered an alteration of a thesis or of an antithesis—this we shall neither affirm nor deny—but we should keep in mind that the new is more than a synthesis of thesis and antithesis, for it is above all, when viewed instrumentally within the ensemble of the *totum*, a corrective which operates as such at a distance, whether in the past or in the future. The new reaches out in a multilinear direction, and in so doing, keeps alive the *totum* of which it is a part.

It follows naturally that the element of negation, so heavily stressed in the exercise of dialectic, is of lesser importance in our way of presenting things. Once completion of the diverse within the One is at work, parts behave like the pieces of a puzzle. They complete, rather than negate, one another. Nothing is really negated, since nothing is really dialectically defeated. In accepting this internal balance as a warrant of survival, the constitutive elements play a part, each of them, since each of them is instrumental for the survival of the *totum* and appears as a positive factor in its welfare. Those who see reality as structured in dialectical terms have introduced this semantics of "negation" that not only emphasizes the differences which exists among the parts—most certainly an observable phenomenon—but also their alleged opposition. With "to negate" a term of combat has been chosen: the very use of the term promotes the sense of separation. Yet, there never is total separation between opponents. Dialectic is peripheral and in no way disturbs the monism of the *totum*. The One is disturbed neither by the plural nor by the introduction of the new. The latter is in its very being something positive, a new expression of the *totum*. The term "negation" is misleading, then, for plurality forms the essence of a fractured *totum* and can only be viewed in a positive light.

The use of the term "to negate" comes from the fact that the individual, in and because of his own individuality and his sense of separation from others (which is more apparent than real), is inclined to use a terminology which stresses division rather than oneness. The individual at times feels his own state as monadic, and as a result uses a semantics of forcible separation for any activity performed by man, whether this activity is directed towards another man or not. To call the cutting of a branch from a tree for the purpose of making a walking stick an "act of negation" is of course one way of looking at it, yet the cutting of a new cane may also be viewed as a positive action. I once knew an eighty-year-old shepherd who, while watching his sheep in the *compagna romana*, spent the hours slowly and carefully carving walking sticks out of pinewood. Each cane was a small masterpiece. It was a new creation, for which the term "negation" would have been less suitable.

One may wonder whether the obsession with a semantics of

negation does not reflect in man the ordeal he went through as a newborn infant. Yet even that is a question. Must the cutting of the umbilical cord, which made him truly an individual, be viewed as a separation? To remove itself from the tree does not make the seed something independent, for—as we stated at the beginning of this chapter—one who walks away from the tree still carries the tree within him. No one can completely escape from the seed that was his beginning and is still his now.

To conclude, we shall not deny the value of dialectic to explain the relation of man to man, man to group, nor man to matter, but in the light of the principles here defended, it becomes apparent that dialectic is an interplay of parts and that it can in no way break up the One nor the communication which is the mark of the One. Between foes of any sort communication is always possible because they are themselves part of the One.

Pain as Symptom of Belonging to the One

IF communication between parts is the basis of the One, diverse forms of communication will result in diverse forms of the One. "We" the dead, the living and the unborn, bound together in the One and each fulfilling a function of completion in the global survival of the *totum*, are constitutive of the *totum humanum*. But there is also a oneness of the *living* only. The enclosure of the living *totum* is not the same as the enclosure which contains all the fragments. Although the dead still belong to the *totum* as a construct, they are no longer in touch with the living on a conscious level. Death is a decrease in communication. The function of the deceased is real and it is also "present," as we have already noted, but we have no cogent way of demonstrating that they are the way we are. Although it would be most fitting, in the philosophical vision here developed, to be able to say that the *totum humanum* being one, all its parts, dead or alive, are interrelated, and that they are so in a conscious way, there is no conclusive evidence to corroborate this point of view. The living remember the dead and carry them in their consciousness. We do not know with certainty whether the dead remember us. It would be more rewarding, therefore, to turn aside from problems of immortality and instead to focus upon the living *totum,* a dimension that we can observe. There we observe a phenomenon that is one of a pending separation of the individual from the *totum* and is at the same time a sign of his belonging. This is the phenomenon of *pain.*

In examining pain, we shall do so from the outside; we shall see it as an external percept and not make use of introspection to discover its nature or what it denotes.

When looked upon in this way, pain appears as that which is unwanted. This is obvious in the case of suffering men. But how can it appear as unwanted unless the sufferer is also aware of that which is desirable and wanted? The anomaly of pain can only reveal itself through the implicit awareness of the normal state of affairs. And of this normal state of affairs, one of health or the absence of pain, the individual in pain can only be aware through the fact that he is in touch with the *totum,* which is by definition healthy. The sufferer knows what he is missing because he is related to the others who have what he does not have. When in pain, he becomes aware of what the others are in not being what they are, but he does so only because in some way he is bound to the others. The tie with the *totum* lies at the origin of pain. Man feels pain because he is a fragment. If there were a living being which was not a fragment, it would never know the malaise of pain.

One may wonder, of course, whether being a unique fragment, an individual has not the right to be different. He undoubtedly does have that right, but only within certain limits. Beyond a certain point, to be "different" becomes intolerable. Pain signifies the "intolerable limit." And in doing that, it also shows the power of the bonds whereby we belong.

If we look more closely at this belonging that is revealed through pain, we observe that it is the sort of belonging which is in danger of being disrupted. Although death, or separation from the living, can in no way be considered a necessary issue of pain, it must be viewed as a possibility. Pain is the red light, the signal of the abnormal. Death is the abnormal par excellence, it is the breaking point—or, more precisely, the point of no return. It is probable that the instant of death, or radical separation from the living *totum,* includes a pain that is maximal but of short duration.

Our speculation is strikingly confirmed when we observe moral pain. We shall call moral pain a malaise which cannot be easily located in the organism. In most cases, it involves a belonging which is either disrupted or in danger of being disrupted. It does not necessarily involve total separation or death. The immigrant suffers, as does the divorced man or woman, the orphan and the prisoner. The last-mentioned suffers less from the quality of the food and surroundings than he does from being closed in, or deprived of communication. Separation is the epitome of suffering for the child. Since the family is the most natural *totum* we know so far, its absence or disintegration is a great cause of pain. Moral pain in most cases (though not in all) is symptomatic of separation from the One and demonstrates the power exercised by the One—whether the family, the school, or the nation—once communication has set in and made the One what it is.

What has been said about pain cannot be said equally about pleasure. Pleasure does not, like pain, posit me as fragment, nor does it in the same way point towards the *totum*, because it does not point at an "absence of. . . ." The lack of comformity with the others which is the essence of pain and indicates our belonging is not felt in the movement of pleasure. Pleasure is absorbed in the self, and it indicates our dependence only to the extent that the other is instrumental to the pleasure. This makes it clear why the young and the healthy do not fear death: they lack the awareness of retention within the *totum* through pain. The young do not feel their body as a suffering body—that is, something which is out of place within the full health of the *totum*. Yet, the fact that they feel that vigorous independence does not of itself make the young independent. No less than the old and the sick, they are held within the confines of the *totum humanum*. Only through the absence of health does dependency in its ontological depth come to the fore—I am not like the others—and with it the painful sense of belonging.

Although pleasure does not denote the oneness of the *totum* with the same force as pain, its importance should not be denied. It is very well possible that pleasure may not be identical with happiness, and Aristotle may be right in not giving it this status of importance and dignity. We have no intention of discussing this here. However, if instead of asking what the function of pleasure is, we reverse the question and ask whether the *totum* of the living will function if pleasure is denied, the answer seems to be in the negative. A world without pleasure would immobilize the activity of its members and reduce man to a plant, the only form of life we know where pleasure is absent. Pleasure is definitely the impelling force, if not the aim, of life. Pleasure is instrumental in the hands of the *totum* as a means of achievement, and most people will agree that its highest form is the pleasure of creation in some way or another. The *totum* itself is more than pleasure, of course, but looking at it from afar, the Observer seems to see that the myriad instants of pleasure give the individual fragment the illusion that such activities are engaged in for their own sake, while in fact these moments are instrumental. There is an incessant delusion: the individual takes for aim what in essence is only means. For the *totum* which wants to be and to survive, the pleasure of the individual is instrumental. It gives the impulse to action, but its results transcend the moment.

Creation is often, though not always, connected with pleasure. Its product transcends the moment, whether the creation is biological or artistic. Not only are both concerned with the production of the "new," but they also are in many cases accompanied by a certain amount of self-forgetting. Paradoxically, in this very oblivion of the self, something new is conceived. The pleasure of creation is the loss of the self and the involvement with a future conceived in that very instant, a future which is "not-I." Ecstasy results in the birth of the new. Such is the will of the *totum*, or what is commonly called instinct. One is carried away, yet Life goes on anonymously. This anonymity of Life is nothing but the *totum* erasing the individual self. Pleasure at its highest, as is also true of intense pain, brings individual man to the brink of the unconscious. During moments of the most acute pain or pleasure, the self as an independent entity is submerged in the *totum*, which, as we already know, constitutes for him the unconscious in depth.

From all this it follows that pain and pleasure, each in its own way, attest to the great link with the totality of the *we*. Pain demonstrates the participation in a more unequivocal way than pleasure, as we have seen, but if pleasure does not at first sight have the same cogent force, it nevertheless evokes an awareness of the *totum* in two ways: first, when through excess it becomes pain, it denotes the *totum* by indirection; and, second, when carried into ecstasy, it loses itself in the undifferentiated *totum*.

When we consider the *totum* as an organic whole, we cannot

help discovering that pain and pleasure run through it both as warning and as inducement. The *totum* is doubtless more than a mass of suffering humanity or a hunting ground of pleasure—this is a rhetoric which cannot be sustained—yet it is no less certain that both feelings pervade it. Men run away from pain incessantly, just as surely as they rush into pleasure wherever they can. If one were to close the circle and consider the *totum* as a container, the immense mobility of its inner constituents would appear to take two directions: one, away from pain; and the other, with no less vigor, towards the rare moments of pleasure. For better or for worse, the *totum humanum* is a closed container indeed. We observe a universal play of pain and pleasure, keeping the *totum* on the alert, and at the same time denoting the compact structure of the whole. There is no exit except through death.

3

The *Totum* and the Perfect

The Perfect Technician and the Imperfect Man

THE interlocking of the diverse is one of the most impressive sights that is offered to the Observer as he contemplates the ontological ensemble of the *totum* in its monistic structure and its internal articulation. There is joy in the contemplation of the diverse. And there is joy because the encounter of parts completing one another appears as that which henceforth shall be called *perfection.*

The word *perfect* derives from the Latin verb *perficere*, denoting "that which is achieved." Derivatively, yet most frequently, the term is used to indicate that which is capable of achieving its end. Thus a perfect tool is a tool which is capable of accomplishing that for which it was made. In this sense Aristotle considered perfection to be an attribute of certain things.[1] The more restricted the end, the easier it is to have a *perfect* tool: it is a far simpler task to make a perfect hammer than to make a perfect missile.

Using the term "perfect" in the same sense, we can also speak of a perfect technician when he is capable of accomplishing the particular job which he sets out to do. We stress the term *particular,* for it clearly denotes that the aim of the technician is limited: his aim is to do this and to do this only. When observed carefully, the limitation appears to lie in the origin, and in the action itself as a result. Repairman *X* is by his very skill limited to do this,

---

[1] *Metaphysics,* 1021 b.

and only this, and as a result he has only this to do. And yet notwithstanding this obvious limitation, we call him *perfect*. To be
exact, in calling Peter a perfect repairman, we implicitly want to
make it clear that perfection is restricted to Peter as repairman,
but from the point of view of the Observer, who views the ensemble
and sees the function of Peter within this diversified ensemble, the
job, however perfect, appears to be a limited part. However skilled
he might be, he is really *sub specie totius*—viewed from the stand-
point of the *totum*—a very narrow kind of being. For notwithstanding his qualifications, he appears to "us" as one who is
deficient in many ways.

Yet this study is not so much concerned with the "perfection"
or imperfection of the technician who is only a technician as it is
with the qualities of a different nature which individual men can
discover in one another. These qualities, for want of a different
term, we shall call *moral*, although this does not imply that at
this stage a definite meaning can already be given to the word.
"Moral" as we use it here simply denotes the behavior of men to
the extent that it is fitting or not fitting within a certain *totum*. We
shall call a behavior "moral" when as a result of that behavior
the life activity of the *totum* runs smoothly.

If we look closely at the meaning of the term "fitting," we see
that it signifies to be different in structure in such a way that what
is lacking in one part is present in another, with the result that
because of this, a certain function can be accomplished perfectly.
Taking up our post of Observer and looking down upon the diversified expanse of the *totum humanum*, we notice that the *totum*
has built-in the diversity of the fragments, together with their
capacity for mutual completion. (We shall later explore the question of whether even the rebel must not be seen as part of the
diversity.) It is this diversity of the *totum* in its ontological depth
and the interlocking of the parts which entitles us to consider the
totum as perfect. The *totum* is perfect because it is diverse and
being diverse, generates within itself its own corrective. All this
can be put more briefly: A totality is perfect when it provides
its counterpart within itself. This is what the diversity *within* is
for: it provides a counterpart.

We shall not claim that moral and perfect are interchangeable
terms, but it may appear later that the morality of the parts pre-

sumes the smooth interlocking of the diverse within the oneness of the *totum*.

One point which needs clarification with regard to the diverse in the realm of human behavior is that this behavior has a physical ground. There is a close connection between the physical makeup of the individual and his behavior. How close it is, is still a mystery. Science has not been able to resolve with sufficient precision the influence of heredity and environment respectively on the molding of the physical constitution, or the relation between a man's physique and his conduct.[2] A healthy, well-nourished kind of person may very well be less hostile and less resentful than an individual who through illness and undernourishment bears suffering within his own body and as a consequence hates not only himself but society as well. Psychosomatic studies lead us to the conclusion that the individual lives his body, and that in living his body he creates his character as a manifestation of that peculiar and unique way of living his body, differing from individual to individual.

At this point we face serious opposition coming from the philosophical tradition which propounds a dichotomy within man him-

---

[2] This is not to deny freedom, the nature of which will be examined later. For the moment we merely want to stress the unbreakable link between a certain physique and a certain behavior. How the actions of a man proceed from his being is a most complex question. In the opinion of this writer the traditional answer—*operari sequitur esse* ("as a being is, so it acts")—should be reversed and understood contrarywise: individual man in order to survive proceeds toward that which he is not rather than toward that which he is. His conduct is a protection, that is, it is a movement toward the not-himself, which results in an exchange, an exchange which is necessary to save him. Need is an ontological concomitant of the fragment qua fragment. It is not a pathological deficiency but an essential qualification of all being which is such or so. This need in its uniqueness dictates conduct. This conduct, which in later pages we shall call vocation, must be seen not merely as a contribution to the *totum* but also as the fulfillment of a need, hence as individual self-protection. Individual X, therefore, will not act X-wise but rather Z-wise in a never-ending attempt to survive and to avoid onesidedness. (Death is onesidedness in the extreme.) Shall we say, then, that a most neatly structured individual (within) will take refuge in some poetic occupation (without), or that a chaotic type will escape into a career with more logical and mathematical demands? Most probably.

self. Such a position presumes a natural split between matter and "spirit," at the same time presenting matter, or the body, as the recalcitrant element in man and spirit, or the soul, as the element which is in charge of disciplining matter. That all this is done on theological grounds is obvious. For centuries it has been a handy semantics for the castigation of the bad people—those who give in to their bodily lusts—and the reward of the good, or those who keep their impulses in check. This makes us wonder whether the ethical purpose did not in some partial way create the metaphysics. Could it not be that God has made individual man one, and that man himself has broken up this God-given unity? At times philosophers and theologians invent two to explain one. But if there is no more cogent argument for the dichotomy of body and soul than the urgent need to bury the mortal remains and to place the immortal element in heaven, we shall not be persuaded to abandon our contention that the individual merely is and lives, and being such, lives such, or in being so, lives so.

If individual man is a unity in his "suchness," it naturally follows that he does not easily alter his fundamental structure. Changes in conduct or "conversions" do occur. Yet where they do, they will never be found to be an all-out creation of the new, lacking all connection with the past. Sartre's claim that freedom is ablaze with incessant creation simply cannot be defended. It seems more to the point to recall Nietzsche's description of moral qualities as lying buried in the "granite of the soul," for the metaphor not only eliminates the dualism but also beautifully emphasizes the fact that the intimate structure of the unique is as solid as stone. If moral qualities can be altered, they evolve slowly. They should never be pictured as detached from their ground, which is indeed the rock, the physical constitution, unique and such.

Examples of famous conversions might be adduced to argue that on the contrary, a total break with the past is possible. Augustine himself might be cited as one who changed in a flashing moment of insight from a profligate to a saint. It will appear to any attentive reader of the *Confessions*, however, that Augustine's fundamental nature didn't really change on that momentous day in Cassiciacum. He was and remained the same man, with a tremendous sensibility, a deep sense of beauty, an unremitting passion. It was only the object of his love that changed: God, and God in Christ, replaced women. In the figure of Christ, Augustine discovered beauty, not merely a moral beauty but also an intellectual splendor. To the errant lover turned believer, Christ appeared extraordinarily beautiful: "He is beautiful in heaven and on earth, beautiful in the womb, and in the arms of his parents; beautiful when he performs miracles and when he offers himself to the scourge; beautiful when he lays down his life and when he takes it up again; beautiful on the wood of the cross, beautiful in the tomb, beautiful in heaven. Understand the canticle with the mind, and may the infirmity of the flesh not turn your eyes away from the splendor of his beauty." Augustine was first, foremost and always a lover; if he had sublimated his sensuality, he had hardly transformed the texture of his soul, whatever he himself thought.

Replacement of the fragment, then, is and remains the instrument of alteration of the whole. One does not so much change the individual's character as replace him. Directors and administrators know very well that upon the discovery of certain limitations in an employee it is useless to lose much time in giving advice or to nurture grandiose hopes for improvement. The individual in question is simply replaced. In doing so, those who are in charge merely follow the age-old pattern of the *totum*, which replaces through the acts of procreation those who pass away—the difference being, of course, that replacement of the living by the living does not require the death of the former occupant of the job, but only the reappointment of men into jobs to which they will be better *fitted*. But the two movements of replacement have something in common, since both show that the structure of the human *totum* is fractured no less in time than in space, and that in time one is redeemed by one's children, while in space, one is redeemed by one's fellow men.

In conclusion we shall say that individual man is *atomos*, or undivided fragment, as we have previously defined him, that this atomos is such or so, and that as a result his behavior is such or so. The ontologically diverse may very well be the ground of moral diversity. If we have observed in previous studies the *totum* and its unequal fragmentation, with a resulting ontological inequality, "we" look once more and, as Observer, note that the diversity is reflected in the behavior of men, hence in the qualities or moral "suchness" *with which they approach one another.*

The Interweaving of Qualities

EVERYONE has observed how men tend to be humble or proud, aggressive or peaceful, hesitant or decided, prudent or imprudent, temperate or intemperate, chaste or erotic, selfish or charitable. Though these traits may be mixed or even concealed in some men, the most memorable human beings are those in whom some traits are predominant. The sight of this diversity from afar is a pleasing one: we think of Bruegel's magnificent tableaux in which every form of humanity is striding or stumbling by, and suspending any judgment of "sin" or "sinfulness," we love them all. Let us look, for example, at the painting entitled *The Combat between Carnival and Lent.* It is the tableau of a town fair, with participants of every size, age and occupation involved. The variety is dazzling: the king of the carnival perched on a barrel; a musician striding along with his violin; Flemish wives baking pancakes, spilling out of the church portals; monks strolling in the background. All is action. While other Flemish painters were still occupied with staid poses—portraits or religious themes—Bruegel, influenced no doubt by his predecessor Bosch, developed a technique whereby, bent over a town as the Observer over the *totum,* he discovered people just as they were, in their most natural poses. The natural at times looks foolish, and if it could be said that folly is pervasive, it could be added that in some ways it is the symbol of the *one* holding the *diverse* together. Bruegel's colors further enhance the sense of unity: they are brilliant and variegated, but in the center an island of light dominates and unifies the picture, spreading out towards a darkish brown on the edges. It is no wonder that one critic calls the painting a *summa*,[3] for it is a pictorial *totum* of humanity, where the universal (if it may be so called) is visual and additive and propounds the diverse within the one. One does not condemn, one observes. At times, it is true, Bruegel's own symbolism will condemn, as in his painting *The Tower of*

---

[3] Robert Delevoy, *Bruegel* (Ge- | neva: Skira, 1959), p. 53.

Babel, where he shows how the attempt to build a tower reaching to heaven is miraculously prevented by the confusion of languages. Too extreme a diversity hampers achievement, and vanity is punished. Bruegel can be a caustic, if always a loving, observer.

The vision of the Observer extends beyond the scope of the painter, for it goes beyond the mere sense percept, seeing more than the eye sees. He relates the variety of human behavior to the ontological diversity from which it originates. Only on the basis of the one *totum* ontologically fractured can the manifold of human qualities be understood. And in doing this, as he should, the philosopher-Observer already reaches beyond the scope of the painter. Since no canvas can represent the myriad ways of human conduct, the painter's attempt remains limited. The vision of the philosopher, if less incisive than the colorful work of the artist, confronts a diversity in oneness that is endless. The range of the qualities is infinite because there is no limit to the ontological substratum, or fractured *totum,* which is the foundation of human virtues and vices.

Once the individual behavior comes to the surface and manifests itself in a particular way, it "calls for" an opponent. Qualification *A* will encounter qualification *B,* which at first glance may appear to be its opposite: humility and pride (in the other man), charity and egoism. This "calling for an opponent" must not be understood in a Hegelian sense—a thesis looking for its antithesis as the first step towards a dialectical movement; it must be seen, rather, as the result of the elemental structure of the One distributing its parts and endowing them with diverse qualities. Once the parts are *there* with their qualifications, they will indeed appear as "opposed,"[4] but they will also appear as incomplete:

---

[4] In claiming that the parts appear as opposed, the Observer uses a term which is ambiguous to say the least. The term *opposition* strictly speaking signifies the attitude (or possible attitude) of fragment *versus* fragment, but it is an attitude seen by the fragment whether that fragment is involved or not. From the point of view of the Observer, who is uninvolved and looks at the disparity of fragments from above, it will appear that there is no opposition, but merely diversity. In using the term "opposition," as is done frequently in this study, I would like it to be known that the Observer does not recognize this attitude in anyone who wants to take the stand of the *totum* or of the Observer.

men as fragments call for one another, and one kind of human behavior needs another kind of human behavior in order to be completed and understood. The following examples will, hopefully, clarify this point.

The humble man keeps his rank in word and deed: he is *humilis* —or, as the Latin word signifies, keeps himself close to the earth (*humus*). But humility takes shape only in the wake of what, again in Latin, is called *superbia*, a term for the attitude of the arrogant man, who considers himself above (*super*) others. Humility and pride are closely related. Not only do they both originate in the depth of the *totum*—as we noticed above—but it also appears that the one illuminates the other. The ontologically diverse becomes intelligible only through its being diverse. The signifying power of the human mind, and of the language itself speaking through the human mind, can attribute meaning and intelligibility only through the different. It is not essential that this different person or thing be actually present or fulfilled—the proud man need not be *there* for me to understand the humble man—but he must be *there* as *potential*. Hence we can say that as soon as there is the one, there is the other, whether as actual or as possible phenomenon.

This "positing" of the opponent has actually a corrective function. Humble men alone do not produce the fullness of life in the *totum*: they are there to serve as an amendment of the proud and to be corrected in turn in their own limitation. This interlinking with one another is not always fulfilled in a perceptible way, since it often has an atemporal character. Although plunged into a space-and-time dimension on Bruegel's canvas, it reaches beyond the here and the now in reality. In some invisible and remote way one quality inclines towards its counterpart in order to create it, and in creating it, to restrain it. The one *totum* needs the diverse in order to be.

We see a similar phenomenon in observing the charitable and the egotistical man. We again forsake the abstract in favor of observing the concrete tableau of acting men, who in a variegated way display charity or the lack of it. It will appear that those we call patient and charitable are possible because others are harsh and selfish. Egoism calls for the birth of the forgiving man. (Egoism is viewed here not with any moral judgment in mind but

merely as a commitment like any other.) The one gives the other
its origin; but, strangely enough, in the act of creating one another, they attempt to resist one another as well. It is of no importance to "us" that they repel one another—as very often may be
the case; what matters to the Observer of the balanced *totum* is
that within its diversified composition, there is the "one" when
there is or would be the "other."

The objection could be made at this point that charity does not
always counteract selfishness but at times is lavished upon other
charitable people. Nothing could be more true. But this does not
contradict our point, for the charitable deed is defined not by what
the receiver is but by what he could be, and also not by what the
giver is but by what he could be. The deeper meaning of the act of
charity must be sought in the fact that man is not a machine, that
he does not merely hand out an object to another machine, like a
robot in a factory. This reaching out from one machine to another
is not charity. Charity comes into being only when the handing out
of the object takes place between fragments of the human *totum*,
fragments which are living, free and responsible—bandaging the
wounds of others and helping those who suffer, although they
could, conversely, inflict wounds or refuse to help. It is upon this
possibility of proffering or refusing help that the concept of charity rests. The charitable deed is such because it could equally well
not be in the agent, or (and) it could also not be in the receiver.
Its appearance therefore is a correction at work towards what is or
could be selfish in the agent or in the receiver. Vice and virtue
need one another not necessarily as actual and existential fact, but
at least as potential counter-tools of fulfillment. As in the example
of pride and humility, we observe an incessant correction at work.
The act of charity, or better still the act of forgiving, is the eternal
corrective of the *totum* and its way of survival. One thing is clear.
Qualities have no complete meaning in isolation but can only be
grasped when viewed in their mutual connection. If I seem to
belabor the point, it is because not enough attention is commonly
paid to this link, and qualities are treated *as if* they were independent entities.

Such, then, is the world of men. It is a world of diversified
behavior which appears to us under the aspect of qualities (good
or bad we do not as yet know)—as the unavoidable concomitant

of the parts and of the way they relate. Clearly, only when there is a multiplicity of parts within the one *totum* can we speak of "qualities." This diversification is not limited merely to those qualities which are opposed to one another, as are pride and humility. They can be diversified without being mutually exclusive —for example, humility and temperance. If they appear as mutually exclusive, however, such as humility and the lack of humility, the opposition, impossible within one individual, will not be destructive when fulfilled in two different individuals. The two, in being diverse, create a tension, but this tension is absorbed by the *totum* or collective, which in this very way finds its balance. Balance here, as in the sphere of noesis, results from part meeting part in an encounter of mutual completion, regardless of the fact that this mutual completion is not felt or sought as such by the individual man himself.[5]

One thing appears from the foregoing discussion, and that is that diversity is not composed merely of "virtuous" deeds. It clearly follows that sin, or what is commonly called sin—we shall define its nature later—is no less part of a world structure than virtue. One virtue is built upon its opposite, and this opposite is at times embedded in the context of sin.

This does not lead us to the claim that in view of the necessary and fruitful tension between sin and sanctity, sin should be committed, any more than the claim that the poor will be always with us is a plea for poverty. We merely state the fact that in a human world, sin *will* be committed, and although we might wish that there would be no poor, the fact is "that there will always be poor"; so, too, there will always be sinners. This simply *is* the composition of a fractured *totum* and of the mutual exigency of its parts in a way which is both ontological and semantic.

Our description of a variegated world has not yet evaluated its activity in terms of good and evil. The presentation has been pre-ethical in character. If the terms "virtue" and "vice" have been used in the previous pages, it was for want of a better semantics, and I pointedly refrained from giving them a moral connotation. This abstention cannot, of course, be prolonged indefinitely, unless

---

[5] For application of mutual completion in the realm of knowledge or noesis, see above, Vol. I, chapter 2.

we wish to be merely descriptive and stop with the view of the *totum humanum* as a cluster, with an interdependency of parts within. The difficulty with the use of "virtue" and "vice" in a "pure" description indicates that we will have to catch up with our terms and indeed enter a domain where certain acts are either good or bad. We are not there yet, although even now, prematurely, terms are used which belong to an area of normative ethics. Whatever may be the norm later formulated to distinguish what is good and what is bad, we can see in advance that the Aristotelian position of virtue, with its *via media*—the golden mean—is unacceptable.

The Failure of Aristotle's Golden Mean

VIRTUE is defined by Aristotle, as a habit which completes our rational faculties and inclines them towards the good. Virtues are —so we are told—acquired by practice. Just as we become lyre players by playing the lyre, so also we become just by doing just acts and temperate by performing temperate acts.[6] Aristotle's metaphor of the lyre players is too beautiful to omit: it has both simplicity and cogency.

From then on, however, the Stagyrite moves on less solid ground. Having attempted to show that it is in the nature of things to be destroyed by defect and excess, he concludes that they are preserved by the mean.[7] What is proportioned ($\sigma \upsilon \mu \mu \epsilon \tau \rho o \nu$) is salutary, and thus it is precisely the art of avoiding extremes which makes for virtue. This position constitutes the golden mean. Aristotle is now ready for a new and more elaborate definition of virtue: it is a state of character, concerned with choice, lying in a mean—i.e., the mean relative to us—this being determined by a rational principle, itself determined by a man of practical wisdom.[8]

A careful reading of the definition shows that the ultimate judge is the prudent or wise man, hence that ethics is dependent upon reason. It is also made clear that this middle position is an excel-

---

[6] *Nic. Ethics*, 1103 a.
[7] *Ibid.*, 1104 a 20.

[8] *Ibid.*, 1107 a.

lent position, hence a summit: *akrotes* (ἀκροτης).[9] Some actions obviously do not need a mean, since they are always evil—such are theft and adultery. We are also told that the mean must be understood as "relative to us," hence that what may be right for one, e.g. in the amount of food, may not be right for another.

Is Aristotle now satisfied? Obviously not, for he continues to correct his theory and by his incessant retouching betrays his dissatisfaction with it. Towards the end of the *Nicomachean Ethics*, he confesses that moral judgment is something extremely difficult, something that is partly felt and partly rational. It is something singular; and more often than not, individual intuition counts more than calculation and reflection. "To strike the mean is difficult in the extreme."[10] The truth of the matter is that in the latter part of his presentation Aristotle is gradually tearing down the whole construct, thereby implicitly agreeing that the mean as a summit of excellence or perfection is not to be found.

Aristotle's approach in the theory of the mean can be linked to other areas of his thought, as, for example, his presentation of the class or category as that logical entity of which one becomes part to the extent that one has something in common with other members of the same class. The Aristotelian category as discussed in the *Logic* does not view man as a unique and irreplaceable existent but presents him in the clear-cut concept of a rational animal. This fits every man and all men. Man as rational animal is a universal, and is as such nonexistent in reality. What is thus presented as an abstraction may not always be easy to realize, but at least it makes possible the portrayal of the ideal man, although this man is never involved in the complexities of lived experience.

The theory of the mean is a similar experience. It works in the abstract—that is, it is easy to say in theory how one should be neither a coward nor act rashly, and that courage is the right attitude because it is the one preserved by the mean; but one soon discovers in practice that the realization does not fit the dream. And it does not do so because the individual existent is infinitely more complex than is his abstract definition. Man must be seen in the concrete; he cannot be detached from his existence.

Although Aristotle did not overlook the social element in man—

---

[9] *Ibid.*, 1107 a, 2–7.   [10] *Ibid.*, 1109 b, 21.

indeed, he wrote extremely pertinent commentaries on man as a political animal—he ignored the basic ontological structure of individual man, who, when observed in the concrete, appears as a part and fragment. Hence man cannot make solitary claims of excellence or of the attainment of the summit, but must be seen as *contributing* to the attainment.

The Redemption of Man

MAN stands perpetually under the burden of being man, by origin imperfect. This imperfection is the ground for his original sin; that is, though it is not in itself evil, it is that which gives rise to evil. Thus, it can be said that to be portion or fragment is to stand on the threshold of sin; for only a fragment attempts to step outside itself in an effort to overcome its original imperfection, and in so doing, risks infringing the rights of others. The *totum* as *totum* cannot sin, since the *totum* is by hypothesis "perfect" and self-contained. It could sin only if it in turn should assume the role of fragments *vs.* a more encompassing *totum*. Original sin in our study presumes this ontological imperfection of man.

The profound awareness of this inner limitation of man has created existential philosophy. From Pascal to Sartre it has taken different shapes, but in whatever shape—the sense of the absurd, the anguish of freedom, the hope of salvation, the dread of nothingness—the diversity of moods has betrayed the profoundly unhappy consciousness of individual man and his yearning to transcend the imperfect. All of this is authentic, and no one can deny the tragedy of the isolation which immures each individual. *Altitudo levavit manus*—with a cry of anguish and a plea for salvation men lift up their hands, revealing the helplessness of the fragment. Theologians may find in the lifting of the hands a gesture of worship or of invocation. What concerns us as philosophers is that the stretching out of the hands in prayer or in despair is basically an act of dependence. The structure fashions the gesture; for the fragment, in not being a monad, reaches out for completion.

Man *participates* more than does a plant. He does so through his senses, which are possessed by the sort of fragment which needs to move in order to live. No doubt a plant is a fragment as well. It does not feel, however, since it does not move. Notwithstanding this external immobility, the nutritional and reproductive needs of the plant are met. Through its roots it is attached to the earth, where it finds its food, and in the wind the seeds of its propagation spread out. Although the plant depends upon an equilibrium in nature, it can do little to change the balance. It falls in the wake of a drought, for it cannot set out to search for water. Individual man, as a sense-endowed fragment, is able to move towards the wellsprings of his salvation.

This reaching towards the other may prove to be the act of Cain. The imperfect stretches hands towards the imperfect and in this act is liable to sin. We shall discuss sin later. Our purpose here is to observe the happier possibility whereby the imperfect man, in reaching out, may attain perfection together with the other. This return of individual man to his fellow man is not a return in the full sense of the word, since he has never been totally removed from him. This is what the existentialist has not sufficiently seen. In his groping towards the other, the existentialist, starting from the self as the absolute point of departure, has never demonstrated with total satisfaction the existence of the other. This has not been a problem for the position we defend, since the other, as tied to the individual self in the pre-ontological oneness of the *totum*, must always be present. What does concern us is the insight that individual man, in his movement towards the other, returns to the other as to his redemption.

This is the core of our discussion. The redemption of man is man. We use the term "redemption" in its original meaning as "a way of liberating someone from a liability." The liability from which individual man has to be rescued is the limitation which we have discovered and called his *original sin*. The imperfect is redeemed by the imperfect. Once more Bruegel comes to mind, because we see that his central intuition as an artist was a panoramic grasp of the frailties and splendors of mankind, all portrayed together in one detailed, interlocking tableau. I think here of his magnificent painting of the blind leading the blind. The pessimists among us might say that this symbolizes man's adventure, which will end with all of us, one as blind as the other, stumbling into a pit. My thesis posits the addition of a sighted man coming to the rescue; the imperfect man is able to lead the imperfect man because the multiple is by essence, once the parts are unequal, self-corrective.

A better example, perhaps, than Bruegel's representation is the mutual redemption in which Raskolnikov and his friend Sonia, the prostitute, are involved in Dostoevsky's novel *Crime and Punishment.* The long process of salvation which takes place in the assassin goes hand in hand with the moral recovery which takes place in the life of Sonia. For not only is Raskolnikov indebted to her constant advice and care and ultimately redeemed by her love, but, in making her the instrument of his redemption, he has given her a vocation, thus rescuing her from prostitution and even transforming her—in a way which we shall discuss later—into a saint.

An example from actual life is that of Chartres. When in 1194 the cathedral burned to the ground, the loss was felt as irreparable by the citizens. Yet out of their grief grew the urge to make something new and even more beautiful. In less than forty years, by 1220, the cathedral was for all practical purposes finished. Everyone—rich and poor, laborer and burgher, noble and cleric—had contributed his talent to building what Rodin has called "the acropolis of France." We shall call Chartres "perfect" in the sense defined in these pages, since perfect as an attribute fits the *totum* and the action performed by the *totum* as well. I could also use the term *complementary-additive,* applied earlier to those achievements in the realm of science that result from a multiplicity of fragmentary sources. The moon landing is, of course, the crowning example today. Chartres results no less from the complementarity of many artists and artisans converging in a perfect achievement.

We shall keep in mind, however, that the action transcends the living and the present. Paul, in a beautiful metaphor, describes the moment of the advent of Christ as the "fullness of time." The same can be said of every magnificent achievement. It comes in the fullness of time, not merely the achievement of the concurrent contributions of the living, but also a termination of the activities of bygone ages—their faith, their skills, their discoveries. Masterpieces are a culmination, and they culminate because they are cumulative. Where this slow growth is lacking, a perfect work is not possible, for the achievement of the collective is self-sufficient only when it comprises the acts of the dead as well as those of the living. If man has revealed himself to be a fragment torn from the whole, it now appears that the return to the *totum* is nothing more than the return to the labor of the collective, whether this labor be so called because it is the sum of the work of the living, or whether it results from an addition which reaches farther into the past and includes the dead no less than the living. An accomplishment which *appears* to be that of one man will be found to result from the fact that many stood behind him. Chartres, whether looked upon as the work of the living or even more remotely as the achievement of those who were no longer, is the perfect work. In this accomplishment the imperfect man was redeemed through his contribution, for with the other, just as imperfect as himself, he achieved the perfect.

During the reconstruction of the cathedral there was a rule that obliged the workers to go to confession before mounting the scaffold to begin the work of God. This was a sign of profound faith, no doubt, and of the conviction that to build a cathedral is not the same thing as to build a chateau for one's mistress. It was also a recognition that individual, imperfect man is a sinner. Yet from a philosophical point of view, which is the only one which interests us at present, the need for confession does not appear to be so urgent, even granted the religious character of the work. It was commonly believed in those days that sin is that which conflicts with the will of God; yet even so, it does not per se hamper the performance of the individual artist. The question can be asked whether the collective labor is not the moral redemption for individual sin, especially when the labor itself is the accomplishment of a holy undertaking, in accordance with the will of God, as the building of a cathedral was presumed to be. (It will be our claim, however, that the holy undertaking need not be a cathedral but can very well be a humanitarian task, such as the search for the remedy against cancer, in which thousands are collaborating.) The labor is one, made up of the contribution of the many. Within the oneness of the action the sinfulness of the agent is annulled.

Here the objection could be made that the achievement of "perfection" as it exists in the collective or *subtotum* is far from uniform. Nothing could be more true. Some groups build cathedrals, and others build concentration camps. In placing the achievement of the perfect in the *totum* or in the work of the *totum*, nothing more is said than that the *totum*, of whatever shape, should be considered prerequisite for perfection to flourish. Perfection in a fragmented *totum* requires the plural as that which is capable of providing its counterpart. To have a counterpart within, hence to provide for a corrective, means perfection fulfilled in the abstract; it does not necessarily present us with an optimum in the concrete. Although the achievement of certain groups is greater than that of others, it is the diversity within the oneness which supplies the infrastructure of the perfect. Upon occasion the inner corrective within certain groups has been missing, or suppressed by fear, and the result has been total evil. It follows that to place the plural as the necessary condition of the perfect does not exclude the possibility of collective sin. Sin as committed by a group does exist, and later on we shall discuss its nature. But even then it will be noted that the *subtotum* that is responsible for the evil deed because it suppressed the corrective within, can and will be redeemed by the other (*subtotum*) within the englobing *totum genus*.

This, then, is the redemption of man by man. It neither excludes nor includes a divine redemption. Let us merely say that even those among us who believe in God as the explanation of our existing world must not see him as incessantly retouching his own creation. That creation undergoes constant repair, no doubt, but it carries its means of repair aboard. It is unjust to promise eternal happiness to the hungry and suffering, when material help might be more to the point. The intentions of those who in the past preferred to send the invisible to the rescue rather than go themselves were not, perhaps, as bad as they seem now. Everyone moves and acts within the perspectives of his own epoch. But religious redemption can no longer be considered the remedy for frustration. On this Marx was right. Whatever may be his other limitations, he saw correctly the responsibility of man for man.

Is God Perfect?

IT remains for us to examine in the light of our new insights the concept of *perfection* as it is understood in the traditional sense of the word, that is, as all-inclusive. Perfection as the all-inclusive has been attributed by the theologian to the Christian notion of the Deity. Thus, God is charitable, humble, just, honest, wise, intelligent, and omnipotent. His perfection appears to be the sum-total of all the qualities which we have shown to be diffused among all human beings. God, then, would be a *totum* solely in himself, since he would condense all virtues by way of accumulation; yet he would be greater and better than any *totum*, since by hypothesis he would be unfragmented.

At this point some difficulties arise. First of all, one may wonder whether in the absence of real fragmentation, the multiplication of qualities reflecting the ontological diversity of the fragments still makes sense. In a presentation of that which by hypothesis is Unfragmented, there is no need to expatiate on its inner components, since there are none.[11]

We are also told that God is alone, that the divine order can no longer be considered polytheistic. Yet it appears once more that if one eliminates the ontological manifold of the gods, one must also abandon the notion of the distribution of divine qualities. The believer in Olympus endows the gods with a variety of virtues and vices, for on Olympus there is fragmentation, and with fragmentation, the character of the unequal, of the such and the so. Zeus is power, Apollo is beauty and intelligence, Dionysos is life and instinct, Aphrodite is seduction and femininity. Yet upon abandoning this picturesque variety, the Greeks gradually constructed the concept of a divine order totally wrapped up in itself and hidden to human curiosity. Aristotle's god had no qualities except *to be*. He is left among the stars, self-contemplation his sole occupation. "It must be of itself that the divine thought thinks—since it is the most excellent of things—and its thinking is a

---

[11] When theologians, in an attempt to clarify the concept of perfection in God, see in Him the human attributes, yet see them as fulfilled *modo eminentiori*—"by way of supereminence"—they merely confess their ignorance. To claim that the human attributes are present in God, but without the human distortions, may appear to be a fair answer to some. To many, it will appear to be a very negative approach to that which by essence is supremely positive; and to all of us, it will appear to leave the problem what it was, namely, mystery.

thinking on thinking."[12] Yet the Aristotelian god did not break all ties between himself and the universe, since the same god is very much loved, and through the fact of "being loved" brings a world into motion just as the beloved woman moves the lover, although ignorant of her power.

The concept of a God whose only contact with the world is one of attraction appeared insufficient to Christian theology, whose notion of creation desperately required an efficient cause. There was an urgent need to reconstruct the concept of deity. In this reexamination the notion of perfection as the sum-total of human virtues was placed in God. It is not our task to trace at length the variations of this approach. A long line of scholars, from the early church fathers on through Scotus Eriugena, Bonaventure, Meister Eckhardt, Anselm, Albertus Magnus and Thomas Aquinas, have contributed to its articulate expression. As far as our study is concerned, following the method of descent, we have no way of making the kind of detailed diagnostic of the divine order which so many scholars of the past have audaciously attempted. Our method did give us a theory of how the collective or *totum* discovers God, but even this attempt could not clarify the internal nature of the deity.[13] We have not altered our fundamental stand, except to stress the fact that perfection cannot be considered an accumulation of virtues unless it is accompanied by an ontological fragmentation as its corresponding infrastructure. If we are reluctant at present to posit fragmentation of the deity, we shall also prudently avoid placing perfection in God as his essential attribute. All that can be said, it seems, is that the Deity should be accepted in an elemental way without further discourse or analysis, without a detailed attribution of qualities, but left by itself as depth and mystery, as *Ungrund* and *mysterium tremendum*. What is unfragmented is also unqualified.

---

[12] *Metaphysics*, 1074 b, 30.

[13] In chapter 8 of my previous volume, I have attempted to show that the concept of God is discovered by a global intuition of the *totum humanum* as such, that this intuition is in no way the privilege of the individual himself (the only exception being perhaps the mystic), and that as a result the only acceptance of God's existence in the individual happens through faith. "We" know and see that in which "I" believe.

A Concept in Oscillation

ALTHOUGH it may appear that the trend towards conceptualizing the Deity has generally been towards a synthetic understanding, it cannot be demonstrated that this trend is the only one, nor that the reverse is forever excluded. No doubt synthesis is the way of comprehending God in Plato's concept of the deity, in Aristotle's Pure Act and in the Christian notion. However, once men had reached this particular stage of condensing the plural into one, men no longer "understood" in a clear and visual way, hence their attempt to dilute this form of the One. "God is infinitely far away and infinitely close," wrote a Flemish poet.[14] Some leave God at a distance, their notion of the divine blurred and synthetic. Others bring their God to the level of man and represent him in the shape of the imperfect and the limited; hence the need for the theophany, or the incarnation of the deity, in human form and for the manipulation of matter in the act of worship.

Upon leaving the dimension of the invisible, the God-man takes the shape of the imperfect and of the finite, making it possible for men to hear, see and touch him. Mary Magdalens are possible only when God has become man. But there is another way of making the sacred tangible, and it consists in making the tangible sacred. Although Socrates' description of the ascent of the soul from the admiration of beautiful forms on earth to the vision of absolute beauty as a form of essence is a moving narration, we shall readily confess that what only the eye of the mind can behold has never, for any length of time, enthralled mankind as a whole. Such a reality, however eloquently defended, is obscure, and the images contemptuously cast aside on the way to the Absolute are worth pausing to admire, whether a work of art, a spectacular landscape or the shapes of beautiful bodies. Similarly in the domain of religious worship, although God remains an object of their belief, many want their vision to be caught by the stone of the altar or the flicker of the candlelight. Incarnation extends beyond the body of the God-man into matter, and the tangible is sacred.

---

[14] C. Verschaeve, *De Dichter Joannes a Cruce* (Bruges: 1926), p. 12.

What if the tangible alone is sacred? Such is the attitude of the idolater. The idolater is not an atheist. He is the one who, observing the multiplicity of the imperfect in this creation, reduces the divine order to a similar domain and a similar dimension. For him God is many just as the *totum universum* is many. The prophets of the Old Testament kept the attention of the Jews focused upon the One, as did the founders of Islam in their attempts to protect the faithful against the seduction of idolatry. In both cases the result was touch-and-go. The story of the Golden Calf represents only one of the many rebellions of a vigorous race against the cult of the Invisible, and the Koran took infinite precautions to prevent a return to idols or "false gods." The mosque must be empty of images or statues, a mere enclosure, and within the enclosure, empty space to invoke Allah. The believer is constantly reminded that Allah is great, but he is given the promise that paradise is populated with houris as well, with whom undoubtedly some believers are more familiar than with the notion of God. And so it goes in the different forms of monotheistic cults. Man believes that there is but one God, yet constantly looks for salvation in a more palpable way and often trusts his eyes more than his belief.

In our times—the epoch of the death of God—the collective effort of men to replace God by the acts of men themselves cannot be ignored. Neither divine truth nor divine holiness is thereby explicitly rejected, but the inference is nevertheless made that there is for man no other truth than what centuries of research have uncovered and no other "perfection" than what the many through the addition of the multiple imperfect have managed to achieve. It is only natural that the truth of men should be the truth of God—as seen by men, of course—and that the perfection of the human *totum* should partake of the divine sanctity as achieved by the infirmity of men. What matters is the acceptance of the additive power, be it in the realm of truth or in the realm of moral achievement. Collectives or *subtotum(s)* are definitely unequal in their achievement; yet, in principle at least, they carry their own corrective. In that sense, and in that sense only, can the perfect be achieved. Behind the interplay of men must be seen the one *totum humanum* upon whose surface they incessantly move towards one another as parts. Undoubtedly the desire for perfection finds a mythical fulfillment in God, however vague, but it must find its present actualization in the works of men. Feuerbach's *Homo homini Deus* finds no literal application in the strange intertwining of the multiple imperfect, for men cannot be called gods, yet their work in the collective is the Promethean attempt to compete with the gods. Prometheus, of course, is no longer an individual: he is the collective.

4

Movements To and From

The Ground of Love

WE have observed the compactness of the *totum humanum*, its oneness and what we have called its perfection, which can be said to occur when its constituents are considered as acting and in their actions are seen to be completing one another. It is now our task to focus upon this movement. "We," coming down upon the fragments from afar, note that the movement is either of fragments toward one another—we shall call it *contraction*—or of fragments away from one another; this separation we shall call *distention*.[1]

Rather than attempt to say what the two movements might mean as invisible—or what are sometimes called "metaphysical"— forces, we shall only observe them in their outward expression, as they terminate in man. It would be similarly hard to analyze Nietzsche's Will for Power as an invisible force. We do not know whether it is physical or metaphysical, yet we do know that according to Nietzsche it is present in man and manifests itself there. So without attempting to solve the invisible aspects of the movements under study, we shall observe them in their outward manifestation and visible expression. This is consistent with our

---

[1] I am at loss to find the right language here. The problem has its origin in the fact that at this stage I do not want to use a terminology which denotes the way these movements are felt by the individual man himself. Although we shall do this in the pages to come, it is important for us to remain faithful to our method if we want to reap the fruits which it is held to contain.

method, which is a "visual" one: we paint what we see, the diverse as well as the one, the contraction of the diverse and its distention.

The coming together is no doubt a return to the primeval and elemental oneness of the *totum*. That which is by essence finite and fragmentary tends to approach the finite and the fragmentary in order to complete itself, and it will do so with those entities with which a form of interlocking can be achieved. The trend towards unification, as we have seen, follows the channels of communication. Yet that which tends to unity with others to form a closed circle will at the same time keep the other at a certain distance. Both movements—contraction and distention—must be present in a *totum* whose fundamental structure is fragmentary but united.

If we are to follow our method of descent, this phenomenon of coming together must be viewed both in time and in space. The small *subtotum* of the family offers a simple example of cohesion in space, for this group, made up of father, mother and children (and possibly extended by other relations), forms a naturally closed-in *totum* which lives and works together. It is equally obvious that the cohesion of the family extends in time. Its members are linked by ties of blood to those who came before and are still to come after. Inheritance laws, according to which the possessions of one family are inherited by the children and later by the grandchildren, recognize this law of cohesion that bridges time. The unit called the family reaches into past and future and obtains an atemporal dimension.

This coalescence of fragments does not fulfill itself only in a family but reaches beyond these borders into the formation of a variety of larger collectives and groups. The bases of these collectives are multiple. They may be biological and result in a unit called tribe or race, they may be geographical and lead to what is commonly called a nation, or they may be a combination of the two. This contractive movement towards the other as complement of his need and imperfection and of the other's need and imperfection will at times be called love.

Love as Need

BEFORE proceeding we must keep in mind that a phenomenology of descent, in the very act of observing and describing, reveals the meaning buried in the phenomenon. The Observer views the fragment as imperfect in its ontological dimension and connects the movement from *A* towards *B* and from *B* towards *A* to this deficiency. Although the Observer does not attempt to use introspection as the means of revelation, he is able to diagnose "need" on the basis of the imperfect and "desire" as the result of need. It is erroneous, then, to depict need and desire as intrinsically evil or the source of evil.[2] Need, as a structural qualification of the fragment and of the imperfect, is natural and just as naturally leads to desire as its sequel. Without need, there would be no desire; the two go hand in hand.

We discover the element of need in all manifestations of love, in the love of man for woman, of woman for man, of children for their parents, and of parents for their children. In addition, we see that the obsession with the unique that underlies all these pages pervades the domain of love as well. Although a man can claim that he loves all women, the fact remains that love in its fullness is directed toward one person. The unique calls for the unique. The need of *X* is a desire for *Z* and no one else, just as in reverse the need of *Z* implies the desire for *X* and no one else.[3]

We do not claim that love is only need, or that need always means love. We merely say that love presumes need. If the objection should be made that love can manifest itself where no need

---

[2] This statement is made against the derogatory implication of Sartre's analysis of man as "*l'homme du besoin*," that is, of man living in a world of scarcity, which is also, as a result, a world of perpetual danger. See Sartre, *Critique de la Raison Dialectique* (Paris: Gallimard, 1960), pp. 165 ff., 688; Desan, *The Marxism of Jean-Paul Sartre* (New York: Doubleday & Co., 1965), pp. 83, 218.

[3] We have no clear explanation as to why this need is directed to *X* and not to *Y*. We can merely remind the reader of a point made in a previous chapter, where it was said that the deeper motive for it originates in the unconscious and cannot with precision be brought to the surface. We should add that this need of the unique for the unique, however sincere and authentic, cannot always be viewed as lasting and perennial. But this is not our present concern.

seems to be present in the one who loves—the love of the missionary for his flock, or any man of charity for the poor and the hungry—we shall answer that actually a twofold need is represented
here: the immense need of the giver to share his wealth or his
time or his energies as well as the need of the receiver. The *totum*
manipulates its constituents intelligently and places the needy on
both sides of the track. There is a need to give no less than a need
to receive. It is precisely in this abundance of love that mankind
is redeemed as a whole. Its parts move towards one another in an
atmosphere of *need for . . .*, hence of *love with. . . .* Man alone by
himself is *destitute*: his mobility towards the other is love as a
cure for his ontological need.

It is of course evident that a need-to-be-fulfilled does not always
imply love. I approach a doctor or a lawyer with a particular
purpose in mind. The use of a professional function (that is, of a
function which is acquired as a skill) is part of the mutual instrumentality which locks the imperfect with the imperfect. I use the
doctor and he uses me; here we shall not speak of love. We shall
reserve the term *love* for that occasion when one reaches beyond
the professional to the grounds of the natural and the human. I
love him or her as a person. At times the use of the function becomes love for the person benefited: a patient can fall in love
with her doctor, or a student with her professor. In such examples
the need reaches beyond that for mere professional skill and becomes the need of the person as such. Nor can one exclude the fact
that natural function (such as the function of a mother towards
her child) is often conducive to love; but here again love of the
child reaches beyond the mere function for the mother herself.

When love is present, that is, when a need transcends the function and reaches the person, it is accompanied by emotion. This
feeling may be neither intensely romantic nor sentimental, but it
does imply in most cases a feeling of happiness in the presence
of the beloved. One looks for the beloved or for any signs that
remind one of him or her. This is not to say that love is a happy
adventure all the way. Disenchantments are innumerable, but men
always keep on trying, and in doing so, follow the eternal law of
the incomplete seeking its complement. The basis' of love is the
fragment and the ontological limitation of the fragment. Since it
is part of man's structure, the power of rapprochement between
human individuals does not rest entirely with their own decisions.

To reduce the unhappy endings, man can and must direct this force, as we shall see, but he does not originate it. The path is there as a datum, but man must choose to tread it.

The claim that love is totally gratuitous, as if there were a form of love which can give without receiving anything in return, is not realistic. Such a love cannot be found. The tragic aspect of love is that it both gives and demands. There are, of course, situations where love returns to the giver not as a reward to him as an individual but as an enrichment to his collective, as in the case of the man who gives his life for the *totum* to which he belongs. Even such a love is not gratuitous, although, as we shall see later, the donor might be heroic. Love for the nation contains the sense of need and of expectation, the expectation that this plot of land with geographical borders that enclose its distinctive way of life will protect its inhabitants. In the light of the principles examined so far, then, love appears as the movement, on the basis of need, of the imperfect towards the imperfect as towards its ideal completion, regardless of the function.[4]

Man as Anti-Man

BESIDES the movement within the *totum* which we have called contraction, there is also the movement in reverse, or distention,

---

[4] At this point it might be objected that we are once more in conflict with the traditional concept of the Deity. This notion represents God as totally self-sufficient, but in so doing, it fails to see that an Entity which is totally self-sufficient does not will to create. (On this Aristotle once more appeared to be very perspicacious.) The question then becomes this: can God still be called self-sufficient if He wills a creation? One only wants what one in depth needs. We have two alternatives: we must either accept in God a Love for the creation He wants, thereby cancelling His self-sufficiency, or grant Him self-sufficiency and let Him ignore a creation which He does not love because He does not need it.

Is this the final answer? Probably not. Perhaps our attention must be turned to the possibility of an alteration in the concept of the Deity, who should be seen not as remote from His work but as present in it. God becomes, then, the real and totally invisible and noumenal entity, the eternal *metaphusis* which carries the *phusis* in its multiple expression. *Phusis* is understood here as nature in its visible manifestation, and God as the only metaphysical entity, for ever unknown to individual probing but not totally impervious to the intuition of the *totum*.

whereby individuals withdraw from one another. This withdrawal takes a variety of forms. A man may withdraw from his fellow men simply because of the need for solitude and physical repose. Or he may wish to protect an existing partnership, whereby he is compelled to keep Z at a distance in order to maintain a partnership already in existence with X. At times withdrawal denotes aggression: one separates because one hates, and in this mood of hostility men attempt to harm one another.

This mood, in the opinion of some philosophers, is built-in, constituting part of the human definition. "Man is such that he can at any time become anti-man."[5] Individual man lives in a world of scarcity, and for this reason finds in every other man a present or potential enemy. Clearly this philosophy places the individual as center, not as contributing part and fragment of. . . . The same idea was already present in the famous Hobbesian axiom: *homo homini lupus.* The practice of men fighting like wolves is as old as man himself, but its theoretical formulation had to await relatively modern times. It is only natural that Hobbes' observation coincided with Descartes' discovery of the Self as absolute point of departure and as center. What has been revealed to itself as the center must and will oppose itself to any other self-enclosed center.

The most extreme form by which individual man asserts himself as center is murder. Murder presumes a will to kill, an underlying hatred. Just as love lies behind the procreation of the new and the protection of the old, hate is at the origin of this extreme act of self-assertion at the expense of the other.

Competition is a more common example of the individual fragment considering itself as center. This time one does not per se aim at the destruction of the other, but only towards doing better than those moving within the same *totum.* "To do better" does not mean to change one's inner nature towards a more moral attitude. It can mean to perform better, to be more successful in a contest—intellectual, political, athletic or cultural. It can also mean "to have more," for man discovered long ago, or thought he had discovered, that what-he-has commands what-he-is. This is not entirely non-

---

[5] Sartre, *Critique de la Raison Dialectique,* Vol. I, p. 689; see my comment in *The Marxism of Jean-* Paul Sartre, pp. 219–21, 224, 248, 265.

sensical, for in many cases this will indeed account for what-one-is: the power to be depends on the power to have. It is no wonder that there is a restless competition on the level of having and that men struggle to improve their status through material possessions or visible accomplishments. The competitive element in man cannot and should not be lightly dismissed. The laws of inner tension between parts may be a condition for the movement of the *totum*. The process might be compared to the operation of a missile. Resistance from part to part gives impetus to the machine as a whole. It is because element X is driven into a position occupied by element Z that there is for the total component, or the vehicle, no other issue but to move ahead. Competition creates a similar tension. The will to-do-better and to-have-more creates an opposition between the constituents of the same *totum*—one wants to occupy the spot of the other—and results in most cases in what is commonly called progress of the *totum*. Since all want to-do-better, it may seem logical to conclude that the collective as a whole will fare better. This is why in any contest the winner must be defined as the one who triggers the others into emulating himself. Although the Roman general might have considered himself to be the undisputed victor when he was drawn in his triumphal chariot, he only succeeded in increasing the number of his rivals and preparing the revenge of the conquered. Grandeur imitates grandeur. While we called the feeling which lies at the origin of murder or assassination hate, we discover at the origin of competitive action what we shall call envy. Within the fabric of the *totum*, which is both one and many, envy appears to be, within limits, a fertile ingredient.

This fertility is purchased, however, at a certain price. For although competition seems prima facie to be beneficial—and it often is—the fact remains that in many cases it consists in the fierce combat of man against man, with no concern whatsoever for the state of the *totum*. It is no less obvious that both democracy and capitalism sin through competition more than do other political or economic structures. A major concern of democracy is the securing of popular consent, while the driving force in a capitalistic world is individual enrichment. What happens is that democracy in its parliamentary form, through a ruthless competition for the votes of the masses, becomes demagoguery, while a laissez-faire economy results in the exploitation of the poor and the weak. That these abuses are endemic to the system cannot be shown. That they are often present is clear to anyone who dares to see things as they are.

What has so far been forgotten both in the theorizing on the concept of competition and in its actual practice is that the activity in which the agents compete, and which, once all is said and done, will place them in a certain order of superiority or inferiority, is not really an individual performance. Although to all appearances the action of an individual is his own, and by hypothesis free—we shall discuss the nature and the amount of freedom later—the reality is that it is not just an individual act but is communal as well. For it is performed by an agent whom we have refused to conceive as the center of a world, but upon observation from afar have seen to be only a part and a fragment; that is, an entity which is made by the *totum* acts with and through the *totum*, and as a result must to a great extent be seen as living for the *totum*. This implies that in fact the action, although individual and private at first glance, is actually communal in origin. The individual agent is not its total cause. Those who carry the individual agent in their midst in one way or another influence, help or even compel him to act; hence they are, no less than the agent himself although in a different way, the cause of the action. As we have stated before, Michelangelo contributes to the making of the Renaissance but is in turn himself made by it. The Australian aborigines could not have given birth to the future painter of the Sistine Chapel, although they may have produced some other exceptional talent. But if that is so, the *reward* of the action (or the pain which is its eventual result) must be seen as returning to the true agent, or what we have called the total cause.

For one thing, the nature of this reward may be the joy of creation itself, the ecstasy connected with reaching a peak of achievement.[6] This obviously is experienced by the individual agent, but it also affects the *totum* as a whole, and the work becomes the glory

---

[6] Notice that in a game or in any play, although there is a certain amount of competition, the prime intention is not to win—even less to reap monetary profit —but to confront a worthy opponent. What this means is that the reward lies in the action itself, not (or at least not necessarily) in that which follows the action.

of the collective which carried the individual artist to his achievement. The Sistine Chapel belongs to Julius II as well as to Michelangelo.

In most cases the reward includes not merely the pleasure of artistic execution, but also money, fame and whatever other tangible results go with the success of the undertaking. Since the action is communal, one might argue, the reward cannot go exclusively to the individual agent. Monasteries and communes have grasped this insight, however ineptly it may be realized at times. The world at large will not imitate them too closely, yet a trend in this direction is perceptible. What comes from the *totum* returns to the *totum*, the individual agent himself being merely the transitory tool of the ultimate interests of the *totum*. What actually takes place in depth is an incessant recycling from the One (*Totum*) to the One (*Totum*) through its internal multiplicity of fragments.

But if the intrinsic perfection and benefit of the *totum* are the aim, the direct and exclusive intention of the individual agent cannot be solely personal profit and (or) elimination of the opponent. Competition well understood implies achievement of the good for its own sake. Hence one must attempt to do the best one can, not to do better than *X*. Competition then is no longer a struggle to the death but a striving for excellence. It must not threaten the unity of the *totum*, as it constantly does, but instead it should protect and enhance it. Above all, competition must not kill the individual agents, as now in so many ways it slowly and surely does; rather, its stimulus should give them a joy in living and the climate conducive to perfect achievement.

This correct understanding is even more imperative when the work itself is by nature a collective enterprise—or, to be exact, presumes an approach whereby several persons work at the making of a particular object, be it a cathedral or a missile. Competition was then—when cathedrals were the object of the collective endeavor—or is and will be—when missiles are in question—an act of cooperation. Although the individual contribution must not be overlooked, the total achievement nevertheless aims at the benefit of the *totum*, and this is what matters primarily.

It is precisely this statement which modern man, and by this I mean the man who came onto the scene in the West some three hundred years ago, has challenged. What has mattered for him has been the growth of self-awareness, with fierce defense of the self and ruthless competition as a result. One who considered the Self supreme and absolute found it logical to practice competition in its most extreme form. And it is in this way that the West has built its strength and its power; but it will not be in this way that the results of this gigantic effort, technical no less than cultural, will be implanted upon the rest of the planet. What was born in a spirit of antithesis or opposition must be communicated in a mood of social consciousness. On a shrinking globe the movement which we shall call contraction will take over the movement called distention.

Oscillation from Love to Hate and Back

CLEARLY the movement of distention and the way it is felt by the individual in the form of desire for solitude, or a feeling of envy or even of hate, is no less vigorous than its opposite, which we have called contraction, with its manifestation of love in the individual man. It is these phenomena which a descending phenomenology observes on a visual and expanded level. The Observer is confronting a quasi-photographic phenomenon, not an abstract structure. This is indeed a "tactful" ontology, for in leaving things as they are, it shows them as they are. The Observer sees and does not, as yet, judge. He sees, as a further part of his picture, that love and hate, or the movement *pro* and the movement *anti*, reveal their presence in one and the same individual. Individual man is made both for association and for disassociation, and he knows that "there is a time to love and a time to hate." He moves away from the person he deeply loves and reconstructs his own self in solitude—even, sometimes, in hate—so that he might love again. The same holds true on a social level, where at times one approaches one's fellow men with relish, and at other moments with reserve. We observe the same phenomenon when the fragment is a collective: so at times the mood of a nation is violently nationalistic and at other periods is more accommodating and internationally-minded.

In most cases the *totum* keeps its balance by distributing the diverse moods, or attitudes, among its diverse tenants. This distribution constitutes its survival. If parts move towards or draw away from one another, the mood of love or hate expressed by this mobility is created by the *totum*, which is thereby protecting its oneness. Fragments are restrained from their movement in one direction or the other by an invisible grip. Of this grip we see the results. Over a span of time and over a certain expanse of space, the *totum* introduces a variation of moods through a variation of fragments. The result is an oscillation of hatred and love, hatred so that men or nations may survive through the quickening of competition, and love so that strife may be overcome and the disintegration produced by hate alone may be avoided.

Notwithstanding all his claim of rationality, the fragment, whether individual self or collective, in most cases succumbs to the mood, and once in the mood of love or hate, finds "reasons" for its attitude. Reason is a tool of self-defense par excellence. The *totum* does not reason: it is neither rational nor irrational. But the fragment within must use reason as one of its most efficient weapons, and if very intelligent, writes its *Apologia pro vita sua*. Apologetics, however, always come after the act.

This study is not a history of ideas. If it were, it would be easy to show how the diverse trends described above have been fulfilled in the realms of politics, economics, international relations and even in philosophy itself. However, it is not at present our intention to implement the principles which our study brings to the fore. Let us merely observe that whether in the grip of contraction or of distention, the individual can in no way be considered a substantial and independent entity. Such was the approach of a philosophy which was and is made by an individual semantics—that is, by a semantics which is constructed on the scale of the individual. When everything was defined by an individual and from the individual's point of view, the result was that the sense of the interdependent and the collective was totally missed. In a phenomenology of descent, the individual is not ignored, for he is unique and "irreplaceable"; but he carries the indelible meaning of the fragment in his very being, hence also the implication of being such only because there is also one who is so. He is unique within the they. And the they are together as the one is.

There is wisdom in the individual when he accepts this structure for what it is and plays his part, knowing very well that he is neither originating nor terminating the movements of love and hate, which always were and always will be. There is one limit to that movement: and that limit is the *totum*.

Once the individual is born into the ambit of the *totum*, he cannot ignore the fact that he is moving on a surface which is by nature limited and that within that enclosure he is not alone but must play a game which is relational. Any one of his actions can be destructive. At times the urge to protect the self through competition produces a combat unto death. It is this combat unto death which we shall now observe. In doing so, our study has to take into account what a phenomenology of descent seems to detect, the slow but gradual shift from the individual to the *totum* as center.

The Parable of the Two Parachutists

> Two parachutists have been dropped during the night in an equatorial jungle. They belong to hostile camps. The region where they have been dropped is totally deserted and inhospitable. The parachutists know of their plight. They are aware that if they are to survive, it must be through mutual aid. Yet they can also exterminate one another. The question which can be raised is this: will they move towards one another for death or for common survival?

In attempting to answer this question, we cannot ignore Hegel's masterly description of the master and slave struggle to the death, but at the same time we must be clearly aware that the situation of the two parachutists is not and cannot be purely and simply a relation of master and slave.

Let us recall briefly the Hegelian dialectic leading to the situation of master and slave. The individual *Self X* in Hegel's vision can only build itself up ontologically as *Self X* if and when it is recognized as such by individual *Self Z*, and vice versa. This need for *recognition* is essential in Hegel. When two individuals meet in the broad frame of human history without further specifications of time and space, this encounter has to be one of combat. This combat—whatever its nature, whether physical, economic, intellectual or artistic—must be one which implies total risk, for without total exposure to injury, even to loss of life, no total victory can be gained. It is Hegel's thesis that the winner of this combat will be the one who shows the greatest detachment from life. In his very abandonment to death, he will win, while the other, because of fear and too great an attachment to life and to the "thinghood" of this world, becomes a thing himself and as a result is the loser.

Herewith an unequal relation is built up, one of master and slave. The master obviously is the one who comes out of the combat victorious, while the slave deserves to be named the loser. It should be well understood, however, that the one is only what he is through the other. The concept *master* implies in its very definition the concept *slave*, and the reverse is no less true. Hegel continues—this may be of lesser importance to us, but it is given here merely to complete our brief summary of the Hegelian narration—by saying that the slave is so deeply shaken by fear in the depth of his soul that in the midst of his depression he begins to work. At first his labor consists merely in working for the master. Yet gradually he becomes indispensable, grows in stature through his hard labor, and in so doing, dominates material reality. He is no longer attached, but in this domination of the world he acquires detachment, and over the years (the centuries!) appears as the one who ultimately will overcome the master and in turn become master.

The first question which must be raised is this: to what extent is recognition essential for the genesis of the self? Hegel places recognition at the beginning of this dialectic, without questioning his right to do so. The self as shown by Hegel is a self in combat, as if strife were the only instrument for the construction of the self. We deny this, for it is an implication which cannot be stated as universal. Although it is undeniable that at times strife does indeed sharpen resistance and that continued resistance does increase the acuity of self-knowledge, it need not follow that the self comes to the fore then and then only. Two things are forgotten. (1) It must be kept in mind that the self is shaped through being born *in*. . . . Before any horizontal dialectic can arise—and this is what I see as the Hegelian approach—there is and was beforehand a vertical placing of the part within the group. This action comes from the many which constitute the *totum* (not only from the parents) and has molded the child long before the time came for the self to provoke the other in a duel, on a horizontal level, whatever the nature of the duel may be. What we want to make clear is that, contrary to Hegel, ontologically and chronologically the *Self X* is to a great extent constructed before its specific encounter with *Self Z*, and it is constructed *such* or *so* before its own explicit awareness can interfere and manifest itself. Only belatedly will the individual, in looking back upon a long life, discover that what he is he was to a great extent *given* to be. This Hegel seems to ignore. If he expects more from the power of the anti-man, it is because he has not seen the impact of the *totum* upon every self which it brings forth.

(2) But there is an even more crucial point. If the *Self X* matures and grows and in this growth asserts itself more forcefully, so that it provokes the other to a duel of sorts, it may appear at first glance that the mood which expresses this is one of hate or of fierce opposition. But this is not necessarily so, for it is not necessarily true that one survives through hate rather than through love. And this leads us into the core of the problem.

> The two parachutists, lost in the equatorial jungle and threatened by annihilation, confront what may be worded simply as a problem of survival. And the question then becomes: What does and does not promote survival? To ensure survival must one move against the other unto the threshold of death?

We can, first of all, exclude the sort of bravado of which Jules Romains spoke in *Verdun* and by which he implied that if there were no women, there would be no war. "The idea that women are there, as on the walls of an ancient city, and that they look, that they judge. . . ."[7] Things being what they are, bravado cannot be totally ignored, for there is in men a certain defiance of life, more pronounced when it can be observed. In the case of the parachutists popular admiration is precluded, since there is no

---

[7] Jules Romains, *Les Hommes de Bonne Volonté, Verdun* (Paris: Flammarion), p. 231.

witness whatsoever, and there never will be. Recognition that results from bringing one's opponent down to earth is excluded.

We can also exclude as irrelevant the Hegelian duel of master and slave to the extent that it aims at producing a way of living for the master which is in comparison better than the way of living for the loser. The problem here concerned is not of how to be better than the other but much rather a question of "to be or not to be." What matters in the case of the two parachutists is just this: to live rather than not to live at all. The parachutists want to live before attempting to live better and to compete with one another with that aim in mind. Where life itself is at stake, competition to be ruler or to be more powerful makes no sense at all. (Here we touch upon the ultimate explanation of why democracies die: they succumb, along with the internal competing which goes with them, when and where poverty is rampant and life itself is in jeopardy. Democracy, and any political or economic structure where laissez-faire is accepted and promoted, can only survive when a way of life is firmly established in which scarcity is at least partly overcome.)

> This is, then, the situation of parachutist *A* and parachutist *B*: they make their way through the wilderness. They are life-on-the-brink-of-death and do not need one another to enter into combat for recognition. There is at that moment not enough incentive to die. Defiance of death is mostly for life's sake, whether one's own life or the life of the *totum*. If the parachutists in moving towards one another run a certain risk and in that sense could be said to move towards death, it is in most cases with the hope of escaping death. Death is instrumental to life. One gives one's life, and in doing so, promotes the life of others. This is purposeful indeed. But the parachutists, although belonging to opposite camps, do not promote life in laying down theirs, and are not therefore inclined to do so. If they are not disposed to die, can we say with equal conviction that they are not disposed to kill either? The answer is yes. Whoever is not disposed to die is in no way disposed to kill. Parachutist *A* has no will to kill; hence the death of parachutist *B* is not a probability, and the reverse is also true. One survives through the life of the other, not through his death. What matters is to live "until" . . . rather than to live "better than." . . .

Just as—and here we agree with Hegel—just as murder does not solve the problem of recognition, it cannot solve the problem of survival. The fact is that considering the menace of death in the immensity of the forest, parachutist *A* needs parachutist *B* and vice versa.

It is this element of mutual *need* which deserves our careful attention. Although Hegel in his master and slave dialectic has not overlooked this mutual dependence, for it is clearly recognized that the one *is* only through the other and that, without the slave, the master would not attain his status, he has not seen that the antagonism which is so fierce between the two is actually a link which is stronger than hate and that perhaps it is of a totally different nature.

In order to understand the deeper relation between individuals, we must keep in mind the fundamental premise upon which this whole study is built: the *totum humanum* constitutes a *oneness*, and the parts or fragments within that unity are human individuals who can constitute the oneness because of the channels of communication between them. Man as part, therefore, is prestructured and predisposed to approach man as part.

From this it follows that behind the physical fragmentation the oneness is always present. The one runs through and operates at the level of the diverse. The manifestation of the general interlocking is by way of a whole network of communications, with the intensity of the interlocking on a par with the closeness of the communication.

The one *totum* is present in the two parachutists, and its first intent will be to introduce a de facto communication in order that the two may use one another instrumentally for survival.

The same closeness can be said to exist in the Hegelian dialectic. Here, too, the one is made up out of the communicable and out of the mutually "utilizable." Hegel has placed such a strong element of antagonism and opposition in his dialectic of master and slave that the closeness might not appear to be as great as it would, or possibly will, be in the case of the parachutists moving through the wilderness towards one another. But even in Hegel the closeness is there, and it is Hegel's regrettable omission not to have stressed it sufficiently. There is in the master and slave relation, perhaps to a lesser extent, a need of one for the other based upon the fact that both are parts of the same One.

> The great difference in the two cases is that while in the master and slave dialectic we have a duel, the issue of which results not merely in being but in being *better*, in the jungle the test is not and cannot be one whereby one attempts to be better than *X*, but rather, one whereby one merely attempts to be. But when survival in its naked form is at stake, the unity of the living is closer than ever. For here is the oneness of the *"we living"* in their defense against the inorganic. Life against the menace of the jungle is a solidarity of the *totum humanum* against the *totum inorganicum*. The anti-man in man is transformed into anti-death, and in order to offset the danger presented by the inorganic in such forms as hunger, disease and wild animals, men come together.

When it comes to the question of semantics, what word to use for the need present in the master and slave, or what word to use for the much more intense need for one another in both of the parachutists, we are at a loss to find any other term but *love*. Love can and must be defined as hitherto in this study; that is, as the movement of fragments towards one another resulting from their inner *need* for the other as other. From the point of view of the individual, it is an existential living of the ontological imperfection, and a reaching toward the members of his own class. Class, of course, must be defined as it constantly has been; that is, as a physical oneness made up out of fragments which are interrelated through channels of communication. The *totum humanum*, therefore, is a closer oneness than the *totum inorganicum*. I shake hands with my friends, I cannot do so with things. I can love a woman, I cannot love a tree, at least not with the same hope for reciprocity. I can speak with another human being and he can speak with me, but I cannot do so with a table; nor can I, with the same clarity and precision, with my dog. The channels of communication and their closeness regulate and dictate the oneness of the class. It is within this oneness that love must be considered as the movement toward X resulting from a need. The intensity of the need dictates the intensity of love.

In this sense it is natural that the master appears to us as the one who has obtained, and perhaps even maintained, his status through an ascendancy over the slave, but only because there is the slave can he do so. Only because there is the one whom he will reduce to thinghood can he assert himself to lordship. He needs and loves the slave as one without whom he would not be. The slave, although oppressed and repressed, likewise needs the challenge of the master to emerge slowly yet forcefully to the rank of the master. There is here a primary relation of love in the sense of elemental need.

> Such a relation becomes even more pronounced when the parachutists are in dire need of survival. They desperately need one another, and this need is incomparably more urgent than would be the case if merely a question of status were involved. They love one another.

This is not a love where the sentimental occupies the throne (and it should be stressed that feeling must never occupy the center). Nor is it a love where sex plays a role. Nor is it even a love which may be lasting, as love is sometimes mistakenly represented to be. Love defined as need is not, and should not necessarily be presented as, eternal; for the mutual need may not be permanent.[8] What is at stake here is the survival of the parachutists, and on the basis of this mutual need the movement towards one another. To the extent that mutual need is a form of love, their approach is one of love. Here (as in varying degrees in other cases) love is the cry of individual despair toward any and all who are able to save. This spells the end of competition as destructive force.

> It should be stressed that love is not, and in this case never will be, an element revealed through introspection. Love is observed here, as the march toward one another through the jungle is observed, together with the fight against hunger and thirst, against the cold of the night and the heat of the day and all the other sufferings. The need for one another is a perceptible phenomenon:

---

[8] We shall later examine what makes *lasting* love.

it comes to the fore not through self-conscious reflection but as a bond arising from common action which results in the ultimate finding of one another. This encounter is an achievement, since from now on their chance for survival is enhanced. It was, and appears to be from the viewpoint of the individuals themselves no less than from the viewpoint of the *totum*, which from afar follows the happenings as that which happens within itself as part of itself. When they meet, they meet as friends. To kill one another serves no cause. To inflict death for the motive of the fatherland has lost meaning. The solidarity of the men in danger is solidarity of life against the menace of destruction itself. Life is the totality of the living, the *totum*. This is the moment in History where Life turns against its origin, which was matter, and refuses to die. The parachutists meet as living. They drink the wine and eat the bread together. This is the new eucharist.

It is now clear how (and why) the parachutists meet. They meet as friends, although they are enemies. They meet as friends because one possesses what the other does not and the latter possesses what the former does not. They are for one another the missing tool, or completing element. To find one another in friendship and love does not mean that the mood of the relationship with one another will always remain the same as at the moment of discovery. "Mood" is used here to define the innermost attitude of the human being and the need which corresponds to this attitude. The mood of friendship and love will at times give way to one of self-protection, upon occasion even to the point of hate. Hence although love or friendship may not be lasting, it fulfills a purpose and satisfies a need.

The meeting of the parachutists—we should add—is also one of dignity. It is not one in which they confront one another in the Hegelian way, as master and slave, victor and vanquished. No doubt inequality exists between the two parachutists, but there is no relationship of victory or defeat. The Hegelian opposition of master and slave results from an optic which stands on level ground and misses the view from above. In the light of the optic presented in this study, we can no longer give to the one the name of master and to the other the name of slave. These names carry a connotation of contempt. The hierarchical structure, with its implication of superior and inferior, is at an end. In an optic of distances there is ultimately neither winner nor loser, but a surviving *totum* alternating love and hate for its final end, which is the avoidance of total destruction.

Cube and Cube-Formation

COMING back once more to the phenomena of contraction and distention, we observe that under the stress of the two movements, collectives are born. To what extent the rupture of the *totum humanum* into collectives or *subtotum(s)* affects our ethical judgments we shall inquire later. Let us first observe their origin and growth.

When a movement of individuals is accomplished on a spatial level—and no other movement is known to us—we notice that any move *toward* implies a move *away from* as well. Grouping implies estrangement from those who don't belong. The grouping itself is here understood not merely as an active coming together but as something which is because it always was. Contraction, then, is the pressure to come together or, if already in existence, to stay together.

Occupying the promontory which by hypothesis overlooks the *totum*, "we" now observe the partitioning of the *totum* into uneven portions, the limits of which are indicated by nature, or at times by the hand of man as a result of contract or agreement. These may be called a nation, or a tribe or race, or sometimes a culture group. Survival brought them into existence. The *totum humanum* is diffused over an expanse which, although spherical and hence limited, is nonetheless full of geographical obstacles. It was the impossibility of communication that broke up the oneness of the *totum*, for we have seen that oneness is not based upon logical class or any category of elements which constituents have in common but upon the possibility of their communicating. This rule, written against the Aristotelian concept of class, once more finds itself fulfilled. Where contact broke down, unity vanished, not in its pre-ontological structure or potential connection but in its promise of fulfillment. Since there was no way of reaching certain individuals because of geographical obstacles such as mountains, rivers or oceans, the "others," on the opposite side of the mountain or river, became strangers or foreigners. Men established the group where the common life could be lived; that is, where communications were possible. The male avails himself of the female within reach. This act, which is at the origin of the family, is followed by others aimed at securing a living. Similarly in the founding of nations, the collateral support which we have so persistently described found its application within certain limits; that is, within the same valley, at the crossing point of the same rivers or on the edge of the same forest, wherever a man found men different from himself on whom he was able to place the burden of what he himself could not accomplish and with whom he could exchange the product of his labor. Wherever there was facility of communication, the possibility arose of enlarging the size of the collective or *subtotum*. Units were formed within the immense unit of the *totum humanum*, and these smaller units, gradually closing in upon themselves, moved away from everything which was not themselves. The qualifications of the *totum humanum*, such as compactness and closeness, interlocking and perfection, were present on a smaller scale. Whether we call it city or tribe, nation or empire, culture-group, or whatever, it is and remains a portion of humanity, enclosed upon itself, to a certain degree estranged from others, yet part of the englobing *totum humanum*.

Our method allows "us" to turn as on a pivot and to apply to the time dimension what we have discovered in space. Again we observe a partitioning over a certain length of time, a portion of history we shall call a *period*. The existence of a period, such as the period of the Reformation or the period of the Roman Empire, is not under debate; what is less obvious, however, is the moment when a period begins and ends. Borderlines in time are less accurate than they are in the realm of space, and it would be sheer naiveté to indicate them with mathematical precision. Yet if we were sufficiently detached from a time sequence and could somehow transcend the succession of events without being involved in them, we might be able to discover the beginning and the end of a period; that is, of a certain duration in time characterized by a way of living, sometimes by a number of events, and generally speaking by a set of values typical of that era.

If we consider the collective diffused in space, together with the quality of enduring which makes it historical—that is, the collective with its unique characteristics as it lasts over a certain period of time—we obtain a unit shaped somewhat like a cube. Our term must not be understood mathematically, as if the surfaces constituting the cube were squares of equal dimension, for the boundaries of our so-called cube are not so clearly defined, nor can they be demonstrated to be equal. Yet upon observation it may appear that in many cases as in the cube, where the squares are equal by definition, so also in the *subtotum* or collective its degree of permanence is directly related to the territory it covers. In other words, the spatial expansion of a nation or of a cultural group often equals its endurance in time. The Roman Empire is a classical example, and although we are told that it was continually on the verge of collapse, the fact is that it did not collapse but survived for approximately eight hundred years. This length of time reflects in the temporal sphere the amount of space it occupied. Size seems to be pivotal. What was immense, through sheer volume and through the power of resistance which goes with volume, made the Roman Empire seem indestructible quite apart from the other qualities of organization which the genius of Rome had instilled in its culture. The Eternal City was for many in those days a matter of the deepest hope and the deepest conviction. Sadly enough, the invasion of the Goths and the sack of Rome proved that eternal it was not. That smaller nations have often shown great resistance to destruction or conquest is beyond doubt; yet on the whole their existence has been constantly the threat of destruction and their independence in most cases of short duration. Their history has had a "geographical dimension," in the sense that their endurance in time could be prorated on the basis of their expansion in space. Even when their political independence was not immediately at stake, they fell prey to cultural and economic pressures. Holland, Belgium, and the Balkan states are cases in point; their independence, as history has abundantly shown, has been precarious, while larger nations such as India and China, notwithstanding internal turmoil, have never totally disintegrated but have preserved their identity and to a great extent their territories. A strange physical law seems to apply to the history of groups: volume is a warrant of longevity. Perhaps it is in the light of the same law that the imperialistic trend of nations must be explained. Imperialism aims at the increase of the geographical extent of a nation's territory or, what is equivalent, its economic influence abroad. The ultimate purpose seems to be that the expanse of land a nation occupies and the number of inhabitants it contains to a certain extent decides its capacity for endurance.

This consideration tends to account for the fact that separatism, however ardently hoped for by smaller collectives, is in most cases unwise. A smaller unit will always have a shaky hold on existence once it appears that its existence is rightly or wrongly considered an obstacle to the welfare of a major totality. Yet the philosophy defended in this study must respect the right of smaller nations to be themselves simply because the dual law of contraction and distention accounts for the cohesion of fragments to a certain time and place regardless of the number of the fragments. Further study of this phenomenon will have to be pursued in a later work.

The compactness of the cubic unit results from both contraction and distention, the terms which we have already proposed to describe the movements of coming together and moving away from. As felt by the individual, contraction was called love, or need. When love is directed to the collective and its accomplishments, the term *nationalism* is sometimes fitting. Nationalism denotes the cohesion of the collective on a spatial level and often results in a hatred of other, foreign nations or collectives.

When we look at the same collective expanding through time yet attempting, notwithstanding the flux of time, to keep its inner stability and to produce what we have called the cubic unit, we observe that a new element comes into the game. This element is called tradition. Tradition is cohesion through time just as nationalism in certain groups is a cohesion on the space level. Tradition can also be called a form of love. It is a love of what was with the hope that what was is also that which will be. It results in a certain sameness of living and thinking which, tested on the touchstone of time, has appeared to be the best way of surviving. This cohesion through time resists change just as nationalism as a form of cohesion in space withstands its own destruction and defies the incursions of foreign countries. A "conservative" is usually an individual who is eager to protect, sometimes more than is necessary, both the cohesion in space, or nationalism, and the cohesion in time, or tradition.

In fragmenting the *totum genus humanum* into cubes or cubic units, we have kept the discussion on a general level and made no explicit differentiation between a nation, a tribe, a race or a culture-group. Now that our study proceeds more and more in a definite direction, we shall be more specific in the use of the term cubic unit and reserve it for a culture-group, that is for a collective which although englobing several nations and of itself politically heterogeneous, has nevertheless a fundamental unity because its internal channels of communications are open and numerous. This unity encompasses its ways of living—dressing, eating, etc.—and also its ways of evaluating what is wrong and what is right. The first mode of uniformity we shall call etiquette (or ethics in small matters), while the other mode, obviously of greater importance, we shall call ethics. As we proceed, this overlapping of the ethical with the spatio-temporal cubic unit will appear to be paramount.

5

Natural Law
in Modern Semantics

The Will to Be

To be means to survive, and to survive implies that a remedy for a threatening situation has always been forthcoming. There seems to be at work within the immense framework of the *totum* an incessant attempt to correct its own failings, what we shall call *an effort of self-preservation*. We have pointed out how in its very ontological structure the *totum* through the act of procreation of its members prevents its own extinction and how on a spatial level men are juxtaposed and through mutual completion overcome the limitations of individual finiteness.[1] Whether this knowledge of "how to survive" is distinct from the effort itself is not clear. The traditional distinction between to know and to will is inessential at this point as long as we are prepared to accept the fact that survival as elemental instinct includes both knowledge and drive. The *totum* is endowed with a technique of survival, which we have previously called the first universal.[2] What is critical here is the insight that the technique of survival as a fundamental universal reaches farther than the mere ontological fulfillment of replacement in the line of generations or of completion by way of spatial juxtaposition. For we discover on the basis of the technique of survival that the *totum humanum* has introduced a way of living among its constituents which seems to be essential for that particular purpose.

So, for example, it is obvious that in everyday communication

---

[1] See above, Volume I, chapter 1. | [2] See above, pp. 112–115.

language is necessary. People are interrelated through sounds. These sounds have a meaning attached to them, and through them the dialoguers convey their knowledge, their needs, their desires, their decisions. Communication through language is the privilege of the fragment within the *totum*. What is self-sufficient does not converse. But men speak to men. That this exchange of thoughts and desires must happen in truth is an essential requisite for the fragment and for the *totum* as a whole. A function of mutual completion cannot be fulfilled where and when truth is repeatedly and willfully hidden or distorted. The Observer from afar sees the rationale for honesty.

We see also that although people disagree and at times fiercely compete with one another, they do not kill indiscriminately. Here again, the *totum*, although heterogeneous in its internal composition, becomes homogeneous in a certain attitude: live and let live. There are exceptions—murder, execution, war—but even those that have been generally accepted, such as execution and war, are repugnant to all and unconditionally rejected by many as solutions to the problems they were supposed to solve. Fragments within the *totum* are made for coexistence.

A third universal mental set, or attitude, concerns the enduring quality of the *totum* through time, as related to sex, or that dimension in man which provides for his own replacement. Here again, there seem to be certain rules which the fragment cannot infringe incessantly. The claim is not being made here that the only purpose of sex is procreation, but it is a fact that if sex is entirely diverted from procreation, the sojourn of the *totum humanum* upon this planet is due for an early ending, unless the continuation of life can be provided for differently.

The behavior in these briefly mentioned examples presumes the ontological structure of a fragmented *totum*. It is because the *totum* is made in such a way that it must act in such a way to survive. The structure engenders the technique. This technique we shall call "natural law." Although it urges a way of acting, natural law must first be understood as an integral part of a way of being. The "way of being" implies a "way of living." This is consistent of course, but it should be stressed that the first part of the conditional proposition is a conditional imperative; that is, a way of life must be followed *if*, and only if, survival of the *totum* is desirable.

The *totum*, then, is made up in a certain way, and this way of being fractured and juxtaposed in time and space in turn dictates a certain technique which is an attempt to regulate the behavior of the constituents. It is immediately apparent that this technique regulating the way of living of the human fragment cannot be placed on an equal footing with the laws of nature. Once it is accepted that rocks are hard and heavy, it is natural for them to behave as things which are hard and heavy. They merely follow what is called a law of nature. Men are obviously not stones. Yet it is no less certain that if they want to preserve the *totum humanum* of which they are the constitutive parts, they too will have to submit to certain regulations. There is, however, a difference between men and stones. Men know what they must do; rocks do not.

Natural law presumes consciousness. Terms such as "laws of nature" or "instinct" presume ordinance and regularity but no awareness. Yet the presence of this "awareness" introduces a new dimension, for it now becomes apparent that since the *totum humanum* is what it is—and for this way of being it has no particular responsibility—it participates in the formulation and execution of its own natural law. The *totum* with its way of being made up out of the many formulates and executes its way of living in and through these many. We observe here the operation of collective judgment, which introduces certain ways of doing or of not doing things, such as the prohibitions of killing indiscriminately or of lying. The fundamental universal obtains a more conscious application: the *totum* knows how to be and how to survive, but it knows it only in and through many masks, the voices of the individual fragments, each expressing in its own way the urge and the know-how of the *totum humanum*. Individual man contributes to the formulation of the technique of survival. This formulation results in conventions which concretely indicate what to do and what not to do in order to be and to survive. Conventions express what the many have found to be most useful for the preservation of the *totum*.

We are so accustomed to convention expressed negatively, in "Thou shalt nots," that we all too often forget its positive aspect, which we shall call devotion to the *totum*. We will discover later in this study that this must be considered as the commandment par excellence, for it will appear that negative commandments are motivated by this more fundamental sentiment, which is commonly

called love for one's fellow men. Yet, however cogent this underlying motivation may appear to be in explaining the origin of
obedience to negative prohibitions, it is not the internal motivation itself which interests us, but rather the motivation to the extent that it comes to the surface and is as a result observable. Devotion to the *totum*, or love of humanity, will be seen to find its
culmination in the saint.

This, however, is to look ahead. We have now the less romantic
task of examining convention as it relates to the practical behavior
of the mass of mankind. We observe that what is accepted and
practiced at present did not necessarily originate in the present.
Yet it is the *totum* of today which protects the acquisition of the
past. This *totum* of today will not forgive infractions of its morality, since the latter is part of its tradition, and on the basis of
this tradition, received and tested by the atemporal *totum*, the
existing *totum* survives and controls its own survival. By this we
do not imply that changes never take place. As we shall see later,
there is no doubt about the fact that they do take place. But whatever they are, they are the result of the incessant testing by the
technique of survival of its own achievement.

So far natural law appears as a strategy of *self-defense* belonging to the *totum* and resulting in a certain number of statements
which are concerned with practical behavior. We are not yet able
to be more specific concerning the nature of these "commandments" and the "conventional" behavior they produce, but it is
easy to understand that they do affect the individuals or constituents of the *totum*. It is the nature of this impact which now
merits our consideration.

The Will to Be and Its Impact upon the Individual

WE have used the term *self-defense*. Let us look for a moment at
the word *self*. In a general way it stresses distinction from. . . . It
is usually used to separate the individual from others and from
anything which is not him-(*self*). But it is equally applicable to
a *totum*, which, although made out of many, can be considered as
a unit. We speak of America it*self* or France it*self*. The introduction and use of the term emphasize separation and some form of
autonomy. It is a plea for distinction. Natural law could be called,

then, a strategy of self-defense, for this clearly implies that the *totum humanum* as *totum* defends it*self* through its technique. Yet no less obviously will it appear that the totum, in protecting it*self*, does not always synchronize with the wishes of the fragment when it takes care of it*self*. For the technique of survival of the *totum* in executing its self-defense does not directly aim at protecting one individual, although the health and welfare of the *totum* ultimately reaches that one as well as every other individual. The result is that conventional behavior that arose as *self*-protection of the *totum* presents itself to the individual as obligation, that is, as something which ought to be done even when it does not suit his wishes. What appears to the *totum* as common sense, something everyone should expect and take for granted, appears in many cases to the individual as restraint.

When we present obligation as a restraint imposed by the *totum* on the individual fragment, we should add that to a certain extent the fragment obliges itself, insofar as the fragment is *totum* as well. For the technique of survival originates partially at least from the contribution of the fragment itself, returning to the same fragment as an *ought*. The interesting point here is that what originates as unique comes back as uniform, for this is precisely what law implies. Law, which is nothing but the dictates of the *totum* in its technique of self-defense, obliges in a uniform way. In certain modes of behavior the glory of the diverse requires the discipline of the law. The very fact that we are unique and diverse requires a coordinating factor which has grown out of and is part of "us." Law is the ascesis of men, made by men for men. It is the restraint coming from the *totum* to its constituents, called obligation when it reaches those constituents.

If law is the reduction of the unique to the uniform, it is so with this important amendment: law clips the wings of the unique only to the extent that it forbids the fragment to wound the *totum* —through dishonesty, murder, etc. It does not restrain the flight of the unique insofar as the unique self devotes itself in a unique way to the *totum*. On the contrary, this commandment is the greatest of all. Yet this positive approach we shall reserve for later in our discussion of freedom. For the time being we shall limit ourselves to that part of the law which does indeed impose restraint and uniformity.

From our observations it appears that the law affects the fragment, not the *totum* as such. The *totum* itself is morality, since its mores, created by itself and called convention, are law, as issued by the lawmaker. It is understood, of course, that the same *totum* may fall under a more encompassing *totum* and as such be subject to a more encompassing law. An obvious parallel can be drawn here between the theory as propounded in these pages and Kant's position on the *holy*. Thus, the German philosopher writes in *The Metaphysics of Morals*: ". . . for the *divine* will, and in general for the *holy* will, there are no imperatives. 'I ought' is here out of place, because *I will* is already of itself necessarily in harmony with the law. Imperatives are in consequence only formulas for expressing the relation of objective laws of willing to the subjective imperfection of the will of this or that rational being,—for example of the human will."[3] As we have seen, the *totum* is perfect and holy like God, although not exactly in the same way. It cannot sin as *totum*. Likewise God is by definition Norm and the Holy.

Yet we should make it clear that this study is not a defense of the categorical imperative. The parallel with Kant does not mean total similarity. For the imperative according to which individual man unconditionally, merely out of a sense of duty, commands himself to act in a certain way is clearly not part of our thesis. Law in this study is a communal affair. The individual is unique, no doubt. Yet the *totum* in certain areas wants the unique to conform. The *totum* commands. The commandments resulting from the *totum* can be called "imperatives," but they are not to be represented as if the individual were commanding himself and doing so in exclusivity, as Kant's third law of the categorical imperative implies. The individual does not command himself; he is under command of the encompassing *totum*. He commands himself only to the extent that he is part of that *totum*.

I should add that Kant's notion of the imperfect is notably different from the one presented in this study, in that for Kant the imperfect has definite moral connotations and presumes that man is sinful, or at least very much inclined to be so. Our concept of

---

[3] Immanuel Kant, *Fundamental Principles of the Metaphysics of Morals*, trans. by Thomas K. Abbott (New York: The Liberal Arts Press, 1949), p. 31.

the imperfect, on the contrary, is based upon the ontological fragmentation of a *totum* which was and is organically one. We shall not deny that this form of the imperfect can be a prelude to sin. But it remains true, nonetheless, that the imperfect as attribute of the fragment does not per se include sinfulness, as seems to be the case in Kant's world, which has overtones of Augustinian pessimism.

Actually a more optimistic note is struck in the view we are presenting. This is so not only because the notion of inherent sinfulness is discarded but also because in being part and fragment of the *totum*, I share in its lawmaking prerogative and thus in its sanctity. Every fragment is holy to the extent that it is part of the *totum*. And to the extent that it is holy, it is autonomous.

The Will to Be and the Will to Be Different

IF in earlier pages we have been vague as to the specific content of natural law, it is simply because we have been purposely limiting ourselves to a discussion of principles. These principles were seen to be an unavoidable consequence of the ontological structure of the *totum*. If the *totum* wants to survive, it must choose the means to that end. Natural law as technique of survival is such a means, and as such it is eternal and absolute, if the *totum* itself is to be eternal and absolute. To conclude from this that the *content* of natural law or the commandments (that is convention as imposed) is absolute and unchangeable would not be warranted. At this point it would be well to recall two things: (1) the fragmentation of the *totum humanum* into cubes or spatio-temporal *subtotum(s)* as discussed in the preceding chapter, and (2) the methodological approach proposed in chapter 1 of this volume.

Actually, one includes the other. The view from afar, encompassing the expanse of time and space, reveals how diverse conventions are. One who is willing to share in that vision will in some ineffable way reap the fruits of vision. There lies in the tradition of a *totum* a wisdom resulting from the slow attrition of time on people and things, a wisdom which is sometimes dull and monotonous, yet which for all its lack of luster and glory has carried life to the present and will carry it into the future. At the same time one realizes that although one lives in one epoch, there is a strange alternation of epochs. The crest of the wave on which we are swept along may very well not be a crest at all.

For any balanced understanding of where we stand here and now, it is sometimes imperative to ponder the past in the concrete, calling to mind the man of the via San Pancrazio or the chief of the Balubas, and to prophesy the future, watching the man of the electronic age move between the planets. This is where the vision of the Observer comes in. There is in this attitude, of course, no startling revelation, no exact intimation of what is right and no clear-cut answer to all ethical problems. The vision of culture-groups is like the vision of living things: their unique character is hard to grasp and cannot be categorized with absolute clarity. But if unique-ness is indefinable, there is somehow an awareness of the "eternal" embodied in the "temporal." The difficulty, of course, is that the eternal cannot easily be detached from the time and place where it is lived. The "eternal" technique of survival is *lived*. Individual men, living their lives within the *totum*, are the termini, within their own being, of all the power-lines which descend to them from the periphery of the *totum*. Suspended in time and place as the termini of these forces, they incarnate the eternal technique in a temporal and contingent form, and in their unique ways constitute convention. But man is also the force of which he is the terminus: he makes what makes him. Natural law has an unchanging intent but a changing content.

Take, for example, the well-known commandment "Thou shalt not kill." We note that in the past men have killed for a variety of reasons, many of which would appear insufficient in our times. One might even be inclined to call such or such an epoch "cruel." But what does the word *cruel* mean? Cruel in this case is a judg-ment made by those of a later epoch, whose own times do not feel the need of such drastic measures to protect their own integrity. What appears as cruel to our epoch may not have appeared so to our ancestors. Cruelty is a judgment of the future upon an activity of the present and of the past (and some day, no doubt, the Hiroshimas, Dresdens, Pragues, that are a part of our way of liv-ing will undergo an evaluation which will be anything but flatter-ing). Obviously, convention is bound up with a particular collec-tive or cubic unit. In line with the opinion that has been developed here, this group which we judge as "cruel" is moral. It had its own mores, which were the guarantee of its own survival, and to break with those mores was an act of immorality. Whether or not the infraction of the mores, a reaction which the *totum* sometimes produces within its own midst, may result in a new morality does not concern us for the moment—we shall explore this later; what matters at present is the insight that one cannot condemn another epoch for not doing what we are doing. The Observer cannot claim that the cannibal commits a sin when he indulges in the custom of his tribe, yet the first of those seated in the circle around the fire who refused the cup of blood may well be called a rebel and a reformer.

We shall later discover the function of the rebel, as the first to break out of the circle, to be a crucial one. In the meantime, we are able to see how, in the light of the diversity of mores and morality, each cubic unit with its particular conventions may be perfect within its own lived structure of *totum* but imperfect when viewed comparatively. Once placed in a line with other *subtotem(s)*, any one *subtotem* must be seen as deficient. This does not mean that it is immoral in one way or another but that its own structure being what it is, its structure-obligations, or ensuing conventions, will be different, and by this very fact will have their limitations. The life of the megalopolis cannot be placed on the same level as that of the Indian tribe on the banks of the Amazon, and however much can be said in favor of technology and sanitation, much can be said as well in favor of a more casual existence without the tensions and haste of the Western culture-group. In this study we shall not judge civilizations and call one better than the other; we shall merely say that they are different. This is the way they are viewed in a phenomenology of descent, as opposed to a philosophy which, judging from the point of view of the subject, takes itself as the norm by which to evaluate persons and events. Only the self-oblivion which is part of a phenomenology of descent will allow the Observer to see the different without automatically placing it in categories of better and worse.

In conclusion, we shall say that natural law is the technique of survival, including both the capability and the urge to be, and that this technique of survival contains a set of commands, the sum-total of which we have called convention. Although convention is always there, it varies in its formulation; hence the three fundamental commandments which we have mentioned at the very beginning of this chapter as being essential to the survival of the *totum* and a necessary condition of its endurance must not be regarded as imperative in the same way and with the same cogency everywhere and always. There are other "commandments" which are at times considered to be part of natural law.

Natural Law and Private Property

THE believers among us claim that it is God who creates the *totum humanum* and puts it upon this planet with the clear implication that this earth should be both its habitat and its instrument for survival. Those who do not see a divine intervention in the human presence upon this earth may call the latter a result of "chance." But whatever may be the remote origin of mankind as a whole, it is undeniable that once here, the *totum* wants to remain in being and that this earth is instrumental to that end. To the extent that this earth is instrumental for its survival, one can assume that the *totum* owns the earth. As we have seen, only the *totum humanum* is and survives unconditionally, while that which is ontologically a fragment survives only as fragment and in no other way. Hence, since the individual is essentially part and fragment, ownership of this globe must go to him as part and fragment, and total ownership must go to that total complex of relations which constitutes the *totum humanum*. Only what *is* unconditionally owns unconditionally.

The partitioning of this earth and the distribution of its fruits can only result from the decision of the *totum*, which is the ultimate technician of the mode of survival and of survival itself. The *totum* is and knows how to be. The more concrete expression of this knowledgeability we have called "convention."

In most collectives, the convention seems to be that either through inheritance or through exchange the individual has acquired the use of a portion of the land and its fruits for an indefinite time. We call this private ownership. All through history private ownership appears to have been a great stimulus of individual effort, since it is directly concerned with the increase of personal possession. It is undeniable that those countries which have practiced this kind of convention over a length of time have been among the most powerful. Private property and its usual concomitant, the right of inheritance, has given individuals an impetus to work which common ownership has not been able to achieve. When one looks at the phenomenon more closely, however, it appears that the motive for this industriousness was self-protection. The individual works for himself and for his family, and as a result, he works harder. The motive need not be considered base. Yet one cannot help noticing that this attitude promotes hostility because of the self-interest involved. Although to compete *is* to complete the *totum*, since it tends to increase the wealth of the collective involved, we also see that in its immediacy, competition makes man "anti-man." Although this is not always clearly expressed, the underlying assumption nevertheless is that in a society where private ownership is the rule, individual man competes with individual man and only the stronger wins.

Ironically enough, this economic system has been most successful among those called Christians, for although Christian countries constitute only sixteen percent of the earth's population, they —the Christians and the Jews who live in these countries—control seventy-five percent of its wealth. Although the method, sometimes called economic imperialism, is not always easy to reconcile with the words and teaching of the Gospel, it has so far been, on the whole, a rewarding experiment for the West.[4]

One can very well visualize situations where "free enterprise" must be curtailed if the *totum* as such is to survive. One such possibility would occur when a nation is in the very early stages of its development, with poverty rampant and illiteracy widespread. In such a situation only control of a laissez-faire economy will enable the nation to protect the poor and the weak. When a minimum subsistence level is out of reach for many, only common possession or the firm control of private ownership can safeguard the *totum*. The tension of the anti-man or the formation of the antithetic which goes along with private property is permissible

---

[4] On the conflict between Christian belief and daily practice see Yves Congar, "The Place of Poverty in Christian Life," in *Concilium*, Vol. 5, No. 2 (May 1966), pp. 28 ff.

only when minimum living standards for all have been attained. Once the *totum* lives at a level above bare survival, its government should grant greater liberty to individual activity, and by the same token propel the *totum* to greater wealth. Common possession aims at bare survival, private ownership at the creation of wealth.

Another possibility where private property may become an evil occurs when—and the case is not at all rare—the wealth of a nation has accumulated in the hands of a very few. Through their wealth these few have placed themselves outside and above the *totum*. They must once again be brought back into the fold, since the power of the fragment cannot be permitted to replace the power of the *totum* unless it is delegated to do so. If at that level of concentration private ownership is not reduced by law, it will be by violence. On this history has judged. Revolutions are nothing but group decisions to bring power and wealth from the hands of the few into the hands of the many. Although one may regret the violence that goes with it, one cannot deny the fact that a sociological event like a revolution is in many cases a natural sequel to prior abuses.

A severe limitation of the prerogatives of individuals must lie, then, at both extremes of the spectrum. It belongs at the birth of a nation which is underdeveloped and cannot divide its resources fairly without strict control, and it belongs equally at the end of an economic growth in which an economy of freedom for all has resulted in the creation of immense fortunes for a few, for the accumulation of financial power is a threat to every other power.

The transition from wealth-in-the-hands-of-a-few to wealth-diffused-among-many does not per se require a revolution. A more peaceful route is the replacement of the multimillionaire by the industrial giant. Although this is rarely mentioned, industrial complexes constitute a prudent form of communism in many cases. The industrial complex is in fact a collective of individuals who, whether they like it or not, work for the benefit of their industrial *totum*. The success of the *totum* benefits the members, but it does so only indirectly, since it is only in working for the totality that they will be rewarded. In the days of private artisans the work was performed by X and the reward reached X as an immediate result; X was both actor and collector. At present X is rewarded only through the collective or industrial *totum*. The circle has widened, and although X receives his salary, he does not receive it directly from the buyer, but only as an entity contributing to the achievement of the *totum*. The *totum* manufactures and the *totum* sells. There is a strong trend toward the collective in every industrial outfit. Every payment and every reward ties the individual closer to the collective of which he is a member. He can leave, no doubt —and in most countries there is no obstacle in his way, except the loss of seniority and stock options—but he can leave only to join another group. The survival of *X* lies within the *totum*.

Once more the *totum is* absolutely while the fragment *is* only conditionally. The existence of the part is and persists through the ensemble, and any outsiders, such as the immensely wealthy or the politically powerful, must be reintroduced into the fold either by force or by legal procedure. Inequality is considered the potent lever of efficient performance, but inequality or uniqueness must be restrained when the *totum* is in peril. Such are the ethical implications resulting from an ontology of a fractured *totum*. Looked at from afar, a certain mobility or what might be called a cyclical movement seems to be the rule: what started as common possession in the genesis of a collective evolves into a practice of free ownership and private property, to return once more to a form of socialism once the wealth becomes concentrated in the hands of a few. Wealth moves from the common to the private and back again according to the morality of the epoch, a morality which itself is dictated by a technique of "survival," but *nowhere can it be demonstrated with cogency that either form belongs exclusively and totally to natural law in its original form of technique of survival.*

Natural Law in Its Historical Setting

WE have now reached the point where it is possible to put our concept of natural law into its historical framework. This will show us how our understanding of natural law contains a defense both of the individual and of the totality, a trend that in the opinion of this writer will be characteristic of the times to come. The following pages are in no way intended to be a detailed assessment of the historical evolution of the concept of natural law. Only that which is of interest to our purpose will be treated.

In 534, on the order of Emperor Justinian, a body of Byzantine lawyers undertook the codification of Roman law. The purpose of this compilation was to present a body of laws which would be universally valid.[5] The presupposition was that this could be done because the concept of human nature is always and everywhere the same. Natural law is eternal because the concept of nature as fulfilled in man is eternal.

It is immediately apparent that such a concept of human nature is a postulate which runs counter to the definition of the universal as we have presented it. The traditional position sees the universal as that concept which, abstracted from the real, is by essence the same in all the beings of whom it is predicated. It is a result of separation, since it omits what is unique and picks out what is similar in all. The notion of universal proposed here is that which results from the addition of entities, resulting in a sum-total which contains both the similar and the dissimilar. Such a universal is not unchangeable but, on the contrary, is ever on the move, since it is a reflection of the real, of which it is the additive replica. Mirroring the real literally and totally, it develops with the real. The incessant change of the fragments builds up a new image of the collective. It is this image of the collective that is the universal, which is an additive universal. What characterizes the Codex, on the contrary, is the presumption that human nature is stable, and that as a result mores are stable as well.

In the writings of the church fathers the same emphasis persists. One could say that in relating natural law to God as its origin, the character of its unchangeability was even confirmed. Natural law becomes supreme and overrules all other laws and customs. From this time on natural law is presented as *in corde scripta*— "written in the heart"—and as containing an *innata vis* (innate drive) towards the knowledge of the law itself.[6] The church fathers have a tendency to produce a greater separation between the concept of natural law as proposed by the Romans and that "revealed" by Christianity. Roman law becomes Christianized. For Augustine above all the glory of Rome and its worldly achievements was gone, together with its philosophy. Many passages of *De Civitate Dei* echo the sound of the crumbling Empire.[7]

---

[5] A. Passerin d'Entreves, *Natural Law* (London: Hutchinson's University Library, 1951), pp. 17–18.

[6] *Ibid.*, p. 35.

[7] *De Civitate Dei*, V, 18.

The medieval scholastics took a more optimistic view, as it appears from the writings of their most authoritative interpreter. According to Aquinas, God stands at the origin of things as their Maker and Creator. He is also the rational guide of man. Insofar as He guides all things to their end, He is the Eternal Law, and insofar as the creation proceeds to its end, it participates in the Eternal Law. This participation in the heart and mind of man is called natural law.[8]

It is reason which enables man to discover the distinction between good and evil. Through reason he "lies in the middle between two hemispheres,"[9] able to explain and justify ethical commands. Aquinas sees reason as man's great asset, enabling him to avoid being overwhelmed by sin, as Augustine's pessimism would have him be. Not only did St. Thomas take a more optimistic view of the intrinsic value of man but he was more accommodating on the concept of the evolution of natural law. According to him, natural law can change either by addition or by subtraction. The whole concept becomes more pragmatic, as history for the first time plays a part.

Yet for all this, Aquinas' view cannot be called rationalistic, since man is never considered to be self-sufficient but is forever dependent upon grace. The obligation of natural law is divine not only in origin but in fulfillment as well. Man is not considered to be autonomous even in the collective structure of the *totum*. We should add—and this is no small matter—that the emphasis is more upon what one *ought* to do than upon what one is permitted to do: *duties* are emphasized over and above *rights*. Obedience is the virtue par excellence, and institutions, political and religious alike, are structured hierarchically, with all the power at the top in the hands of one man or of a few only.

It took centuries to change this climate of opinion. Philosophy echoes an epoch, and it was not until Descartes with his *Discourse on Method* and *Meditations* that the importance of the individual subject was emphasized. His *Cogito* was the glorification of the individual self as that which has matter at its command and stands opposed to a world of matter. To man as a center the world is

---

[8] *S. Th.*, I, II, Q. CL, art. 1 and 2.

[9] Dante, *De Monarchia*, III, 16.

an object of knowledge. Later on, in the writings of the Encyclo-
pedists, the status of man is stressed even more: he is born free and
equal to his fellow men. Through Rousseau's theory of the social
contract, for example, individuals willingly and consciously ratify
their agreement of living together, showing themselves prepared to
abandon some of their privileges for the benefit of society. This
was one attempt, if not the best possible, to reconcile the state
and the individual. On all fronts a growing attention was being
given to the individual as such. The discussion of *duties*, so characteristic of the Middle Ages, was giving way to a discovery of
rights and *liberties*.[10] Hobbes and Locke still managed to hold
both rights and duties in balance. See, for example, chapter VI of
Locke's *Second Treatise on Government*, 57 and following, where
Locke makes it clear that we are *born free*, yet regulated by law,
since "where there is no Law, there is no Freedom." People therefore are *subject* to the law, but this law is not so much a limitation
as the direction of a free and intelligent agent. But when on July 4,
1776, the Declaration of Independence was signed in Philadel-
phia, the meaning was unequivocal: "We hold these truths to be
self-evident, that all men are created equal, that they are endowed
by their Creator with certain inalienable Rights . . ."; natural law
was a law of *rights*. This was no less forcefully expressed in the
first amendments to the Constitution, or Bill of Rights, once the
War of Independence was over, although there was a hint of duty
in the statement that "the enumeration of certain Rights shall not
be construed to deny or disparage others retained by the people."

At about the same time, on August 26, 1789, the French Assembly adopted the *Déclaration des droits de l'homme et du citoyen*.
Once more the emphasis was upon freedom and equality, although
this time the oppressor was not a foreign country but forces within
the nation itself.

We are a far cry from the scholastic concept of natural law.
Yet there is more. Amidst the multiple events of those tempestuous
days, we should mention the "Culte de la Raison," which was a
movement to replace the cultus of supernatural religion by a worship of Reason. This reached its highpoint on November 10, 1793,
when Notre Dame cathedral was dedicated to the goddess Reason;

---

[10] Passerin d'Entreves, *op. cit.,* | p. 59.

a large number of priests together with Bishop Godel unfrocked themselves, and Mademoiselle Maillard, an actress at the Opera, impersonated the goddess of Reason. All of this was significant of the mood in which the revolution took place, and most of all, of the times which prepared this greatest of all revolutions. It was a revolution of the individual man fighting for his rights, and he did so on the basis of reason and of reason alone, excluding revelation as a source of knowledge.

Never in this long procession from the ancient, through the medieval, up to and including the modern period were either duties or rights emphasized to the total exclusion of one by the other. Both are an intrinsic part of the concept of law, and nowhere would it be possible to establish a society without at least a minimum of both. It will be given to our times to implement the realization of both rights and duties on equal terms. Ideas have their epochs. It is in reaching their fulfillment that they constitute an epoch. The epoch of "Les droits de l'homme et du citoyen" with its onesided emphasis on rights is gone, as is the medieval phase of blind obedience that preceded it. In taking a critical look at both of these periods, we have no intention of disavowing the role they played in their own times. We wish only to examine their value for the future. In our view ethics is a question of opportunity, and "convention" belongs to the cube which in its temporal dimension we have called a "period." It may appear by the end of our examination that in our times we will see at work the complementarity of a twofold movement: on one hand the corporative trend embodied in the concept of the *totum* and on the other its limitation through the defense of the *unique* fragment. The remaining sections of this chapter will be an attempt to elucidate this by means of a more detailed study of what it means in concrete terms to be in authority and of what it implies for a fragment to act as a fragment.

The Future of Authority

ALTHOUGH this has not been explicitly stated, it has nonetheless been sufficiently implied that in our philosophical approach, authority belongs to the *totum* and the *totum* only. It is vested in the hands of a few only as delegated by the *totum*. This delegation of authority can be by tacit consent of the *totum*—this is usually the case when the *totum* has neither the background nor the education to set up a political election—or it can be done formally and explicitly—authority is entrusted to a government by the people. To be fragment of a *totum* absolutely precludes any status of superman, the status by which a human being, transcending the totality, dominates and governs it from beyond and outside. There is nowhere any philosophical warrant for such an entity. Yet this was the basic form of authority cultivated during the Middle Ages by both Church and State.

The concept was supported by two kinds of sanctions. The first, "supernatural" in origin, is contained in the famous *Omnis auctoritas a Deo*—all authority comes from God. This formula, undemonstrated and nowhere clearly explained, laid the foundation for the mythologization of ecclesiastical and political authority. Political structure and church hierarchy alike were built up in the form of a pyramid. The average man was a subject, in the Latin sense of the word *subjectus*, or lying under, while above him, in layers which became gradually narrower and narrower, different forms of authority were installed until it was finally embodied in one individual, pope or king or emperor. The life of the *totum* was regulated from above, and the individual man was taught and retaught that his salvation lay in obedience and blind submission to God, as present in the political or ecclesiastical authorities "above" him.

The second foundation for the idea of the Superman was a very natural one. Authority has power. Whoever has power is looked upon with respect and fear. The awesome power vested in the pope or king unavoidably gave rise to a "personality cult." This form of personality cult is, of course, not an exclusive feature of medieval conventions. It is in no way alien to socialistic and democratic countries alike, for to side with the man in authority is for most people the easiest road to success.

The demythologization of authority that started with the French and American revolutions will continue in our times. This demythologization consists in giving authority its proper status, which is one of instrumentality towards the welfare of the *totum*. The hierarchical structure which must be demythologized is a complex one. It includes a distribution of functions in which terms such as *higher* and *lower* are borrowed from spatial dimensions; the result is the strange situation wherein one looks up to what is higher and down to what is lower. Only the powerful man, or the one who considers himself invested with a divine character, holds a high place. Height and power become synonymous. We say about someone: He is in a high position, meaning that for some reason he deserves special respect and attention. But, here again, this way of making a statement and of looking at one's surroundings is only made by the subject as such. The subject, whether he looks up (which is at present the case) or down, makes a judgment from his point of view. He evaluates others to the extent that the others are harmful or beneficial to him, and he does so in spatial metaphors which betray an optic of the subject. Not only does he take a look at the surrounding world from his own angular optic, and from that subjective point of view judge the others to be above or below himself, but he will also be inclined to judge the richer and the more powerful to be "better." To be better is not always applied to what is morally better; in most cases it applies to what is successful. The rich and successful are doing "better," and the one in authority is "better off" than the one who is "under" him.

If, on the contrary, we choose a point of view of descent, it will appear that the *totum humanum* is indeed fragmented, unequal and different—clearly the president of a nation does not fulfill the same function as the carpenter—but it no longer appears that *A* is better than *B* because he is more influential, or worse because he is less influential. The subject is no longer there, to measure what is above or below himself, or to fear what may threaten him. Spatial metaphors concerned with that which is above or below lose their bearing if one presumes that there is no longer an individual subject, center of the universe of man and of things. There is no center. There is only the *totum* and the diversity of the unique within the *totum*, all of them equally valuable because of their unique character.

Inequality there is, no doubt, and we have no intention of denying this ontological trait of the segments within the totality, but this inequality is not one of better or worse, but one of difference. The leader of a nation is not better than his carpenter, but he is different from him. The danger of Plato's Phoenician tale lies not in his accepting the different and the unequal—with all this we gladly agree—but in his placing the gold at the top, as if it could not with equal right be found at the bottom. In placing the gold at the top only, Plato shows his disregard for the brass, to which he assigned all the humble functions. In this he is wrong. In a world of the unique and the different as seen by the Observer there is no humble job. Every function is unique because—and this is paramount—the better and the worse lie in the achievement, not in the function itself. There is no longer a hierarchy in the function, but only in the fulfillment of the function. Not every one fulfills his function with equal skill. It follows with no less certainty that if we reject the idea that quality is inherent in the function, we reject with equal vigor the semantics which for centuries have mythologized the function. It cannot be demonstrated that authority comes from God any more than that the function of the carpenter can be said to be divine in origin. Even those who want to reduce everything to the First Cause or the Supreme Lawgiver need not abandon their belief in the divine origin of Law, for clearly the One who would create a *totum humanum* would also want an entity to coordinate the internal communications of the constituents of that *totum*. Such an entity, which we shall call an *authority*, is part of the division of labor, which itself is a consequence of the ontological inequality within the organic structure of the *totum*. There is no noumenal quality attached to one function more than to any other. The formula *ex opere operato*—working by the action done—was for a long time a mask behind which clerical or political figures could hide: as long as the rite was correct, the one who performed it could be anything. This is no longer so. People want the performer to be as good as his rite.

We are now ready to define the place of authority within the *totum*, that authority delegated by the *totum* as a *function*. It is a function, and like all functions within the *totum* it is instrumental to the welfare of the particular *totum*. More specifically, the function of authority is to protect the oneness of the *totum*, not through any suppression of the unique but through promoting the communication and cooperation of the diverse. Authority, therefore, should never attempt to render the diverse uniform. On the contrary, the function of authority is to protect diversity as the ontological requisite of the organic totum. Thus, it should respect the creative and free expression of the unique and attempt to discover the vocation of the segment within the *totum*. Above all, it should incessantly attempt to keep open the channels of communication between the diverse and tear down all walls, for in the world of the future there is no place for ghettos.

Such, then, is the primary function of authority. This function has nothing noumenal about it. The carpenter or the mason is as divine—or as human—as the king. The events of the last three centuries have fostered greater respect for the individual man, each individual man. He is as imperfect as ever and "no better than his fathers," but in our times an attempt is made to let him be and live and work. One is aware of his presence, and in being aware of his presence or his being *there*, one respects his right of being there. This is how, on a visual span, individual man appears to the Observer, and how over the centuries he has shown himself to be, simply by becoming what he is now. Both the French and American revolutions have forcefully dramatized this evolution, without for that reason having produced it all by themselves. Revolutions, however violent, are surface movements and merely express at a certain moment in history what has already been going on in the depth of the *totum* over a considerable length of time. They are symptoms of a *totum humanum* getting hold of itself and reestablishing the balance.

A secondary function of the man in authority is to restrain any individual or any group of individuals whose actions threaten the welfare of the *totum* as such. The lesson of the revolutions of the last two hundred years is clear: the rights of the individual are sacred. Although this has not been everywhere implemented, the idea has taken root in many places. In America especially the trend has been to protect the individual and his rights. It is in the light of this protection that one can understand the mentality of the American nation which, in theory at least if not always in practice, has constantly attempted to protect individual rights. In economics the laissez-faire approach, with its tolerance of individual achievement and personal profit, has succeeded in building up an economic power which is probably the greatest in the world. Respect for the individual has protected the defendant on trial as in no other country in the world.

We begin to observe, though, that as a result of this twofold protection, economic and juridical, a twofold abuse threatens the *totum*, the power of money and the power of crime. In both cases one can detect the consequences of a use and abuse of individual rights. But if their origin is common, the circumstances and persons involved produce different results. The criminal, in the act of his crime and in calling for extreme interpretations of the protection offered to him when he is on trial, attempts to go beyond his individual rights. So also does the businessman who, taking advantage of the freedom from restraint afforded by a laissez-faire policy, increases his power at the expense of the poor and the weak. Both have their defenders. The defender of the business world is considered in most milieus to be a conservative, while the protector of the criminal calls himself a liberal. Ironically enough, both defenders are in favor of liberty, but they want it to be granted to a different sort of individual.

This is where the secondary function of the man in authority comes in. It is becoming clear that if capitalism has succeeded for itself, it has not succeeded for the nation. It is the function of the man in authority to curb the power of business no less than the power of crime. In doing this, authority must of course have the power to enforce. Without coercive power its function of promoting the *oneness* and the *diverse* within the one would be in vain. Authority should be able to prevent the fragment from becoming the *totum*, yet enable it to remain unique in its fragmentarity. In curtailing the power of money and of crime, the authority of the *totum* marks the individual as fragment. And this is as it should be.

One point should be made very clear. Authority itself, once it is delegated, remains embodied in the fragment. Authority which is delegated acts in the name of the *totum* but it is not the *totum*. And it is on the basis of this principle that the individual members of a totality remain participants in the exercise of the delegated authority. This participation occurs in a variety of ways, and it cannot be demonstrated that the political structure exemplified in the Anglo-Saxon countries is the only way. To specify the ways in which power should be delegated is the function of the political scientist, not of the philosopher, but the philosopher can offer certain underlying principles that must be kept in mind in any consideration of political structures. Our view can show, for example, the obstacles to the current popular demands for total participation in the decisions made by such totalities as nations or universities. These are, first, ignorance and second, the lack of communication.

The first obstacle does not imply that the constituents of a *subtotum* are not capable people. It is merely that we should keep in mind that not everyone knows everything and that a division of labor is merely the ontological consequence of the ontological fragmentation of the *totum* and the unequal distribution of talents. The administrative function, for example, requires a skill which not everyone can claim to have, or for which not everyone has the time and energy. It may be that an individual will be better suited to expanding his energies on the law, medicine, masonry, physics, or philosophy. The recent creation of a new profession of court administrators is an attempt to take certain burdens off the shoulders of the judges in order to free them for their proper task, which is to preside over the trials themselves. The need for division of labor is basic in this study, and no form of government, however democratic, can fail to take it into account, for it is part of the deeper structure of the *totum*.

Lack of communication is another obstacle to total participation. How shall we convey our wishes and our needs to the men in authority? On this topic we have already made some suggestions, and it is not our intention to repeat what we have said before.[11] Among other things the computer will make a referendum among the participants easier, hence will become a means for fuller communication. Our remote forefathers were able to give their opinion as they sat around the fire. Closer to us, towns in New England hold "town meetings" for an exchange of views. The concept of time has changed, however, and in most parts of the world there is not enough of it available for such forms of dialogue. This is where authority comes in and decides for "us," if and when the conversation of the many has become an impossibility.

What Does It Imply to Act as a Fragment?

THE paradox of a fragment is that being fragment, it must act as one. The individual, viewing the world from a particular angle,

---

[11] See above, pp. 122–125.

goes into action, and through his act, considered partially, is liable to hurt the other. What it means to act as fragment may reveal to us where we stand in the historical shifting of the concept of natural law.

(1) To act as a fragment does not preclude the inequality of the fragments (either as individual or as *subtotum*) within the *totum genus*. Inequality, as we conceive it, does not per se contain any evaluation of better and worse, but merely a qualification of *such* or *so*. The inequality is made up out of contraries, or entities which are ontologically different, not out of moral variables, a distinction which would imply that one is better than the other.

(2) The acceptance of being a fragment does not exclude the use of one's talents to an optimum or restrain attempts towards creativity and high achievement. Of course, no individual, however talented, could become a *superman* if the latter is considered identical with the *totum* and, as a result, above and beyond its rules.

Similarly no group of individuals could consider itself a super-race which, as "cube extraordinary," considers itself above and beyond any other culture-group, hence empowered to dictate its laws to other collectives.

(3) Entrance through birth into the *totum humanum* implies a presence beyond the present moment, hence the possibility to survive. This privilege simply to be is a fundamental right, what we shall call the first right. What is structurally interlocked in the ontological order is so morally. Hence what is right for X becomes a duty for Z. The other is my ought and my right is his ought. Right and ought (or right and duty) are no less interlocked than are men themselves. As soon as individual man emerges as part of a *totum*, he is affected by the presence of others, and the ought which the others impress upon him through their company, whether remote or near, becomes incumbent on him. The ought is created by the presence of the other. Just as in previous chapters the other was considered the redeemer, he appears no less forcefully now as the one who is "right." The self is "right"; again, not in the sense of being faultless or correct, but merely in the sense of being a unique and irreplaceable self that is endowed with a will to be and, as such, worthy of respect.

In the light of all this, it will appear that the obligation coming down from the *totum* and reaching the individual man merely states that the fragment ought to be what it is. It seems consistent to speak of a situation in this world which could be described as the phenomenon of "fitting": man as fragment is the entity which "fits"; he is the one among the many juxtaposed to each other. However explosive he may at times appear, he fits on a horizontal level as that entity which faces the others, and he fits on a vertical level as that which comes from . . . and is productive of. . . . Within this framework man is placed as the one on whom is incumbent a law which is nothing but the will of the *totum*. But if an individual is subject to the law, he expects by the same token to have his rights—or, better still, to be "his right."

It appears that it is no longer possible to visualize the individual man as having duties and no rights, or rights and no duties. Whoever has no rights has no duties. At the present time, we have reached this level of theoretical consciousness even if we have not yet seen its practical fulfillment. It is no wonder that as a result, modern man is becoming exigent. The theory of right propounded in these pages must be brought into relation with the concept of anti-man. It now clearly appears how man becomes anti-man. The defense of rights is the defense of self, and where rights are lacking man more than ever grows into the mood of *anti*.

(4) To act as a fragment presumes the acceptance of the *totum genus humanum* as the ultimate *totum* and its survival as the ultimate absolute. The existence of the *totum humanum* encompasses the fragment in time and space. Since the *totum is* unconditionally, it takes precedence over that which *is* only relatively and conditionally. This does not signify that the power of the *totum* entitles it to crush the fragment, nor does it mean that the *totum* is in any way better than the fragment, but it does imply that within the fragment *simply to be* is prior to *being such*.

When we use the term *simply to be*, we allude to the entrance of the individual man into the *totum humanum* through birth —the only way so far known. On the basis of this coming into the world, the individual fragment enters into the oneness of the *totum humanum*. He is part of the complex unit of interrelated fragments called the human totality. It is the fact of being able to relate in a variety of ways that makes the individual fragment a human entity. This is what we have in mind when we speak of *simply to be*, to be human.

When we use the words *to be such*, we allude to the fact that *within* this global *totum*, which is, as we know, a fractured *totum*, the newly born is unavoidably different from. . . . He is human, but he is human in such or such a way. He is American or French or German, he belongs to the Western world or to the Oriental world, he lives in 400 B.C. or A.D. 2000. Returning now to our previous statement according to which *to be* precedes *to be such* within the fragment, we understand its implication; namely, that to *be human* is prior to being American or being French or being Western or being anything else.

Before elaborating upon the consequences of our proposition, we must at first answer an objection which will inevitably be made at this point. The claim can be made that *being such* is the unavoidable concomitant of *simply to be*. The individual man is always caught within a *subtotum*, which shapes him into being either Chinese or American, French or German, part of modern times or of Roman antiquity, etc., etc. This is indeed its way to be: the *totum humanum* survives because of the diversity within it and the incessant correction that results. Consequently the diverse cannot be eliminated.

Yet the actualization of the totum and of its diverse expression does not preclude the fact there is a theoretical priority of *simply being* over *being such*. In line with the view here proponded, what matters above all is the survival of the *totum humanum*. The diverse ways in which it survives—be it as American or as Russian, as Greek, Roman, Congolese or Brazilian—are accidental. By accidental we mean contingent to historical and geographical circumstances, hence transient and not absolute. Although the *totum humanum* survives through the diverse, the diverse itself is by no means the same always and everywhere. The collectives called nations have an unstable foundation, and although the collective itself as a means of survival is indeed a way of being, that way is not the only one. What is Etruscia today may be Rome tomorrow, and what is the Roman Empire tomorrow may become Gaul at a later date. The instrumentality of the *totum* changes, yet the ultimate purpose—that is, the survival of the *totum humanum*—remains.

This principle has far-reaching consequences. If the instrumentality of the diverse, although always there, somehow is a contingent one, the principle given above, according to which *simply to be* transcends *being such or such*, obtains a strong confirmation. What matters in the human fragment is not so much to be either American or Russian or Chinese or whatever else one may be in time or space, but to belong to the oneness of the *totum humanum*. For this is the only enduring absolute. And *belonging* in our case means to be interlocked within the whole structure of the human community. In the ultimate sense, one is human before being anything else because one is always, in the genesis of life, born into a *totum humanum* with the fragments of which one will live, create and procreate. What the physiological conditions are which make that interlocking a reality is not for the philosopher to consider. We shall turn to the sciences for that. The philosopher merely wants to stress that oneness implies relation. This potential interlocking of man with man precedes any other coloring of the *subtotum* or cubic unit which surrounds the individual fragment. This ontological priority is undeniable. Although the priority is not a chronological one (upon its birth the newborn always enters into a group, or the *subtotum* of a certain group), it must rule the life of any individual fragment.

For if there is an ontological priority of the *totum humanum,* natural law, although diversified in its applications over time and space, deserves unconditional assent. Prior to all obedience to any convention as existentially realized, there must always be a prior consideration of the natural law as the nonexistential technique of survival of the *totum*. It may seem paradoxical, yet it is nonetheless correct to say that here the nonexistent commands the existent; or, more concretely, that natural law as a technique of survival protects the human being as a member of the *totum humanum* before any specification or distortion which might result from *being such or so* (English or French or Japanese, etc.). *The belonging to the* totum humanum *transcends all belonging, and the commands of natural law as the deepest technique of survival transcend all conventions.* What this natural law in its nonexistential purity implies is a secret of the *totum humanum* itself, and for this reason belongs to what we have called the generic truth. Yet whatever may be the conventions of any particular "cube," no "convention" may contain the right to kill indiscriminately, nor can it prohibit the most elementary right to live. Hence, although stealing might be prohibited by the convention of a certain epoch

—it would be disastrous indeed if stealing should be introduced as a *modus vivendi*—no law of any epoch or of any place can be such that it would require the individual to die rather than to steal. To steal rather than to-die-from-hunger can never be a sin. This is a sacred priority, for just as the State can disappropriate a private property for public reasons, so also can an individual in extreme necessity get hold of the elementary things to live when the normal method of exchange is not available. For this is a case where the *being human* takes precedence over the laws of the *being such or so* (English or French or Japanese, etc.).

Although this study is not explicitly concerned with legal philosophy, it does lay the groundwork for some legal applications. For example, it is in the light of the precedence of *simply to be* over *being such* that the conflict between natural and positive law that at times arises must be resolved.

Positive law is a particularization of natural law that is promulgated by a particular authority. It is, by nature, clearer and more precise than the fundamental law prescribed by the convention of natural law; it has obtained legal sanction within the community, and it has legal coercion, with infractions being punished. To follow the positive law is a way of *being such*.

One question that has been asked again and again is whether or not positive law must be related to natural law. Our thesis would make their interrelationship mandatory. If natural law is as we have described it, it cannot be practiced without the further specification that is embodied in positive law. In order to be lived by, natural law must not only be made more precise; it must also be made binding. However strong the "conventionality" of natural law may be in itself, it needs to be particularized in positive law. Yet in taking the shape of the particular, it becomes caught within the "angular" view of the lawmakers themselves, hence contaminated by the frailties of their judgment. Although all positive laws aim at the defense of the *totum* and the individuals within that *totum*, they, more than the elemental conventions of natural law, are contaminated by the vicissitudes which went into their making. At times positive laws are even corrupt, because their aim was not the general interest but the defense of a few. Sometimes they are a result not so much of bad will as of ignorance, as was that blind obedience so often encouraged in the religious life, or its counterpart, the adulation of authorities in the political sphere. The individual fragment within the *totum* must learn to judge the impact of positive law against a background of the more enduring natural law. It is above all this lack of independent judgment which resulted in the cooperation of the Nazi torturers with their leaders. In perpetrating the extermination of the Jews and other prisoners, they were merely "obeying orders." That these orders, or "positive laws," were the most serious offense against natural law ever committed apparently did not occur to them. They had forgotten that any positive law and any command presumes a deeper law, the law of the *totum* itself, which because of its internal fragmentation carries within itself a structure-obligation called natural law.[12]

---

[12] Although no one has any intention of defending the mass murders of Auschwitz, the legal grounds on which the condemnation itself of the Nazi criminals was based—*nullum crimen sine poena*, "no crime without a penalty"—is debatable. Crimes of so monstrous a character cannot be permitted to go unpunished. On the other hand, the fact remains that it is a fundamental rule of positive jurisprudence—that is, of a jurisprudence which does not claim the natural law as its basis —that no punishment can be meted out unless a law is broken: *Nulla poena sine lege.* The question now becomes this: on the basis of what sort of positive law could the Nazis be brought to trial? What gives the assembly of judges seated at the international tribunal of Nuremberg the right to judge the Nazis? What positive law accounts for it, presuming of course that no natural law can back it up? Why should evil be punished? Why and how must evil be defined? Why should the victor be entitled to condemn the loser? Why must Dresden go unpunished, and Yokohama? Why must the concentration camps of Siberia go unmentioned? No clear answer is available to these questions for anyone who rejects natural law as the ultimate safeguard of the *totum.* There are plenty of answers, of course, for anyone who, rejecting natural law, replaces it by the law of the strongest and by the age-old motto *vae victis*—"woe to the vanquished!"—but this is not what is here understood by natural law.

6

The Phenomenon of Sin

IN discussing the problem of sin we shall not dwell upon its theological significance but shall attempt to keep the topic within a philosophical perspective. If the results concur with the "Ten Commandments," this may be one more indication that the split between the natural and the supernatural has been unduly emphasized and may be eliminated in the world of the future. If we do not completely concur with the prescriptions of the Decalogue, it may suggest that we have moved into another phase of development, where the teaching of Moses must to a certain extent be considered obsolete. To what extent, we may not be able to set forth with precision. Yet the persistent attempt in this study to move the supernatural into the natural dimension is already in itself indicative of our view that God is not above but within His creation and that worship of the deity consists not so much in a search for one's Maker as in a respect for His work. To worship Him and at the same time to destroy His creation is a contradiction. In the future it may very well be that the religious man will show a kind of devotion differing from that of the past, and it will be the task of our last chapter to outline this new form of "sanctity."

In his evaluations the moralist is neither preacher nor playwright. If he becomes preacher and claims that crime does not pay, he may oversimplify his case, for again and again it can be shown that sin does (at least partially) pay. If there were no reward attached, people would not sin. If, on the contrary, the moralist becomes a worldly playwright and represents sin as a pleasant diversion with no evil consequences whatsoever, his description will again appear to be onesided, for even where sin is depicted as a farce—for example, the many comedies turning upon adultery—it can be an amusing spectacle only if the less happy consequences are overlooked. In a comedy these consequences must be played down, for its purpose is to amuse and not to teach. The moralist is neither preacher nor playwright. He does not usurp their functions, for it is his task to look at life as it is.

Consistent with the approach outlined in earlier chapters, we shall be looking at various phenomena—adultery, murder—from the outside and shall not ascribe to the agent any intentions beyond the "present." We observe that what the agent has in mind appears to be the present "instant." "Sin" is committed by the individual (or by the collective) for a satisfaction without delay and with a disregard for the consequences. The sinner (the one who commits the act—we have not yet precisely defined him) is a man of the instant. By the term *instant* we do not understand the indivisible atom in a duration of time, but rather that dimension of the action that is viewed strictly within its own duration and is prescinded from what precedes the action and from what follows it. As such, it is the act as wanted by the agent. It will appear that for a better understanding sin must be looked at in the light of a broader time-dimension. The examples which we shall consider will merely confirm that particular insight. Paradoxically enough, the understanding of both preparation and consequences will place the sinner at the pivotal center of a time-space quadrant, so that a more complete vision of sin will appear to be not the act alone but that which is built around the act. It will appear towards the end of the chapter that if our method overlooks the intention of the agent, it does not overlook his position. Perhaps the revelation of his position at the center of the vortex will be indicative of his intention.

We shall make our point clear through the study of two fictional characters, Emma Bovary and Raskolnikov, and one historical event, known as the Middle Passage. In proceeding to do this, we have a particular philosophical point in mind and will therefore not be sidetracked by literary or other considerations. As we proceed through our three examples, it will be seen that each new encounter throws more light upon our point of view.

In choosing the career of Emma Bovary as our classic adulteress, we note that Anna Karenina has equal claims to the title and might have been selected save for the fact that Tolstoi is more didactic and definitely wishes to teach a moral lesson. Gustave Flaubert, while not avoiding this issue, wants above all to show the deed and its consequences. In *Madame Bovary* the deed speaks for itself. It leads the perpetrator to her destruction with almost mechanical necessity, while Flaubert himself is invisible. There are no prejudgments, no visible strings: Emma propels herself to the final judgment. In Tolstoi's novel one is more aware of the author's intentions and moral evaluations. Emma had her moments of delight, Anna had none. And although in both cases the ending was disastrous, Emma had known the sweetness of love no less than its cruel consequences. Above all, Emma, more than her Russian counterpart, was able to forget; she lived for the instant and for the instant alone. She had no interest in the daily routine of life, or in monotonous surroundings. The ocean interested her only when it was stormy and the landscape when it mirrored her emotions. Emma lived for the extraordinary, discarding anything that was not an object of immediate gratification and avidly looking for those rare moments of high tension, regardless of the consequences. The life with her father was a boring existence, but once married, she found life with her husband no less insipid. The relations with her lovers were still in the distant future, and yet without knowing it or being conscious of all that this would some day mean to her, she was expecting them. A first encounter, or what may be called an initiation, was the ball in the chateau to which Bovary, as the local notable, was invited with his wife. At this ball she met the rich and the happy. "There was an air of indifference about them [about the men she met], a calm produced by gratification of every passion; and though their manners were suave, one could sense beneath them that special brutality which comes from the habit of breaking down half-hearted resistances that keep one fit and tickle one's vanity—the handling of blooded horses, the pursuit of loose women."[1] She met a count

---

[1] Gustave Flaubert, *Madame Bovary*, trans. Francis Steegmuller (New York: Modern Library, 1957), p. 57.

who was in her eyes handsome and rich. This acquaintance did not last, but was nonetheless one of those extraordinary moments which, however short, leave a memory which by far outlasts the evening. "Her visit . . . had opened a breach in her life, like one of those crevasses that a storm can tear across the face of a mountain in the course of a single night. But there was nothing to do about it."[2]

The romance with the notary clerk, although merely sentimental, was a step nearer to things to come. In the person of Rodolphe, a bachelor and rich landowner of the neighborhood, however, she would find everything she longed for. This was her hour of triumph, and love so long repressed gushed forth in joyful effervescence. There was neither remorse nor anxiety: Emma lived in the "instant."

Paradoxically the "sinner" seeks a stabilization of the "instant." Although Emma's deed was a break with bourgeois conventionality, she wanted bourgeois security. She wanted to have a ring as a sign of everlasting love and to escape with Rodolphe to foreign countries. These things were impossible demands as far as her lover was concerned, for he did not consider them to be in any way connected with his present pleasures. He too was living for the "instant" and not for what the other might wish to be the result of the act. His refusal to elope was a consequence which Emma had to accept. The affair ended with her illness.

Emma did not languish long, however, and in a new adulterous affair reached out once more for the "instant." This time it was more than ever passion, and less and less love. Expecting the maximum from every meeting, she experienced growing dissatisfaction. "Each disappointment gave way to new hope; each time, Emma returned to him more feverish, more avid. . . . There was something mad, though something strange and sinister, about that cold, sweating forehead, about those stammering lips, those wildly staring eyes, the clasp of those arms—something that seemed to Leon [her lover] to be creeping between them, subtly, as though to tear them apart."[3] She became as surfeited with her lover as he was tired of her. Adultery, Emma was discovering, could be as banal as marriage. Abandoned by her lovers, persecuted by her creditors, Emma ended her life by taking poison.

---

[2] *Ibid.*, p. 63.　　　　[3] *Ibid.*, p. 321.

The book reached its climax with the love affair of Rodolphe and Emma. This is the "instant" par excellence, that act which the agent wants without the consequences. In observing the case of Emma, we see that her absorption in the affair with Rodolphe is total. She is wholly engrossed, as few sinners are, in her own act. There are before and during the affair no worries, no solicitude as to what the affair could eventually mean for her, for her husband and for her child. Emma desperately wants the romance and all that goes with it. As a classic case of rapture with total oblivion of the future, Emma could be considered a prototype of the sinner. For her transgressions she is given the harshest punishment, nothing less than death by suicide—an ending which to many readers has appeared uncalled for.[4] Yet to understand this ending, we must keep the following in mind.

We have observed how the *totum* builds up a technique of self-defense and how this technique expresses itself in a set of conventions. In terms of these conventions adultery is "forbidden." The rationale behind the prohibition is that procreation is part of the technique of survival. If children result from an encounter, they must be protected and educated. Both procreation and the resulting responsibilities can only be fulfilled within a stable union, where happiness and security for parents and children are possible. Adultery is considered an immediate threat to the *totum* that is the family, and a remote one to the larger *totum* or collective.

Both Anna Karenina and Emma Bovary are a confirmation *per absurdum* of this abstract concatenation of ideas. Their authors do not demonstrate that marriage is the only way of procreation, nor that it must be monogamous nor that polygamy would be an impossibility. We cannot deduce from their stories that every adultery must lead to a tragic ending. They do not attempt to do any of these things. They merely illustrate the fact that whenever the technique of survival or natural law in its elemental dimension

---

[4] "While I have read you without reservations to the end, I have criticized the last pages. You have hurt me, you have literally made me suffer. The expiation is out of proportion to the crime!" (Lamartine in a letter to Flaubert.) The text was quoted by Flaubert's lawyer, when the author went on trial in Paris on January 31, 1857 for alleged immorality in his work. Tolstoi, equally criticized for having given a similar ending to Anna's career, claimed that he could not do otherwise.

has worked out a scheme for procreation on the basis of monogamous relations in a certain culture-cube, such as that of the Western world, adultery constitutes a threat to that relation and at times is tragic in its consequences.

What matters to us who attempt to grasp the novel philosophically is the understanding that although Emma wants the act alone, or what we have called the "instant," and closes her eyes to the consequences, nevertheless the consequences relentlessly follow. As soon as the individual sinner performs the act, the *totum* takes over. The individual self, wrapped up in the "instant," ignores, or attempts to ignore, the consequences. The *totum*, however, confronts the act and the consequences. This confrontation, which is in itself already a sequel to the act, must not be considered to be a revenge on the part of the *totum*; it is merely a result of the fact that over the centuries the *totum* has freely but effectively immersed itself in a conventional mode of life. As such, the conventionality of the *totum* forms an opposition to the act.

Adultery is considered a threat to the stability of marriage and to nothing else. To the extent, and only to the extent, that it is a menace to the family can it be considered "sinful" and will it be opposed. Even where adultery is subject to no juridical sanction, it is still treated with disapproval because of the threat of divorce it contains. If and when the time comes that the *totum* chooses other forms of reproduction than those used at present, the convention that protects the family as a stable unit will no longer have meaning and the way will be clear for adultery. When this time will come is not for us to decide. What does matter is the understanding that the convention of our epoch protects, very forcefully at times, what it needs now in order to be and to endure.

The agent is engulfed by this silent but powerful opposition of the *totum* and its conventionality. At first glance, it may appear to be coming to him from the outside. It does indeed. It does to the extent that the *totum* surrounds him in the many individuals who belong to it. But it comes from within as well, to the extent that the sinner himself is the *totum*. The opposition from without creates a malaise for the agent, for it compels him to secrecy. What is forbidden must be hidden, and this is often awkward and expensive. But in addition to these problems, which engender a more complex way of living, the agent suffers from within.[5] Some writers have called this unhappy feeling "remorse." Yet this is not always a fitting term. Few adulterers feel sorrow about the relation itself, or what we have previously called the "instant"; they merely regret the "disapproval" and the endless problems which this "disapproval" entails. Observed more closely, the unhappiness of the sinner will appear to be nothing but the pain of nonconformity, just as a headache or any other physical discomfort is, in depth, both a sign of nonconformity in the biological order and an irrefutable sign of one's belonging to a particular *totum*. Individualism is an asset. It is the quality by which the fragment is unique and behaves in a unique way. This individualism turns into pain, however, once the uniqueness in bearing and behavior becomes a threat to the conventional. The question is not whether the convention protecting marriage is right or wrong in an absolute sense of the word—by absolute we mean here eternally and universally—the question is whether at present it meets disapproval and opposition. On this there can be no doubt. This disapproval is felt by the sinner as pain, however loud his claim of independence may be. Undoubtedly many people bear remorse without visible strain, but very few can have the pleasure of adulterous love over any length of time without any worry whatsoever. It is this torment which constitutes the topic of innumerable novels and plays.

We have remarked that this pain of separation is equally a symptom of belonging. It is only because one belongs to a *totum* and to the conventionality which that *totum* has created that one suffers through dissent. If there were no firm belonging to the *totum*, there would be no pain in dissent. This last observation explains the ending of *Madame Bovary*. It is clear by now that sin is a break with conventionality and as such is opposed by the *totum*. It is also clear that sin, although wrapped in the instant by the individual self, overflows this narrow space-and-time dimension against his wishes and in one way or another confronts

---

[5] "No matter: she wasn't happy, and never had been. Why was life so unsatisfactory? Why did everything she leaned on crumble instantly to dust? . . . Besides, nothing was worth looking for: everything was a lie! Every smile concealed a yawn of boredom; every joy, a curse; every pleasure, its own surfeit; and the sweetest kisses left on one's lips but a vain longing for fuller delight." *Ibid.*, p. 322.

the *totum*, just as the *totum* confronts the act. It is at that crucial moment that the sinner faces several possibilities: a return to the conventional, which for Emma would involve a return to her life with Bovary and a break with her adulterous life; the decision to produce a new set of conventions or a new social structure with different obligations; or the refusal to belong any longer to a *totum* which carries such a conventionality with it. Suicide is one way of refusing to belong. It is self-exclusion, of course, yet it is dictated remotely by the conventionality of the *totum*. Unable to live under a conventionality which is by nature impersonal and heartless, both Emma Bovary and Anna Karenina see no other solution than suicide, which in a certain sense is their act but which in its roots must be seen as an explusion from the *totum* by the *totum*. Neither woman can endure the conventional and the *totum*, nor can the *totum* endure them. This may not be the conclusion for every case, but it was the only one that both Tolstoi and Flaubert could discover.

Crime and Punishment

MURDER is that act whereby one man kills another without sufficient reason. In the semantics of this study it is the action of one fragment eliminating another fragment. Life eliminates life. The apparent result of such a deed is that one fragment remains untouched, and if the deed remains secret, goes on living as if nothing had happened. Yet the fact is that whoever kills, kills within the *totum*, and hence destroys a member of that *totum* of which he is himself a part. In that sense murder is suicidal. Can it be that that form of suicide reacts upon the agent and transforms him into a victim?

When the statement is made that the act of killing recoils onto the killer, we do not merely claim that its immediate results may prove embarrassing, such as in some cases the presence of the *corpus delicti*. This is indeed an impediment, but it is one which although resulting from the deed, remains external to the agent, and so can eventually be disposed of. The consequences which we want to look at are those which are less readily disposed of, for the act that results in the death of the other is, so to speak, petrified; it cannot be undone. However much one might wish that an action had not been carried out, regret cannot erase the past. Individual life develops like a tree. What goes into life goes into the tree and remains there. Any action is an addition to the suchness of the individual fragment and accumulates within as an indestructible part of his makeup. The lightheartedness with which murder is shown on the screen is regrettable, for it seems to ignore the cumulative effect on the uniquely lived make-up of the one who commits the act and is shown surviving for a time. He does survive, but he survives as mutilated. In appearance he is intact; in reality, every action leaves its mark on the agent; it marks him with a force equal to the power with which it strikes the victim. Sometimes this reaction is called remorse, but it must be admitted that there are murderers who claim to have no remorse. Raskolnikov, the murderer in Dostoevsky's *Crime and Punishment,* showed no remorse in the first weeks and months after the act, yet he was profoundly unhappy. The malaise reaches deeper than remorse, and the explanation can only be that the act of killing the innocent appears to be suicidal. The *totum* disrupts the *totum,* with the murderer being that part of the *totum* which kills yet survives, and the victim that part of the *totum* that is in agony and death. To the extent that the agent is part of the *totum* which survives and witnesses the harm he inflicted upon the *totum,* he can be said to be the one who witnesses the pain of his own destruction yet survives. Murder marks the agent as does any action, but as destroyer of the *totum* it marks him ever more deeply. Although the voice of the Lord talking to Cain must have no literal interpretation in this study: "What hast thou done? The voice of thy brother's blood crieth to me from, . . ." the fact remains that from now on Cain dwells on earth as a fugitive. Finite time-and-space dimensions are favorable to human beings, since they can be on the move and incessantly place between themselves and the act a certain number of days, months and years, and unlike the oak, which cannot move to other regions, can cross mountains, rivers, and even oceans. But this mobility that is the privilege of the human individual does not undo the deed, for his life, like that of the stationary oak, is of one piece and absorbs its own past. The incessant mobility of the fugitive is a sign of his unrest and of the fact that his deed stays within him. The assassin is on the move until the authorities get hold of him. In many cases he provokes his own arrest; in others he successfully evades it; but in none does he escape the fact that he committed the deed and that the deed returns to him.

The deed not only recoils onto the agent but also reaches beyond him to the group or collective to which he belongs. It is possible that the deed reaches down to his descendants, although we are not yet sufficiently equipped to see exactly how and where the genes transmit the action of the individual man. To commit a murder does not go "unnoticed," especially when the deed is multiplied, for it alters the individual man in depth, whether he knows it or not, whether he has regret or not; and since it alters him, it will affect, in one way or another, those whom he brings into life.

We have observed with regard to Emma Bovary that sin is the action of the "instant." Sin is possible only because the agent has a fixation on the "instant," be it the instant of pleasure or of profit or of pride which goes with the act, and it is just this fixation on the instant which makes it impossible for the agent to see the consequences. His vision ascends from himself as center. Not only does he not take the viewpoint of the other, but even when taking his own point of view, he does not see, or sees only vaguely, what will in the long run do himself great harm. He attends only to what will give pleasure or satisfaction now. The assassin is caught in the instant of his act, but once the act is performed the *totum* takes over and the consequences of the act will unavoidably unfold. Murder is more "harmful" than adultery. Of this there can be no doubt. Hence the malaise, or the form of reaction which the sequel of the deed takes in the agent himself, will be greater.

From the preceding, it can be seen where the *totum* itself stands. In order to judge the position of the *totum* adequately, we shall recall its omnitemporality and its ubiquity. The constitutents of the *totum* are within the ambit of the *totum* everywhere and always. As a result the *totum* is omniscient within the expanse of the *totum humanum* and can be said to possess that *scientia visionis* which theology has in the past attributed to God; in our terminology, this prescience is a vision of descent. The *totum* as *totum* with its profundity in time knows the sequel of the deed.

If we apply our principle to Dostoevsky's novel, we can say that the *totum* knows from the beginning the last encounter of Raskolnikov with Sonia, where Raskolnikov as a convict breaks down and for the first time loves Sonia, and through her, his fellow men. Dostoevsky makes it clear in the very end of the book that the love for Sonia in the heart of the convict was also a love for mankind as a whole, not merely in an abstract way, but very concretely for the convicts with whom he lived. This last encounter is (and was) known by the *totum* when the murder was committed, just as a traditional theology represents its deity as endowed with the vision of things to come. That vision of the things to come in no way hampered the act as a free act. The omnitemporal and ubiquitous *totum* knows through its perceptive fragments the murder and all its consequences, yet it does not in this act of vision prevent the murderer from committing the crime. One thing is certain—and this may be indicative of human behavior— the fragment in its ignorance, whether this ignorance be willfully protected or not, is free-to-sin, while the *totum* as *totum* aware of the act and at the same time of its consequences cannot and will not commit the sin. It looks as if one who knows and knows well is no longer free to sin, while one who is ignorant is free-to-sin. Only one who is totally stupid can feel absolutely free. We would reaffirm here a Socratic stress upon knowledge in the domain of ethics, without wanting to press it unconditionally; for there are indeed individuals whose attitudes betray an obscure knowledge of the consequences, yet who nonetheless commit the murderous act.

From the preceding it appears that there is only one way to prevent sin, just as there is only one way to repair sin within the agent himself, and this way is the same in both cases: it consists in bringing oneself onto the level of the *totum*. If the would-be assassin can break out of the fixation upon the instant, which is the moment of sin, and consider "from above" what the act once posited implies as its unavoidable tragic sequel, the act may be avoided. Murder, like any sin, reaches far beyond the instant, but this aspect is ignored by the agent. He lacks wisdom, that quality which enables us to see the sequel of the deed far beyond the deed and to act in the light of this far-reaching vision. The wise man is a man of distances. He measures from afar what will happen to his victim, to his family and to himself. This is his prescience which will affect the future action, since it is precisely that "vision" which transforms the future act (the possible crime) in the future which will never be. To the extent that he "sees," he may be said to be divine.

If things do not happen that way, however, and the murder is committed, redemption can only be achieved when regret takes over, regret that is more than unhappiness because of the suffering the action has brought in its train—which was the case for Raskolnikov almost to the end. The regret must be a condemnation of the crime and presume real repentance. Repentance is *self*-condemnation and shows itself through humility and love. The resurrection of Raskolnikov was promised only at the very end of the book. For the first time the crime becomes an external fact. He could not even analyze that strange phenomenon, but he knew for the first time that life had taken over and that something quite different would gradually work itself out in his mind and in his behavior. His salvation was the acceptance in humility and charity of the *totum*. This insight that the murder was inherently wrong, not because its chain of effects are troublesome for him but because they are a threat to the other, was the beginning of his redemption. To this Dostoevsky alludes only in the last page of his book. It has taken him the whole novel to bring the individual "sinner" to that ultimate and redeeming understanding. Once the sinner has the insight of the *totum*, his renewal is not far away.

A last question arises, concerning the relation in depth of the act of murder with the final regeneration of the assassin. The question can be formulated thus: is it possible that the murder itself, which the *totum* knows to be infallibly connected with the regeneration of the assassin, can and must be considered as the remote yet necessary step on the road towards this redemption? Is it possible that although there is no awareness during and before the act that this final repentance will someday come to pass, there is nevertheless a subconscious finality woven through the lives of men such that the future indeed commands the present moment and that, although the present act is immoral, the final outcome is known subconsciously to be beneficial?

In order to explore this question and its answer, we must first clarify the issue. The subconscious in the individual lies beyond the domain of present awareness, and hence within the ambit of the *totum*. It is the *totum* as a whole which survives and outbalances its fragments in space, distributing the diverse and the unequal in such a way that survival is possible and realizable. From the point of view of the totality this incessant corrective action in the realm of space is paramount. But there is no strong reason to deny the same corrective action in time: what is cast down will in one way or other be raised up again, not necessarily in itself but perhaps in its counterpart. This resurrection—if not in the same individual, at least in the other—is imperative if the *totum* as such is going to survive. The renascence need not take place within the fallen individual, for atonement may very well be achieved by another, who may be one in the same family or even a total stranger. We shall speak of conversion only when atonement reaches the sinner himself as was the case with the main character of *Crime and Punishment.*

Accepting this state of affairs and the return of the sinner to the insight that the convention protecting the life of the innocent is sound and that his act in breaking that convention was unlawful, the *totum* knows what the individual who is ignorant of the future does not yet know. It is precisely this ever present awareness, some-where, sometime, which constitutes the atemporal and aspatial *totum* as present everywhere and always. In this special way, then, the *totum* knows that where murder was committed, the deliverance is as present as the act of murder itself. And since both conversion and repentance are known in the prescience of the *totum*, they can be said to be infallibly connected. But—and this brings us to the answer—what is considered to be infallible cannot, because it is known to be such, by the same token become the dominant motive. Raskolnikov cannot commit the murder *in order* to be redeemed, although "we" (of the *totum*) know that in committing murder he will be redeemed through the action. Things are as they are, how-ever much one might wish them to be different. The tragedy of murder calls for redemption of the sort which set Raskolnikov on his way to a complete renewal; in this sense redemption calls for murder. This must not be understood in the sense that one commits a murder in order to become a saint; it is merely that the depth of redemption presumes the depth of sin. "Deep calls to deep" (Ps. 42:7).

The Middle Passage

So far we have observed examples of ethical behavior which are related to and performed by individuals alone. We shall now turn our attention to an act performed by a collective and reaching another collective. Examples of this that are all too familiar to us are the extermination of one people by another and the forced immigration of one collective for the advantage of another. The counterfinalities of both deeds—the extermination of the Jewish community by the Nazi regime and the captivity and enslavement of the African Negro—are still among the major concerns of our "day." Both lie within our own time-space cube, but since the perpetration of one of them is more remote, we shall be better able to focus upon it: the Middle Passage, or the transportation of captive Negroes from the west coast of Africa to America from the years 1700 to 1808. For years the subject of this transportation was rarely brought up, as if not mentioning it could bury the dead forever, even though its immediate effects were almost as brutal as those of the Jewish holocaust. It is only with the struggle for civil rights that the true facts are slowly coming to light, as the *totum* struggles to correct an earlier inequity of its constituents.

The Middle Passage was the route from the west coast of Africa to the West Indies, the longest leg of the journey made by the slave ships. This run was the third side of a triangle, the two others running from England to Africa and from America back to England. The shipping companies, mostly English or American but for a long time French and Dutch as well, carried rice and rum from America to Europe and cutlery, textiles and fire-arms from Europe to Africa; but the most profitable cargo by far was that of the slaves. Liverpool in England and Newport and Salem in America were the most important bases for these ships, and eventually those ports were the most serious competitors.

The slaves, in most cases already made captive by Arabians or by the Africans themselves, were brought to the coast, to be purchased by the sea captains. On the ship the Negro males were shackled two by two, and they had to stay together for the entire length of the voyage. Kept apart from the women and children, they spent most of the time below deck, except for a few hours a day. They had no coverings, and were all forced to sleep on bare planks. There were two methods of "packing" the slaves, "loose-packing" and "tight-packing." Captains selecting the former method gave the slaves more room and better food, in the hope of reducing the death-rate. The "tight" packers, on the other hand, saw more profit in carrying a greater load, even though a far larger proportion of lives would be lost as a result of the intolerable conditions. The tightly packed "cargo" was inserted spoonwise, with not enough room for a man to lie on his back. On some trips less room was allowed for a slave than for a man in his coffin. Six feet in length and sixteen inches in width was the average space allotment.

The dangerous moment was the loading on the African coast, for there was often fierce resistance. "Africans did not submit tamely to being carried across the Atlantic like chained beasts. They often showed that 'they would rather die than be enslaved.' "[6] Once they were aboard, the trip was even more painful. The captain tried to cut it short, for the longer he was on the ocean, the greater the number of dead that could be expected. The slaves spent the night and most of the day in their tight quarters, but for a few hours they were brought on deck for what was called "dancing the slaves." Those with irons made what movements they could, while the women and children were permitted to roam around the ship. But in foul weather, all remained below, crouched in their filth. Many died of disease—dysentery, scurvy, and smallpox. But this was not the only cause of death. Suicide was prevalent; many jumped overboard if given a chance to do so or died from voluntary fasting; or they faded away from what was called "fixed melancholy." They had lost the will to live.

There are no precise statistics as to the toll exacted by the Middle Passage, but a careful comparison of the losses on different ships has led to estimates of 12.5 percent during the voyage, 4.5 percent before the embarkation and 33 percent during the acclimatization to the New World, for a total loss of 50 percent. In other words, out of every two slaves seized in Africa only one survived. Considering that the total importation of Negro slaves into the New World was approximately five million between 1700 and 1808 (date of the official abolition of the trade in the English Parliament), we have no difficulty in calculating the number of victims which this trade inflicted. It is comparable to our more

---

[6] *American Heritage*, February 1962, Art. by Cowley and Mannix, p. 25; see also D. P. Mannix and M. Cowley, *Black Cargoes, A History of the Atlantic Slave Trade, 1518–1865* (New York: Viking Press, 1965).

recent example of man's inhumanity to man, although stretched over a longer period of time.

As we observe this sin of the collective, we see that no less than in individual sin, the *collective* agent is so deeply engrossed in the "instant"—in this case, his immediate financial profit—that he has no concern for that which unavoidably follows the "instant." Here again there is or was total ignorance of the results, which sooner or later would reach out to the agent himself. There is, however, an important difference in the consequences of individual and collective sin. In the case of sin committed by the collective, the counterfinality of the action—those remote consequences which were not at all wanted by the agent but which nonetheless will follow with mechanical necessity—is slower to appear and strike the primary cause. The collective is slower moving into action, as is the process of the act itself when it runs through all the constituents of the other *totum* (its victim), with the result that before the act returns onto the agent himself—i.e., the individuals who committed it—he is no longer there. The deed hits back, as can be normally expected, but it does so only at the descendants. In the use of an individual semantics, the term *descendant* is wholly intelligible, for he is the one who descends from, who is not yet but will come later. In this semantics, the division of time into past, present and future is legitimate, but it raises serious questions about the accountability of those present for their ancestors and to their descendants. From the point of view of a generic semantics, which ours is in this discussion of collective sin, *the descendants are part of the same space-and-time cubic unit.*[7] The *totum* of the West is one through time and space by virtue of its internal relatedness and communication. We grant it an ontological oneness, not exactly the same as that given to the individual man, yet not totally dissimilar. We can attribute qualities to the *totum* or *subtotum* almost as we do to the individual agent.

Consequently when it is shown that the consequences of the action reach the descendants, one may say that the action has returned *onto the agent to the extent that the descendants are one*

---

[7] On the uses of the double semantics, see *The Planetary Man*, Vol. I, ch. 6, *Rules VI* and foll.

with those who committed it. I shall call the West guilty, not in
the sense that each one of its constituents committed the act of
enslaving the African, but in the sense that there is a continuity in
a multiple way—biological, financial, cultural and national—between fathers and sons.

That all this has happened in recent times is now obvious. The
transportation and its effects, conveniently buried and "forgotten,"
have now been exhumed and brought into view. A malaise has
arisen. The "conscience of the world," as it is commonly called,
has begun to disturb the pleasures of profit. The malaise arising
is a form of remorse. It must be understood as the awareness of a
totum that its behavior was, or is, in contradiction to the conventions of a more comprehensive *totum* which surrounds it geographically or historically. It is no longer acceptable to have
slaves and to treat human beings like animals simply because the
color of their skin is black. This consciousness of the no-longer-
being-acceptable and of the action conflicting-with-the-conventions-
of-a-certain-epoch provokes pain. In varying degrees, the West is
going through a period of pain, or remorse, at the present time. It
is, at the very least, no longer so morally confident; it agrees that
things should no longer be as they have been. The deed of the
past is "regrettable" not only because it harmed the victims but
also because in the long run it has become harmful to the agent
(and his descendants). Sometimes the guilt-feeling of a group can
include as much regret as remorse. The deed, in our case the massive transportation of the Negro to the New World, should not
have taken place because in the long run it is the source of great
trouble even for the white man. Regret is a less admirable attitude
than is remorse and no doubt brings less expiation.

It is at this moment that our look from above is of paramount
importance. Taking this point of view that transcends time and
space and in visual noesis comes down upon the events of the last
centuries taken collectively, one sees that servitude was the destiny
of Africa during the last four centuries. It is a servitude which
reaches far into the past and includes not only the forced transportation of Africans to the New World but also the colonial exploitation by Europeans of African nations—also a domination of
one *totum* by another *totum*. The black man carries a trauma of
suffering and inferiority which cannot be healed within a century

of rehabilitation. The trauma of inferiority is perhaps the most serious consequence of the sin of profit, which stands at the center. It is the profit of the white man which has been chosen ruthlessly and must be seen unremittingly as the center of ever widening circles. If the ethical could ever be outlined in a diagram, this might be the way to do it, presenting *temporal* succession on a plane of *spatial* simultaneity.

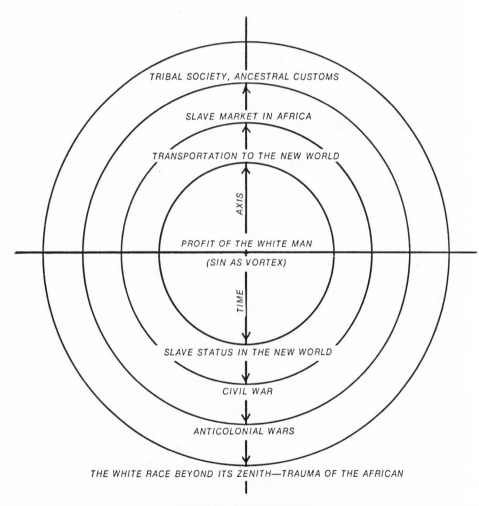

TRIBAL SOCIETY, ANCESTRAL CUSTOMS

SLAVE MARKET IN AFRICA

TRANSPORTATION TO THE NEW WORLD

AXIS

PROFIT OF THE WHITE MAN

(SIN AS VORTEX)

TIME

SLAVE STATUS IN THE NEW WORLD

CIVIL WAR

ANTICOLONIAL WARS

THE WHITE RACE BEYOND ITS ZENITH—TRAUMA OF THE AFRICAN

DIAGRAM—COLLECTIVE SIN

From the diagram, it appears very clearly that the profit of the white man, who was technically superior, lies at the start of the commotion which threw the African into a state of despair out of which he has not been able to free himself.

To the Observer from afar, it will appear that sin causes a vortex, at the center of which lies the act called sin and around which a series of events move as around their axis. Some seem to orbit nearer the center, others are more removed, but all of them seem to be irresistibly drawn into this orbit regardless of the suffering and pain of hundreds and sometimes thousands of people. When the sin is not merely an individual action like murder but one which takes on gigantic proportions, like the one under study, then the vortex reaches over centuries in time *and* continents in space. It becomes a world event and dominates history.

It appears with no less cogency that the sin of the white man carries with it what often has been called atonement. The word is correct, but it should not be understood as something which affects the feelings of the constituents of that *totum* we call the Western world from within. Atonement has no necessary connection with feelings of guilt or remorse; it merely indicates what is the sequel to the act, the unavoidable result of the "sin" of profit. It must be seen as a redressing of the balance. It is not possible for the *totum* called the West (the term is, of course, extremely broad and even somewhat undetermined geographically and historically) to hoard within its own frontiers a wealth which it has conquered with the help of the African while the latter was still a slave. This is a disturbing experience for the white man when he lives with the black man and sees the results of his work at close quarters.

Atonement, then, in the case of collective sin reaches those who in one way or other are one with those who committed the act. The *totum* as a whole committed the act and as a whole must atone. Once more history has judged. This judgment is unemotional and unrhetorical; it is not necessarily formulated in words but merely inscribes itself in the accomplishment of mankind as a rhythm of repair, which is the infrastructure of survival. This sequel to the action, though it could be called guilt, is not the actual guilt of the one who committed the act, but that of the individual who is in one way or other related to the culprit. But—and this is important to remember—this guilt of the collective reaching the individual may become the real guilt of the individual in a narrow sense, if and when he refuses to pay back the profit which his ancestors have extorted from the black man. In this operation feelings are accidental, and collective restitution is more important than individual remorse.

The Self as Center

IN the three cases under study it appears that through the action which we have called sin the agent places himself at the center of a succession of events, which either precede and prepare the action or follow it as a result. If we assume the time-and-space equation which was given in chapter I as part of our methodological approach, it appears even more clearly that the agent is the center because in this reduction of the temporal dimension to the spatial, the act with its antecedents and its consequents stands in the midst of an immense blot on the one-dimensional plane of space. The act itself, divorced from what precedes and from what follows it, we have called the "instant." This "instant" presumes an agent, whom we shall call the sinner. We are at present not concerned with his responsibility, which we shall discuss in our next chapter. Limiting ourselves merely to what we have observed so far, we see the act as the center of the chain of events which surround it, and behind the act we see the agent. The agent makes the profit or enjoys the pleasure, but what leads to it and what follows it injures the *totum* in one or in several of its members. The position of the agent is clear: he stands at the center of a series of events which his action provokes. His position betrays his intention. His intention is threefold. (1) Negatively, he has no intention to serve the *totum*. Sin is a refusal to serve. It fulfills the "I will not serve" which rabbinical literature places in the mouth of Satan. Yet the individual self in its ontological structure is relational, it is part and fragment of the *totum* and finds its salvation as contributing and complementing entity. Sin ignores this ontological structure. (2) The agent intends the act to be self-satisfying. Such is indeed the nature of the "instant": it satisfies the individual self, regardless of the consequences. In choosing the instant, the agent chooses himself. (3) Although his intention may be to confine the act within its own limits and to exclude its harmful consequences, the fact remains that in some way or other his act reaches beyond the instant. To claim that one wills the act and not its consequences is of no avail. Whatever may be his wishes and his hopes, the agent, in positing his act, must take the responsibility for its consequences—assuming, of course, that the act is his own.

Since the three examples given in this chapter fulfill this description, we can now apply the term "sin" to all of them. In all three cases, the agent appears to be engrossed in the "instant" and unwilling to confront the consequences of the act. The act can be forgiven no doubt—and by this we mean it can be so far erased as to be considered as not having taken place; but forgiven or not, the phenomenon stands at the center of a series of events that orbit around it and can not be undone. The effects remain. The nature of the consequences differs from one act to another, but in all cases the first reaction starts in the "instant," even though it escapes the "visual" domain of the "sinner." The suicide of Emma was present in the surrender to her first lover, just as prison life in Siberia was "in view" when Raskolnikov committed his double murder. The "perfect" crime does not exist, and it does not exist because no human being can prevent the consequences of his own act. They transcend the "instant" and belong to the *totum*. To the extent that they escape the agent's control and belong to the *totum*, he himself will not escape. It is of no avail that the agent denies any connection with the act he commits. Here Pilate is a prototype, for the washing of the hands is the eternal gesture of one who at the same time wants and does not want the deed: in fact, he wants the deed undone as soon as it is accomplished. Every sinner is addicted to this naive behavior, for it is his firm hope that once the deed is done, he can turn his back on it and consider it as never having happened.

The same must be said of the Middle Passage. At the moment that the black man was made captive in the African villages and loaded onto ships to be a slave of the white man, the riots of the American ghettos were born. The trauma of the black man was present *then*, although there was no way of predicting in detail the far-reaching consequences. The centuries of slavery, with their moments of paternal benevolence and those of brutality; the civil war; the drama of liberation—all start in the "instant," although not foreseeable in every detail. This ignorance of consequences must not be confused with ignorance of the fact that the act is forbidden. The agent knows the action as "condemned" and opposed by the *totum*. It is a recognition of this opposition that in all three cases, as in all sin, there is an urgent need to keep the deed secret. In the case of murder, the agent wears a mask: he is no longer what he was, he no longer wants to be recognized. He tries to hide from the *totum*. Sin is a break in communication. And yet at the same time the whole move towards secrecy is a clear admission that one does not break the ontological link with the *totum*. Shame confirms the ontological structure of "fragment." A lonely sinner upon an empty planet would neither be ashamed nor secret about his "sin," for he would not be part of . . . and he would be unaffected by opposition either from within or from without.

Collective sin, no less than individual sin, looks for secrecy, for the collective unity involved in mass murder both approves and disapproves of the action. The Nazis, in carrying out their "final solution," made great efforts to make their sin disappear. Cremation, the burning of the remains in open pits, and bone-crushing machinery were so many means put at their disposal by modern technology to rid the world of the visible traces of their acts.[8] This was of no avail. The repercussions of any action in a world where everything is interconnected cannot be kept secret, although in some cases of individual sin the responsibility of the agent cannot be juridically demonstrated. Opposition to the sin, whether collective or individual, comes both from within and from without: both the sinning "fragment" and the encompassing *totum* oppose the act.

The opposition of the *totum* takes place variously but with one common element: those outside the action judge those inside it. The disapproval of the slave market took centuries to arise, while the disapproval of the "final solution" was immediate. In the judgment of the first act, time was a requisite, while in the condemnation of the Nazi persecution, time played almost no role. "We" who do not belong to the Nazi regime but live in the same

---

[8] On the failure of secrecy, see Hannah Arendt, *Eichmann in* *Jerusalem* (New York: Viking Press, 1963), p. 211.

epoch condemn the act. This condemnation comes from the outsider, or what we have called the without, but it is the outsider on
the spatial level. Opposition to the slave trade took place in a
time dimension: those who are without-in-time condemn the act.
We are told that the Portuguese captains took certain precautions
which astonish us today. Before embarking on the agonizing voyage from Angola to America, they baptized the captives by force.
This may surprise us, children of the twentieth century; it did not
surprise the Portuguese of that time. What is natural to one epoch,
or at least is not wholly repugnant, may no longer seem so three
hundred years later. Those of our time and place oppose the slave
market situated then, in the past, no less fiercely than they oppose
the extermination of the Jews taking place there, within another
collective.

The act of reprobation by which one group attempts to correct
another group is a necessity for the health of the *totum humanum*.
The survival of the *totum* requires the incessant redemption of
one by the other. Only in making right what was wrong will the
totum escape annihilation, although the one through whom redemption comes by way of atonement is not necessarily the same
as the sinner. It is "our" task to condemn and atone for the
extermination of the Jews and the cruelties of the Atlantic run between 1700 and 1808, just as it will be the lot of our children
some day to discover and expiate "our" sins. To condemn is not to
limit oneself to words only: it implies the duty, in this case, to
repair the harm done to Africa, the looted continent, and to the
descendants of the slaves torn from that continent. In that sense,
the white man is responsible for the black man. What this means
in practice is not for us to explore. As philosophers we shall write
it down as one more instance of exchange and mobility within the
totum, which—one and fragmented—hangs timeless onto this
planet but incessantly corrects itself in time.

Dimensions of Sin

IT is important to keep in mind that the three cases under consideration are concrete events, whether fictional or real. The power
of the concrete event is absolute in the sense that it is a happening,

and that once there, it can not be treated as if it were not. Concrete events, even when they are clearly in conflict with the conventions, cannot per se be universalized. Yet they can be instrumental in formulating certain norms that are applicable to other cases. There are some who would deny this possibility of universalizing from the concrete. For them the existent itself is the only absolute. They may accept fiction as a portrayal of what is, and that is all. Yet in their reading they unconsciously universalize, for they set that concrete story against other events of life, perhaps of their own, and through this process draw their own conclusions. Others reject both philosophy and fiction and will accept only history, what has actually happened. Here again, it is difficult to study history and not attempt to discover what is and is not transferable to our own times. The reader of the lives of great men will learn only to the extent that he detaches what is valuable from the past and brings it into the present. Reading history or good fiction is a form of vision.

It follows naturally that one cannot apply all the characteristics of one adultery to another, much less claim that every adulterer commits suicide. The case of Madame Bovary has tragic consequences that are certainly not the fate of all adulteresses. Many disturb the *totum* hardly at all. The technique of survival rests upon an "experiment" of the *totum* which has discovered over a length of time that certain acts constitute a threat. These acts are "forbidden," or as we have said, they are "opposed" by the *totum*. This opposition on the part of the *totum* results from the potential harm which threatens the *totum*. It is apparent that an act can only be said to be sinful to the extent that it contains this threat. If and when it can be shown that an act which is usually considered sinful does not contain this threat, the claim that it is sinful must be tempered. It is in this relationship of the concrete event to the *totum* that we find its morality.

In this light, murder or the killing of the innocent is total sin because it causes total evil—destruction of life. Since this definition is absolute, we cannot relativize its moral implications. Murder cannot be permissible in one country and not in another, or at one time and not at any other time. The cases of both Raskolnikov and the Middle Passage stand condemned. Although killing was not the intention of the slave captains, we must in this judgment keep in mind our definition of intention as not merely what the agent explicitly intends but also what the act unavoidably implies. The intention of the agent is measured by his position. Whoever stands at the center of the act is responsible for the events which prepare or follow it. The Middle Passage must be considered equivalent to murder. We are not indifferent to slavery itself, which has been practiced for centuries, but we shall keep in mind that the holding of one man in slavery by another, although illicit in our times, was not considered as such in times gone by. We can state absolutely, however, that the murder which has often gone along with it is total evil, always and everywhere wrong.

Adultery is not murder. Although in most cases it is a serious threat to the integrity of the particular *totum* that is the family, this cannot be demonstrated to be so in all. In the realm of physics induction presumes the presence of certain similarities in matter and from there concludes with mathematical certainty to a certain outcome. When observing the behavior of men, one can also detect certain similarities, but one cannot as in physics be mathematically certain of the same outcome. Adulteries differ in frequency, in time and place, in passion and intensity. They are unequal, and they are so because of the inequality of the love which inspires the act. Notwithstanding this diversity, they have a common trait. In a world of monogamous relations they can, once revealed, disturb and injure the legal partner. We cannot assert, however, that this is always the case. The possibility of an adulterous act which has neither harmed the particular *totum* to which the agent belongs nor injured the *totum humanum*, but has on the contrary been of some benefit, cannot be totally excluded.

This does not mean that it is our intention to develop an ethics of the isolated individual. The relational structure of individual man has been so repeatedly underlined—man is a fragment, completive of the *totum* in and through the uniqueness of his contribution—that we should not have to repeat that there is no ethics for him considered in detachment. Ethics comes into being through the collective and is for it; it can not provide satisfaction for the whims of the individual.

Yet "sins" such as adultery might be considered in the following way. Natural law and the conventions it expresses contain a negative and a positive statement. It is negatively stated in the well-known formulas which were used in the Ten Commandments:

"Thou shall not. . . ." "Thou shall not. . . ." etc. This is the customary way of teaching morality, one which can not be totally ignored. But ethics consists of more than prohibitions; it also contains a positive law. Man is not merely ordered to refrain from destruction but encouraged to contribute in a positive way to the welfare of the *totum*. This positive element in its fullest flowering will later be seen to be sanctity; but here it can already be stated that there is a positive law of charity which, more than any other law, protects the cohesion of the *totum*. And it does so in a constructive way, not merely by forbidding. It is a fundamental law, for unless the individual has this benevolence toward the *totum* in his heart, he will be incapable of any enduring achievement. (Even bad men at times have this benevolence in their hearts and do good things!) Furthermore the commandment to love appears as a universal law, a law that is not caught within certain limits of space and time and does not belong only to one or to some cubic units. The law of charity transcends any convention originating at a certain time and in a certain place.

If this is true, then there must be certain circumstances where ethics in its positive and constructive aspect overrules commandments which merely forbid. It can happen that what appears as immoral to a certain *totum* does not appear as such to the totum at large. In such cases the convention of a certain epoch is superseded by the convention of the *totum humanum*, and what may appear exceptional to some is in fact not exceptional. Thus, certain acts that are prohibited by the convention of this particular collective, such as "Thou shall not commit adultery" or "Thou shall not steal," are differently viewed in the light of a more encompassing law, that law of charity which is the ultimate law. The de-universalization of the law is only apparent. What happens is that individual man transfers his obedience from a particular *totum* to a more encompassing one.

The one who makes this transfer is the individual self. It is his responsibility to judge whether or not the law incumbent upon a particular *totum* does more harm than good. It is one's individual conscience—and this is exactly what individual conscience means —which will judge that a higher law, in this case a law of charity, allows oneself to posit an act which in the estimate of a particular *totum* is wrong. The following examples may clarify this point.

One great danger to modern life is the dissolution of the family unit. Although divorce may be beneficial to both partners, it is in most cases harmful to the children, who are profoundly disturbed by the fact that two people whom they love do not love one another. Even more distressingly, divorce destroys the sense of the absolute in the mind of the children. Children are like growing nations: they need to confront an absolute. And although they will someday outgrow that form of the absolute, they need for the time being the image that parents provide. Since divorce upsets this balance, it must be avoided, if at all possible, and can only be considered as a last resort. In order to save the *totum* of the family, a temporary departure in the form of an extramarital relation may be advisable. There are women who love their husband and their children and have no intention of severing this connection, yet who can be saved from total breakdown only through an extramarital relationship. There are women who can not possibly live with a man, yet desperately want and need children. There are others for whom intercourse becomes a practical impossibility, at a certain age, yet they must allow their husbands some sort of sexual relation. At times prostitution provides an answer. The function of the prostitute should be reexamined with great honesty, for it may appear that she does not deserve the contempt with which she is treated in many quarters. Were she properly recognized, her person and activity would not be regulated by crime syndicates. A nation which believes that it has solved the problem of prostitution may discover that it has merely replaced it with a greater number of divorces—or, worse still, with a flood of rapes and assaults.

In any of the examples mentioned above—all of which are drawn from real life—it appears that the adulterous act is the answer. Yet let us make it clear. That answer does not introduce an ethics of exception. There is no exception in this philosophical approach. There can be no superman who is above and beyond the law. But there is an act of charity which saves the *totum*. And in this light, adultery could be tolerated by the "injured" party as a lesser evil for the sake of the *totum*, or be committed (at times) for the sake of charity on the part of the agent. If the agent does not choose the instant with the intention of selfish enjoyment regardless of the consequences of his act, it becomes more problematic to categorize the act as sin. Any attempt to demonstrate that the act is a sin must show that it is merely egotistical and in its consequences destroys rather than contributes to the welfare of the *totum*.

From all this it can be seen that the individual self, judging whether or not a deed must be accounted moral or immoral, confronts a serious task. This task we shall summarize by way of conclusion. (1) The individual conscience can never alter the nature of certain acts which are always and everywhere wrong, such as murder. (2) The individual conscience, confronting the permissibility of certain acts which conflict with the conventions of his own time and place—such as adultery, stealing or draft evasion—must still be viewed as being fallible. For individual opinion is always based upon an angular vision, resulting in a limited judgment. We have previously denied the possibility of infallibility in any one man, whether he be a man in authority or a simple citizen. We shall abide by this view and conclude that the conscience of the individual, in denying the application of a particular law to his own case and appealing to a higher law, does so with great risk for himself and for others. (3) Inasmuch as the benefit of the *totum* transcends the well-being of the individual, it follows that the *totum* itself is entitled to set aside the "opinion" of the individual. Hence it can de jure overrule the individual conscience; it can oppose as criminal any form of disobedience to its own conventions and eventually treat it as such. Whether or not it should de facto behave in this way, we choose not to answer and shall leave it at that.

Erotica, or the Revenge of Man

It is a complex task for the individual conscience to find its way through the labyrinth of modern erotica. Clearly sexual behavior has changed. For a long time the West, dominated by a Platonic and Augustinian concept of matter, viewed both matter and the body as sinful. Sexual pleasure was considered to be of a lower order, and the act of procreation, even when its intent was to bring forth new life, ranked far below virginity. The priest and the nun were placed upon a pedestal and looked up to with wonder and admiration because of their continence. The reasons that the world has moved into a new phase of sexual morality are multiple, and it is not for us to trace them all. Yet two of them merit our attention.

It can be safely said that the decline of faith in the supernatural, or what I would like to call the "supernatural in isolation," has resulted in a renewed emphasis upon the visible, with *nature* viewed as intrinsically good. Even the believer will claim that incarnational values have pervaded "matter." In his opinion Christ has not merely redeemed the "soul" but sanctified the body. Libido is part of this physical constitution and must be seen as nature-wanted-by-its-maker. Augustine's dualism of a *heavenly* and *earthly* city has fused into *one* city, which is one because it is *natural*, and while it may or may not contain heaven, must attempt to provide it for all.

It is the voice of the nonbeliever, however, which has given the new trend its strongest impetus. According to Nietzsche, Christianity has accomplished its function of refining the barbarians and their mores through asceticism, and a return to the Greeks is needed. Discarding outmoded notions of *sin*, man must become more carefree and Dionysian. "I conjure you, my brethren, remain true to the earth, and believe not those who speak unto you of superearthly hopes . . ."[9] The joyfulness of life need no longer be submerged by guilt. On the contrary, a holy *yes* to life is needed. Men must no longer be angry with their bodies and with the earth. "Let your bestowing love and your knowledge be devoted to be the meaning of the earth! . . . Let it not fly away from the earthly and beat against eternal walls with its wings!"[10] If Nietzsche's outcry was extreme in its form, it proved to be prophetic in content.

A similar vision is present in Sigmund Freud, less direct perhaps, but more technical in its presentation. Repression, the core of Freud's philosophy, makes man human and shapes him into a civilized being; yet, through failing to recognize the realities of human nature, it has been the cause of useless suffering as well. To repress does not mean to eliminate—the unveiling of the unconscious through the interpretation of dreams is the proof of that. Man should accept the realities of his nature and not repress

---

[9] Friedrich Nietzsche, *The Philosophy of Nietzsche* (New York: The Modern Library), pp. 6–7.
[10] *Ibid.*, p. 81.

what does not need to be repressed. Psychoanalysis aims "to strengthen the *ego*, to make it more independent of the *super-ego*, to widen its field of perception and enlarge its organization, so that it can appropriate fresh portions of the *id*. Where the id was, there the ego shall be."[11]

In the light of these new ideas—all of which are not so new, but which the somber vision of an Augustine had hidden from the West—sex appears not merely as an instrument for the perpetuation of the species but also as a source of personal happiness. One of its functions is to produce life, since no other means are as yet available, but another is to satisfy the need for union between the sexes. This unitive function is creative of happiness. This new insight has been accompanied by discoveries in science which can help to put it into practice. Contraceptives are part of a modern and future way of living. No doubt, they still can be improved, but whatever their limitations, they clearly are here to stay and no condemnation has succeeded in dislodging them from the mores of our times. What will be our attitude toward the modifications in process?

(1) The principle which was and is fundamental in these pages is that to act as a fragment presumes the acceptance of the *totum* as the ultimate absolute. There is only one sin, and that is the sin against the *totum* and against oneself to the extent that one is part of the *totum*. The survival of the *totum* is the cornerstone of our ethical vision. The modes of survival change, yet the ultimate purpose remains. There is no other enduring absolute. Since conventions and imperatives resulting from the quest for survival do change, it is only natural that they occur in the domain of sexual behavior as well as in other domains. Not only the individual him-

---

[11] Sigmund Freud, "New Introductory Lectures on Psychoanalysis," vol. 22, trans. James Strachey, in *New Introductory Lectures on Psychoanalysis and Other Works* (London: Hogarth Press and the Institute of Psychoanalysis, 1964), p. 80. See also Winfrid Huber, Herman Piron, and Antoine Vergote, *La Psychanalyse, Science de l'Homme* (Brussels: Charles Dessart, 1964), p. 210; Norman O. Brown, *Life Against Death* (Middletown, Conn.: Wesleyan University Press, 1959), p. 3. Cf. H. Marcuse, *Eros and Civilization* (Boston: Beacon Press, 1955), whose theory of the surplus-repression is also an accusation against capitalist society and its social "domination."

self, but the *totum* and *subtotum* have their moments of fertility or procreation and their moments of restraint. This rhythm is dictated by the need of the *totum* or *subtotum*. When the *totum* is threatened by extinction, as it may be in times of war or of epidemics, procreation is the dominant rule. At other moments, when overpopulation is a threat, restraint is the rule. Contraceptives are a way of slowing down the tempo of procreation. They are a technique, no doubt, and like all techniques, are neither good nor bad in themselves, but merely matter touched by the mind of man and placed at his disposal. Their immorality cannot be demonstrated.

If control of births is part of the ethics of today, so will be any technique which encourages this. It cannot be proved that there is anything wrong with implanting the husband's sperm, or even the sperm of a donor, in the wife. Nor can it be proved "immoral" to implant an ovum taken from another woman into the womb of a woman who cannot produce an ovum of her own. The same can be said about the technique of freezing which would make it possible to preserve ovum or sperm in banks for later use.

(2) To separate sex from procreation on a partial basis, as the previous point presumes, does not exclude the birth of children altogether. But if children are not excluded, neither are the structures in which they are growing up and being educated. The family remains as a particular *totum* to which children belong. As long as we have not reached Plato's dream of a common life, where marriages no longer exist and children are given over to public nurseries for their education, we cannot live and act as if we were already there. Although we are at loss to prophesy how life in the future will propagate itself, any shape it does take will be structured. Structures are the protection of the *totum*. They vary from epoch to epoch, as our discussion on natural law has clearly implied, but they are the varied expression of an enduring preoccupation with the need to be and to endure. What matters is to replace mores by mores, and it is of no importance to the defense of the thesis under consideration whether the mores of the future will keep some of the simplicity of the tribe or whether they will be scientifically controlled. The confusion in some sensational writing of the present consists not in promising a different world, but in speculating upon a world with no restrictions whatsoever.

The philosopher avoids speculating upon such naivetés. The society of tomorrow will be a society of men (not of supermen), which will either survive in a structured way or disintegrate in chaos. We of today should live like men of today: sexual ethics cannot be made prior to scientific fact, whatever the discoveries of science may be tomorrow.

(3) The scientific discoveries in the field of sex raise still other moral questions. If the conventions of the past have attempted to regulate sexual intercourse, it was with the clear intention to protect the unborn. Since the use of modern contraceptives has taken care of that, it seems natural to conclude that further restrictions are meaningless. If the act has no consequences, or—to express it in our semantics—if beyond the instant there is nothing, it can no longer be forbidden. Such is the argument in favor of what we shall call promiscuous love.

In examining this case from a moral viewpoint, we shall from the start distinguish it from the behavior of a couple who live together in a stable way but without the legal sanction of normal wedlock. From a philosophical point of view such a couple stands under no accusation except one of imprudence and lack of foresight. Once more the structure in one way or other is a necessity, for although here it does not seem a requisite for the unborn, who by hypothesis is not expected, it is and remains of great importance for the partners themselves. In order to grasp this, we shall remind the reader of our definition of love as need. The partners need one another, and the fulfillment of this mutual need creates their happiness. Observation seems to show that only in stability will this be fulfilled. If stability, together with the legal sanction of stability, is a protection of the unborn and of existing children, it is no less a protection of the partners themselves. Without some sort of stability or structure, happiness will be fragile, and we shall come close to what we have previously called sin, which is nothing but the act of the instant, or the selfish act, where the individual thinks only of himself and the partner is discarded as mere instrument. Hence, although the philosopher may not be able to demonstrate the need of religious or legal sanctions for the benefit of two people living together, he may point to the danger of love without any guarantee whatsoever. Still in line with our definition of love, we observe not only that love is in depth a need, but also that it lives upon need. It is important, therefore, that in my attempt to extend love, mutual need for one another be kept alive. It matters for both partners to need one another, and this need will sustain itself when it is kept alive through some accomplishment in which both partners are involved. The care and education of the child are an obvious example, as is sex itself. But to discover in the other not merely a sexual or domestic partner but a partner in a cultural dialogue as well is an even greater safeguard. To endure, love seems to want more than love: in some strange way, it becomes instrumental and tends towards an accomplishment which is other than itself.[12]

If stability of any kind is lacking and promiscuous love is engaged in for its own sake (children are excluded—we have agreed not to protest about that), the eventual result is going to be that the partner is excluded as well. In most cases promiscuous love is narcissistic, for the act is by definition self-oriented. Yet the individual man is not a center, however much he likes to think that he is. If he establishes himself as a center, he is going counter to the ultimate definition of love as need, the need to give and the need to receive.

(4) Certain manifestations of conventionality belonging to one place are considered sinful in another; or they are frowned upon at one time and not at another—for example, polygamy, simultaneous or in succession (the latter not infrequent in Moslem countries). Our role here is clear. Tolerance of the diverse is the ground rule of an ethics which claims to be planetary. In a world which is totally open and contains no more *terrae incognitae*—unexplored areas—no other attitude is possible except that of accepting diversity in the moral order, just as in the cultural and economic.

Can one extend the concept of a planetary ethics beyond the limit of tolerance and practice as well as accept the diverse? It seems here that one must consider the *totum* to which he belongs. In a society where monogamy is the rule, polygamy is the infraction. But no moral objection can be made against someone mov-

---

[12] It is because of this ultimate recognition that the child was called by Claude Farrere, "the last of the gods" in his book of the same title, *Le Dernier des Dieux*.

ing to another section of this planet where polygamy is an accepted mode of living and himself becoming polygamous. Immigrations take place for a variety of motives. This might be one. But in reverse, to export the rules of monogamy and impose them upon a culture where polygamy is still the practice is harmful in most cases because local mores have a deeply grounded motivation which a zealous reformer must attempt to understand before presuming to "correct" them. No wonder, then, that missionaries who were carried away by religious zeal have attempted to change the cultural pattern of foreign lands, only to discover that their efforts were to no avail or that their converts became uprooted in their own tribe.

One thing clearly appears from the foregoing remarks: the *totum* opposes the sinful act because it wants to prevent the series of events which follow it. This reaction of the *totum*, a particular *totum* or the *totum humanum,* results from the look beyond the instant. Its global reaction is the sum of the reactions of the many. The plural is that out of which the One is made. Conventions, or the structures which they imply, are a protection of the One and a restraint of the-unique-and-the-selfish. Nietzsche's dream of a world in which there would be no sin is utopian; structures are a necessity, but wherever they are, there will be infractions against them. An awareness of the consequences of these infractions helps individual man to avoid sin. We call this knowledge. Taboos will not save man. Nor will religion, unless it helps him to understand the beauty of totality and of the individual's place within the total creation. What matters above all is the wisdom to see the future as present, that is, to see the sequel of the act as unfolding in the instant. There is a sense in which every man is the Observer as well as the Actor. It is crucial that the Observer should see the consequences in advance, before he is destroyed by the Actor in the deed.

The Sin of the Proselyte

IN February 1863 a letter from Emperor Napoleon III appeared in the *Moniteur*, the official French gazette. The emperor declared that Algeria was not a colony in the real sense of the word, but an Arabic kingdom (*un royaume arabe*). Therefore, the letter went on to say, the structure of the Moslem society should be preserved and a fusion of Europeans and Arabs should sooner or later take place. Such was the foresighted plan. As is well known, it was never fulfilled in its own time. The settlers were firmly opposed to any fusion with the native population and even more so to the idea of "un royaume arabe." The Catholic clergy itself, although well-intentioned, had no grasp of Islamic culture, and even less of the Moslem religion. What their bishop, Charles Lavigerie—later to become cardinal—had in mind was a Christianization of North Africa. This would be only a beginning. His ultimate aim was the building of a Christian empire "from the shores of the Mediterranean to the Great Lakes." The plan was ambitious and aggressive to say the least, as was the man behind the plan. Brilliant, intelligent, relentlessly energetic, incessantly forging new plans, manipulating things and events with a masterly hand and men as if they were things, Lavigerie considered himself chosen by Providence to convert the Arabs and the African Negro as well.[13] His plans were not always clear, and the term "Christian civilization," constantly used in those days, was ambiguous, for it was not obvious whether the emphasis was on "Christian" or on "civilization" or on both as being inseparable. Yet whatever the terms used, there can be little doubt about the ultimate intent of Lavigerie and his followers. Their aim was to win over the Moslem population to the Christian Gospel.

In this they have failed. In examining this failure, one feels no lack of admiration for those who gave their lives for this purpose —their charity and heroism were unbounded. The question which deserves attention at this point of our study is whether or not Lavigerie and his followers should have attempted the propagation of the Faith in the Islamic countries.

Observing things from afar, we see first of all that all kinds of proselytism—religious, political or cultural—must equally be seen as a movement of expansion. The particular *totum* wants to enlarge itself. This self-enlargement is a move of self-protection: in order to be and to endure, the particular *totum* propagates. In

---

[13] "Those are the ones who make the mothers cry!" Dorme in an account of Lavigerie.

so doing, it is merely following the eternal law of survival that it is dependent upon multiplication. That which has a greater number of adherents has greater chances of survival. The number of adherents can be increased through more births within the group or through conquest or conversion. In proselytism, multiplication takes the form of expansion through conversion.

Proselytism generally presumes a certain ignorance, an ignorance of the values of the one who must be conquered.[14] The proselytizer is convinced that his own stand is the only one worth considering and that any other position is indefensible. Up to a point he is a fanatic, in that he knows his own position and no other. Like the fanatic, he fights under the standard of the absolute, and as a result, whatever may be the fragilities and imperfections involved, fights with vigor. Decadent nations or tribes neither conquer nor have children. Where there is no will to be, there is no will to propagate. The same can be observed of religions in decline. *So far* a look at world history reveals that the will to expansion has been a hallmark of the strong.

The future will show, however, that on a planet which has reached its frontiers, proselytism and conquest are dangerous occupations. It will show, furthermore, that unlimited fertility can constitute a menace as well. As a result, the vigor of a nation or of a religious group will demonstrate itself in a different way. Instead of dreaming of quantitative growth and of world expansion, the particular *totum* will aim at qualitative improvement. The proselytism of tomorrow can only be one of mutual illumination, not of mutual conquests. The era of conquests is over; the era of enlightenment of the diverse by the diverse has started. *But this, of course, presumes that the diverse be respected in its uniqueness.*

It is precisely this lack of attention to the peculiarities of a race or a tribe which has made the proselytizing of a religion or of a political system unsuccessful or even harmful. Examples are manifold. American democracy, once it becomes an article of exporta-

---

14 "Infidel" is a derogatory term. It is used by the Christian for anybody who does not belong to the faith, and in reverse it is used by Moslems for Christians, who are "dogs of infidels." To be a Gentile in the eyes of a believing Jew is not a flattering epithet. To be called a Jew has not always been a compliment either.

tion, is caught in a similar dilemma. America has wanted to propagate a concept of democracy, but it has exported only itself, and all too often it has shown no grasp of anything different. The constant failure of American-type democracy in the newly developed or the underdeveloped countries should open our eyes, but it does not. Such is the defect (and the power) of all proselytism; it is unwilling to see the different and to respect the diverse. Although the intention of the proselytizer is a noble one in many ways, the execution is in most cases a failure because it is the faithful replica of *one* program, *one* idea and *one* mode of action. There is no adaptation, no flexibility, but only a fierce defense of the same concept everywhere and always. Anyone who questions the American way of life in politics is labeled "fascist" or "communist."

As far as Christianity is concerned, no harm results from teaching a gospel of charity or from enabling the minds of the illiterate to open to their fullness—nobody will call that sort of a missionary a fanatic. The difficulties start as soon as people feel compelled to present these magnificent ideals in Western wrappings or through devices totally alien to the native. For a long time the missionary thought he needed the apparatus and the philosophy of the West in order to deliver his message. But in selling the form with the content he degraded the content.

The concept *Christian* is made up additively: it *includes* rather than *excludes* differences: it is the diversity of Christians who together make up the *universal* concept of what a Christian is, and it is the same diversity seen as *totum* which understands exhaustively the density of a concept.[15] The individual himself knows that this way of understanding is never totally exhaustive —it is only angular vision—and he knows that the notion of Christianity needs the plural to obtain its full meaning. He sees the concept of Christian as being incarnated in a variety of ways, and for all his impotency, recognizes that through the diverse one invariable constantly emerges, that of charity and forgiveness towards one's fellow men. Beyond that, it would be difficult to demonstrate that the apparatus of a certain mode of Christianity, however much respected and respectable, is the only one and

---

[15] See above, Volume I, pp. 110, 119–122.

must become an article for export. It would be even more problematic to demonstrate that the apparatus itself is more important than the spirit which it contains and is supposed to convey.

Charles Lavigerie was no anthropologist. His knowledge of the Bantu races was slight, as was his acquaintance with the world and culture of Islam. He could not but think that conversion would mean the acceptance of the gospel message together with the structures of the church in which this message was contained. This would have entailed a profound alteration of the African mores and customs.[16] We have seen the extent to which Lavigerie succeeded. Proselytism in the Islamic countries is no further along than it was one hundred years ago. In certain milieus the missionary has perhaps introduced a spirit of rapprochement and of mutual understanding.[17] But as far as religious belief or practice is concerned, the Arabs are still what they always were, Moslems. While the concept of a Christian empire floundered, the dream of an "Arabic kingdom" has not. So contemptuously decried one hundred years ago, it is at present a reality.

---

[16] See de Montclos, *Lavigerie, Le Saint Siege et l'Eglise* (Paris, 1965), p. 489.

[17] The whole question, of course, then becomes whether Christianity should be more than a "rapprochement" of races and of people, and whether the Gospel is anything but a teaching of mutual understanding. On this we have at present no answer to give.

7

On Freedom

The Ground of Freedom

IT is generally believed that freedom is an asset. The word works like magic upon the hearts and minds of people even before any attempt is made to define it. We shall try not to disappoint them at this stage, but as befits philosophers, we must nevertheless specify its meaning. For we should not confuse the feeling of freedom with freedom itself, however pleasant or even euphoric that feeling may be. The sophism is common: human beings often believe that they are free because they feel free. Yet this belief based on feeling is not an argument. This is one more reason why we should not succumb to an introspective method but instead should observe freedom from without in order to make certain that it is present within. To observe from without and to describe a phenomenon as it appears from without, as has been our constant method, enables us to make certain observations concerning the workings of freedom that are based more on fact than on feeling.

To the Observer the *totum humanum* appears as both one and diverse. Since it appears that notwithstanding the oneness there is diversity, we are able to conclude that diverse fragments have something by which they appear to be "themselves." We shall tentatively call this "being themselves" *freedom*. The label can only be used if and when the One appears to be such that it does not prevent the constituents from being themselves. To "us" observing the *totum* from its periphery, the diversity comes to the fore through the mobility of the parts, which go out in a variety of directions and communicate with one another. We shall call this mobility of parts at variance a *diversified mobility*.

Diversified mobility implies that there is a diversity both on the level of space and on the level of time. The diversity on the spatial level manifests itself by the fact that the fragments are ontologically unequal. Here the accent is on *diversified*. On the temporal level, diversified mobility implies that for the fragments there is no compulsion to remain what they are, no binding uniformity forcing them to move into the same direction. The accent here is on *mobility*. A certain amount of change is undeniable, as the fragments become fully "themselves." We will later see whether the creation of something entirely new is involved in this change. Whatever later examination reveals to us, we can already say that both to be diverse and to change, or to appear such to the Observer from afar, is contained in the words *diversified mobility*. *Diversified mobility* constitutes the ground of freedom.

The quality of being free, or the quality of being "oneself," cannot cancel the fact that the fragment is still a fragment. Although diverse, the fragments under examination (be they the individual selves or fragments of larger sizes, such as groups or collectives of different sorts) are not independent. They are dependent upon one another within the *totum*. By way of descent one can discover that what is born in time is dependent in space; and that that which comes into the world through the other (who was) can only survive through the other (who is). A conception of the fragment as something which is and acts totally cut off from its past or from its surroundings would be a contradiction in terms. Limitations of a physical sort are imposed upon the fragment as being part of the One. The fragment is not the *totum*. In the light of these observations the Sartrian understanding of freedom as absolute would be unacceptable.

When applied to the constitutive elements of the *totum*, freedom, or the quality of "being themselves," cannot possibly be the same as license or freedom abused. Diversity is the privilege, even the prerequisite, of the heterogeneous, but it must never become a threat to the *totum*. Diversified mobility shows itself as the ground of freedom only to the extent that the diverse in motion is integrated in and towards the ensemble.

From all this it can be seen that if freedom is ever present, it can only be conjectured as an attribute of the fragment. Ontologically it implies belonging, yet it excludes enslavement. We cannot within the structure of this universe discover freedom as an attribute denoting total non-belonging. Our semantics confirms this understanding, for one cannot be "different" unless there is some entity to differ from. The fragment is free because although rooted in the *totum*, it has mobility within the *totum*. The *totum* itself as *totum* is neither free nor unfree: the *totum* merely is and survives through the internal fragmentation and the "freedom" of its components.

Freedom of the Group

WE shall discover that these observations apply to group-fragments as well as to individual fragments. By group-fragment we understand any particular *totum* or *subtotum*, whether political, cultural, religious or racial. Reacting upon such data as soil and climate and to the particular purpose which it wants to achieve, each collective has "chosen" its own character, its own tradition and its own way of living. This way of living includes a set of conventions, covering the deeper problems of ethical behavior, and in most cases an etiquette as well, concerned with decorum and the niceties of pleasant living. This "choice" has taken centuries to come to the fore and is the result, like all collective judgments, of the addition and incessant correction of many individual evaluations, which in turn are rooted in the depth of the unconscious One that holds together that particular group-fragment.

In recent years there has been an increasing awareness of the right of each collective to be itself and shape its own future. On the level of nations this has been called "self-determination"; in our terminology it is the "freedom of the group," their "being themselves." Whatever may be his limitations, Charles de Gaulle with his slogan *l'Europe des Patries*—a Europe composed of fatherlands—had a rich insight into the equilibrium between oneness and diversity that must be achieved. The fatherlands must be protected and their diversity allowed to flourish within the one continent, for what has developed through the centuries must not be totally absorbed by the larger *totum* that is Europe. This explains in part his keen distrust of the United States, which, he felt, was encroaching upon the self-determination of France.

Spatial mobility must no longer refer to the expansion of a nation beyond its own borders, either as a physical presence or as a "spiritual" mentor. Such a mobility took place in earlier times, when whole tribes were on the move to carve out their places on this planet. This must no longer be the case within the shrinking confines of our earth, for when it is, trouble erupts between the conflicting group-fragments, as in Israel, Czechoslovakia, Nigeria, and Vietnam. Perhaps some day whole groups will decide to expatriate themselves to other planets, but in the meantime, spatial mobility will have to be confined to the diversity and subsequent movement of the fragments within the *totum*.

This movement takes place in time. If the nation or group-fragment has its own identity, built up by its own constituents, this does not mean that the choice is final. Conventions change, for the "freedom of the group" points not only to the originality achieved by a particular *totum* within a more englobing *totum*, by which it contrasts with other collectives within the same ensemble, but also to its originality on the move, as it incessantly reaches out into new directions. This is how the freedom of the group appears from afar. The diversity of fragments is the condition of its freedom, for this provides the possibility of change. We shall later discuss the function of the rebel as an instrument of this change, but for the moment we wish to see how this change is an expression of the group and is under its command.

If the group has freedom, it must have an identity that it determines itself. As it moves in time, something seems to take hold of all of its members and pull them along, even those who don't want to "move with the times." The beginnings of a revolution, the most radical form of change of the group-fragment—the storming of the Bastille in 1787, for example—are the result of a group decision.

The group is born before "my" articulate awareness of it and before I run onto the Boulevard towards the Bastille, yet in its decision it englobes all of us and provokes the response of each one of us. The entity "group," in some remote and invisible way (invisible to the individual perception), sweeps all individuals onto the Boulevard St. Antoine. It is a group decision, motivated by the circumstances, although one that does not necessarily coincide with my individual choice. It may force me into action, at times to the detriment of my own interests or while appearing "unreasonable." To the extent that the group takes a clearcut shape, it may even seem to be a prison, and then of course the term *destiny* comes to mind; yet it is in fact nothing but the group acting in self-defense, as a group thinks it must, even at the price of some of its unwilling "fragments."[1]

What appears unintelligible to the individual may very well be intelligible to the *totum*. What looks like destiny to the individual man is merely a disposition of certain means towards an end that is visualized by the group as a group. In fact, there is no destiny in the full sense of the word, but there is a freedom of the group, which formulates its decisions above and beyond the choice of the individual, even though the latter may at times bitterly resent it. The group or *totum*, whether existing in its elemental and natural way or in a man-made form (for a particular purpose), confronts a problematic situation and adopts a solution. We call it a "choice." This choice often appears as a mystery to the individual existent, but it compels him, nonetheless, as destiny.

From the preceding analysis it follows that when a revolt takes place against authority—be it Stalin or Louis XVI, or the Grand Inquisitor, or the Curia—that revolt has lived silently in the hearts of men long before it found its explicit formulation through praxis. The group was born but its members were unaware of its birth. The individual belonged to the rebellious group and did not know it. His conscious cooperation will be free—the extent of this freedom we shall examine later—but at the same time his actions are made possible by the global freedom which surrounds him. When Sartre describes skillfully and in great detail the rush of the rioters on the Boulevard St. Antoine towards the Bastille, he overlooks the fact that the individual's conscious response is a response to the group as to an ontological entity-that-already-exists. Sartre forgets that individual freedom responds to what is. The fact is—and we are not approving or disapproving but merely

---

[1] This passage comes from my book *The Marxism of Jean-Paul* | *Sartre*, p. 276.

observing—that in rioting the individual is swept along by forces coming from behind him. The impulse seizes him because of an urge emerging from the *totum* itself, an urge which is in depth a drive for survival. The individual no doubt contributes: he consciously corresponds to the global decision. But as a fragment of the *totum* he was already involved in its preconscious origin.

We have emphasized that the freedom of a *totum* comes out of and at the same time limits the freedom of its constituents. The mobility of each group is, in turn, restrained by the One of which it is a part. No rebellion of a collective against its own past can totally erase that past, since it is in many ways tied to it. Nor can it ignore certain commands which are essential for survival. It cannot and will not tolerate any group-fragment being a threat to the larger whole. To think of a revolution as a total break is naive. No revolution is omnipotent and unlimited: it merely brings changes where and as it can. Freedom remains mobility within the One, no less and no more. The One is limit and judge.

Freedom and the Individual

IF we have seen and described a certain compactness of a particular *totum*, a close communication of its constituents, a common way of acting and even a kind of common plunge in a certain direction, this does not preclude the profound diversity of the individuals within that collective. For within the unique character of a group (be it nation or tribe, race, church or even country club) there is a uniqueness of the individual fragment. This individual fragment has "depth within him unfathomable, and infinite abyss of existence."[2] He is unique within the unique *totum* of which he is a part.

"At the moment of (man's) entrance into the *totum—totum universum* and *totum humanum*—he is marked forever. His birth is his destiny."[3] The uniqueness of the individual's birth lies at the beginning of his journey through life. The motion of his life

---

[2] John Henry Newman, "The Individuality of the Soul," *Sermons* (London: Longmans, Green and Company, 1920), p. 134.
[3] *The Planetary Man*, Volume I, pp. 37–39.

is the continuation of that which was his, and his alone, at his birth. The term *curriculum vitae*—life course—is a particularly apt one to signify the path or the achievements of a life, since it points to its mobility: life is a journey, a "run." Tertullian was well aware of this when he defined the Christian as one who is searching and journeying, not as something achieved and completed once and for all: *Sed tu, peregrinus mundi huius. . . .*[4] Of course, Tertullian had in mind the ephemeral existence of man in a world which was a mere prelude to the beyond, but whatever may have been his reasons, Tertullian was right in stressing the pilgrimage of the individual fragment within the contours of an enclosing *totum*, a wayfaring that could not be predicted in detail. Under the global span of their particular *totum*, the many wander in different directions. These directions can take many forms. They cover the entire *life course*, but at times may appear more dramatically through an act of agreement or disagreement, submission or revolt, teamwork or discord. Whatever form they take, they are a way in which and through which the individual asserts himself and is himself.

The unique mobility of the fragment does not mean exemption from all physical impacts, genetic or environmental, or from all control. Robinson Crusoe was by no means a monad. Too much was salvaged from the wreck to consider him even remotely a self-sufficient entity—not to mention the fact that in keeping himself alive, he carried onto the shore the product of centuries of the West. For in bringing himself onto a remote island of the Atlantic, he remained what he was: fragment of a *totum*. To be part of . . . is endemic. Nor can it be said that he is from now on exempt from all control. Although he can physically commit a murder— he has all the tools at hand—the very fact of being part of a *totum* which may not and will not be maltreated should keep him in line. We shall presume that it did, and that it was an act of mercy to kill a few natives in order to save his man Friday.

At this point the objection might be made that ants in many ways display some of the diversified mobility that we have been describing. If we observe their activity, we see a skill that is truly amazing. They build intricate housing under the ground, provide

---

[4] Tertulliani Opera, *De Corona* (Turnhout, Belgium, Brepols, 1954), p. 1061.

for their own reproduction and subsistence, and have an involved system of communication. Can we not say, then, that the anthill is a *totum*, made up out of the diverse and displaying a division of labor similar to that of human communities? If it is true that there is mobility and diversification and that ants can be said to be fragments of a fractured *totum*—and it is—can we not say that ant and man are equally free—and equally unfree?

Although the presence of a diversified mobility in the anthill seems undeniable, we are not able to apply to it the term "freedom," for there are some important points of difference between ant and man. We have seen that fragmentation runs both on a horizontal and on a vertical line: the fragment is juxtaposed as well as preceded and succeeded. Observed in juxtaposition, ants are alike and human beings are not. Human diversity is something which affects the individuals themselves, and not merely groups of individuals differentiated in terms of the particular function they perform, which is the case with the ants. Ants considered as ants are not unequal to each other: all inequality consists in the difference in function. This assertion is based on the observation that once engaged in a function, all ants *act* alike. They act alike because they are caught up in their own functioning. The human fragment, on the other hand, is aware of his act before it is done; or, more precisely, he can be considered as looking at himself and at his own action as objects. The ant lives its actions rather like a somnambulist; but it does not, it seems, ever become aware of the actions as its own, looking at them with a view to changing them. In other words, the ant is engrossed in itself and shows no capacity for transcending the instinct which causes its activities and keeps it in being. Ants are alike because they act alike within the same function.

The "freedom" discovered so far is merely the unique movement of the individual man within the ambit of his encompassing *totum* wherein others, too, "run" their own course. To "us" from without it appears to be a unique mobility, differing from the mobility of any other fragment. We shall have occasion later to explore this concept of freedom and clarify its content more thoroughly. It already appears that the method used in this study, a phenomenology of descent, discovers the multiple within the *totum*, while a phenomenology of ascent, the approach of Sartre and of the early Heidegger, discovers the multiple within *man*.

The existential approach is but a revelation and an awareness of the possibilities which the individual self confronts within *himself*, but we also need a way to view the self within the *group*, as he is related to the other, who, when viewed from without rather than from within, may turn out to be man's salvation rather than his hell.

Unique Mobility, or Mobility-Ahead-of-Itself

WE have admitted that the mobility of each fragment is somewhat restrained by the *totum* or *totum(s)* of which it is a part. The freedom of the individual is marked out by his givens, genetic and environmental, coming to him not only from the present but from the past, through his particular collectives: nation, race, religion, family, school.[5] If this man-as-product were all that there

---

[5] If we accept this impact of the past and of the milieu, it naturally follows that men differ from one another, but it does not follow that one is superior or inferior. Inferiority is a term used by the West for anyone who does not meet its standards of logical and mathematical skill, technical knowledge and ruthless competition. Evaluation in this case is made by the West on *its own terms*. But who proves that these terms are the norm? No one. The black man who lives in the West, as is the case with the Negro living in the United States, resists this evaluation, and rightly so. The Afro-American—as at times he likes to be called, and personally I believe it to be a fitting name, for he is indeed Africa within America—does in fact recognize this descent from a remote past and is justly proud of it. His efforts to study his history attest to the recognition of this presence of the past in himself. The Afro-American resists the levelling: he is right, for in doing so he protects himself and his own past. The controversy between geneticists and environment-

alists cannot be solved by the philosopher, since it lies more in the domain of biology and sociology. But from the point of view of the Observer, who by hypothesis is not tied to the *now* and takes what we have called an atemporal position, the two factors of environment and genes seem indistinguishable at the very beginning of the genesis of man as man, for the simple reason that in the early stages of mankind what environment and climate incessantly inflicted upon individual man must have ultimately transmitted itself. Climate, milieu and occupation have in the long run left some imprints which were slowly transferred, such as color of the skin, bone structure, nervous system. At a certain time certain characteristics were slowly acquired and transmitted. They are persistent even in a new environment in which the individual impact does not work upon sheer nothingness but upon a genetic residue which-was-already-there. This does not exclude the possibility of a new mutation over a length of time.

is, then we would have to say that indeed, he is no more free than the ant. But we have observed something different: whatever his self is, man seems perpetually to be ahead of it.

This man-as-product we shall call *Alpha*. Alpha by no means comprises man-in-full. Further observation discloses something that needs to be added, for which we reserve the term *Beta*. This dual form of expressing differing aspects in man must not be understood as reflecting an ontological dualism; it is merely a means of designating in the one and same individual that-which-is-product and later on that-which-assumes-these-influences-towards. . . . It is in this "assuming towards" that the unique mobility or ground of freedom will get its distinctively *human* character. It is here that we must seek the possibility of change and creativity without which there would be no chance of ever discovering freedom. We speak merely of the possibility of the new, for it looks as if we shall still be able to speak of freedom when element *Beta* assumes *Alpha* and consciously assents to man-as-product without any noticeable attempt to alter the inherited bundle of influences. The cautious man might do so. He would still be free. But to tell the truth, the cautious man is not creative, and although he may be what we have called man-in-full, he is not the most conclusive argument for our thesis.

It is now incumbent on us to take a closer look at this "assuming towards . . ." which we have considered to be the hallmark of the free man, or what we have called man-in-full. To assume the act as yours may be considered to be an observation which only introspection can reveal. Such is the existential approach that is so familiar, as in what Sartre would call *le projet* (the Project). However much Sartre's insights have inspired the present analysis, his mode of approach has been ruled out from the start through our insistence that only a phenomenology of descent, observation from without, would be used. "We," standing outside, shall still be able to observe the assumption of the act, for it can be seen that to assume it as one's own occurs only when one is ahead of it—aware of it in advance—by the simple fact of planning and of having planned. To plan clearly implies to break the causal link between past, present and future as an unavoidable ordering. It shows to the outsider that the individual man who performs the act is, through planning, sufficiently detached from the past to be able to alter that past and to an extent command both it and the future. There is no need to look for dramatic examples of this phenomenon. Everyday man will do.

John plans to go to Chicago. This fundamental project immediately entails a series of actions which cannot be omitted if the main project is ever to be fulfilled. He telephones the airline for a reservation and arranges his work so as to be free on that particular day. On the morning of his departure, he finds transportation to the airport. He checks his luggage. He walks towards the airplane, smiles at the air hostess, chooses his seat, fastens his seatbelt, etc. The life of this man, like the life of every individual, appears to the Observer as a chain of brief actions. Most of these acts involve a certain mobility which is unique, yet—and this belongs to the fragment as unique—while positing the act *John runs ahead of his own mobility.* Once a man has a project, be it a career or some more limited endeavor, almost immediately he starts making smaller plans which lead to the fulfillment of the more encompassing one, so that in carrying out certain actions, he is almost continually ahead of the act. And it is because he is ahead of the act that the act is performed. When John leaves his house and jumps into a taxicab, he is already at the airport by way of intention. When he deposits his luggage on the scale, he is already in Chicago where he will pick it up. Man appears to be mobile on two levels. The life of an individual is a fabric made up of a multiplicity of actions, and this life course, in which the unique mobility of the individual consists, contains a mobility-ahead-of-the-act-itself. Just as there is in the individual life the chain of actions which we see, so also there seems to be an underlying being-ahead-of-the-act which is a vital factor in the uniqueness of the individual's whole life activity. The visible execution of his actions can only be the outward movement of a ceaseless planning which gives the course of the individual's life its originality and its possibility of change. To the Observer from without, this planning is a disclosure of the fact that the individual takes his actions upon himself, for it reveals that man is not mere product but is aware of his act before it happens, and being thus "ahead of it," he is able to alter it. In taking the act upon himself he posits it as his own. He is responsible.

We willingly concede that this point, at which to all appearances the cause-and-effect sequence breaks down, remains noumenal. It is here that the Observer is brought face to face with freedom as freedom and is able to lay hold of what follows, since by hypothesis there is nothing which is a necessary sequel. This point from which the creative originality of the individual issues is a labyrinth as well. If we have touched freedom, we have not—to use a Cartesian distinction—grasped freedom. In its deeper nature freedom remains an X. Rather than give it a metaphysical status, we are better advised to consider it a physical entity which is incapable of measurement. It *is*, yet its nature at present escapes us and we are not able to define its presence in the way we describe and measure other data of the senses. It is and remains the point from which man's originality issues, the source of his responsibility, but within the domain of the nonquantifiable.

At this point of our observation the difference between the anthill and the human *totum* comes clearly into the foreground. One can see the components of both collectives moving in different directions, yet something is missing with the ants. They are diversified on the spatial level, it is true, with different ants fulfilling different functions, but they show no signs of diversity on the temporal level. They seem to be prisoners of their own act and their own function and never to be ahead of the act, hence never to break out of the fixed path which their instinct has traced for them once and forever. Man, on the other hand, is seen to be both *Alpha*—the given, that-which-is-already-there, different from everyone else—and *Beta*, the assumed, that-which-will-be, the subliminal movement by which he is ahead of himself and guides that-which-is towards what-is-not-yet-but-will-be, in which he differs not only from others but from his old self as well. Unlike the ants, man is capable of turning aside from the preordained and of discovering the new. He innovates in time. He is free.

Freedom and Angular Truth

IF the mobility of man is connected with planning for the future, it is also tied to the way he sees that future, or to his particular vision or angular truth. Individual X walks within his own light as within a moving circle, and although the impact of the future regulates his act, as that which attracts it, the future as seen and attracted to is not remote. Individual man may be an "entity of distances," as Heidegger asserts, but his consciousness and clear awareness illuminate a definite, limited circle, beyond which the darkness and the unknown future lie. For if the future comes to individual man from afar, he himself sees it only when it is within the reach of his knowledge. This noetic reach of the individual man is what is called in the film world a "close-up."

Close-ups can be absorbing, but once they are known as close-ups, they no longer compel as absolutes. One who knows that his vision is angular is aware by the same token that another vision is not only possible but even probable. This myopia affects the project which we have called *Beta*. If it could be shown that the future event is the only thing that can be done, with the total exclusion of everything else, there would no longer be an assuming of the available *Alpha* by *Beta*. The Absolute then confronted would take control of the act, and nothing would be left of individual freedom. It is only in this sense that there could be a conflict between the existence of God and man's freedom: it is not God's existence that is an obstacle to human freedom (on this Sartre is wrong, I believe) but the prospect of His eventually manifesting Himself. Only a hidden God can leave man "unique" and "free," for the individual can move freely and construct his life course in a variety of directions only because he is not brought face to face with the Absolute. No doubt there are within his ken absolutes other than the prospect of a God revealing Himself: love for a woman or for the fatherland may at times impose itself upon the individual vision with blinding force, concealing the other values in this world and making the beloved "the whole world" to the lover. Whether or not values which impose themselves as absolutes wholly eliminate freedom, we shall not decide. But one thing is clear: it is possible for us to speak of freedom only because all of man's knowledge is derived through an angular vision, and he has at the same time a confused understanding of the fact that the partial vision which is his own could not be the only one.

Responsibility and the Totum

ONE might consider presumptuous the attitude of the Observer who discovers freedom and its consequent "responsibility" without actually being able to describe it very precisely. The presumption seems less, however, when we consider that such an attitude is one which, however paradoxical, the *totum* itself has been taking all along.

It is a fact that the particular *totum* shapes its constituents in many ways. To be born in the Congo is not the same thing as to be born in Sweden. In this event, for which the individual can in no way be made responsible, lies buried most of what he will be. The group has chosen for the infant what clothes to wear, what education to get, what opinions to have or not to have, what religion to practice or not to practice, what books to read and what political views to embrace. Although it is the hope of the Planetary Man to break down the zealotry of the group-fragment, this hope, like all hope, runs ahead of its fulfillment. For the present the group-angular vision triumphs and the vision of individual man is profoundly impregnated by the vision of the particular *totum* in which he is born.

As a result we must admit—and I believe that most sociologists will confirm this point—that *totum A* shapes man-as-product *a*, while *totum B* will mold man-as-product *b*. Environment and heredity play a large part in what the individual will be. Clearly it is from there on (the French phrase *à partir de . . .* would be most suitable in this case) that element *Beta*, the personal interference and potency of creating the new, will start. If freedom and responsibility are part of the destiny of man, they can only be understood against the background of belonging to a certain culture-unit. Responsibility is caught within a cultural ensemble, and although it is present everywhere, it is present differently. Whether belonging to *totum A* or *B*, the individual will be held responsible by it. He will be treated as responsible by his own *totum* and consequently be repulsed or seduced by it.

The mode of approach practiced by the *totum* may appear cruel to some. It is indeed, for the judgment of the *totum* ignores nuances. Always prone to find a culprit, it finds what it wants. Yet the "presumption" of responsibility is at bottom an act of self-protection. For this is what matters above all: the *totum*, made up of a diversified mobility, cannot survive as human *totum* unless the fragment is considered to be responsible. "We" the Observers do not adequately comprehend freedom, or that by which individual man is himself and master of his actions, but on the basis of the "evidence" we presume it to be there. "We" the *totum*, with no less fervor but with much less philosophical anguish, discover the culprit. While individuals argue, the *totum* acts. Like the surgeon it discovers the cause and proceeds to root out the diseased organ. Yet in presuming freedom without ever totally comprehending it, the human *totum* inflicts upon its constituent the consequences of a quality which he may not yet totally possess but which some day, under constant prodding, he will make his own. What appears inhuman at first sight will, over the span of centuries, appear to be most human, for it is responsibility that in the long run distinguishes man from his dog. Man will be fully man only when he stands up and allows himself to be counted for his actions.

In the meantime we shall side with the *totum* and "accuse" the fragment whenever we see the "diversified" action doing harm to the *totum*. The act of accusation can not be dropped, for this would cancel the force of the antithetic by which a phenomenology of descent discovers entities which are diverse and unique, yet part of the *totum*. To be a possible object of blame is the mark of man, for in the strength of the antithetic lies the implication that the selves are selves, and by the same token that they are free and responsible.[6]

Freedom as Totum-*Oriented*

THE Statue of Liberty which the immigrant observes as his ship navigates into the port of New York is a symbol of this fundamen-

---

[6] There is one reservation in this consistent act of presuming and of giving man his responsible status: one can only be expected to respect the mores of the *totum* if and when one has been accepted into that *totum*. Those who have been excluded by the other members can hardly be made responsible for the mores and conventions of that particular *totum*, unless of course it concerns commandments which have a universal application and pervade all groups.

tal *presumption*, for the immigrant is given notice that he is arriving in the land of the free. While the liberty here has primarily political implications, it is grounded in the freedom that we have discovered philosophically. It is because individual man is master of his actions and assumes them as his own that we have called him free. But whoever is master of his actions must be treated as such and cannot be lowered to the status of an ant, since he is not fragment of an anthill. Political and religious freedoms result from the fundamental presumption of freedom philosophically warranted. We shall treat men as men because we know that they are responsible. Whoever rejects freedom philosophically has no basis on which to establish it politically and is fully entitled to treat men as ants.

Freedom as signified by the Statue of Liberty is a privilege and a right, but it carries a duty with it. Of this there can be no doubt. In making this assertion we merely translate into moral terms the ontological structure of the fragment, which is one of belonging to. . . . Nothing born in time (and disappearing in time) can be termed absolute, although it can provisionally be endowed with this dimension. There are moments when absolutization can be a necessary operation of life on this globe, as during the last three hundred years in the West when individual man was being "liberated" and given a standing. It is imperative now that he be brought back to the fulfillment of his ontological structure, which is one of belonging. It is this fundamental belonging which ultimately dictates the direction of the responsible act. The individual fragment set free and treated as such is himself, but being himself, is more than ever instrumental vs. the other components of the totality.

Instrumentality implies that one is used by the other just as one uses him. The qualification of "just as" is crucial, for in the intricate interlocking which makes up the *totum*, I can only make use of you to the extent that you are allowed to make use of me. The time is over when one could presume to use the other as animal or as tool, with one "side" enjoying a monopoly. Man can employ and be employed only with due respect for the status of a free being and for the unique vocation of each individual. (Both qualifications amount to the same thing.) Mutual instrumentality is a fact.

It follows that it is the vocation of every man to direct his unique mobility into some measure of service. The use of freedom in some form of service is his assignment and his vocation. The multiple diverse becomes a variety of functions. Individual man is *called*, his vocation is the call to accomplish his unique function. As such *his* freedom is relevant: it is the unique way to participate in the achievement of the noontide of mankind. What this accomplishment will be we cannot claim to know. It can perhaps be expressed negatively as nothing but an escape from annihilation.

The individual does not use freedom for himself alone, then, for survival does not center around one individual as around a god. The *totum* has no center. If man transcends the ant, it is on the basis of free cooperation, not on the basis of noncooperation, for the discovery of freedom neither detaches the fragment from the *totum* nor obliterates its relational structure: to be a man is only to be a *free* ant. In that word "free," of course, lies a distance which cannot be measured in a million years. The human *totum* cannot return to its primeval origins. It must survive as a human *totum*. Yet it will only survive as human if the individual is treated as free and unique, and it will survive as *totum* only if that unique freedom, far from being self-centered, is directed to the welfare of all.

It is now apparent that we cannot look for freedom as a property of the *totum* as such. The *totum* has no center: it is merely the cohesion of the interdependent. It merely is and survives through the freedom of its members. Freedom is a property of the fragment. The *totum* becomes free and responsible, however, when it plays its part within a more encompassing *totum*, for then it asserts itself as diverse with respect to its neighboring collectives. It becomes itself *totum*-fragment, with all the characteristics that distinguish the fragment.

We have seen that a pronouncement made by the group and expressing what we have called the "freedom of the group" sometimes presents itself to the individual as a dictate or command. The *will* of the group can be compelling to the members within its enclosing walls. But from the point of view of the Observer, by hypothesis on the promontory of the neutral or the nonbelonging, that same will appears only as the manifestation of the particular *totum* (or *totum*-fragment) being its own self, or that which at that phase of history makes it different from other collectives. In its pronouncement the group is both compelling and free, for it is compelling as *totum*, but free as fragment.

8

Rebels and Reformers

The Rebel and the Absurd

THE concept of the rebel has sometimes been identified by poets and others as a protest against the absurd. Such a sense of rebellion is clearly present in Dylan Thomas's "Do not go gentle into that good night." The first strophe in particular revolts against what cannot be removed or changed by human means, such as death.

> Do not go gentle into that good night,
> Old age should burn and rave at close of day;
> Rage, rage against the dying of the light.

The confrontation of what cannot be overcome is accompanied by despair, a despair which is also rancor.

> And you, my father, there on that sad height,
> Curse, bless, me now with your fierce tears, I pray.
> Do not go gentle into that good night.
> Rage, rage against the dying of the light.[1]

The sense of rebellion in the poem of Dylan Thomas is magnificently expressed and obsessive as a dream, and we admire the poem as an expression of a deeply felt and universal emotion,

---

[1] From *The Poems of Dylan Thomas*. Copyright © 1952 by Dylan Thomas. Reprinted by permission of New Directions Publishing Corporation, p. 128.

but it leads us only to a senseless beating against the gates. Nietzsche would say that anger against the inevitable is an extreme case of resentment, a mark of inferiority and repression. Rebellion that takes the form of anger against the futility of it all is not the form that we shall be considering, for in a philosophy of descent we do not recognize the absurd as an authentic expression of what man is within the englobing *totum*. On the contrary, if we follow the sequence of things and events which leads to individual X, we find a concatenation of cause-and-effect. We recognize that man, although a being of exceptional value, is nevertheless part of and dependent upon nature. This does not deny freedom as the source of the new, nor does it totally explain freedom. But the view that man is explicable within a *totum universum* makes Nietzsche's yea-saying to the earth seem a more suitable response than is a curse against the dying of the light.

The attitude of Camus's "L'Homme Revolté"—"the Rebel"— is a more positive one than that of Thomas's dying man, for although the rebel protests, his protest does not imply a renunciation. He rebels against the state of affairs he discovers in this world, which is one of suffering and of "senseless" evil, but he courageously stands up to the evil and fights it. Furthermore, the combat of man against evil is conducted in the name of a certain nature, which is the nature of man as commonly expressed. Rebellion is therefore not an egotistical act; it may very well be the act of an individual who is not himself oppressed but revolts in the name of all those who share in human nature. Camus's sense of rebellion transcends the merely speculative and approaches the world with a purpose. This we applaud. We admire Dr. Rieux, who personifies that spirit and together with his fellow workers devotes himself to the fight against the plague in the city of Oran, when he might better have fled.

Yet for all its merits, *The Plague* caters to a semantic ambiguity. Camus's rebel is not really a rebel but rather a man in revolt against a poorly constructed universe.[2] Since he is revolted man as well as man revolting, his brave service is carried out in a

---

[2] The French title of Camus's book is *L'Homme Revolté* (Paris, 1951), while the translation into English is *The Plague* (New York: Alfred A. Knopf, Inc., 1954).

spirit of sad futility. Such is Camus's vision, which once more proceeds from the subject and considers as evil that which inflicts suffering or death upon man. It might lift some of the gloom if, placing man within a surrounding universe, we visualize the concatenation of things and events as they come from afar and shape one's destiny. Acceptance of death becomes an acceptance of the fragmented *totum* as we know it. From this more removed point of view, recognition of a limit need not be nonsensical, nor must suffering be seen as an absurdity, since it is a part and even to an extent a defense of life.

Portrait of the Rebel

WE have seen how the *totum* is organically structured in its oneness and how its salvation lies in the internal diversity of this oneness. Without the unequal the *totum* would decline. This ontological structure is at times threatened by inertia, that is, by the continued imposition of a certain number of laws and customs which are no longer necessary except for the few who profit by them. The ultimate redemption of the many is warranted only by the disappearance and replacement of these customs. The man in charge is the rebel.

The rebel sees what others do not yet see and is aware of a need which others have not yet felt. Furthermore, he has the audacity to act upon his vision. His first movement is a questioning, for where there is no questioning, there is no rebellion. The Indian pariah neither questions nor rebels. The Catholic, in certain phases of the history of the Church, did not question. Not only was reform excluded, but so also was any question about the need for reform. The rebel, however, questions the conventionality of which he is a part, and as a result, challenges the *totum* into change. He does this in a particular way, through doing what is forbidden.

This "forbidden" act is, in our terms, that which must not be committed by anyone belonging to a particular *totum*, as a result of one's belonging to that *totum*. The problem is that certain actions are forbidden by one's own *totum* but are condoned by a more encompassing one and may even someday belong to the conventions of one's own collective. The rebel takes the risk of deciding when this is the case and of committing the act forbidden in his own time and place, in the belief that it is not forbidden in the light of the future. He has the audacity to declare that he is the future. To some of his contemporaries Christ was immoral, since he broke with the mores of his day and claimed that he himself was "the light." So also was Francis of Assisi, who puzzled his family and friends in his rejection of the bourgeois life and his embracing of poverty; yet today he has a place in the gardens of polite society as well as in the hearts of hippies.

Martin Luther is another example. His arrival on the scene coincides with the birth of the Cartesian man, who is man aware of himself. Until then, the church had been the custodian of men. The church is and always was a *totum*, but it was not then a *totum* as this study defines a *totum*, that is, a sum of the unequal. In Luther's day the church saw itself as the sum of the equal or uniform. One was a member of the church in the way one is a member of an Aristotelian category: only what one has in common was considered and not what one has as uncommon or singular and unique. Such was, and still is, the strength of an institution, ecclesiastical or not. The church had fairly well succeeded in rejecting the eccentric, through excommunication, incarceration or even physical elimination. It would most probably have done the same thing with Luther if historical circumstances had not prevented it. As it happened, however, the world was ready for his larger vision. Luther was, of course, called a heretic instead of a rebel, since the term *heretic* is more appropriate when rebellion is directed against the dogmatic structure of the church. The semantics do not alter the fact that he fulfilled the function of the rebel.

Obviously the rebel—or the heretic, as might be the case—does not necessarily start a revolt with the clear insight of what should be done to replace what his rebellion attempts to tear down. The solution or its understanding will come only later, and sometimes with exceptional force. Luther did not really foresee where things were going when he nailed his decrees to the church door at Wittenberg. Nor does our observation exclude the possibility that rebellion in its destructive phase may be accomplished by one and reconstruction or reform by another. The rebel is not necessarily the reformer. And although in some cases, as with Luther, the two categories coincide, they do not necessarily do so. This is particularly true when the function of the rebel is carried out by a group. For rebellion does not necessarily have to be fulfilled by one individual. It may also be accomplished by a group, although a group of individuals still constitutes a fragment rebelling against the *totum* of which the individuals are a part. To rebel-in-a-group within a *totum* often means to start a revolution. The French Revolution, for example, originated as a group within the larger *totum* of the nation, with the aim of destroying the structure of the *ancien régime*.

Whether it be a solitary mission or the performance of a group within a more encompassing totality, the task of the rebel is one of correction. He is born out of the impossibility of tolerating a state of affairs of which he was either victim or the witness of victims. He is instrumental, for through his behavior, he responds to and acts out the unconscious wish of the group. As agent of change, he is wanted by the *totum*, but at the same time it fights desperately against him. Since the *totum* clings to its own survival, it wants to be what it is; but to be what it is, it also wants the change that helps it stave off the rigor mortis of death and nonbeing. It both wants and does not want the rebel, hence puts into action all the means at its disposal to eliminate him or to neutralize his impact. The rebel is thus condemned to be solitary, seemingly at odds with his *totum*; for the latter, especially when it is highly institutionalized, cannot transcend its own angular vision. Within this vision it rewards its followers and excludes those whose vision does not coincide with its own optic, giving its present rewards according to a logic of standardization that stresses what men have in common. And yet it is the inequality, the existence of the singular and the individual, which makes possible the survival of the *totum* and protects it against the apathy of decay. The reward of the rebel is postponed, often until after his lifetime.

For the rebel serves the *totum* in acting as its prophet. He is the future of the *totum* living now. Falling outside of the "angular" grasp of his own times, he lives within the vision of times to come. Hence, although responding to the need of his *totum* and—as in the case of Joan of Arc—hearing "voices," he is in the eyes of his contemporaries just that: one who hears voices, a misfit. The case of the condemnation of the Modernist "heresy" is an example. What the Loisys and the Turmels wanted was merely a reformulation in modern semantics of what the rigid presentation of Christian dogma had held for centuries, propounded in a scholastic mold. It was a case of angular vs. Angular, with the weaker fragment being the unavoidable loser for the time being but not forever. To the church, Loisy and Turmel were hearing voices and had to be condemned. To the *totum* the voices they heard were those of the future, of itself speaking.

It is through the unrest caused by the unaccepting, the rebelling, the outsiders, that the *totum* itself slowly evolves towards a new set of conventions. The evolution is not without resistance. At times the elimination of the heretic is considered, with the hope that this will save the collective of which he is a member. Such was the method of the Inquisition, and of all groups using fear as a means to ensure conformity. Expulsion does not always work, however; it merely postpones the ultimate and necessary change. The execution of Giordano Bruno did not eliminate the necessity for freedom of expression, nor has the condemnation of Galileo caused the sun to revolve around the earth. Consciously or unconsciously the rebel is a reformer. He is chosen from afar by the future of his *totum* as a tool of innovation, and it is on the basis of this function, and of this function only, that he will be judged.

In the fulfillment of his function, the rebel is not likely to succeed unless he realizes what can and cannot be hoped for. He knows that a certain amount of suffering is part of life, certainly in his own but also in the world he hopes to change, for there will always be a tension between dream and reality. Descartes has already stated it for us: man, although finite in his knowledge, is infinite in his wishes and his hopes. Individual man, aware of his fragmentary status, will always suffer the pain of not being omnipotent. The road is short from Descartes to Hegel's unhappy reflections, in which man and the collective are shown to project a myth to cure the incurable. This "realization" of man's imperfection is part of history, literature, and philosophy, but it must be ever discovered anew. The rebel carries limitation within himself. He must not expect things to happen exactly as he wishes. For this will not be, and impatience for the impossible will merely poison his soul. The true rebel is stoical and unselfish. He is not disturbed by those things that are not in his power to alter, for it is foolish to "long in the winter for the fruit you can only have in the summer" (Epitectus). Forgetting himself so far as hoping to benefit from his own reforms is concerned, he often dies, as we have seen, long before the seeds he has planted begin to bear fruit.

Morality and the Rebel

AT this moment we must recall our earlier defense of the conventional. It was stated that convention is an expression of natural law, with the aim of protecting the *totum*. It was made clear that one cannot live without the structures of the *totum* and that its dictates must transcend the whims and the wishes of the individual. Tradition, it was said, is in itself a selection, an empiricism of the species. As such it is not less important than change. But when, we ask, is an innovation such that tradition must give in? When is the rebel right, and his immorality no longer sin?

If we follow our previous line of reasoning, the logical conclusion seems to be that an innovation is *moral* once it is accepted by the group. The innovator who prods the group into accepting changes that will ultimately benefit the *totum* can no longer be considered the unwelcomed outsider. On the contrary, he is the redeemer. The whole problem, of course, is to discover within one's own time the *true* rebel and to distinguish him from the one whose sole aim is to destroy anything within reach. The uniqueness of the false prophet, who also breaks with the mores of his time, cannot be considered to be beneficial to the *totum*, at least not in a direct way. What matters is to distinguish the "immorality" of the false prophet from the "other-morality" of the true rebel, to recognize the redeemer when he comes. There are several criteria that must be applied in determining whether or not the rebellious action is ultimately a moral one.

First, one must ask whether the action profits the *totum* as a whole or only the agent.

If the act of the rebel profits the *totum* as a whole, his function serves a purpose. It is justifiable in the light of a higher morality, that is, it breaks down the mores of a particular *totum* with the intention of replacing them with better ones. The Observer, by hypothesis uninvolved in the conventions of any one epoch, cannot deny the rebel the right to improve the world in which he lives and to make room for a better one.

It is true that the rebel's function is one of great complexity. When closely observed, it appears to be both destructive and constructive, as loving, yet as hating too. It may even go so far as to appear as one of death, with the rebel incarnating the anti-man. Yet he wants life, and his opposition, when looked upon by the uninvolved, appears as ultimately constructive, and his hate as a form of love for the *totum* in which he moves. It is through the work of the rebel that we are able to explain the pivotal movement from one epoch to another. The *totum* slowly turns on its axis from an old way of living to a new one, with the rebel as the propelling force. His ambitions are not always so vast, of course; but whether large or small, they reflect the same intent. He performs a function and nothing more.

But in performing that function, he lives for it and is oblivious of himself. His aim of renewal becomes sinful only when it is concentrated upon the instant and provokes actions which disrupt the mores for his own pleasure and profit. Such a man must be put aside, for he is betraying his sacred function, which is that of a fellow servant.

The second criterion that must be applied to the rebellious act is whether it threatens the deepest law of the *totum*, which is the law of survival.

A rebellious act cannot be considered to be beneficial if it constitutes a menace to the life of the *totum* either in the present or in the future. The morality of the act must be evaluated by the amount of harm it does or does not do both to those who are and to those who will be. Consequently, a "rebellious" group which advocates the use of lethal drugs must be viewed as immoral, even if the drugs affect those who-will-be more than those-who-are. So also, a "rebellious" group that attempts to ostracize those-who-are and belong to a certain tradition in the name of those who-will-be is acting immorally. A global judgment concerning the morality of a rebellious act we shall call the *last judgment*. This judgment ought to be placed not at the end of time but above time. It is this supratemporal character which gives such an evaluation its collective strength and its character of objectivity. The young must not be privileged at the expense of the old, nor must the power of the old crush the initiative of the young.

It is in this light, the survival of life as a whole in the *totum,* that we must view the question whether or not the rebel can use violence to protect or achieve his rights. By violence we mean violence in the usual sense of the term, that is, the use of physical force exerted against an individual (or group) through assault on him as a person or through occupation of his property.

Force can be used aggressively or defensively. Aggressive violence takes place when an individual who himself is not under any threat uses force against another individual. Such an act is clearly destructive of the *totum* and cannot be tolerated. As far as defensive violence is concerned, we shall be consistent with the views presented above, according to which each human individual has a basic right to be and to survive, and state that when under attack, he has a right to protect himself even if this defense results in violence. The ambiguity is still not clearly resolved, for the meaning of the words "to protect oneself " needs clarification. Self-protection must be understood as a momentary protection of such basic rights as those of life and possessions. (No general rule can be given as to whether violence is better than a totally passive attitude when self-defense is at stake. Greater evil can result when violence is used as self-defense. On this the individual facing a concrete case will have to decide for himself.) Careful attention must be given to the word "momentary," for its meaning is of major importance in our evaluation of the use of violence. By "momentary" we mean the amount of protection (through violence) which is required when facing an aggression which could not be foreseen, or if foreseen could not be prevented. This excludes any advance plan for the use of violence in the acquisition of basic rights, under the motto of self-defense. Acquisition of basic rights, except for a sudden need of self-defense, must follow the methods of grouping and organization. We shall insist that the emphasis in all methods of rebellion must be upon persuasion and upon all other means which respect the totality as such, when and if some components of the latter do not agree with the new values. The rebel must gradually instill these new values, and over a length of time make them representative of the *totum* rather than of only a few. Ideally, he is an educator rather than a destroyer. Violence does not make him a rebel, it makes him a sinner, because he is injuring a part of the *totum*. This is not justifiable even if that same part of the *totum* has injured him by indirect violence. It is a sad irony that even the exponents of nonviolence become violent in their attempt to get the philosophy of nonviolence across. It is a commonplace to see the anti-war demonstrator become a fierce fighter in and during the street riots and by the same token belie his deeper vision of respect for his fellow men.[3]

We must concede that our position, although normatively correct, is not descriptively cogent, and by this it must be understood that although violence must be considered an evil, the fact remains that looking at a world from afar, as has been our constant attempt, we observe that all through history violence has in fact led to the acquisition of rights. Revolutions have been bloody, and in being bloody, they have been successful. Politics in many cases are unethical—I regret to say, yet I must be honest enough to say it—and being unethical, they have succeeded where a more honest line of action would have failed. All this is undeniable. There are innumerable instances where the normative is overrun by the descriptive.[4]

Has this in the long run made for a better world? Our question with its qualifying phrase lays stress upon the length of time, and in doing so puts the emphasis where it belongs. For with a philosophy which considers the benefit for the *totum* as a whole, one modifies the question. Even when successful in its immediate result, has the use of violence made for a better world? Has dishonesty in politics or deceit in business, even when rewarding a

---

[3] Our principle of justifiable violence on the grounds of self-defense only goes for the police forces as well. Their self, of course, does not merely include their self(s) as individual men, but also the community of which they have charge. For the guardian, self-defense means defense of the community itself, not merely of himself as a person.

[4] Sartre's view on that point was made clear to me in a recent meeting. "Some people are surprised that I seem to favor violence," he said. "Actually I am by nature very much opposed to violence. But I have learned over the years that the leading class, or anyone in power for that matter, will not give up its oppressive power unless under threat." (April 12, 1969). I presume that Sartre had in mind "threat of violence" or violence itself.

demagogue or a shrewd business executive, been a blessing for the *totum*? The answer is no. Immoral methods merely create an immoral climate. Likewise the use of violent methods keeps violence alive as a tool of victory. Someday the deceit will be defeated by deceit, and brutality will be crushed by brutal means. Violence invades the fabric of a *totum* and impoverishes it the way some diseases imperceptibly alter the constitution of a body and keep it in poor health. Since history has shown violence to be successful, we know no other way. But now we are the victims. We are paying for the people who won their rights by violence.

Even if we have seen violence succeed, on a short-term basis, we should not too easily take for granted the failure of the nonviolent. The contrary has often been shown to be the case. When the rebel has been rejected, excommunicated, imprisoned, expelled, or perhaps even executed, authority has merely been using its power. Its intentions are not under discussion at present. Whatever they were, it is obvious that the deed of the rebel cannot be considered undone, although he himself is no longer a factor to be considered. Once Joan of Arc had been executed on the public square of Rouen, her judges felt a sense of relief, for with the Maid's disappearance it became apparent that order had been reestablished. There is, however, an ambiguity in the term "apparent," for what is apparent to you may not be to me, and what was apparent to Cauchon was definitely not so to posterity. Angles of vision differ, and there may be a total lack of communication between the way the same action is viewed now and the way it will be viewed later. There is another error on the part of the authority who feels safe and justified once he has eliminated the rebel. Even though his judgment concerning the ethical content of the rebel's act may not be mistaken, it often constitutes a misreading of what lies beyond the visible facts. The rebel may be wrong in what he does but not in what he signifies. When he proposes the use of certain drugs which are definitely harmful to his own health and that of his descendants, the action must be considered wrong in the ethical view of this study. But the fact that people do take drugs and that to some they are necessary as an escape from a world which seems orderly, correct and hygienic, yet is in fact impersonal and ruthlessly competitive, should tell us something. Similarly, although we have condemned violence as a means of obtaining rights, we should heed the message of the riots in the American ghettos. Although the act of the rebel is something we cannot "live with," it stands as a warning. Most individuals in authority observe the phenomenon, not the warning. To the noninvolved man, the warning is still visible.

The Homecoming of the Rebel

WHATEVER may be the fate of the rebel, the beginning and the term of his excursion is and remains the *totum*. It can rightly be presumed that he draws strength from his convictions, yet his vocation is and remains a provisional one. He is not what he appears to be, happily independent and self-sufficient. He is the moment of correction and nothing more. But no moment lasts forever, and this is true whether the rebel stands as an individual or as a group in revolt. The rebel-reformer disappears qua rebel. The need for the rebel to be annulled in his very function of rebel is so essential that once his function is fulfilled, he must go. Eventually the French Revolution began to guillotine its own leaders, and the liquidations of Marat and Robespierre were only natural, although the way this was accomplished is questionable. The survival of the rebel qua rebel is harmful, for if he refuses to disappear he belies his ontological function of instrument. What is not law-abiding becomes destructive.

If the rebel-reformer does not return home—and this is sometimes the case—he becomes the founder. If he cannot succeed in reforming the *totum*, he may withdraw completely and start a new one. Luther, whatever his original intentions, was driven to embody his vision in a new totality. The Lutheran church in certain ways became as rigid as the Roman church and grew into a *totum* with a carefully organized sacramental and liturgical life, an intellectual theology, and its own political vision which was a new relationship between church and state. All of this grew and spread so widely in the course of twenty-five years that the old papal structures could no longer integrate with the new church, whatever effort of unification was made.[5]

Whether or not this founding is temporary and will last only

---

[5] Cf. J. M. Todd, *Martin Luther* (London: Burns and Oates, 1964), chapter 44.

for a few centuries, until the original *totum* brings the reforming process to completion, is something which we are not yet able to say. One thing appears certain in the transition from the function of rebel to that of founder: the individual once more betrays a deeper urge, that of multiplication. Proselytism, like sex, aims at perpetuation of itself; but in so willing, the fragment confesses to being what it is, fragmentary and finite, ever in search of some form of permanence beyond its own narrow limits in time and space. Like other forms of procreation, creation starts when the individual is expelled from the original *totum*, whether his expulsion was a self-willed act or the forced result of his rebellion. The creation is not necessarily that of a new *totum* in the strict sense of the word; it may as well be a new vision which will later call for followers and admirers. It is upon being expelled from the Synagogue that Spinoza started the more systematic writing of his *Ethics*. Dante began the composition of his immortal trilogy only after he had been banished from Florence. The unwanted make themselves desirable, and it was an exile who fashioned the common language of Italy. But when the exiled are accepted and everyone speaks their language, they are no longer there.

It seems that the end of all rebellion is stability, or what we have equated with the *totum*, that which is unconditional and survives. When all is said and done, it appears that the rebel walks in a circle. Bent upon correction, which he may or may not accomplish, the rebel strays away from the *totum* only to rediscover it later in one way or another. His return shows that in most cases tradition may stand correction and that once completion and correction are achieved, the mobility of the rebel, more unique than most, reveals itself as having been only instrumental.

9

A New Image of the Saint

The Saintly and the Profane

THE term *saint* comes from the Latin *sanctus*, which is the past participle of *sancire*, "to establish by law." That which is established by law is sacred. This original meaning has been kept in the current signification of saintly as "that which is august and exceptional, hence that which is holy and divorced from the profane and from the ordinary." With the Romans *sanctus* was an epithet for the gods, and Christianity continued the practice. We are told that God alone is most segregated from the ordinary. He is *sanctus*: he is holy.[1] The same quality is attributed to Christ, as also to the church which he founded. Even the members of the church are supposed to be "saints" in this general meaning of the word. Saint Paul used the word "αγιος" and implied that through baptism the members of the Church became saints (sacred and consecrated) simply by virtue of their belonging to the Church. Later on, the term was applied more selectively, so that not every member of the Church was called a saint, but only those who after formal and close investigation were found to have led "perfect" lives.

This chapter is an attempt to bring the term *saint* back into the world of the profane, while still preserving the signification of elevation attached to the word by its religious use. Thus, the saint is the one who in some way transcends the mediocre.

---

[1] The English word *holy* comes from the word *whole*, that which is in totality and contains no imperfection.

This definition is still too imprecise to be valid. Obviously an intellectual genius transcends the mediocre, yet is not called a saint. Raphael, da Vinci, Rembrandt, Picasso can hardly be called average, but this does not make them saints. The multimillionaire who works unremittingly to calculate the needs of the market and the ways he can provide those needs is uncommon, yet however much he may be venerated by some, he is still not called a saint. Each of these—the genius, the artist, the industrialist—is different from the ordinary run of men; none is a saint. This is not to condemn but merely to say that the saint has something which none of the others has. The genius sees new ways of ordering things, the artist brings forth beauty, and the industrialist, in gathering wealth for himself, perhaps improves the material standing of others. The saint does not per se condemn intellect, beauty or wealth; yet there is something else for which he works primarily. The saint has *his* absolute.

A Variety of Absolutes

GROWTH is nothing but a reevaluation of absolutes. Such is the greater part of the maturation process of individual man, and of the inner growth of the *totum* as well. If we observe the etymology of the word "absolute," we note that it comes from the verb *absolvere,* to untie. This brings to mind the common application: to untie one's guilt, to absolve, to forgive. But the original meaning also contains the connotation "to detach from. . . ." The past participle of *absolvere,* or *absolutus,* can be that which is physically detached, or that which is detached from its own guilt, or— and this is the most frequent use of the word—that which is detached from all limiting circumstances, hence that *which counts always and everywhere.*

This last meaning of absolute as unlimited acceptance can be applied in three different ways. When the absolute can be understood as something which must be believed, we shall call it a *credendum.* For the believer the existence of God is such an absolute. When the absolute is understood as something which must be done or not done, we shall call it an *agendum* or a *nonagendum.* An example here is the commandment: "You must not kill."

Finally there is the absolute which we shall call a *habendum*, that which must be obtained or protected at all costs. Towards the acquisition or safeguarding of the absolute habendum, the absolute which we have called agendum is merely instrumental, but as such it is conditio-sine-qua-non. In that sense you must not kill (nonagendum) for the protection of the *totum* (habendum).

For some people their family constitutes an absolute, for others it is a certain woman, for still others it may be political freedom, or the nation or the race. Some believe that money is everything. Any one of these "objects," although by nature finite, can and does assert itself with the power of the "absolute": to acquire it (habendum) the individual is prepared to do anything (agendum). He is even prepared to give his life for it, since by definition the absolute is that which counts more than anything. Although absolutes may differ, there is one common factor: in each one the act returns to the agent and is somehow rewarding. It is easy to see the compensation given the man who sets forth to conquer a woman. Closely observed, our other absolutes—political freedom, protection of the nation, the spreading of the good news —may also be found to contain some reward for the agent himself. Of course, the danger of losing one's life is always there, if the absolute is truly an absolute, but this danger, real in some cases, often remains remote.

The struggle to safeguard an absolute can become nationalism when the object is the nation. It can also take the shape of proselytism when the believer has the conviction that his dogma constitutes salvation for the rest of mankind. When the candidate is not only enthralled with his object but also obsessed with it to the extent that he ignores anything else it is called fanaticism. The fanatic lives his absolute in a desert: he sees nothing else.

Whether this attitude is destructive is not our immediate concern, but what is obvious to any observer is that the absolute as habendum or agendum means power. That which confronts the viewer as what must be obtained and protected at all cost has made the martyrs. It has also built empires. Whether it has made the saints we shall have to determine. One thing appears certain, and it is that any collective where the members no longer carry within their vision an object for which they are prepared to die is itself in decline. To many, sophistication may seem preferable to naiveté, but it also signifies the fall of the absolutes and the aging of the *totum*.

Contamination of the Absolutes

FOR a complete understanding of the notion of absolute, we must return for a moment to what has been said concerning multiple "vision" and the resulting multiple truth.[2] In showing the ontological fragmentation of the *totum*, which results in a noetic segmentation, we pointed out that truth is present in three degrees: the angular vision with its truth quantum for the (individual) fragment, the generic vision with its truth quantum for the *totum*, and finally the absolute truth that can only be the vision of God. The presence of a certain amount of absolute truth within the angular vision was not denied, but it was made clear that an angular vision (and its truth quantum) was by essence limited and condemned to be only a corrective balance for another angular vision. We shall not elaborate upon that point here, since this has already been done.[3] Yet its importance is undeniable, for it implies that however absolute may be the truth quantum within the angular or individual vision, this vision and grasp of the absolute truth by the individual is always individualized. Although "absolute" (truth), it will not and cannot be identical to the "absolute" truth as viewed by another individual. The acceptance of the ontological fragmentation and the ensuing angular visions signifies the end of identical absolutes. The presence of the absolute within the angle of vision is contaminated by the ontological segment of which it is the angular vision. If the limitations of the fragment led to an argument for the collective in the earlier study, it was a defender of the individual as well, for a philosophy of the angular unique is a defense of the unequal and of the impossibility of imposing the absolute as visualized by individual X upon individual Z. The knowledge of the individual has its own truth quantum. (To have its own truth quantum is typical of beings

---

[2] *The Planetary Man*, Vol. I, chapter 3.

[3] *Ibid.*, pp. 79–81.

which have consciousness, yet are somewhere or sometime. To be somewhere or sometime—the dimensions overlap—means to be caught in the angular. We further observe that anything which moves in space is altered in space and that a truth quantum moving in space with the individual who carries it is no exception.) This uniqueness of the individual vision does not prevent it from being relevant, although not all encompassing, and contributing, although never totally self-sufficient.

The application to the moral problem under discussion is obvious. What is contaminated in the realm of knowledge by the very structure of the individual self is similarly contaminated in the realm of action. The truth which one confronts becomes one's own truth, and it is that for which one chooses to live and to die. This does not mean that this absolute (or that which I must do or have at all costs) is necessarily unworthy simply because it is shaped in the angular vision of my own optic. We merely want to point out that it is not unselfish. The absolute which one confronts becomes one's own. It protects its owner in giving him a reason for which to work, to live and eventually to die. Whether or not this absolute is mere myth, and will later appear to be so, is at present of no concern. What matters is the insight that this absolute, be it a credendum or an agendum, pays its returns and like a financial investment, in one way or another comes back to the investor.

We should add, though, that such an investment contains some risk, for if it is true that the confrontation of the absolute is a strong stimulus, its acquisition (or protection) means combat. War is violence for the defense of a piece of land and all that it stands for. The murder committed out of passion is a fight to the death for a woman. Each one of those objects—that woman or that land—is sublimated into the power of the absolute, and although in by far the greatest number of cases the acquisition or defense of an absolute does not demand such extreme sacrifice, it remains true that to strive for it is to emulate, and to emulate is to rival. We meet here the same rules which regulate the movement of love and hate; the reaching towards an absolute is a form of love and includes hate or potential hate as well. Whoever loves Joan as habendum hates anyone who emerges as a threat to the possession of that "absolute."

Absolutes and the Collective

THESE observations concerning the individual as fragment can also be noted of any particular *totum* when it is considered as fragment of a more encompassing totality. A particular *totum* has its own vision, and that vision is the coordination of the many individual visions. The individuals constituting the *totum* do not cancel their angular visions, but there is a certain coming together into one vision or dominant panorama. But that vision, the coadunate of many visions, returns unto its makers and enslaves them to its own content. If it can be said that the multiple make the One, it must be said in turn that the One makes the individual fragments constituting it. When from afar we observe the confrontation of the individual with some of the absolutes which are believed to be his own, we notice that quite often they *are* his because he *was* a fragment of that particular *totum* and shares in the vision of that *totum*. If God is an absolute credendum for the Christian, the reason must be found in the fact that the Christian was born into that group and took his part in and of it. Whoever is born into a group confronts the objectives and tenets which that group has chosen, and anyone stepping into an existing group automatically steps into its angularity (or what we called the generic truth of *that* group) with the vision which it embraces. God as absolute credendum is an essential part of the group that calls itself Christian. With that *totum* the acceptance and defense, even the propagation, of that absolute is so pervading that within this group all other absolutes pursued by its constituents—women, money, pleasure, freedom—must be seen as lesser. Another absolute which might be called a group absolute is the defense of a particular nation, with its accompanying feeling called nationalism. Here again the absolute habendum is strong and easily overruns the other goals, although it does not claim to eliminate them. It will merely insist that it is within the fulfillment of the dominant absolute—service to God or defense of nation—that all other objectives must take their place. Caught in the prison of the *totum*, the individual inhabitant soon discovers that the interest of the *totum* transcends his own.

At this moment an important observation must be made concerning the presence of the absolute in the collective. Coming back once more to the example of the deity as the absolute of a *totum*, it must be stressed that if the texture of the concept of the deity is human, its peculiar humanity reflects the stage of the *totum* which over the centuries has elaborated the concept. The originality of the angular is influential in the forging of the vision of the *totum*, but it is so only as the chemical element is present in the ultimate composite. That ultimate composite, possession of the *totum*, has an identity. Hence when viewed within the span of a larger *totum*, the generic in turn becomes angular, and from that point of view may no longer be an absolute absolute, but an absolute which is "amendable."

Similarly in the domain of political structures, the concept of nation is understood differently within different nations. It is part of the American naiveté to attempt to inflict its concept of democracy upon every other form of collective. If a certain form of government is the absolute of the Anglo-Saxon world, it does not follow that for that particular absolute, other forms of government and their followers must be prepared to die. An absolute is of one's own making. The individual lives for it and may eventually die for it because that absolute is considered to be the warrant of survival of the *totum*. But one must remember that this absolute will only protect when it is accepted as absolute, superior to all other absolutes. This presumes a certain innocence of alternatives. When and if at a certain moment in history the absolute appears as "amendable" and is in the process of being absorbed by a larger *totum* and replaced by a new absolute, it will no longer be preserved; at that moment one no longer dies for it. The absolute ceases to be and is in need of replacement. One no longer dies for Florence, one dies for Italy (perhaps).

Yet as long as this moment of truth has not arrived—and it should not emerge too soon, for it robs the child of its fervor and the group of its vigor—it will appear to the Observer from afar that the group no less than the individual is fierce and aggressive in the pursuit of its absolute. A nation in the process of growth aims at power and is self-assertive. It wants to develop its economy, its culture and its technology and to protect all of them through its military power. The movement *anti* is a form of hate, born out of the need of self-protection, or what in our semantics may very well be called self-love. Hate is born out of self-love.

Hence wherever upon this *totum universum* we discover a

particular *totum* at times called a nation, we observe that for its parts (or inhabitants), that nation stands as an absolute, and anything else as instrumental and conditional towards its growth. A form of maturity will be reached as soon as the individual fragments of that *totum* visualize their absolute as contaminated and selfish. At that moment the defense of the absolute may very well be broken. Its force may not be dead, but its ruthless aggressiveness, or its anti- movement, may be blunted.

The Saint, or the Planetary Man in Ethics

MEN live in the light of their absolutes, which compel them to action in order to acquire something or to protect that which has already been acquired. In most cases they appear to be motivated by some personal profit, although this profit need not be considered to be immoral. The absolute usually belongs to an individual because of his belonging to a collective or a particular *totum*. Whether the individual confronts his absolute because of this belonging or whether the absolute was of a more private nature or concern, we can say that the pursuit of it involves the self. To the extent that this self-defense affects the status of the absolute itself we have called the absolute *contaminated*.

When the individual attempts to protect an absolute which belongs by essence to the collective—the independence of a nation or the spreading of a doctrine—greater abnegation is required than when one labors for a more personal object, such as the protection of his own family or service to the woman of his dreams. But even so, the self-denial which is required for the defense of the absolute called nation or church is not total, for although real sacrifice is involved, a reward will somehow follow.

The question may be asked: is there anyone who surpasses the majority and has a grasp and a love of the *totum humanum* as such? Is it possible to discover a human being whose total engagement is with the *totum*? This would imply (1) that his activity does not return towards himself but is directed at least in intention towards the other as its primary and exclusive preoccupation, (2) that the individual self or fragment does not assert himself beyond or against the *totum* of which he is a member, be it the particular *totum* or the *totum genus*, and (3) that he is nonaggressive and does not aim at the destruction of the *totum* or of any of its members in order to protect himself. If such a man exists, could he be the Saint?

We have earlier defined the planetary man as that entity which is nowhere and never, hence "non-engagé." The orientation of his noesis was one of nonbelonging, and his ultimate aim was the overcoming of the angular in the conquest of absolute truth. He was a god in the depth of his aspirations. If and where this appeared to be out of reach, his aim was modified; the goal became generic truth, and the whole process of his growth was shown to culminate in the acceptance of the *totum qua totum* and of the diverse within it as parts. His was the insight into truth as eccentric and relational, for he had the understanding that no angular truth could possibly be exhaustive and terminal; it could never be more than corrective. But within that function as corrective lay the essence of truth itself. In his detachment from the subjective, the Planetary Man wanted to reach the objective, which is nothing but the sum and result of the multiple subjectivity, or angularity, or partial visions. His noesis was unselfish, since it was a transcending of the singular and a conquest of the additive universal as lived by the *totum*.

The saint is the planetary man in the realm of ethics. What earlier was a movement of the mind towards the *totum* becomes now a movement of actions done for the good of the whole. This activity can be called saintly when it is noncyclical (its primary motive is not the self) nonassertive (its primary motive is not personal survival) and nonaggressive (it does not aim at the destruction of the other). Only when the individual is moving towards the welfare of the commonwealth shall we call him a saint. It is the *direction* of the mobility which counts, for it is from the trajectory that the Observer will know the missile. The absolute of the saint must be the *totum*, and it is an absolute that we shall call *uncontaminated*, since by hypothesis it is not contaminated by selfish motives in its fulfillment. This move towards the *totum* which must be protected at all costs, and which counts always and everywhere, we shall call the absolute *uncontaminated*. The absolute here is neither money, nor pleasure, nor a woman (for the lover): the absolute is the other, any other. Hence the movement of salvation goes from one living being to the other, the other whom we shall call the other-in-peril. The *totum* has a definite shape, the shape of the other-in-peril. Unlike the lover, for whom the woman is an absolute and a reward, the saint is on the move for the salvation of the other-in-peril, but he does not expect a reward for his saving work.

It is apparent by now that the other-in-peril which individual man places before him and surrounds with an aura of absolutization is not confined to any particular *totum*—say, to one's family, nation or religion. Perhaps we could call the missionary who devotes his life to lepers in some lost corner of our earth a saint, but we can do so only when and if his apostolate is not contaminated by proselytism. If his primary aim is to convert the sufferer to a particular religious affiliation, we shall not call him a saint in the full sense of the word, for in that situation "we," the Observer, note that the angular has caught up with the generic and the self has contaminated the absolute. The term *saint* does not belong to a particular religious dimension. It does so only when the religious dimension promotes what is commonly called charity and practices it apart from the purpose of selling its dogma, which is always angular. Proselytism does not per se exclude sanctity, it may even promote it, and many missionaries have led lives of heroic charity; but it does preclude sanctity when it uses charity as the fundamental diplomacy for conversion without for that reason making the other-in-peril any happier. The tacit implication, of course, is that the other will only be happy when he is as *we* are. No greater mistake could be made, for it shows a total inability to enter into the angular truth of the other, or even to suspect that there is any angularity different from ours. In being a man of detachment, the saint accepts the plural and the existence of any angular behavior which does not injure the *totum*.

We are beginning to see that paternal benevolence of the rich towards the poor which is accompanied by a preservation of the system that maintains the division between rich and poor cannot be called saintliness. Charles the Good, who was murdered in Saint Donat's church in Bruges in 1120, was considered to be a religious man and a generous one; yet he firmly opposed the social transformation of the lower class into a more economically powerful class of burghers. The revolution against his rule resulted from the natural growth of a society of serfs into one of independent citizens. The "beatification" of Charles was merely an attempt of the conservative church to perpetuate the status quo, not the honest making of a saint.[4] If it takes the *totum* to make a saint, perhaps it also takes the *totum* to know one.

In positing the *totum* as his absolute—and we know that the shape of the *totum* is the other-in-peril—the saint by definition eliminates the selfish, as well as the antithetic movement that almost inevitably accompanies selfishness. He has no other self than the *totum* itself, which is the identification towards which he is aiming unconsciously. While in the realm of knowledge the planetary man attempts the conquest of the objective—that is, of generic truth—in the realm of action and moral behavior, he pursues the salvation of the *totum*. He too is "nowhere and never" and in the loss of the self has become the *totum*.

It is thus the saint, and only the saint, who is a revenge upon our statement that Aristotle's golden mean is not fulfilled in reality, since it appears that he may be the accomplishment of the Aristotelian dream. For to the extent that the saint identifies with the *totum*, he assembles within himself the balance of virtues. He is holy, for he is whole. By virtue of this, he can be called self-sufficient. His is a self-sufficiency which must be understood as the equivalent of perfection: that which carries within itself its own corrective. The saint by definition carries his own balance within himself and for this reason can be said to be perfect. He moves from the part to the whole, and in the transition upgrades his choice from the *absolute contaminated* to the *absolute uncontaminated*, which is sanctity.

The Existential Test

ONE character in Dostoevsky's *The Idiot* seems to fulfill our definition. His endless charity and unwearying forgiveness shape him into a man who never seems to think of or protect his own self. On the contrary, he constantly wants to help the other. The

---

[4] See Galbert de Bruges, *The Murder of Charles the Good*, trans. with an introduction and notes by James Bruce Ross (New York: Columbia University Press, 1960).

women who surround him and are madly in love with him are never exploited. They look up to him as to the Redeemer. And so also do the men who come into his presence. He appears as the saint, or the totally unselfish man whose sole purpose in this world is what benefits the *totum*—or, more concretely, the other-in-peril.

Everyone admires the Prince. Yet upon closer observation, one begins to see that the Prince has something ethereal and provisional about him. When the moment of decision comes—the moment that he might become too involved—he longs for the solitude of the mountains. He recounts a tale of a time when he stood on the mountain and held out his hands to nature, crying because he could not be part of it.

> Before him was the brilliant sky, below, the lake, and all around a horizon, bright and boundless, which seemed to have no ending. He gazed a long time in distress. He remembered now how he had stretched out his hands to that bright, infinite blue, and had shed tears. What tortured him was that he was utterly outside all this. What was this festival? What was this grand, everlasting pageant to which there was no end, to which he had always, from his earliest childhood, been drawn and in which he could never take part?[5]

Prince Myshkin was not of this world. But not being part of it, he could not reach out to his fellow men. Around him orbit many creatures who are in peril and great need. Myshkin loves them all, yet as a redeemer he fails lamentably. He does not prevent Rogozin from becoming a murderer, nor Nastasia, whom he loves deeply, from being murdered, nor Aglaia from forsaking her homeland in marrying a Polish prince and becoming a Catholic (a fate worse than death in the eyes of Dostoevsky). The author, as he repeatedly states in his notebooks, made a brilliant attempt to create the beautiful soul, but he failed.[6] Towards the

---

[5] F. Dostoevsky, *The Idiot* (New York: Washington Square Press, 1965), p. 432.

[6] F. Dostoevsky, *The Notebooks for the Idiot*, ed. and with introduction by E. Wasiolek, trans. by K. Strelsky (Chicago and London: University of Chicago Press, 1967), pp. 165, 201.

end of the novel, in the eloquent diatribe of Yevgeny Pavlovich, he smashes his own creation. Prince Myshkin is admirable and totally unselfish, but he does not last. His author and creator puts him back on the train to Switzerland and locks him up in an insane asylum. Incessant forgiving and endless understanding has not cured the souls of men. Something was missing. In an attempt to define this quality that Myshkin lacked, let us come back once more to the speculative part of our work.

In our earlier volume the planetary man appeared as the one who moves through several phases.[7] The first phase is one of total detachment, which can be compared to some sort of intellectual abnegation. As a thinker, he shows no preferences. Gradually he proceeds to enrich his soul, and in so doing, understands the eternal balance of human creation, the constituents of which incessantly correct one another and thereby keep the *totum* alive. Yet even this position is provisional. Eventually he transcends the unhistorical plan: the Observer becomes the Creator. Overcoming the conflict of the diverse within, he formulates the universal and the eternal in his own semantics, and by the same token repeats the act of all incarnation, for all creation is a return to the singular. Wherever the infinite is caught within the finite, it loses the power of the infinite. Incarnation is partial defeat. A vision created by the one individual, however planetary, may very well offer unity to the one who sees, but it is still caught in the lens of his own optic. The individual, in accomplishing the synthesis within his own self, puts his own stamp upon the vision. The planetary man, born in the singular, must die in the singular and can never totally identify with the *totum humanum*. Yet notwithstanding this restriction, or better still because of this restriction, he is the Creator. His attempt to transcend his own self and to grasp the larger vision reveals to him the multiplicity of men and the variety of creeds; but in formulating this vision in his own terms, as he should, he creates a new vista, his own. To be only oneself may appear to be a defeat, but in this fractured *totum* of ours it is the only way to behave.

What we observed in the realm of speculative noesis finds its counterpart in the moral order. When the saint has grasped the

---

[7] *The Planetary Man*, Vol. I,   chapter 9.

totum, he becomes truly himself and acts, and in the process of acting, he commits himself. We shall be most reluctant to call someone a saint who is totally inactive. Not that contemplation is a vice—in a world of feverish activity it may very well be a virtue—but when contemplation has degenerated into quietism, it is a form of laziness or escape and does not fit our image of sanctity. The saint as portrayed in these pages is the one who posits the action, just as the creator in the realm of speculation is the one who formulates the vision.

When we make the statement that the saint acts and in the process of acting commits himself, we imply that in daring to act, he chooses the consequences of the act as well. It is an act, and the act is *his*. Commitment is the hallmark of the self. Although Prince Myshkin was the object of admiration, he did not in that sense commit himself.

To what does the saint commit himself? To that which is available, and in being available is also in need of him. He commits himself to the visible. The saint is a man of this world.

Dionysus vs. Christ

WHAT is the meaning of this unusual statement? How shall it be understood when we say that the saint is of this world? In order to clarify the term, we shall at first call upon a philosopher who is well known for his defense of the "earth." When Nietzsche made his statement "God is dead" in the prologue of *Thus Spake Zarathustra*, he did not want it to be understood as a Voltairian attack on the cleric, nor even as a total denial of the Judeo-Christian concept of the deity; what he wanted above all was a radical rejection of the supernatural in isolation. By supernatural in isolation, we mean a "world" which can only be known through revelation, which will be obtained as a reward after death and must here and now be conquered through a special way of life. Belief in that sort of world is ruled out for Nietzsche. That it is likewise ruled out for Marx is well known and needs no special emphasis in our study. Although the dictum "God is dead" sounds negative, it actually takes a very positive stand, for the exclusion of the supernatural is an affirmation of the strength and the self-sufficiency of the natural world. The claim that "there is no longer a god" has the object of making it clear that the act of man originates in the visible and, as far as one can observe, terminates in the visible. Therefore, naturalism in the Nietzschean view is not negative. It is most positive, and puts its trust in what can be seen and what is within reach.

To say that this brand of philosophy is at present generally accepted may be saying more than can be proved. Yet the state of affairs is such that men are no longer pleased with the promise of future happiness and cannot be kept in submission with the hopes of eternal salvation. Absolutes are on the move. Every epoch creates its own ideals, and these ideals are chosen in line with its predominant needs. Men of today, without excluding the hope of immortality and what goes with it, hope for happiness here and now. There lies an absolute clear and firm. The concept of the saint must be viewed as closely related to it. He too belongs to the visible, and he belongs to it to the extent that he makes this visible world and the modicum of happiness it contains available to all.

From this it follows that the saint of our times must not be seen as first a *savior of souls.* (People who worry about saving their souls forget that salvation is not an intent but a result.) Nor must he first and foremost be an ascetic. Self-mortification and contemplation may be admirable when they promote the essential vocation of the saint. Yet looking at these activities from afar, they appear to have no direct connection with sanctity, and if practiced for the sole reason of contempt and hate of the visible, they are senseless. As for the particular form of asceticism commonly called celibacy, this too must be judged in the light of the proper vocation of the saint. Although the individual man under an obligation of celibacy may remain what is commonly called chaste, he does in fact create his own diversion, and by this I mean that he creates his own temptation. Roman women appeared infinitely more seductive to Anthony in the desert than they were in Rome. But in producing his own temptation, the candidate for sanctity creates an ideal to the fulfillment of which great attention must be given, for he must remain chaste at all costs. How much energy has been spent to attain the unattainable, we shall never know. But the sublimation of the Virgin Mary and of many saints attests to the immense effort involved. Yet looking at it from afar, the sim-

ple question to ask is: what for? Is the attitude of the past still
justified as a motive? The answer seems to be that it no longer is.
The myth has changed because the needs have changed. In a world
where millions live in poverty and in disease, the obvious need
is the other-in-peril. The mythology of today calls not for chastity above all, but for a commitment to the visible and to those
who are seen to suffer.

Hence when we are told that in our epoch people are obsessed
by sex and that this is a very *serious* matter, the answer is that the
contrary is true. The fact is that sex has become play. Sex as an
instrument for the propagation of life has lost some of its serious
import in a world which is dangerously overpopulated. In some
way, sex has become accidental. This is not to say that the game
cannot become destructive. That it can and does at times, we have
already pointed out. Yet what matters at present more than anything is the need to keep alive what is rather than to procreate
what is-not-yet. Hence it is natural that sexual morality, however
important in itself, does at certain epochs of history become a
less urgent problem, when compared to the need to alleviate the
suffering of the living. When caught up in one absolute, people
become strangely insensitive to other absolutes. Such are the
limitations of the man-fragment. He practices sex *naturally*, while
both charity and chastity he practices *freely*, for they require him
to overcome himself. Let him then in present and future epochs
overcome himself in the domain of the selfish. Someday perhaps the
mood of the collective will change, and confronting a *totum* under
threat of extinction, man will once more give serious attention to
sex as the tool for the propagation of life and to everything which
in one way or other is concerned with it.

So much for asceticism. In the hands of the saint it is a tool
and nothing more. There are tasks waiting for him which have a
more positive content and greater importance. One is the practice
of excellence: "Let us not level, let us make it clear how expensive and rare virtue is: let us make it clear that Virtue (or talent)
is not something moderately desirable, but is in fact a noble folly,
a beautiful exception and the privilege of becoming great."[8]
Nietzsche's text applies to his concept of the superman. Yet in this

---

[8] Nietzsche, *The Will to Power,* | no. 865.

particular place, it does not portray him as an immoral being, living outside and beyond the laws of the land, nor as the "noble Man" who has the "pathos of distance" and keeps his fellow men down and at a distance, but rather as the one who accomplishes the utmost within the frame of his vocation. In this sense the saint of the future fits the notion, for he too strives for excellence, whether he be a carpenter, a mason, a lawyer or a doctor. His ambitions may be considered mundane, no doubt, since he strives for excellence in and through the visible; he may even appear to be selfish, since he asserts himself. The saint in the existential phase is committed to self-achievement: he is the Observer who has turned Actor.

Yet in uncovering the ultimate aim of this excellence so fiercely acquired, we part from Nietzsche once more. Nietzsche is incomplete, his incompleteness calls for a complement: Jesus Christ is that complement. We do not object to calling it *divine*, to the extent that his message appears as the extraordinary corrective of the West. Even the term *revelation* is a suitable one, when understood as the wide diffusion of the message. In the light of this message, excellence itself must in turn be instrumentalized: it is self-development no doubt, but it is *totum*-oriented. If charity is the message, to whom shall it be done? An answer seems to be given in the Sermon on the Mount: "Blessed are the poor in spirit. Blessed are they that mourn. Blessed are they that suffer persecution for justice' sake, for theirs is the kingdom of heaven." (Matt. 5: 3, 4, 10). At first look this may appear as a praise of suffering. It would be hard to prove that suffering is preferable to not suffering, but most of us could agree that suffering is part of growth and that the individual (or the collective, for that matter) who has gone through a phase of suffering becomes a new man. This is, of course, as much Nietzschean as it is Christian. Nietzsche sees suffering as part of growth, and the means "whereby the European spirit has attained its strength, its remorseless curiosity and subtle mobility. . . . The discipline of suffering, of great suffering— know ye not that it is only this discipline that has produced all the elevations of humanity hitherto?"[9] But if it comes to revealing the attitude one should take towards suffering which is not called

---

[9] Nietzsche, *Beyond Good and* | *Evil*, nos. 188, 225.

for and can be mitigated, Nietzsche and Christ part company. The love of Christ goes towards the other-in-peril. In the choice of the parables—the parable of the prodigal son, of the lost sheep, of the good Samaritan—the same import emerges. What matters is the immediate salvation of the other-in-peril. Nietzsche's love, on the contrary, is selective. His predilection for the strong and the healthy is well known. "Do I advise you to neighbor-love? Rather do I advise you to neighbor-flight and to love of the remotest." (The German text has *Nächstenflucht* and *Fernstenliebe*.) If the meaning seems to be that one should love what is remote, it must not be understood as if the object of our love must necessarily be a person. It could be anything valuable. But it clearly implies that one does not love indiscriminately. Nietzsche chooses, his love is selective and preferential, for ultimately he wants to educate an elite; he has little concern for the humble man and for the other-in-peril. The Gospel, more concerned with the underdog than with the wealthy, comes closer to Marx than to Nietzsche, and it is precisely this original intent, sadly clouded by centuries of religious structures, which must be brought back into fresh understanding if we want to complete our definition of the saint in modern semantics. The saint is of this world and is devoted to the other-in-peril in this world. It is under the mask of failure and suffering that the *totum* shows its face to the saint, and it is upon that encounter that the latter will be judged.

It can be seen now how the image of the saint combines a dual trend, embodied both in Christ and in Nietzsche. More than the Gospel, as we have read it, Nietzsche's vigorous prose has stressed the importance of the unique and of commitment in this world, but he has not understood how the welfare of the *totum* must dominate the selfishness of individual man, and how as a result individual accomplishment must be directed towards the other-in-peril. Nietzsche's rejection of the supernatural in isolation was not a sin, but his rejection of the other man was unpardonable. The internal makeup of the saint in the phase of commitment contains the two trends. He is "a flexible understanding of the many and a selfish drive against the many."[10] He is antithetical within. He is both egotistical and altruistic, self-assertive and yet concerned about

---

[10] *The Planetary Man*, Vol. I,   chapter 9.

other men. Such is the challenge of the future: man will be asked to be himself, but in being himself to live for others. Perhaps the person of Alyosha, however fictional, fits the portrait of the saint in this second phase. Here is another creation of Dostoevsky, this time in his novel *The Brothers Karamazov*. Less violent than his brother Dmitri, less negative than Ivan, he moves through a world of sinners as an earthly saint, not without sin himself, but with real concern for peace and charity and with ideals that are within reach. He tries to fulfill them, unremittingly but not violently. He is patient and disciplined, yet possessed by an intense lust for life, for he too is a Karamazov and a living proof that this earth can not preserve a pure spirit for any length of time.

Sanctity as the Achievement of a Team

IF we have denied an all-encompassing truth to individual man, so also we shall deny him all-out sanctity. Just as we have previously reserved the concept of Truth for God alone, so we shall with equal right say that only God is Holy. This is of course not a proof of His existence. Nor does it say that if there is a God, He is also Perfection, in the way we understand perfection. Sanctity attributed to God is understood here as that which is totally different. God is out-of-the-ordinary.

If we cannot discover the totally unselfish and the totally different among men, it is because the self is both fragment and unique: it is caught within the *totum*, yet in its very structure it delimits and defines. Individual man may be *a* saint, but he can never be *the* saint, just as *a* table will never be *the* table. Like every fragment, a saint stands in opposition to . . . another saint or to a sinner. Since the antithetic implies the diverse, we find within the same *totum* a saint and a saint, a sinner and a sinner, etc., etc. Sinners and saints constitute extremes. They make one another and will always be there. Yet their presence does not preclude the whole gamut of intermediate attainments which are neither saintly nor sinful, but just human and diversified.

The imperfection of sanctity thus obtained by any one saint implies that the definition of the saint as the one who attains the absolute uncontaminated is theoretical. Yet although theoretical, it allows me to discern those who are saintly from those who are not. And I should add that the unique imperfection that is obtained by any one saint is at the origin of a movement which never reaches its end. Sanctity among mortals is a continuous attempt, never a total achievement. As in the realm of human noesis, John must take over where Peter leaves off. But the continuous relay is paramount, for like the Olympic runners, Peter and John are both needed to carry the torch to its destination. The metaphor is of course only partially accurate, since sanctity as a continual attempt of the many must be seen as a simultaneous effort, dispersed in space, as well as successive in time. A saint no less than a sinner is caught in the imperfection of the angular, but unlike the sinner he provides himself, through his movement to help the other-in-peril, with a thrust towards sanctity.

It is now apparent how sanctity at its highest is a team achievement, where each member of the community discovers himself as fragment and promotes, at least in intent, his own movement towards sanctity. This is the true foundation of the monastic life. The sanctity of the communal life must not be understood as a state of perfection, hitherto ascribed to the monks of the Western world by virtue of their vows and irrespective of their behavior; it must henceforth be seen as the total result of a diversified attempt and of a diversified achievement. The sum of all their efforts and achievements will constitute what I shall call a *totum sanctum*. Whether or not it will in the future contain a religious element, considered essential in the past, or even an attempt through prayer and asceticism to bring forth a mystical communion with the deity, we shall neither deny nor assert, but leave out of consideration for the present. Although this may be considered important by some, it cannot be said to be essential in our definition. The predominant characteristic of sanctity as achieved by the individual must remain what it was when we considered it as an adornment of the individual. Sanctity is the devotion to the other-in-peril. That is why, notwithstanding the limitations which everyone can observe, any collective and structured approach such as the Peace Corps and Vista must be encouraged. They are tentative, no doubt, and show an obvious lack of structure and discipline. They have not been able to do what missionaries have been able to accomplish on a purely charitable basis; yet they are a step in the right direction, on condition that they have no nationalistic interest to protect or any form of political structure to advertise. They may very well constitute the seed of a monachal institution of tomorrow, where both altruism and the need for an ideal can find its wishes fulfilled. Perhaps the day will come when individual man will discover God in his fellow men. This may be the ultimate discovery, and for mankind as a whole a redeeming one.

Monastic life of whatever form or shape presumes a coordinating function. There must be a man in authority. His office has nothing divine or mythical about it. Leadership, however important, is a function among other functions. The task of the leader consists in making the heterogeneous work together, and with that aim in mind in discovering the uniqueness and the special aptitudes of the other members of the *subtotum* and combining their activity with the activity of the other individuals (or collectives). To award to this function any higher "rank," as has been done in the past, must no longer be the case. Although insignia distinctive of the function are acceptable (as also are titles which indicate the function), these insignia must not reflect a hierarchical structure. Titles such as Holiness, Excellency, Grace are totally obsolete. It is against the misuse and veneration of authority that the youth of our times are rebelling. They have an insight into the value of the "baser" metals and rightfully refuse to bow down before the gold that is wrongfully placed at the top. There is neither top nor bottom, only diversity.

To demythologize authority does not mean to discard it. Authority is a product of the *totum*. The multiple ways in which it can be established is not the topic of our discussion, but once granted and given to an individual or to a group of individuals, it has the power to command. Authority must have authority. As a consequence, obedience remains a necessity, not as a passive attitude of blind submission but as an acceptance of the other's function. To live within a *totum* implies the acceptance of a function which coordinates the other functions and regulates the communication between them. To live in accordance with this attitude means to be obedient. Obedience denotes neither passivity nor inferiority, but must be seen simply as a practical necessity, for without it a *totum*, whether large or small, degenerates into chaos.

Meditating upon the pragmatic link between authority and other members of the community, we can only say that the use of the permanent vow as a means to maintain an individual within a collective is not defensible. And the main objection simply is that there is no permanent state for the individual himself. We have in previous pages outlined the successive phases of sanctity, a phase of total unselfishness in the service of his fellow men and a phase in which the individual asserts himself more forcefully. Although the point was made that the first phase had a more theoretical character, its fulfillment is not totally excluded; but if not forever, it is the least possible for a length of time. If now we apply the succession of these two phases to the case under study, we observe that the monastic life, or that which will in one way or other replace it, may very well be a period of unusual dedication. Yet the exercise of devotion results in a growing awareness of one's unique qualifications as well. With age a man becomes more self-conscious and in some ways more selfish, with as a result a slow but unavoidable detachment from the communal life. Alyosha Karamazov once more comes to mind. If one wants to touch the world, he must become part of it. Whoever really loves the world must abandon seclusion. Alyosha kisses the earth and leaves the monastery.

Saint and Hero

WE have defined the absolute as that which must be obtained at all cost, or, if it has already been attained, as that which must be preserved at all costs. When it was seen as something which benefited the agent, we called it an absolute contaminated, contaminated in the sense that the risk was for the agent's own benefit. We gave as an example that of the lover who would do anything to obtain the woman he loved. This does not imply that this disposition is totally selfish and contains no abnegation whatsoever, for within the deed, that is done for a "selfish" end, we can discern a certain amount of detachment. The lover is detached enough from life to give it up rather than to live without the beloved. Still, we shall not call him a hero.

If we modify the case, however, and imagine an individual who performs an act which seriously threatens his life but benefits the *totum* to which he belongs (family or nation or any other *totum*) we shall call him a hero. He is a hero, but not a saint. The saint strives towards the absolute uncontaminated; he lives and dies for the *totum humanum* and has no personal gain in mind. The hero in most cases, though not in all, is prepared to die for his family or for his nation.

To understand fully the importance of the role of heroism in a *totum*, let us keep in mind that the absolute which the hero intends to protect at all costs is not necessarily something which will last forever. It is not being eternal which makes the absolute. The absolute is the obligation of that time and of that place because it is the necessary condition of an optimum survival for that particular *totum*. History has shown that no absolutes (be they social, political or religious) keep the same form forever. The growth and the alterations of the *totum* itself dismantle the roof under which it has lived for a certain length of time and replace it with a different one. Those who died for a city in the past die for a nation in the present and, altering or consolidating their absolutes, will die for a continent tomorrow. What ultimately dictates the rise and fall of the absolutes cannot with certainty be disclosed— this belongs to the mystery of the we-language semantics and is impenetrable to individual insight[11]—but we can surmise that they change with the changing needs of survival as smaller states fuse into a larger one or immense empires break up into smaller units. Yet whatever may be the duration of a nation, the individual who gives his life for it may be said to be a hero. Once there are no more heroes or martyrs, the *totum* is beyond its zenith. Decline may not be imminent, for the power contained in inertia is beyond estimate, but the absence of heroes within the *totum* nonetheless signifies the beginning of the end.

The decay of one absolute does not mean the decay of all absolutes, but it does show that replacement in some way or other is in the offing. Man as man cannot survive unless he is protected by some absolute, which is actually the *totum* calling for its own future. Once this future as exemplified in the present is no longer desirable, the heroes disappear from the *present* stage. There is,

---

[11] *The Planetary Man*, Vol. I,   chapter 6, *rule IX*.

then, we confess, a certain fragility in the life of the hero (and of the martyr), since the absolute for which he gives his all today may not deserve a total sacrifice in the future. If absolutes belong to the angularity of the epoch and will inevitably be altered as the times change, this still does not diminish the immense value of heroic deeds. A Thomas More is truly a "man for all seasons."

But what, one may ask, of the individual who gives his life for any other-in-peril, regardless of his creed, race or nation? The soldier who throws himself on the hand grenade to save the life of his comrades is such a hero, for although the protection of the others is the protection of his unit as well, the motive must be considered humanitarian in the full sense of the word. This was not merely a defense of the nation but a protection of man as man, of the *totum humanum* itself. No greater act can exist than to give up one's life for one's fellow men. The absolute is truly uncontaminated.

But whether he confronts an absolute that is contaminated or uncontaminated, the hero is limited by another circumstance. He is dependent upon the occasion. The occasion makes the hero and not the hero the occasion. Only a series of circumstances creates the external setting in which he will become what he is. Without the plague-ridden city, Dr. Rieux would never have become the hero he did in fact become in Camus's novel. Unless one is in combat, the chances for throwing oneself on a hand grenade in order to protect others-in-peril are rather slim. The hero who sacrifices his life may be called at that moment a saint. But he is a saint of the instant. Often the rest of his life has been quite ordinary, or even, in the eyes of some, immoral; but at that instant he gave his life and became the hero. At times the word *instant* must be taken literally, for the decision was a split-second one; at others it covers a certain length of time during which a number of events prepared the setting for the heroic deed. But in any case the deed was unpredictable, not only because the events themselves were unpredictable, but also because the potential hero looked upon from without did not appear to have what at that particular instant he was going to display. The devout man who prays daily may turn out to be inferior to one who says no prayers but, when the moment comes, gives his all to save the other-in-peril. The hero may have been a sinner. But he could be hero as well. Time and time again it has been shown that sinners are the stuff out of which heroes are made, because if, for better or for worse, an individual was daring enough to violate the conventions, he may also be imprudent enough to run other risks. One who is preoccupied with his personal salvation, be it eternal or temporal, takes no chances either way.

The Kamikaze and the Samaritan

ALTHOUGH the merit of the heroic act is not cancelled because the absolute "to be protected at all costs" is provisional, the fact remains that such an absolute can elicit an act which is at the same time heroic and murderous. When, during World War II, a Japanese suicide pilot sent an American destroyer to the bottom of the sea, the act was considered by the Japanese people to be heroic; yet the same action was not looked upon with admiration by the American Navy, which did its utmost to kill the Kamikaze pilot before his plane could reach the deck. What was heroism for those in Japan was murder for those on the deck of the destroyer. It had to be prevented at all costs. The evaluation was radically opposed depending upon the point of view, and with good reason.

The planetary man as Observer detaches himself from one side as well as from the other and observes both from afar. He is neither in the airplane nor on the deck, for he can have no one "point of view." Clearly, within a *totum* made up of fragments, each endowed with a certain amount of freedom and carrying within itself the urge for survival, conflict is unavoidable. Whether conflict must be resolved by force in an age which has moved beyond the tribal is another question, the study of which we shall postpone until later. Our present observation is not an approval but a simple statement of fact. There will always be conflict. At present there is force. The Observer sees that in the case of the Kamikaze the moral evaluation was made from opposite standpoints. The fragment (individual or collective), caught within the angular and unaware of his imprisonment, erroneously believes that his judgment is objective. In truth, as seen by the outside Observer, it can only be subjective.

Could it be that the Kamikaze and the American destroyer are outdated? Could it be that the two opponents are being invited to ascend to the plane that is nowhere and everywhere and share the point of view of the Observer? This plane, which some may be inclined to call amoral, is not amoral but belongs to a morality of a higher sort. It is the true "beyond good and evil" (not the Nietzschean) which belongs to the *totum* as such, the supratemporal and the supraspatial.[12]

At that level one does not judge unilaterally. Like the Alpinist who has reached a refuge and is safely protected from a sudden storm, the one who has reached the detached position of the unprejudiced is able to evade the emotional impact of the angular. This is the true planetary attitude, the definition of the divine. Only a god can fully maintain this objective position, and it can only be called naiveté to believe that the gods are on one side rather than on the other. Their sense of justice is "objective," hence uninvolved. But how can the individual—who is not, after all, a god—in moments of conflict reach that plane of the amoral, or, as we have called it, adapting Nietzsche's phrase to our own purpose, the region "beyond good and evil"? Survival rests upon equilibrium, and the refuge in the storm may be a commitment to nonviolence.

The ascent towards the refuge of the objective is the journey of the saint. In contrast to the Kamikaze, who plunged to his death for a point of view, the Samaritan walks a road that leads to everyman everywhere. In examining his attitude, we do not intend to produce an apologia either for pacifism or for war. It is possible that a concept of internationalism may be built upon this foundation, but at present we merely want to explore the philosophical implications of the Samaritan's attitude. The story itself (Luke 10:30) is so well known that it needs no retelling. Let us merely recall that the Samaritan took care of someone who was regarded as hostile, at times even an enemy. The wounded man must be seen, then, not merely as the other-in-peril, but as an enemy. On the road from Jerusalem to Jericho the Samaritan confronts the other not merely as different—so is every man—but as

---

[12] I do not say extratemporal, since that term has spiritual implications, as if there were a realm of beings which have no domicile in space and time; the supratemporal merely implies that it does not belong to the here and the now and is truly planetary.

an opponent, as an individual who traditionally is seen as that which must be fought, or even eliminated.

Such would be the position of the individual who posits himself as center and absolute. The position of the self as center has been emphasized since the time of Descartes, whose claim "I think, therefore I am" leads one to observe things and people from one's own point of view, discovering in them what is profitable or harmful to oneself. Yet this centric position, from which one attempts to eliminate what is harmful and to absorb what is beneficial to oneself, conflicts with the planetary attitude that we observe in the Samaritan.

In the world of the centric or Cartesian, John judges Peter from out of his own uniqueness, with all its insights and limitations. We know that the individual is ontologically imperfect. This ontological imperfection has moral implications, for what is ontologically imperfect and caught in the angular noetic must evaluate the other from an angular optic. It is from one's own deficiency that one evaluates the other. Naturally, in judging Peter on the basis of his own imperfect being, John does not discover *his* kind of imperfection. Peter is not John, nor is John, Peter. Each discovers in the other certain qualities which are not his own. There is a tendency to ignore this potential in the other and to bring to the fore the absence in him of one's own perfection (which, of course, objectively considered is an imperfection). John sees Peter's limitations rather than his positive achievements. One's vision is even more obscured when the other appears not merely as different but as that "different" element which poses a threat. When Peter's difference is not something which has merely speculative implications, but threatens the observer in his very being, we call him the enemy. Hate results from a centric position from which the other is feared.

The change of position from the centric to the planetary alters the evaluation, which from now on will be made not from within but from above. From this vantage point the different is seen not from the point of view of one's own deficiency, hence as something which is deficient and menacing, but as something which has its own qualities and virtues. Although it is other, it need not be destroyed, since like oneself the other is part of a fractured *totum*. This speculative acceptance of the other in his unique otherness must be protected even when one is committed to one's own group or *subtotum*. No one, even the one who threatens my own life, must be seen simply as enemy. Observed from above, the other is seen to have qualities too. He is "justified." His intentions of survival must be accepted and respected, for this is the beginning of coexistence and dialogue. This rule, so beautifully practiced by the Samaritan, is a universal rule, applying to those at war as well as those at peace. The individual man in a war, although caught in the angular vision of the here-and-now and ready for self-defense, must at the same time be planetary, for he remains part of the immense human totality.

It is customary, in the search for community and coexistence, to look for what opponents have in common, but the speculations in this study lead in another direction. The advantage of stressing what opponents have in common is not really denied, but the point is made that for all practical purposes there are many things which people do not have in common; moreover, even if and when there are certain common elements, they are quite diverse in their existential fulfillment. All this merely confirms the fundamental thesis of this book, according to which the one is made up of the multiplicity of the diverse: that is the way things appear in the concrete, although one can and does discover certain common traits among the diverse.

The question now arises whether this sort of attitude, a tolerance of the diverse in the world of absolutes, does not in fact signify the end of all absolutes. To this we shall answer that the absolute of the one is not the absolute of the other, hence to defend one's *totum* and its patrimony does not imply that one should impose it upon others. A view that accepts in depth the existence of the plural and the juxtaposition of absolutes eliminates the fanatic but not the hero. One can still die for one's national heritage, but one can no longer impose it by force upon others. The imposition of a religion or of a political structure belongs to the past. But what does not belong to the past is the gradual implementation of new modes of living, for absolutes are shifting, and what may appear in our world of today to be a radical impossibility—the integration of different *tota*—may someday be reversed into a need—the mingling of the diverse. There is at present an increasing loss of isolation with regard to the peoples of the world. The primitive tribe was once a self-sufficient segment of humanity, but the areas of primitive culture have been overrun by a Western world that has discovered the power of technology. Colonization and the work of the missions must be seen as an immense unfolding of the *totum humanum*, the result of which has been the intermingling of races and religions. There is no more isolation or separation, and the result has been the fall of many absolutes which had been founded on division and ignorance.

It is at this point that the role of the Samaritan deserves full attention: he accepts in the other what he himself is not and shows by his actions that he loves him for it. This is the self-abnegation of the saint, for the Samaritan, as Goethe pointed out, comes face to face with the opponent in his ugliness. The wounded man is not the Apollo of the Belvedere. He is unpleasant to look at: bloody, beaten, covered with the dirt and dust of the road. He is no longer young, perhaps. Such is the way we see him in the famous etching of Rembrandt. The enemy is ugly because he is enemy: he is ugly in his very essence. Rembrandt's etching catches this truth. In opposition to Nietzsche, the vision of Christ seems to imply that the enemy must be loved and that one must understand the depth of his need and as far as possible provide for those needs. The Samaritan fulfills his function because, although he remains what he is—there is no demand that he should give up his identity—he overcomes the singular and the particular of his own position and moves with understanding into the world of the other and the opponent. Such is the planetary attitude when the other is not merely different but an opponent as well.

Sanctity as Obligation

WE now reach one final question: how "guilty" were those who saw the man lying on the side of the road and, unlike the Samaritan, passed him by? Or, to use an example given by Urmson, must a doctor leave his family to go to a plague-ridden city and minister to those in need?[13] What obligation, if any, is incum-

---

[13] J. O. Urmson, "Saints and Heroes" in A. I. Melden, ed., *Essays in Moral Philosophy* (Seattle: University of Washington Press, 1958). Urmson's approach is very different from the method followed in these pages, but our conclusions are not so far apart. One is also reminded of Dr. Rieux in Camus's *The Plague*.

bent upon him? We have used the term "obligation" in discussing the concept of natural law, where we defined it as the pressure coming from the collective to submit to the conventions. Convention itself we saw as the slow yet forceful creation of a technique of survival. In order to protect itself and to survive, the collective compels you to behave in such or such a way. We shall call this a "must" or an "ought." Obligation does not exist in the abstract, it exists when it affects an individual in a concrete situation. Only the one who faces a red light must stop. Only the one who is a doctor and by vocation committed to protecting life must take his own life into his hands and go to the plague-ridden city. To both agents it will appear that the act has to be done. As you approach the red light, there is a pressure upon you to halt and to save the lives you might destroy if you continue. If you are a doctor in a particular situation, there is pressure upon you to make use of your skills. The pressure is exerted by the collective around you and in you (insofar as you are part of that *totum*) to perform a certain action. The urgency of the pressure manifests itself when the act-to-be-performed is not in fact performed, for this omission evokes the sense of guilt. Guilt is what follows the failure to do something which "ought" to be done.

Let us notice the difference between the two "oughts" under study. The first act, which consists merely in stopping before a red light, is relatively easy, while the second requires much more self-denial. The first act, furthermore, is accepted by the collective without undue praise, while the second arouses admiration. And finally we note that if the first kind of obligation is not observed, the *totum* interferes coercively, while if the second kind is omitted —the doctor does not go to the aid of the city but stays quietly at home—there will be no legal penalty in most cases. (We presume, of course, that the doctor is not under orders, as he may very well be in time of war.)

This threefold difference does not affect the inner structure of the ought itself. There remains the clear awareness that the driver must stop for a red light and the doctor must help those who suffer in the plague-ridden city. The ought affects the doctor, although to discard it will not entail a punishment as does the infraction of a positive law. There is in most cases no positive law compelling anyone to heroism. Yet the refusal to perform the heroic act, when it might have been done, provokes a malaise. The doctor who does not go feels uncomfortable. Those who thought only of themselves the night that the Titanic hit the iceberg live in infamy, while the courageous Strausses who gave up their places in the lifeboat are universally admired. The malaise of the non-hero, which has been called remorse, is accessible to the Observer through its external manifestation only. It appears to "us" that the non-hero remembers. He does not forget the act or its omission. At first he makes excuses to himself and to others. When his defensiveness appears to be pointless, he disappears. This disappearance is a form of self-accusation, but it does not exclude expiation. Remorse is the painful memory of an action. Charity does not erase the act, but in the very act of repairing the evil done, it alleviates the memory.

In conclusion, then, how shall we define the *ought* or obligation compelling individual man towards heroism? There is only one way: heroism issues from a sense of obligation felt by the individual as fragment whereby he is induced to perform the action which protects the *totum*, even though it involves the risk of his self-interest or of his life. No personal reward is in view; the *totum* is served, and the individual only indirectly. The basis of the heroic act consists in its response to the pressure of an obligation. The obligation itself originates in the depths of the *totum* as a mode of correction and repair. As such, it is a hidden force; nevertheless it is strong enough to preserve in being the *totum* which is visible to us.

Similarly, sanctity hovers over the average man—as a dream, perhaps, but not an impossible dream. Once more, the pressure towards sanctity, or the unselfish life on behalf of the other-in-peril, originates in the *totum*. The *totum* contains the multiple: this precisely is its original sin, for it is the presence of the multiple which constitutes the source of the antithetic and of the selfish; but it is the same presence which creates its antidote as well: the antidote is the saint.

It is not clear to this writer why John is chosen and Peter is not. Perhaps we could say that the pressure towards the unselfish act reaches all and everyone, but that in the concret—and that is our constant approach—it is received in a very uneven way among individuals. It looks as if each individual has a "position" which is not merely the proper place where he is situated at a certain time but also contains the reference to others which that "position" implies and the task which goes with it. Obligation towards sanctity reaches individuals in the concrete uniqueness of their "position," and it reaches them unevenly because of their unequal "positions." There is Christ, there is Gandhi, there is X, teaching the ignorant and the poor, and there is the less spectacular saint who in a barbaric world is simply polite and considerate. None is perfect, but as we have seen again and again, the imperfect engenders the different and the different engenders mutual completion. The saint redeems the life of sin, his own no less than that of any other. Boundless charity is nothing other than boundless atonement; and so, when we see a saint or a hero in his daily rounds, we might in many cases suppose that he is as much sinner as saint, serving, in the natural order, as an instrument of redemption for himself as well as others. Sanctity on a natural level—and no other level is of concern to us—is above all the removal, through atonement, of guilt. Hence it is natural that for our times, bowed down as we are by an immense weight of guilt, the sole means of salvation should be sanctity in action; for therein lies the expiation of the actions centered on self and the return to the oneness of the *totum*. The obligation to strive towards sanctity is the obligation to strive towards the reconstruction of the One and the fulfillment of its urge to be and to survive.